STRATEGIC NEGOTIATIONS

STRATEGIC NEGOTIATIONS

STRATEGIC NEGOTIATIONS

A Theory of Change in Labor-Management Relations

Richard E. Walton, Joel E. Cutcher-Gershenfeld,
and Robert B. McKersie

ILR Press
an imprint of
Cornell University Press
Ithaca and London

First published 1994 by Harvard Business School Press
First printing, ILR Press/Cornell Paperbacks, 2000

Printed in the United States of America

Library of Congress Cataloging-in-Publication Data

Walton, Richard E.
    Strategic negotiations : a theory of change in labor-management relations /
    Richard E. Walton, Joel Cutcher-Gershenfeld, and Robert B. McKersie.
        p. cm.
    Includes bibliographical references and index.
    ISBN 0-8014-8697-1 (pbk.)
    1. Industrial relations—United States.   2. Industrial relations.   I. Cutcher-
Gershenfeld, Joel.   II. McKersie, Robert B.   III. Title.

HD8072.5 .W35 2000
331'.0973—dc21   00-060148

Paperback printing   10 9 8 7 6 5 4 3 2 1

Contents

Preface to the Paperback Edition

ADVANCING THE PRINCIPLE OF NEGOTIATED CHANGE

The challenge of large-scale systems change in labor-management relations motivated the development and publication of *Strategic Negotiations: A Theory of Change in Labor-Management Relations*. In the years since the publication of this book we have seen the ideas and concepts applied with respect to the restructuring of collective bargaining, the establishment of labor-management partnerships, the implementation of worker-participation initiatives, and other systems-change initiatives in the labor-management context.[1] We have also been honored to learn of colleagues building on the core theory.

In this preface to the paperback edition, we summarize our views of the lessons learned from these developments, but we also advance a bold additional thought that was only briefly suggested in the first edition of the book. We outline ways to extend the theoretical framework far beyond the domain of labor-management relations—extending into the worlds of joint ventures, strategic partnerships, customer-supplier integration, and cross-functional alignment. The principles even apply in the relations among legislative and executive branches of government, international relations across global centers of trade, and countless other instances where there are interacting stakeholder groups with common and competing interests.

A core dimension of the theory is the importance of always attending to two outcomes in any negotiations—the bargaining around the substantive contract and the bargaining around what can be termed the social contract. The social contract represents reciprocal understandings or quid pro quos around relationships rather than substantive issues. For example, in a strategic joint venture between two companies there will be a substantive agreement around the scale and scope of the activity, but there will also be a set of shared understandings—what we are terming a social contract—around the expected levels of trust, information sharing, and mutual commitment. The parallel negotiation over these shared understandings may be less visible, but it is no less important. Indeed, the early draft manuscripts of the book were titled "Renegotiating the Social Contract." The notion that both social and substantive contracts can be, in effect, on the table for negotiation was particularly salient when we observed union and management leaders negotiating over the establishment of partnership arrangements. The relationship between social and substantive contracts also was highlighted as an unintended consequence of decisions to down-size, reengineer or otherwise restructure organizations where existing social contracts were perceived by one or both parties as having been undercut or violated.[2]

Although it is now quite common in the world of employment relations to see social contracts as important outcomes that must be constructed through negotiated processes, there is less attention given to social contracts in other organizational and business contexts. We argue, however, that social contracts are just as important in these contexts. When a small entrepreneurial firm is acquired by a larger organization, a long-term supplier partnership is established, a public-private partnership is contemplated, or other such alliances are formed, it is essential to track and understand the ways in which the relationship itself—the social contract—is being negotiated. Further, it is critical to understand the inter-relationships between the social contracts and the substantive agreements. Both types of agreements are not just negotiated; they also require ongoing administration where the interdependence between these two outcomes continues. For example, a research and development joint venture may have very explicit substantive agreements around intellectual property, but those agreements will have completely different meanings if the social contract has a long- or short-term time horizon. A social contract that features a short-term time horizon will likely prompt a more guarded approach to intellectual property and less emotional investment in the pursuit of inventive ideas, while a social contract that incorporates a long-term view of the relationship will generally foster more open sharing and joint creation—even with the exact same substantive agreement.

Beyond the dual outcomes, another key dimension of the *Strategic Negotiations* theory involves the links between tactics and two primary strategies—forcing and fostering. In essence, we argued that these two negotiation strategies and combinations of them are composed of individual tactical moves in each of three domains: dealing with the explicit agenda (integrative/distributive bargaining), structuring of attitudes, and managing internal negotiations. A negotiation strategy exists only as it emerges out of the alignment and synergies across different tactical combinations. Thus, the combination of various distributive tactics along with a heightening of uncertainty and the exploiting of internal divisions on the other side combine to create strong forcing dynamics. Conversely, the combination of various integrative tactics along with emphasis on trust and the forging of internal consensus combine to create strong fostering dynamics. When the tactics are consistently aligned with just a forcing strategy, there is the risk of unrestrained forcing taking on a life of its own. When the tactics are consistently aligned with just a fostering strategy, there is the risk of soft or naive fostering dominating. More often, the tactical moves are a complex mixture that sets the stage for sequential or even simultaneous combinations of forcing and fostering.

In the labor relations context, we have found that the terms *forcing* and *fostering* have face validity—parties almost instantly incorporate these terms into their language. Further, the attention to forcing—especially the forcing that is involved in placing controversial issues on the bargaining agenda— serves as an important antidote to many unfortunately simplistic efforts to advance the idea of "win-win" bargaining. Too many parties report attending training on win-win bargaining that focuses only on problem-solving and consensus, leaving them unprepared for the contentious and complicated issues that one side or the other is eventually compelled to place on the agenda and to insist that attention be paid to underlying interests. Similarly, a focus only on fostering leaves parties unprepared for the internal divisions that predictably emerge when representatives are closely cooperating. The unfortunate history of many employee-involvement or quality-circle efforts involves an exclusive focus on fostering that fails to anticipate the contentious issues that inevitably surface when front-line employees are empowered to consider how to improve operations—especially larger systems barriers identified by front-line employees and considered off limits by senior- or middle-level leaders.

Simply put, by validating the legitimate and important role that forcing plays in bargaining, it becomes possible to anticipate potentially divisive issues. By not attending to the forcing dimension, fostering may be pursued in a manner that does not produce substantive results—what we call the blind side of this strategy. Conversely, parties that rely only on top-down threats and intimidation—as is the case with the use of replacement workers and some corporate campaigns—have the blind-side risk of escalating and uncontrolled conflict—conflicts that may sour relations for an unexpectedly long time. Thus, the experience in labor relations suggests that the interdependence of forcing and fostering strategies represents a key practical insight, rooted in solid theory around the way strategy emerges from tactics.

One issue that was introduced in the theory, but only partially developed in the first edition, is the concept of escape. We termed this a *non-negotiations strategy* since it involves unilateral action designed to end or substantially undercut the relationship. We are pleased to report some colleagues are further expanding theory around escape—highlighting not just the role of escape threats as part of forcing, but also the way escape once carried out casts a shadow over other forcing and fostering strategies.[3]

If we look beyond the labor relations context, we see that the interdependencies across forcing, fostering, and escape are poorly understood by many leaders engaged in large-scale systems-change initiatives. In some cases, reengineering initiatives, hostile takeovers, even initiatives by a political party, involve tactical moves that combine into unrestrained forcing strategies. By not anticipating recovery afterwards—a key element of strategic negotiations—these parties fall into forcing traps. Alternatively, partnership agreements, joint ventures, acquisitions, and other initiatives that are rooted entirely in statements of trust, consensus, and cooperation risk the fostering trap of not being prepared for the divisive issues that inevitably emerge among interacting stakeholder groups. Both types of traps reflect incomplete appreciation of the negotiated nature of large-scale systems change.

Seeing systems-change initiatives as negotiated processes has a number of beneficial implications. First, the existence of multiple stakeholders is acknowledged. Stakeholder groups are not just barriers to be overcome nor are they just drivers to be harnessed. They are independent actors with common and competing interests, all of which need to be understood and addressed. Second, the process for addressing these interests involves a variety of tactical moves that have the potential to coalesce into forcing and fostering strategies each of which has its own dynamics. Therefore any change initiative will not be a one-time event, but rather an ongoing dynamic requiring strategic leadership and attention to numerous tactical details. This fact also highlights why these details matter so much—they can quickly combine into strategies. Third, the relevant outcomes will not just be new substantive agreements—they will also include social contracts, which may be explicit or tacit understandings about the social relationships. The discipline of wisely crafting a social contract is frequently not well developed and is, we argue, essential for the effective negotiation of change.

Despite the value of taking a negotiated approach to change, it is neither instinctive nor easy for most leaders to undertake. The alternatives—unilateral implementation or escape—are responses that probably have deep roots in the psychological tendencies that we all have around either fight or flight. It is not the merits of a negotiated approach to change that are hard to advance: it is the incorporation of these principles into daily practice that is the challenge.

Ultimately, the agenda in labor-management relations is an agenda that includes many large-scale change initiatives. Such change initiatives, however, are not limited to settings with formal union and management parties, and the scope of such initiatives reaches well beyond the domain of employment relations. Wherever there are interacting stakeholders with common and competing interests, the strong implication of our work is that a negotiated approach to change is both essential and challenging to undertake.

The overall contribution of *Strategic Negotiations* was, we hoped, to add the notions of strategy and structure to the existing process theory advanced in the 1965 *Behavioral Theory of Labor Negotiations* by Walton and McKersie. This was necessitated because the structural instability and the strategy dynamics observed in recent decades made a focus on process alone incomplete. As we think about the combination of strategy, structure, and process outside of the labor relations context, we find that these interacting elements of the theory hold great promise for explaining complex realities and guiding leaders at all levels. It is to that end that we dedicate the reissuing of this book by the ILR Press. It is to this ever expanding domain of theory and practice that we remain not just scholars and change leaders, but students with so much still to learn.

ACKNOWLEDGMENTS

In writing this new preface for the reissuing of *Strategic Negotiations* we have additional acknowledgments to add. First, we thank what is now over 2,000 participants in the seminar "Negotiating Labor Agreements"—offered since 1996 through the Program on Negotiations at the Harvard Law School—for their ideas, questions, and reports on real-world applications of these ideas. Second, there are numerous colleagues and friends who have further advanced our thinking on these ideas, including participants in the MIT industrial relations theory doctoral seminar, Marjorie Corman Aaron, Marion Baird, Richard Barnes, Matt Bodah, Michael Diamond, Jan Klein, Thomas Kochan, Roger Komer, Elaine Landry, Russell Lansbury, Gerry Lazarowitz, Marty Mulloy, Robert Mnookin, Nancy Peace, Dennis Richeleau, Mary Rowe, Phyllis Segal, Steve Sleigh, Larry Susskind, Michael Watkins, and John Calhoon Wells.

NOTES

1. For example, union and management leaders at the Kaiser Permanente health plan report formally organizing their strategic partnership around the dimensions of the theory.
2. Additional research examining the negotiated process of constructing social contracts has been conducted by Ron Fortang at the Harvard Business School and the deeper development of the social contract as a concept has been the focus of a series of conferences and publications involving MIT, the Sloan Foundation, and a mix of leading employers.
3. See the work of Marion Baird, for example, who has studied the use of escape in the Australian consumer products manufacturing industry—where newly established "greenfield" facilities cast a shadow over ongoing relations in existing "brownfield" facilities.

Preface

This book began with two simple observations. First, during the 1980s and early 1990s, labor relations in the United States was polarizing around cooperative and contentious extremes. Second, the process by which these divergent shifts were taking place was—in both cases—largely one of *negotiated* change. Thus, in setting ourselves the task of understanding the process by which U.S. industrial relations was changing, we have produced a theory of strategic negotiations. By "strategic," we refer to the importance of the transformation involved—major revisions in the social contract between management and labor as well as in the collective-bargaining agreement. The book presents this theory and uses it to analyze 13 case histories of negotiated change drawn from three industries that offer especially instructive contrasts—pulp and paper, railroads, and auto supply.

Like the industrial landscape in American industry as a whole, our 13 cases are diverse in many respects—whether management gave higher priority to tangible concessions by labor or to more cooperative relations with labor, whether management relied primarily on coercion or persuasion and attitude change, and whether management succeeded or failed in its change efforts. The cases also vary in terms of labor's response to demands for concessions and to cooperative overtures—from vigorous opposition to receptivity. Finally, the outcomes vary widely in terms of whether both parties gained, both lost, or one gained at the expense of the other.

In constructing a theory adequate for addressing the changes occurring in the nature of labor-management relations and the diversity in trends we observe, our point of departure was *A Behavioral Theory of Labor Negotiations*, developed by Walton and McKersie and published in 1965.[1] This remains the standard theory of labor-management negotiations. However, the scene today differs from the 1960s in two major respects: both the stakes being negotiated and the processes themselves have changed.

First, the *stakes* are higher and more complex. During an earlier era when arm's-length accommodation was almost universally the basis of management's social contract with organized labor in U.S. industry, labor-management negotiations and theories to explain them could focus exclusively on incremental changes in collective-bargaining agreements. However, in the present era of intensified market competitiveness when management seeks major revisions in these substantive contracts, such as to break past patterns of wage increases and roll back work rules, it must also revise social contracts with labor—either marginalizing or eliminating the union, such as occurred at Greyhound and Continental Air, or making it a business partner, as has happened at the Saturn subsidiary of General Motors and at National Steel. Thus, we need a theory dealing with negotiations that break existing paradigms—both with respect to substantive and social contracts.

Second, the labor-management *processes* and *structures* employed to revise these contracts are more varied, complex, and subtle. In an earlier era, labor-management relations had become routinized around formal periodic, bilateral interactions, followed by predictable patterns of contract administration. In the current era, the formal, institutional aspects of collective bargaining have become entwined with informal, interpersonal interactions around workplace problem solving on the one hand and informal "in plant strategies" as alternatives to strikes on the other. While periodic collective bargaining still occurs, a more continuous form of negotiation can also be observed—which has been referred to as a "living agreement." The bilateral structure of traditional collective bargaining is shifting in many cases toward multilateral arrangements as customers, stockholders, communities, and others seek to influence labor-management negotiations. Other changes are also evident, such as more complex internal differences within labor and management. Thus, we need a theory that comprehends the additional complexities.

The basic idea of *Behavioral Theory* is that social negotiations are comprised of four parallel subprocesses—distributive bargaining, integrative bargaining, attitudinal structuring, and internal bargaining. Although we found that this idea is still applicable for our present purpose, to fully capture the nature of contemporary change episodes, we have expanded the theory in the following ways. First, as noted earlier, we have explicitly attended to both social contract and substantive contract outcomes. Second, we have formalized the treatment of negotiation strategy—highlighting the strategies of forcing change, fostering change, and escaping the relationship. Third, we have broadened the analysis to include the negotiation structure, which encompasses the level of interaction, the number of parties, the degree of centralization, and the channels for communication. Fourth, we have formalized the analysis of contextual economic, legal, social, and historical factors that help shape a negotiators's choices of strategies and tactics. In addition, we have made minor changes to the organization and labeling of the subprocesses featured in the earlier theory in order to sharpen our specification of the tactical role each subprocess plays in each change strategy.

The overall theory of strategic negotiations presented here, like the earlier theory, is offered as a tool for analyzing actual negotiations—to yield discrete insights into negotiating dynamics and to make systematic sense of this complex change phenomenon. However, we have pushed the present theory further—beyond an analytical framework to a set of testable propositions. We subject these theoretical propositions to a preliminary "test"—by assessing whether they are capable of explaining the actual differences we observe among the three industries from which we have drawn our company case histories and among the 13 case histories themselves.

The theory presented here lies at the intersection of several fields—industrial relations and organizational development as well as negotiations. We believe it has the potential to expand the discourse in all three fields. For both industrial relations and organizational development, this attention to the negotiated nature of change should be helpful. In industrial relations, the negotiation approach can extend understanding of how institutions change and the implications of that change process for subsequent institutional arrangements. In organizational development, the negotiation approach highlights the interactions of multiple stakeholders with overlapping but distinct interests—which helps explain active resistance to change and the indeterminacy of outcomes during planned change processes.

We have commented on how the form of the present theory of strategic negotiations differs from the earlier *Behavioral Theory*. We should also place the present theory within the larger body of negotiation theory. Over the past two decades, there has developed a community of negotiation scholars with roots in many disciplines (economics, game theory, cognitive psychology, and social psychology) and many institutional fields (such as labor relations, international relations, urban planning, environmental management, and commercial relations). Each perspective has enriched our understanding of negotiations as a generic process. Generally, they have offered complementary techniques and insights rather than rival theories. The present work is in the same vein. We build on—or take as given—these advances made in negotiation analysis.

Specifically, here is what we do in the present work that we believe makes it distinctive:

- We conceptualize the several types of social contracts between American management and labor that are replacing arm's-length accommodation.

- We explore the interrelationship between negotiating substantive terms and negotiating a new social contract.

- We identify two contrasting approaches to strategic negotiations—forcing and fostering—and specify the tactical operations associated with each.

- We clarify major strategic and tactical risks associated with each negotiating strategy.

- We analyze the factors that shape decisions about whether to force or foster (or to do neither—i.e., to continue negotiating incremental change).

- We show that in our cases, better outcomes are associated with scenarios in which managers used *both* forcing and fostering strategies, either sequentially or combined in the same period.

- We explore the tactical dilemmas and other dynamics associated with coordination of the two broad strategies.

We employ three levels of analysis to make these contributions: (1) a comparison of three industries to identify contextual forces influencing negotiators' choices, (2) a comparison of 13 company histories to learn the relationship between strategies and their outcomes, and (3) a comparison of 20 distinct strategy periods in order to learn how negotiators' priorities and expectations shape their choice of strategies.

How do these contributions relate to the existing body of knowledge about negotiations? First, we can point to a general contrast involving the scope of our theory. Existing theories of negotiation (like the earlier *Behavioral Theory*) focus on creating and claiming tangible wealth or valuable rights. They also analyze a negotiation episode—which has a beginning, a middle, and an end. Our present treatment takes a broader cut—not only by including social contract outcomes as well as tangible stakes but also by analyzing sequences of negotiating episodes (scenarios) as well as individual episodes.

Second, we can point to a few more specific contrasts that help locate the work within the field. Howard Raiffa,[2] David Lax and James Sebenius,[3] and others have invented new ways of analyzing the substantive interests of the parties and formulating alternative solutions to substantive negotiations. While we make no theoretical contribution to this aspect of negotiations, our treatment of another type of outcome—revisions in the social contract—breaks new ground.

Others have made major contributions to our understanding of preconditions and procedures for effective integrative bargaining (or "mutual gains bargaining"), notably Roger Fisher and William Ury,[4] Richard Peterson and L. N. Tracy,[5] and Lawrence Susskind.[6] Our present work adds only incrementally to our understanding of this particular process per se, but it does advance our understanding of how a parallel process of managing intraorganizational differences influences integrative bargaining—often decisively.

The dynamics of threats, escalations, and impasses have been rigorously analyzed by others, including Dean Pruitt and Jeffrey Rubin[7] and Barry O'Neill.[8] While our work reinforces their analyses of these dynamics, we also clarify the antecedents and consequences (both immediate and longer-term) of these dynamics, particularly in our cases containing episodes of unrestrained forcing.

We have targeted the present book for students of labor relations; academics whose specialty is the broad study of negotiations; and scholars, educators, and consultants interested in workplace reforms and the management of change. We hope to improve practice by improving the theory guiding research, course curricula, and the action strategies of managers, labor leaders, and third-party consultants.

This book emphasizing theory and a comparative analysis of cases complements another publication that presents in extended form 12 of the company case histories generated by this research project.[9]

The present rate of workplace change in the United States is slow in view of the pressures on the parties to change. We are concerned both with the need for U.S. industry to improve competitiveness and with the need for U.S. trade unions to find the best ways to serve the long-term interests of their members. By contributing to an understanding of the interests of management and labor, and the processes by which they negotiate their substantive and social contracts, we hope to assist the continuing change process.

The authors wish to acknowledge the generous support provided by their respective institutions—Harvard Business School, Division of Research; Michigan State University, School of Labor and Industrial Relations; and Massachusetts Institute of Technology, Sloan School—and by the W. E. Upjohn Institute.

We also wish to express our appreciation to our assistants who helped us manage the project through its various stages: Margo McCool at Harvard; Annette Bacon at Michigan State; and Michelle Kamin and Cherie Potts at MIT. We are grateful to a number of colleagues who have read and critiqued the manuscript at various stages, including Chris Argyris, Irving Bluestone, Walter Gershenfeld, Gladys Gershenfeld, Charles Heckscher, Harry Katz, Thomas Kochan, and Deborah Kolb. We are grateful as well for the cooperation of the many union and management leaders at the field sites studied during this project.

We would also like to thank Rod Bloedow, Chip Hunter, and Amy Andrews for their assistance during field research on the railroad industry and Don Power for his assistance with the analysis presented in Chapter 2.

Finally, we are especially indebted to two research associates—Kathleen Rudd Scharf, who helped develop and draft the chapter on the paper industry, and Patrick McHugh, who provided similar assistance on the chapter covering the auto supply industry.

NOTES

1. The study was re-published on its twenty-fifth anniversary with a new introduction. See Richard E. Walton and Robert B. McKersie, *A Behavioral Theory of Labor Negotiations,* 2d ed. (Ithaca, N.Y.: ILR Press, 1991).
2. Howard Raiffa, *The Art and Science of Negotiation* (Cambridge, Mass.: Harvard University Press, Belknap Press, 1982).
3. David A. Lax and James K. Sebenius, *The Manager as Negotiator* (New York: Free Press, 1986).
4. Roger Fisher and William Ury, *Getting to Yes: Negotiating an Agreement without Giving In* (Boston: Houghton Mifflin, 1981).

5. See, for example, R. B. Peterson, L. N. Tracy, and A. Cabelly, "Problem Solving in Labor Negotiations: Retest of a Mode," *Relations Industrielles* 36 (1981): 87–105.
6. See, for example, Lawrence Susskind and Jeffrey Cruikshank, *Breaking the Impasse: Consensual Approaches to Resolving Public Disputes* (New York: Basic Books, 1987).
7. Dean G. Pruitt and Jeffrey Z. Rubin, *Social Conflict: Escalation, Stalemate, and Settlement* (New York: Random House, 1986).
8. Barry O'Neill, "Conflictual Moves in Bargaining: Warnings, Threats, Escalations, and Ultimatums," in *Negotiation Analysis*, ed. H. Peyton Young (Ann Arbor: University of Michigan Press, 1981), 87—108.
9. Joel E. Cutcher-Gershenfeld, Robert B. McKersie, and Richard E. Walton, *Pathways to Change: Case Studies in Strategic Labor-Management Negotiations* (Kalamazoo, Mich.: W. E. Upjohn Institute, forthcoming).

Introduction and Overview

This book proposes a theory of strategic negotiations grounded by case histories of labor-management change. The theory covers the full range of adaptive changes currently taking place in U.S. labor-management relations—largely in response to heightened competition. It focuses on how these changes are negotiated among the stakeholders. Case histories are used to illustrate the framework and its utility for analysis as well as to provide a "test" of some of the propositions that comprise the theory.

To introduce the book, we present an overview of the theoretical framework and a chapter-by-chapter preview of what we learned when we applied it to our cases. We also add some comments about alternative approaches to reading the several parts of the book that report our empirical findings.

FRAMEWORK FOR ANALYZING STRATEGIC NEGOTIATIONS

We distinguish two potential sets of outcomes to labor-management change efforts. The first set of outcomes—*substantive contracts*—is very familiar. We use the word *contracts* broadly to include collective-bargaining agreements, formal personnel policies, and well-established past practices. These substantive contracts are embedded in a second set of outcomes—which we have termed *social contracts*. The social contract includes broad quid pro quos between labor and management as well as shared understandings about the "rules of the game."

Traditionally, the dominant social contract between employers and unions in the United States was premised on arm's-length accommodation, while the dominant social contract between employers and employees was premised on compliance. The rules of the game involved periodic rounds of formal collective bargaining, followed by rule-based contract administration. This social contract emerged in the decades following the New Deal and involved an implicit promise of labor peace in exchange for continually rising standards of living.

In the face of global markets and deregulation, we have embarked on an era oriented around *industrial competitiveness* that has shifted the parties' substantive priorities. Management's substantive agenda now emphasizes cost containment, flexible assignment of labor, improvement of quality, and responsiveness to customer needs. Labor's substantive agenda emphasizes job security, protecting past gains, ensuring institutional security for the union, and—in some instances—enlarging the union's role in business decision making. Although some of the agenda items, such as certain cost-cutting measures by management or certain protections of past gains by the union, can be pursued within the rubric of the existing social contract, many of the issues call for a parallel renegotiation of the social contract.

While there are many possible social contracts, we focus on social contracts at two levels—an *institutional level* (between a union and an employer) as well as an *individual level* (between an employee and a supervisor/manager). At the institutional level, we observe new social contracts oriented around either union-management cooperation or containment/avoidance of the union (in contrast to the traditional arm's-length relations). At the individual level, we observe some continuation and even intensification of the traditional social contract oriented around compliance as well as new social contracts oriented around employee commitment. Of particular interest are two combinations of institutional and individual social contracts: (1) *union-management cooperation and employee commitment* and (2) *union containment/avoidance and employee compliance.*

A negotiations perspective is critical in order to understand either sort of change in the social contract. The first element of the negotiations perspective involves the broad negotiations strategy. We highlight three key strategies: *forcing change, fostering change,* and *escaping the relationship.* Of the three strategies, the last—escape—is not a negotiation change strategy. Our analysis will focus on forcing and fostering strategies (noting, where appropriate, the tactical uses of escape threats).

Forcing strategies—in their pure form—can be understood as the alignment of three negotiating processes: *distributive bargaining, structuring attitudes to emphasize hostility toward the other side,* and *managing internal differences to promote solidarity on one's own side while exploiting divisions on the other side.* The core advantage of a forcing strategy is the promise of quick results or the achievement of results that the other party is most reluctant to concede. The core disadvantages are the failure to identify the integrative potential in the situation, the lack of commitment in implementation, and the risk of a "conflict-cycle" dynamic. Thus, the alignment of the three bargaining processes into a forcing strategy carries a number of downside risks or disadvantages that must be weighed against the lure of potential gains.

Fostering strategies—in their pure form—can be understood as an alternative alignment of the three negotiating processes: *integrative bargaining, structuring attitudes to emphasize trust,* and *managing for consensus in both parties.* The core disadvantages of a fostering strategy are the long time typically required to produce results and the risk that "healthy" conflict will be stifled. The alignment of the three bargaining processes promises many advantages, given a long-term strategy and patience regarding the achievement of results.

Change theories often discuss strategic choices solely in terms of what is *desirable* for the moving party. Our research has highlighted, however, that some strategies that are very "desirable" for a given party may not always be *feasible.* For example, no matter how desirable the escape option may seem to managers in capital-intensive industries, it is not very feasible.

Within the constraints of what is feasible, a range of choices are usually available to a negotiator. For example, *structural* factors are often a constraint on what is feasible, but they can sometimes be adjusted to better serve a strategy (e.g., *decentralization* of the negotiations may be promoted to serve a fostering strategy). Needless to say, in the context of fostering, the adjustment of structures often occurs by mutual agreement, while in the context of forcing, structural changes are usually initiated on a unilateral basis and met with reverse structural initiatives.

Given the limitations of pure forcing or pure fostering, most negotiators will employ some mix of the two or use the strategies in sequence (for example, forcing followed by fostering.) It is these *mixed* or *sequential* cases that are both most interesting theoretically and most relevant to practitioners.

Mixed or sequential strategies are complicated first by the social contract in which they are embedded. In the context of a social contract in which the parties rely on compliance mechanisms to ensure performance, forcing strategies are highly consistent, while fostering strategies are likely to be viewed with distrust. In the context of a social contract oriented around employee commitment and union-management cooperation, fostering strategies are highly consistent, while forcing strategies run "against the grain" and are likely to be viewed as a violation of shared understandings.

The broad consistencies and inconsistencies of mixed or sequential strategies are further sharpened when we examine the bargaining processes. For example, integrative bargaining depends on high levels of information sharing but is then vulnerable to subsequent or parallel distributive tactics in which the shared information may be used to gain a power advantage.

OUTLINE OF THE BOOK AND PREVIEW OF THE EMPIRICAL FINDINGS

The three chapters in Part I review the contemporary labor-management landscape and present the theory. Chapter 1 analyzes the new forces in the competitiveness era that are driving the change agendas of management and labor, and Chapter 2 introduces the three strategies—escape, forcing, and fostering—by which managements are pursuing these changes. Building on the concepts introduced in these two chapters, Chapter 3 sets forth the whole theory.

Part II (Chapters 4, 5, and 6) summarizes the change histories of 13 companies or plants drawn from three industries—pulp and paper (4 cases), auto supply (5 cases), and railroads (4 cases). Each industry is considered in a separate chapter, which starts with an analysis of the industry context and then presents the summaries and analyses of the respective cases. The cases in each industry illustrate a diverse set of forcing and fostering strategies and a diverse set of outcomes. These case histories are used to illustrate the concepts of the theory and assess their utility in generating insights. We also identify and score certain aspects of every case to provide comparable data for use in our comparative analyses in Part III.

Part III (Chapters 7 and 8) assesses the factors that appear to have influenced negotiators' strategic choices. Chapter 7 treats this question at an industry level of analysis. We observe that each of our three industries was characterized by a distinct pattern of reliance on escape, forcing, and fostering. In auto supply, all three strategies played important roles; it was the only industry with significant escape activity. In paper, forcing was the dominant strategy, with fostering playing an increasing role by the late 1980s. And in railroads—which manifested the least amount of change effort—fostering was the more prevalent change activity.

Our comparative analysis confirms that certain aspects of an industry's context, such as capital intensity and embedded infrastructure, strongly shape the overall pattern of strategies adopted by companies in that industry. The unexpected finding was that in explaining these overall industry tendencies, the "desirability" factors in our model played no discernible role and the "feasibility" factors (also in the model) were decisive. For management, desirability factors specify how well a strategy addresses the logical (or actual) priorities of the industry's competitive situation. In contrast, feasibility factors determine how possible it is (or appears to be) to effectively implement a strategy in a given industry.

Chapter 8 shifts the focus to the company level (or plant level in some cases), presenting an analysis similar to that in Chapter 7, but more detailed. We compare the strategic choices that launched the 20 distinct change periods identified in our 13 case histories. This analysis provides some level of support for each of several specific propositions about the major considerations that tend to cause a negotiator to force or foster.

Specifically, the propositions we assess are based on the premise that management's choices between forcing or fostering would be shaped by the following judgments:

1. Management's priority with respect to substantive concessions and/or movement toward commitment and cooperation

2. Management's expectations about labor's receptivity or resistance to its substantive proposals and/or its social contract aims

3. Management's assessment of the parties' relative bargaining power

The first judgment relates to desirability and the other two to feasibility. Our analyses generally supported the idea that all three considerations were influential, although the roles each played varied from case to case.

In Part IV, we draw material from our case histories to identify and illustrate the tactical implementation of forcing (Chapter 9), fostering (Chapter 10), and the two in combination or sequence (Chapter 11).

Chapters 9 and 10 provide support for the general idea that given a strategic orientation to either force or foster, there are predictable patterns in how negotiators will manage each of three interrelated negotiating processes—bargaining, shaping intergroup attitudes, and managing intraparty differences. We also discuss the various ways in which bargaining structures may be manipulated to serve a particular strategy. Finally, we identify what we believe are predictable dynamics and risks associated with implementation tactics, such as the risk of escalation during forcing when a negotiator heightens his or her constituents' distrust of the other party.

Chapter 11 explores the tactical dilemmas and other dynamics that are generated when a change strategy consists of a combination of forcing and fostering. Similar dilemmas arise during the transition from one strategy to another—for example, from a forcing campaign to a fostering effort.

At various points during our discussions in Parts II–IV, we take note of evidence that helps explain why the outcomes were better in some case histories than in others. Although we find exceptions, we observe a tendency for better outcomes to be associated with scenarios that contained a sequence of forcing and fostering and/or included a period of combined forcing/fostering. We also identify especially imaginative and effective tactics that appeared to play a role in good outcomes and miscalculations that contributed to poor outcomes.

In the book's conclusion (Chapter 12), we summarize the findings within the framework of the theory and also argue the advantages of viewing workplace change through the lens of a negotiations framework such as the one we have proposed. We describe "realities" that we believe this lens does a better job of identifying and treating than other theoretical perspectives. The advantages include a more discriminating treatment of what is often labeled "resistance to change," clarification of the contingent nature of the power of the party driving the change, and recognition of the many sources of uncertainty in the outcomes of a planned change effort.

ALTERNATIVE APPROACHES TO READING THE BOOK

Not surprisingly, the organization of our book is the one that we believe will make the most sense to the majority of readers. However, experience has taught us that some readers will prefer to read the three parts containing our findings (Parts II, III, and IV) in a different sequence.

The first consideration is the reader's interest in case studies. Most readers will find it useful to familiarize themselves with the cases in Part II before proceeding to the analyses in Parts III and IV. Others may wish to read only the introduction to Part II and then go directly to our case examples, analyses, interpretations, and conclusions in Parts III and IV, returning to the cases selectively to better understand the data from which the conclusions have emerged. We hope some readers will eventually want to dig even more deeply into the cases than is permitted by the relatively brief summaries contained in Part II and refer elsewhere to the extended treatment of these cases.[1]

The second consideration is the reader's proclivities regarding different types of analysis. Both Parts III (about strategy) and IV (about tactics) contain analyses that cut across all of the cases. However, Part III's treatment of strategy is driven largely by the formal hypotheses and is relatively more abstract, whereas Part IV's treatment of tactics is organized merely by the theoretical framework (not by formal hypotheses) and the ideas are more extensively illustrated. Therefore, some readers may prefer to go first to Part IV and immerse themselves in the detailed discussion of the tactics that implement forcing and fostering before they take up our analysis in Part III of how negotiators decide to pursue one strategy or the other.

NOTE

1. Joel E. Cutcher-Gershenfeld, Robert B. McKersie, and Richard E. Walton, *Pathways to Change: Case Studies in Strategic Labor-Management Negotiations* (Kalamazoo, Mich.: W. E. Upjohn Institute, forthcoming).

STRATEGIC NEGOTIATIONS

STRATEGIC NEGOTIATIONS

Part I

The Challenge and Theory of Strategic Negotiations

Part I reviews the profound changes occurring in labor-management relations and offers a theory for making sense of the phenomenon. Over the past decade or more, management has come under mounting competitive pressures to become more efficient and has often taken the initiative to revise in fundamental ways the terms of its relationship with labor.

Chapter 1 sets forth the change agendas of management and labor. In the collective-bargaining arena, management seeks to reduce payroll costs, increase work assignment flexibility, and secure a more sustained effort from labor. Management's objectives regarding its social contract with labor are more diverse. For example, whereas some managements would replace the traditional compliance-based relationship with employees with one based on commitment, others are seeking to strengthen the existing compliance relationship. Similarly, whereas some would replace the traditional arm's-length accommodation with unions with a social contract based on mutual cooperation, others desire an arrangement based on union containment or avoidance.

Labor's responses to management's collective-bargaining initiatives range from resistance to grudging acceptance (depending in part on labor's own reading of whether the company's survival and jobs are at stake). Often, labor's responses also include new demands, such as enhanced employment security and power sharing. Responses to management's initiatives to renegotiate the social contract also vary. When management seeks mutual cooperation with the union and mutual commitment with employees, the union may or may not reciprocate (depending in part on its assessments of management's true intentions and of the implications of such a relationship for the union's institutional security).

Chapter 2 describes the several strategies management employs to achieve its objectives: it may seek to *escape* the union relationship; it may attempt to *force* substantive change and/or a diminished role for the union;

and it may *foster* both new cooperative attitudes and solutions to common problems. Management often seeks to coordinate two or more of these change strategies.

The advantage of this coordination of distinctly different strategies derives in part because each strategy is especially relevant for a different change objective and in part because one change strategy may enhance the effectiveness of another. For example, the possibility that management might escape the existing relationship by transferring operations to a non-union site may enhance its ability to force change without using tactics that risk uncontrollable escalation of the conflict. Also, there is often compelling logic for management to first force the substantive changes especially disagreeable to labor (for example, pay concessions or a combination of crafts) and then foster changes in relations that make it easier to implement new contractual provisions in particular and that promote cooperation in general.

Chapter 3 lays out the theory of strategic negotiations that we have already previewed in the "Introduction and Overview." It provides the framework used to analyze each case history presented in Part II and formulates a number of propositions around which Parts III and IV are organized.

Chapter 1

Management Objectives in the Competitiveness Era: New Social and Substantive Contracts with Labor

What are management's objectives, and how are they driving the change processes we want to understand? As this chapter documents, the changes of interest are reflected in highly contrasting movements in labor-management relations. On the one hand, some of the bitterest industrial conflicts of the past half century have been fought during the past decade, involving the air traffic controllers, Phelps Dodge, Greyhound, Eastern Airlines, and Pittston mines, to mention a few well-publicized examples. On the other hand, recent years have seen unprecedented advances in labor-management cooperation. Saturn, the pathbreaking partnership of General Motors and the UAW, is a particularly ambitious example. But serious commitment to labor-management cooperation can be found in most American industries, including telephone, autos, glass, electronics, paper, rubber, steel, airlines, and copper. Cooperative initiatives in these industries focus on a number of issues relevant to business performance: product quality, employee involvement, training, work redesign, customer service, and even strategic business planning.

What do these divergent trends have in common? The changes involve both substantive adjustments in the terms and conditions of employment *and* revisions in the social contracts that tie labor and management together. The social contracts include shared (or at least acknowledged) understandings about the broad quid pro quos and "rules of the game." We are particularly interested in the social contracts between union and management (at an institutional level) and between workers and employers (at an individual level). Social contracts are typically unwritten, but their elements are often reflected in key documents such as the management's rights clause or the mission statement for a joint union-management initiative.

We explore first the contracts inherited from the New Deal era.

THE PAST: NEW DEAL INDUSTRIAL RELATIONS

The principles of "scientific management" and adversarial collective bargaining—as codified by New Deal labor legislation and the War Labor Board and then routinized through collective bargaining—had by the 1960s produced a relatively stable set of social contracts.[1] Between employees and employers, there was a social contract based on mutual compliance. Between employers and unions, there was a social contract based on arm's-length accommodation. Substantive contracts were negotiated, of course, between employers and unions through formal collective bargaining, but they were also negotiated directly between employees and supervisors through the establishment, enforcement, and revision of informal work standards, norms, and expectations about the behavior of individuals in both groups.

The employment relationship between employers and workers was based on mutual compliance within the terms of increasingly refined substantive contracts.[2] Management institutionalized an approach to managing the workforce based on Frederick W. Taylor's ideas of scientific management and the principles of mass production.[3] Jobs were fragmented and deskilled to minimize training, while supervision relied on discipline and engineered standards to ensure performance. Unions further codified job demarcations in the labor contract in order to place boundaries on management discretion. Workers cooperated among themselves to treat minimum performance standards as output ceilings (while management treated them as floors). Labor and management developed an increasingly detailed set of rules outlining their rights and obligations and prescribing how their differences would be adjudicated. Each party developed professionals who specialized in managing these relationships—and ensured mutual compliance. While the substantive contract (formal collective-bargaining agreements, personnel policies, and well-established past practices) recorded the increasingly specific work rules, the compliance-based social contract between employers and individual employees fueled the increasing legalization and formalization of the employment relationship.[4]

To complement the compliance-oriented employee-employer relationships, companies and unions formulated institutional relationships that were both arm's-length and accommodative. They evolved quid pro quos that satisfied the institutional priorities of each party. Labor provided management with assurances of uninterrupted production (between contract negotiations) and accepted management's rights to make basic business decisions. In exchange, management contributed to an ever-rising standard of living (through wage and benefit increases), agreed to negotiate measures to ameliorate the negative impacts of certain business decisions (such as the introduction of new technology and workforce reductions), and did not challenge the basic legitimacy of organized labor. The substantive agreements were struck in the context of an arm's-length, adversarial, but accommodative, social contract between employers and unions that represented generally accepted rules of the game for institutional interactions.

Firms in the nonunion sector largely followed the wage and benefit patterns set in the unionized sector, with substantive contracts primarily "negotiated" at hiring and promotion. The nonunion firms also tended to follow a Tayloristic approach to organizing and managing work. Thus, employee relations in the nonunion sector were also based on mutual compliance, even though they were not embedded in an adversarial institutional relationship.

THE PRESENT: INDUSTRIAL COMPETITIVENESS

During the 1970s and 1980s, a combination of economic, technological, social, and political forces began to tear apart the individual and institutional social contracts. In their place, negotiations over a new set of social contracts represent core assumptions for what we have termed "the industrial competitiveness era" have emerged.

The concept of industrial competitiveness captures a wide range of external pressures, values, action patterns, and outcomes that stand in contrast with those of the preceding era. The old industrial relations agenda was fueled by economic growth, accommodated by the domestic nature of competition, and reflected the liberal national mood. Now, that agenda is driven by international competition and domestic deregulation and is influenced by a more conservative national mood. While the New Deal framework took for granted rising standards of living and emphasized equitable distribution of wealth, the competitiveness era emphasizes wealth-producing methods and contingent compensation. Whereas unions used to take the initiative in pressing for change, management now initiates much of the change.[5]

The exact contours of the changes are still emerging, but it is already clear that they encompass a wide range of highly contrasting labor-management relations. We feel that the emergence of diversity and the implications of alternative approaches to labor-management relations can best be understood from a "negotiations perspective."

TWO LEVELS OF CONTRACTS—TWO LEVELS OF NEGOTIATIONS

Just as there are two social contracts between labor and management— one at the institutional level (e.g., arm's-length adversarial) and another at the individual level (e.g., based on mutual compliance)—there are important labor-management interactions occurring at both levels. Accordingly, we need to broaden our definition of labor negotiations.

Institutional-Level Negotiations

Normally, when we refer to labor negotiations, we immediately think of collective bargaining. Indeed, what is happening in America at the bargaining table is more complex and interesting than ever. It is these developments—at both the contentious and cooperative extremes—that are most visible and that prompt increased scholarly interest in labor-management relations. Our negotiations perspective, however, encompasses the full range of interactions, including, for example, joint committees, in which the formal terms of employment are set and the nature of institutional relations among firms, unions, and other parties is defined.

Individual-Level Negotiations

Though the present era features many new developments at the institutional level, an equally interesting and equally important game is going on at the individual level. Middle managers and supervisors are under pressure from their superiors to increase the utilization of the human resources assigned to them. They are expected to negotiate lower absenteeism, safer practices, closer conformance to quality specifications, and increased machine uptime or more hours of actual work during a shift.

Supervisors have a wide range of negotiating techniques at the individual level—just as management representatives do at the institutional level. They may seek improvements in attendance, quality, and productivity by using closer monitoring and more systematic discipline and by constantly testing the limits of their power, authority, and rights. Or they may seek to negotiate these improvements by using workers' heads as well as their hands, giving people more say over more aspects of their work environment, and providing more information about the business and more contact with customers.

Workers, of course, do not necessarily accept management's statements about its intentions at face value. For example, management may introduce involvement mechanisms that employees see as a sophisticated form of manipulation, not as a desire to increase mutual commitment. If management wants to convey the seriousness of its intentions, it will likely have to up the ante in terms of the organization's commitment to employees by training, disclosing information, increasing employment stability, and according dignity.

Then again, workers sometimes believe that management's intentions are constructive even when they are harsh and restrictive. For example, in a plant in which absenteeism has gotten out of hand, the majority of employees may accept the need for management to clarify the rules, tighten their enforcement, and administer discipline. Thus, while the nature of managers' techniques conveys something about their intentions, it does not tell the whole story.

Individual-level negotiations are often about supervisors' struggle to test what it takes to negotiate employee commitment and also to decide whether they are prepared to pay the price for commitment by, for example, sharing power and responsibility. We take individual-level negotiations to include the full range of interactions between supervisors and employees over actual day-to-day routines and over the nature of employee/supervisor relations.

MANAGEMENT'S SUBSTANTIVE AGENDA

In taking the initiative for change, management has focused especially on three substantive areas: reduced payroll costs, increased flexibility, and sustained contributions by individual workers.

Over the past decade, many managers have sought to *reduce pay and benefits* in absolute terms or to slow their increase to rates markedly below the historical pattern. This issue has been particularly important in industries in which wages had increased faster than national averages, wage increases had exceeded productivity increases, and/or the cost of health and retirement benefits was increasing at unexpectedly rapid rates. The airline, steel, auto, paper, and meatpacking industries are examples. Research suggests that during the 1980s, anywhere from one-third to one-half of all labor-management agreements in the United States were characterized by some form of "concessions."[6]

Typically, management has won these changes (concessions) only over the vigorous opposition of labor. In some instances, where the survival of the plant or enterprise was clearly at stake, the union was persuaded that it was in its best interests to accept wage decreases. In some industries, the reduction in payroll costs has been achieved primarily by reducing head count without reducing per capita compensation.

The other two agenda items relate to changes in the way employees work. Management seeks *more flexibility* in the assignment of workers—by revising contractual rights and/or by eliciting voluntary actions on the part of workers. It also wants *more sustained contributions* from workers—either by utilizing more effective compliance techniques or by employing practices that elicit employee motivation. The term *contribution* encompasses the full range of potential inputs, from physical effort (working faster and in a more sustained pattern) to creative intellectual effort (improving work methods and giving careful attention to quality).

As noted, increases in flexibility and contributions may be achieved by two contrasting routes—directly revising formal, contractual rights and/or making informal changes in practices. Labor usually opposes management's attempts to negotiate contractual flexibility (e.g., eliminating restrictive work rules) and counters management's efforts to negotiate an increased workload or expanded authority to monitor and punish performance problems. However, when management attempts to enhance flexibility and employee contributions by eliciting positive motivation and voluntary cooperation, labor's responses are more varied. Workers often manifest initial skepticism. Many of them may subsequently respond positively, depending upon their judgment of management's sincerity and the adequacy of other changes to support a new relationship. Union officials usually remain skeptical or opposed for a longer period of time, as they sort out the full range of implications of management's initiatives, including, for example, the implications for the institutional security and strength of the union. We return to this subject in our discussion of social contracts.

An important distinction among the agenda items is that some can be realized through direct changes and others can be realized only through a change in attitudes and relationships. For example, a company can lower wage costs by persuading a union to accept lump-sum wage increases, a two-tier wage system, or employee co-payment of health care costs. Once these changes are agreed to, implementation is relatively straightforward. In effect, the changes are "self-implementing."

Other changes—for example, increased flexibility and employee effort—are more complicated. A new agreement can specify a team-based production organization and indicate that employees will assume responsibility for their own quality performance, but effective implementation of these changes will not be automatic. Agreement on contractual language is only one step in the process of negotiating such changes. This step may be followed by obtaining acceptance and implementation of the changes by workers and supervisors. As such, negotiations occur both at an institutional level and at an individual one. A case in point can be seen in an ambitious set of labor-management structures created by AT&T and the Communication Workers of America (CWA) in what they call "The Workplace of the Future." It will be interesting to track how this mechanism agreed to in contract negotiations influences day-to-day relations involving workers and supervisors.

LABOR'S SUBSTANTIVE AGENDA

The competitiveness era is characterized primarily by management initiatives around a management-defined change agenda. Labor's responses to management's change efforts center primarily on defensive actions but also include identification of new priorities and independent labor initiatives.

Labor's defensive responses include vigorous opposition to

- Wage concessions, unless a majority of jobs are at stake
- Repealing established restrictions on management control over how work is done—again, unless survival of the business and employment are at stake
- Management attempts to more closely monitor worker behavior

Beyond its opposition to new management initiatives, labor in many industries is particularly concerned about *employment security*. The traditional bread-and-butter issues of wages and fringe benefits are still important, but greater attention is paid to preserving jobs that are seen as "good" in comparison to alternatives in the labor market. In the unionized sector of manufacturing (a major focus of this study), wages and benefits are substantially higher than what workers receive in other industries, especially the expanding service sector of the economy. Thus, with the vast restructuring of, and decline in, manufacturing employment, workers who are still in high-paying jobs place top priority on keeping them.

Unions also place high priority on retraining in order to enhance the *career interests* of their members and promote continuity of employment. Major companies in autos, steel, and telephones, with their respective unions, have created joint funds for upgrading the workforce. In the case of General Motors and the UAW, the annual budget for this jointly administered program was, by the early 1990s, more than $200 million.

Some unions have presented management with independent initiatives or responded to management initiatives with their own proposals. In some cases, this involves *programs to improve the competitive position of the industry.* For example, the Bricklayers Union, in conjunction with the major employers' group, has established the Masonry Institute in order to expand the use of building materials that create employment opportunities for its members.

Other union initiatives center on *joint planning at the strategic level.* For example, Boeing Corporation and its major union, the International Association of Machinists (IAM), have met regularly to examine trends in a number of key areas of technology, such as robotics, CAD/CAM, composite materials, and computer-integrated manufacturing. These discussions have been used by a management-union training committee to design programs facilitating career shifts from declining occupations to expanding occupations related to new technologies.

Competitive pressures have also prompted many unions to seek access to business information and decision making. They include the United Steelworkers of America (USWA), Flint Glass Workers, Grain Millers, Communication Workers of America, and Amalgamated Clothing and Textile Workers Union (ACTWU). In the case of the latter union and Xerox, top officials have met regularly for some time to discuss investment decisions.

In an earlier era, unions attempted to "take wages out of competition" by imposing similar terms on firms that competed in the marketplace. However, with declining union density, growing international trade, and the increasing number of situations in which economic pressures threaten the survival of a company and its jobs, unions often must make judgments about wage policy on a case-by-case basis. Making these judgments requires considerably more information and more in-depth knowledge about the economics of individual businesses.

The fact that unions are seeking wider access to business decisions does not mean that they are necessarily seeking more cooperative labor relations in all cases. Indeed, the information to which they gain access may be used to pursue adversarial tactics more vigorously. For example, knowing more about the profitability of different product lines may enable a union to resist proposed concessions.

As we shall see in the following sections, the substantive agendas of labor and management are accompanied by new objectives for the social contracts they want with each other at both the individual and the institutional level.

NEW SOCIAL CONTRACTS AT THE INDIVIDUAL LEVEL

Proposed revisions in the relations between employers and individual workers (or small work groups)[7] can be based on a mutual *commitment* employment relationship, in contrast to the traditional one based on mutual *compliance*. Whereas under mutual compliance, the parties agree merely to comply with certain set terms of employment, under mutual commitment, employees become more broadly committed to the enterprise and management becomes more broadly committed to the well-being of employees.

Today, the mutual compliance relationship is the approach preferred by many companies. Indeed, many companies have reacted to competitive pressures by shifting the terms of employment in ways favorable to management and increasing management's capacity to enforce labor compliance. For example, such a shift often accompanies the conversion of full-time work to part-time, more contingent work.

However, during the 1970s and 1980s, a trend for companies to move toward commitment gained momentum.[8] In these companies, which included both unionized and nonunionized firms, management and labor renegotiated their roles, rights, obligations, and relationships to reflect a higher degree of mutual commitment (in effect, a higher level of interdependence). For effective change to occur, the parties had to agree on their reciprocal commitments.

Both the compliance- and the commitment-based relations can be thought of as social contracts when there is concurrence regarding, or at least acknowledgment (tacit or explicit) of, one or more underlying principles of employee-employer relations.[9] Negotiations occur when the objectives of one or both parties include revision of the social contract.

NEW SOCIAL CONTRACTS AT THE INSTITUTIONAL LEVEL

We distinguish among three distinct institutional-level social contracts, each representing a set of principles that guide interactions. The previously dominant type, *arm's-length accommodation*, was discussed above. This is being replaced by two divergent social contract objectives—one more adversarial, the other more cooperative.

One type, *containment/avoidance*, is the objective of some managements that seek a social contract in which the other party is contained, weakened, or even eliminated. Few unions will willingly join in such a social contract, so it is generally achieved through the unilateral exercise of power by management.

Table 1.1   Management Objectives Regarding the Social Contract with Labor

Employee Relations	Union Relations		
	Containment or Avoidance	Arm's-Length Accommodation	Cooperation
Compliance	Examples: FAA/flight controllers Continental Airlines Greyhound	Traditional New Deal social contract	Examples: Sweetheart deals in trucking
Commitment	Examples: Greenfield plants in the South	Examples: Quality circles in manufacturing	Examples: National Steel/USWA Xerox/ACTWU Saturn/UAW AT&T/CWA

Note: The two major alternatives to the traditional social contract with labor reached by *negotiated* change are compliance/containment (upper-left cell) and commitment/cooperation (lower-right cell).

A third important target of many managements, employee commitment/union avoidance, is frequently reached by means (such as starting up new facilities) that do not include negotiations with organized labor.

In contrast, a social contract objective of *cooperation* involves management and labor's building a partnership (in relevant aspects of the relationship). Such an arrangement has the potential to reinforce and extend the union's institutional strength while conferring a degree of legitimacy on management initiatives. However, a social contract premised on a cooperative relationship may be seen to limit management's independent prerogatives and to create political and practical dilemmas for the union.

COMBINATIONS OF INDIVIDUAL AND INSTITUTIONAL SOCIAL CONTRACTS

What are the various possible combinations of the two individual social contracts (compliance and commitment) and the three institutional social contracts (arm's-length accommodation, containment/avoidance, and cooperation)? (See Table 1.1.) What combinations are most relevant in an era of industrial competitiveness?[10]

Combinations Characteristic of the Earlier Era

Of the six possible combinations of individual and institutional social contracts, one of them—individual compliance and arm's-length institutional relations—is the pattern that characterized the earlier era. We and others have found this to be increasingly problematic in the current economic environment. In the face of growing competition, most managers have rejected the arm's-length accommodation relationship with unions, seeking either containment/avoidance or cooperation. In some cases, compliance-based individual social contracts are retained (and even intensified), but in other cases, there is a shift toward employee-employer social contracts based on mutual commitment.

Another possible combination of social contracts—individual compliance and institutional cooperation—is characteristic of what are termed "sweetheart" contracts between employers and unions. Such arrangements were previously an important topic of study in certain industries (such as trucking, cement, and construction) and may still occur in certain cases today, but neither their frequency nor their features make them very relevant to our analysis. However, the four remaining combinations of individual and institutional social contracts are important and will be discussed in turn.

Arm's-Length Accommodation and Employee Commitment

A combination of continued arm's-length accommodation and new employee commitment represents perhaps the most common variant on the previously dominant social contracts (arm's-length accommodation and employee compliance). Between one-third and one-half of larger U.S. firms indicate that they have engaged in some degree of experimentation with quality circles or other forms of employee participation programs.[11] We can assume that many, perhaps most, of these firms have not revised their institutional relations.

While this arrangement is attractive to many managers since it involves a relatively modest degree of change, there are theoretical and practical reasons to suggest that it is unstable. Because the relationship with the union is unchanged, the union can successfully oppose an effort to gain employee commitment. Moreover, in the case of a quality circle program that is attracting growing numbers of employee volunteers, such opposition is likely since the program will probably be seen as "going around the union." Alternatively, the union may want joint ownership of the program—in which case, it would seek to renegotiate the institutional social contract around a set of cooperation objectives. As such, we predict that this combination will either revert back to the arm's-length accommodation/compliance combination or be transformed into cooperation/commitment or one of the other combinations.[12] In fact, a growing body of research evidence confirms a high failure rate among employee commitment programs undertaken in a setting in which the union-management relationship remains arm's-length.[13]

Employee Commitment and Union Containment/Avoidance

Some managements that seek individual employee commitment have concluded that a union must be either weakened or absent in order for the business to succeed. Examples of this pattern include new plant start-ups in greenfield sites (plants usually built in rural locations on empty green fields). Beginning in the 1970s, many manufacturing companies used greenfield plants not only to escape the union but also to implement work organizations and human resource policies designed to elicit high commitment. TRW was among the many manufacturing companies that pursued this strategy, and its Lawrence, Kansas, cable plant, started in the early 1970s, is one such case. The plant used a team structure, implemented a pay-for-knowledge scheme, and relied on facilitative supervision. Despite organizing campaigns, management succeeded in avoiding unionization while maintaining the team system of work organization.

Other managements work toward high commitment among employees without escaping or dislodging the union. Instead, they merely contain or circumscribe its influence. These managements, which deal with unions without strong traditions or strong national organizations, practice benign neglect, in which management neither challenges the union directly nor acts in ways to enhance its leadership position. When such unions do not respond to the challenge associated with management's individual-level activities, they are likely to become marginalized.

Employee Compliance and Union Containment/Avoidance

A significant trend is toward a tightening of employee compliance and a weakening or an elimination of the union. A highly publicized example was the Reagan administration's handling of the illegal 1981 strike by air traffic controllers, in which the striking workers were terminated, their union was decertified, and FAA management control over tower personnel was strengthened. Another example was Greyhound's aggressive attempts to reduce pay during contract negotiations in 1986 and again in 1990, both of which resulted in bitter strikes marked by violence. Still other examples were Frank Lorenzo's actions, first at Continental and later at Eastern, to tighten control over airline workers and weaken or eliminate the unions representing pilots, flight attendants, and ground personnel.

In these cases, management was willing to take whatever steps were required to mobilize power and defeat the union, including replacing strikers with permanent employees, selling assets, and declaring bankruptcy. It was also willing to sustain the heightened adversarialism that resulted and to escalate the use of compliance techniques in an attempt to secure performance from a disaffected workforce.

Other managements are moving in this direction, but less dramatically. They merely seek to contain or weaken the influence of the union without any hope of eliminating it. USX (formerly U.S. Steel) appeared to fit this pattern during the 1980s. It fought hard for greater control over work practices, accepting a strike in 1986, and then took exceptionally tough actions in administering the contract and managing the workforce during the remainder of the decade.

Unions' response to management's attempts to contain or weaken their influence is typically an escalation of adversarial rhetoric and other tactics to discredit management and impugn its motives. Common tactics are corporate campaigns (programs to create public relations problems and place other forms of pressure on the corporation) and "in-plant strategies" (practices that frustrate regular business operations, such as working to rule and filing large volumes of grievances).

Employee Commitment and Union-Management Cooperation

The objective of many managements is a combination of high employee commitment supported by cooperative union relations.

While many quality circle programs have been initiated in nonunion locations or pursued independently of a union, a substantial number of companies have joined with their unions to support quality of work life (QWL) or employee involvement (EI) activities. These activities were pioneered in the automobile industry by GM and Ford—with the UAW in both cases—and spread to other companies and other industries. QWL activities usually involved joint union-management steering committees and voluntary employee groups formed to solve work environment and production problems. The committees and groups were supposed to avoid issues covered by the collective-bargaining agreement.

QWL programs by themselves do not redefine the individual and institutional social contracts. They can, however, serve as a first step along a path toward a combination of employee commitment and institutional cooperation. Ultimately, the parties must also redesign jobs and work structures as well as share a significant amount of power, responsibility, and information. It is these later interactions that can result in a significant renegotiation of individual and institutional social contracts.

The institutional negotiations with the union may be direct and formal, or they may be tacit, as when management undertakes a unilateral initiative and the union responds by counseling its members not to participate. Supervisors' individual-level negotiations for worker participation are invariably a tacit and continuous process. Management usually finds it relatively easy to negotiate the involvement of 15 to 25 percent of the workforce but relatively difficult to negotiate the conditions under which the large majority of workers will opt to actively participate.[14]

EI and QWL programs and LMPTs (labor-management participation teams in steel) are often established as voluntary. The program facilitators (who may be recruited from both management and the union) are charged with attempting to negotiate the active participation of workers and supervisors. However, if the union and management feel that more active participation by the entire work organization is necessary for competitive reasons, they may negotiate new work systems, including work team structures that change the roles and responsibilities of all employees. They may create structures at several levels of the organization to allow for union involve-ment in business-planning activities.

National Steel Corporation and the Steelworkers is a high-profile example of an effort by management and labor to move their relationship toward commitment and cooperation. In 1986, they reached a labor agreement that the *Washington Post* called "precedent-breaking." The contract stated:

> The management of National Steel Corporation and the United Steelworkers of America jointly recognize that in order for the corpo-ration to meet the immediate challenge of survival and the need for long-range prosperity, growth, and secure employment, both parties must now work closely together in a joint partnership that extends from the shop floor to the executive suite to solve problems quickly and in a cooperative manner.

The key element of the agreement is a cooperative partnership, manifested in joint structures and processes for sharing power and responsibility.

Still other notable examples of movement toward commitment and coop-eration are the Shell polypropylene plant in Sarnia, Ontario (with the Oil, Chemical, and Atomic Workers Union); the NUMMI plant in Fremont, California (a GM-Toyota joint venture with the UAW); Xerox Corporation (with the Amalgamated Clothing and Textile Workers Union); Magma Cop-per (with the United Steelworkers); Rohm and Haas (with the OCAW); and the previously mentioned Saturn subsidiary of General Motors (with the UAW).[15]

Unions often propose their own conditions for a partnership with man-agement, including formal membership on the board of directors or, more commonly, access to strategic decision making by informal briefings or participation in key management planning processes. A good example of this partnership-ownership arrangement is the 1993 deal between Inland Steel and the United Steelworkers. The company agreed to add a director acceptable to the union but not a union member or officer (thereby making the individual acceptable to the company). This model of a director with a special perspective on union-management relations was used in several trucking companies during the 1980s. In order to save these companies from bankruptcy, the workers accepted pay cuts and received stock (held in an ESOP), and the union gained the right to nominate two independent direc-tors to each board.

Where partnership is a response to a severe economic threat to the com-pany, some unions have insisted upon labor's acquiring an ownership stake as a quid pro quo for concessions. They have also obtained a commitment from management to reinvest savings from concessions in the industry. They have negotiated limits on outsourcing and contracting out. Finally, in some cases, the unions have sought agreements from management to stay neutral

Table 1.2 Contrasts between the Traditional Social Contract with Labor and Two Emerging Alternatives

Emerging Compliance and <——— Containment	Compliance/Arm's Length Accommodation	———>Emerging Commitment and Cooperation
Each party is concerned about its own institutional survival.	The parties acknowledge conflicting interests of employees and employers; emphasis is on achieving equity in that context.	The parties place joint emphasis on mutual goals and integrative potential, as well as on increasing the size of the economic pie.
Power and responsibility for managing the business are concentrated in management. Management attempts to diminish the union's role, and the union seeks to maintain checks and balances on management action.	Power and responsibility for managing the business are concentrated in management, which accepts union checks and balances on management action.	There is significant sharing of power and responsibility for improving business functioning, as well as sharing of economic ups and downs and of information and status.
Management discounts and undermines labor's power to punish or reward management.	The power of labor that derives from its ability to withdraw from the workplace—e.g., conducting a strike or job action (punishment power)—is emphasized.	The power of labor that derives from its ability to contribute value—e.g., solving production problems (reward power)—is acknowledged.
Neither side accepts the other's definition of its legitimate role.	Adversarial, but legitimate, roles for unions and management are emphasized.	A mixture of partnership and adversarial roles for unions and management is acknowledged.

Management and labor struggle over both the amount of employee voice and the vehicle for that voice.	The parties rely wholly on union representatives (primarily in formal mechanisms) to express employee voice.	Both direct worker participation and representative democracy are considered important.
Management relies on its power to implement decisions it judges to be in the interests of the business. The union contests whatever it can.	The parties rely on rules for prescribing acceptable behavior.	The parties rely on shared goals and agreed-on principles for prescribing desired behavior.
Management departs from uniformity of practices depending on its assessment of business needs. The union contests whenever it can.	Uniformity of practices is adhered to in order to ensure equal treatment.	Diversity of practices is accepted if consistent with mutually determined principles.
Performance standards are uncertain and based on what management can negotiate in practice.	Performance standards are stable and based on engineering principles.	Performance standards are evolving and are more responsive to market requirements.
Management's view is the same as in accommodation, but with management contesting the union's checks on its action.	Management views labor as a cost to be trimmed in a downturn and provides minimal training. The union ensures that layoffs are distributed fairly.	The parties view human resources as an investment and jointly research ways to stabilize employment and increase training.

Table 1.3   Routes to Achieving Management's Substantive Agenda under Emerging Social Contracts with Labor

Management's Substantive Agenda	Compliance and Containment	Commitment and Cooperation
Reduced payroll costs	Economic concessions forced by management	Reduced payroll costs agreed to by management and labor because they are seen as in their mutual interests
More flexibility	Flexibility increased by bargaining for rule changes	Flexibility increased by informal practices and problem solving
More sustained contributions	Increased effort required by stricter standards and control techniques	Contribution broadly construed to emphasize "working smarter" and elicited by positive motivation

about, or even cooperate with, union drives to organize new facilities or employee groups.

Unions do not always reciprocate management's interests in moving toward commitment and cooperation. In many instances, the unions have actively opposed this development, assuming that it would undercut members' loyalty to the unions. In fact, wariness and ambivalence were the most typical union responses in the 1980s and early 1990s.

SUMMARY AND CONCLUSIONS

American managers largely agree on the substantive changes they need: reduced payroll costs, increased flexibility, and sustained contributions by individual workers. And labor usually resists management's proposals for achieving these ends. In addition, the competitive era has raised the salience for labor of new needs of its own—for example, different approaches to employment security and new inputs into business decision making. Thus, the substantive agenda for negotiations in the current era is rich with novel items full of obvious contentious potential and, in many cases, less obvious integrative potential.

American managements may need the same substantive changes, but they sharply diverge in the types of social contracts they seek. The traditional social contracts initially formed in the New Deal era—based on employee compliance and on arm's-length accommodation between union and management—are being replaced by a variety of combinations of individual- and institutional-level social contracts. The two alternatives that involve the most ambitious revisions and are the most contrasting in form are those shown in diagonally opposite corners of Table 1.1—employee compliance and union containment at one extreme and commitment and cooperation at the other. We summarize in Table 1.2 how each of these new options contrasts with the traditional contracts as well as with each other. Almost all of our company or plant case histories involve movement, if it occurred at all, toward one of these alternatives. In all cases, labor initially either opposed a revision of the social contract or regarded it with skepticism. Thus, the social contract changes, like the substantive ones, include conflict potential as well as, in many instances, integrative potential.

Table 1.3 shows management's several substantive agenda items and suggests the routes by which those changes might be achieved under two combinations of social contracts.

We can summarize the several characteristics of management's new objectives (and labor's customary views of them) that have prompted our effort to develop a new theory:

- The duality of the objectives—substantive and social
- The two levels of social contracts involved—institutional and individual
- The magnitude of the potential changes—and the parties' stakes in them
- The interrelated nature of the many changes sought
- Labor's varied responses to these potential changes—initially and subsequently

Existing theories of negotiation, including that proposed in the 1965 edition of *Behavioral Theory*, do not fully address the paradigm-breaking nature of the current change efforts. Other theories of social change do not take into account the negotiated, contingent give-and-take nature of the change process.

NOTES

1. The term *New Deal system* is used by Kochan, Katz, and McKersie to characterize the dominant union-management relationship that emerged during this period. See Thomas A. Kochan, Harry C. Katz, and Robert B. McKersie, *The Transformation of American Industrial Relations* (Ithaca, N.Y.: ILP Press, 1993).
2. See Richard E. Walton, "From Control to Commitment in the Workplace," *Harvard Business Review* (March–April 1985): 76–84.
3. The link between Taylorism and mass-production technology represents the baseline for the analysis by Michael Piore and Charles Sabel in *The Second Industrial Divide: Possibilities for Prosperity* (New York: Basic Books, 1984).
4. This increasing legalization has been explained as the product of institutional interactions by Jack Steiber and Richard Block, "The Impact of Attorneys and Arbitrators on Arbitration Awards," *Industrial and Labor Relations Review* 31, no. 4 (July 1978): 5; and from a critical legal perspective by Katherine Van Wetzel Stone, "The Post-War Paradigm in American Labor Law," *Yale Law Review* 90 (June 1981): 7. While this book focuses on the present era, we would include the

negotiations perspective (and in particular, the compliance-based social contract) as an additional factor that helps explain the successive rounds of increasingly specific substantive agreements.

5. Note that we are not indicating a bias for or against these features, nor are we saying that these are the only patterns present—this is a description of what we see as dominant social trends.

6. Using a very conservative definition of *concession,* Mitchell found the impact extending to between one-third and one-half of unionized workers during the early 1980s. See Daniel J. B. Mitchell, "Shifting Norms in Wage Determination," *Brookings Papers on Economic Activity* 2 (1985): 575–599. This finding was corroborated and extended in Peter Cappelli, "Plant Level Concession Bargaining," *Industrial and Labor Relations Review* 39, no. 1 (1985): 90–104. The issue is a subject of important debate, however. See Richard Freeman, "In Search of Union Wage Concessions in Standard Data Sets," *Industrial Relations* 25, no. 2. (Spring 1986): 131–145. See also Kathryn J. Ready, "Is Pattern Bargaining Dead?" *Industrial and Labor Relations Review* 43, no. 2. (January 1990): 272–279; and "Comments" by Peter Cappelli and Daniel J. B. Mitchell, "Reply" by Kathryn J. Ready, "Is Pattern Bargaining Dead? An Exchange," *Industrial and Labor Relations Review* 44, no. 1. (October 1990): 152–165.

7. We include interactions between small work groups and managers at the level of "individual" social contracts when the negotiation is between a supervisor and an individual work group. Once the interactions involve representatives from multiple work groups, they move toward what we have termed an "institutional" level.

8. This trend was observed by Walton, "From Control to Commitment"; Eric Trist, *The Evolution of Socio-Technical Theory* (Toronto: Ontario Quality of Working Life Centre, 1981); and Irving Bluestone, "QWL and the Adversarial Relationship," *Work Life Review* 1, no. 1 (July 1982): 10–12.

9. Others have used the term *psychological contract* to refer to these individual-level understandings between employees and employers. Given the social nature of the contracting process and the employee-employer contract itself, we believe *social contract* is the more appropriate term.

10. Our thinking about the social contract has been influenced by the pioneering work of Benjamin Selekman, who advanced a framework for analyzing labor-management relations across a spectrum of relationships, including conflict, containment, power bargaining, accommodation, and cooperation. See B. M. Selekman, S. K. Selekman, and S. H. Fuller, *Problems in Labor Relations* (New York: McGraw-Hill, 1950).

11. New York Stock Exchange, Office of Economic Research, *People and Productivity: A Challenge to Corporate America* (New York: New York Stock Exchange, 1982), 1–52.

12. The instability of this combination is the central thesis of research on employee involvement by Joel E. Cutcher-Gershenfeld, Thomas A. Kochan, and Anil Verma, "Recent Developments in U.S. Employee Involvement Initiatives: Erosion or Transformation?," in *Advances in Industrial Relations*, ed. Donna Sockell, David Lewis, and David B. Lipsky (Greenwich, Conn.: JAI Press, 1987), 1–32. It is of note, however, that one of our cases in the paper industry—Boise Cascade's De Ridder mill—moved to this combination of social contracts, and it was more viable than we would have expected. Therefore, we will attempt to understand why this combination was stable in the particular circumstances of this case.

13. See, for example, William N. Cooke, *Labor-Management Cooperation* (Kalamazoo, Mich.: W. E. Upjohn Institute, 1990).

14. While research studies have documented this plateau in enlisting new volunteers for participation programs, there are notable exceptions in which much

higher levels of participation have been achieved. See Thomas A. Kochan, Harry C. Katz, and Nancy R. Mower, "Worker Participation and American Unions," in *Challenges and Choices Facing American Labor,* ed. Thomas A. Kochan (Cambridge, Mass.: MIT Press, 1985), 271–306.

15. Kochan and Osterman have formulated a conceptual framework for capturing the essence of these examples of commitment/cooperation. They outline the steps required of the parties and of employment and labor policy to stimulate further diffusion of these constructive models. See Thomas A. Kochan and Paul Osterman, *The Mutual Gains Enterprise: Forging a Winning Partnership among Labor, Management, and Government* (Boston: Harvard Business School Press, 1994).

Chapter 2

Change Strategies
in the Competitiveness Era:
Escape, Force, and Foster

Confronted with intense external pressures that call for major revisions in the substantive and/or social contracts with labor, management has adopted one or a combination of three approaches: *escape* the existing labor relationship (e.g., by transferring operations), *force* labor to make substantive concessions, or *foster* substantive and social change. Two of the approaches—forcing and fostering—are negotiating strategies and the primary focus of this book. Escape is a nonnegotiating change strategy, although the possibility of escape has tactical implications for both forcing and fostering.

This chapter explores how each change strategy can be used to address management's objectives outlined in the preceding chapter and how the strategies are sometimes combined. The treatment of these two points continues to lay down building blocks for our theory, which is presented in its entirety in Chapter 3. In addition, we review evidence regarding the prevalence of the departures from traditional collective bargaining represented by the three paradigm-breaking strategies we propose here. This evidence supports the idea that the episodes we analyze in this book are typical of a significant fraction of contemporary labor-management relations.

CHANGE STRATEGIES

When substantive and social contracts are renegotiated, what strategies are employed? How does management utilize the various strategies? What counterstrategies and independent strategies does labor employ? What are the individual-level consequences of strategies implemented at the institutional level (and vice versa)?

Escaping the Relationship

In the present era in the United States, escape from the labor-management relationship represents perhaps the most controversial strategic choice. Escape is primarily a managerial strategy, though we will note ways in which unions also occasionally employ this strategy in this country.[1] If management seeks to escape the union, it can follow several routes. First, within the constraints of the law, it can relocate its operations, closing down a unionized operation and opening up a greenfield site, which it then usually manages in such a way as to minimize the chances of a successful union campaign. Second, and again within the constraints of the law, management can create conditions in which workers elect to decertify the union. Third, management can hire permanent replacements for workers on strike. In this case, the union remains the certified bargaining agent. On a de facto basis, however, the union may be pushed out of the picture, and decertification becomes a distinct possibility if significant numbers of strikers do not return to work. Fourth, management may contract out maintenance, construction, and other support functions, removing work from the bargaining unit. Finally, management may systematically raise its investment in nonunion operations, causing unionized facilities to become increasingly marginal.

The transfer of operations has been the most significant form of escape in the past two decades. During the 1970s, companies in many industries—including autos, rubber, electrical equipment, and electronics—opened new plants in greenfield sites, frequently in rural areas or southern states where unionism was weak. This action has been referred to as the "southern strategy." A more recent and increasingly common variation of the strategy involves opening plants abroad.

Management usually took the escape step after concluding that it could not compete effectively if it expanded or even sustained operations in established facilities marked by adversarial relations and high wage rates. Often, established facilities were subsequently closed, in part or entirely, effectively representing a transfer of operations to locations where management could develop labor relations and practices more to its liking. The availability of this option is determined by the mobility of physical plant and equipment and by labor law (in recent decades, decisions of courts and the NLRB have weakened constraints on closing a business and opening a related operation elsewhere).

Management reaped an additional advantage from implementing this approach, in that the new operations often demonstrated the productive power of a new social contract, especially one based on mutual commitment at the individual level, and thus heightened management's interest in seeking comparable change in established facilities. Moreover, because the new plant was tangible evidence of management's willingness to close down inefficient facilities, the escape maneuver provided a backdrop—enhancing the effectiveness of its forcing and fostering strategies in other locations. Faced with this maneuver, the workers in the closed facility usually had no direct recourse, and the primary response of the union involved was to attempt to organize the workers who were hired at the new site, though unions have also used boycott threats and corporate campaigns with some effect in challenging escape strategies.

Thus far, we have considered only escape as pursued by management. Unions recently have developed their own escape routes through employee ownership and leveraged buyouts. Some employee ownership has emerged in the aftermath of a company's deciding to dispose of facilities; examples include the efforts of General Motors to jettison its Hyatt Clark transmission plant and National Steel to divest itself of its Weirton division. However, unions for United Airlines and Northwest Airlines have taken more direct initiatives, attempting to use their leverage to change both ownership and management. Unions have pursued these escape options in only a handful of instances and with very limited success.

Although escape tactics take many forms, our primary interest is in the most strategic form of escape—transfer of operations by management to escape unionization. Escape in this sense typically is not accompanied by negotiations. It may be, in effect, management's best available alternative to a negotiated agreement.[2] Both the escape strategy and escape tactics have many potential implications for the two negotiating strategies—forcing and fostering.

Forcing Change

The most immediate and direct response to the need for change has been for management to attempt to force economic concessions and changes in work rules and worker behavior—usually at the time of contract negotiations but sometimes by unilateral action during the contract. The ability to force change relies on a mixture of bargaining power and evidence about the necessity for the changes. Management forcing may or may not precipitate a strike or job action, the interactions may or may not become acrimonious, and the initiatives may or may not produce the changes management seeks.

The strategy of forcing change is used heavily by managements whose long-term intentions are to tighten the terms of the traditional compliance relationship with workers and/or to contain or weaken the union. Given these intentions, forcing change is a continuous and dominant theme in management's relationship with workers and unions.

However, a management whose long-term intentions focus on high commitment and union-management cooperation *may* also decide to use forcing as part of its broad change effort. Within this particular framework of intentions, the forcing strategy is employed periodically and for relatively limited purposes.

Even when a management is clear about its general purposes—and sometimes it is not—a union cannot be sure. Therefore, although management may intend that forcing tactics be used to achieve a limited purpose, the union may interpret these moves as indicative of a broader anti-union stance, which sets in motion a polarizing dynamic explored at various points throughout the book.

When management pursues a forcing strategy in order to negotiate stronger compliance and containment, it usually hopes to achieve (1) constrained wage and benefit increases (or reductions), (2) broader rights to operational flexibility, (3) strengthened rights to set and enforce higher work standards, and (4) an ongoing power advantage over the union. In contrast, a management that employs this strategy for limited purposes may emphasize the first or second potential benefit, but usually not the third and fourth.

In its pure form, the forcing strategy means that management focuses on achieving specific substantive changes, even at the expense of its working relationships with its employees and union representatives. In most cases, management wishes to minimize the negative consequences of deteriorated relationships, but as we will see, in some cases, relations become extremely acrimonious.

The viability of the forcing strategy depends in part on the availability of effective bargaining weapons. The most important weapon, the strike, has undergone change in its relative importance. Under New Deal bargaining, the strike proceeded according to a relatively established and predictable routine. At the expiration of the labor agreement, if the parties were at an impasse, the union struck and operations ceased until the parties reached agreement. In some industries, supervisors continued to operate the facilities, but very rarely were replacement workers hired. The generally accepted premise was that the only way a company could win a strike was to endure a long one, and even then it could not be certain of attaining its objectives, as a number of long strikes during the 1950s and 1960s illustrated.[3]

However, this predictable and stable role of the strike—i.e., as a natural part of the collective-bargaining process—has changed. For one thing, most companies see a cessation of operations as a "disaster" to be avoided. Supplying customers on a continuing and timely basis has become increasingly important as a competitive factor. Companies like International Harvester (now Navistar) and Caterpillar, which were shut down by long strikes in the early 1980s (and again in the early 1990s in the case of Caterpillar), are illustrative, demonstrating the vulnerability of market share to cessation of business.

Partly as a result of the increased costs of a strike and partly out of a growing realization that it has become feasible for management to continue operations, more and more companies have taken steps to neutralize the consequences of a strike by preparing to operate their facilities with replacement workers. Prospective replacements are recruited and trained far in advance of the contract expiration and are held in readiness to be hired when and if a strike develops.

Management reaps big gains from these new tactics because it may implement its proposed changes as soon as an impasse has been reached. Replacements continue operations as the company puts these changes into effect. Under the traditional approach, management only gained "relief" when the union and the workers accepted the new terms, often after a long strike, whereas, under the new approach, the changes are imposed shortly after the expiration of the old agreement. Thus, management has, in effect, developed a "social technology" to continue operations with limited disruption during a strike.

In the face of this across-the-board change in how management views strikes and how it responds to the prospect of a strike, unions have escalated the power struggle through corporate campaigns (aimed at embarrassing and otherwise pressuring corporate officers and directors), delays in the approval of settlements at "pooled" plants (in order to position themselves to simultaneously strike a larger fraction of the company), and a variety of other tactics. Unions have also attempted to mobilize public opinion against the employer practice of hiring permanent replacements and pressed for legislation that would prohibit the practice.

Changes in public opinion regarding industrial disputes have further weakened unions' relative bargaining power. For most of the prior era, many members of the public would hesitate to cross a picket line, thereby making strikes in consumer-related industries especially effective. Today, however, the public appears to be much more neutral, and the commonly held view is that a dispute between labor and management is a "private affair"—best left to the parties themselves to resolve. Thus, the airlines, for example, which have been involved in bitter work stoppages during the past several years, have been able to keep their planes flying, both because of workers' willingness to be hired as replacements and because of the flying public's willingness to cross the picket lines.

This analysis of the changing character of the strike is consonant with statistics showing that the incidence of strikes has dropped dramatically in the United States.[4] This country still experiences some major drawn-out strikes, as witnessed by several in the paper industry and a number that have occurred recently in transportation and mining, but unions are no longer able to use the strike routinely as a form of leverage.

Of the three change strategies, forcing is the most familiar one, representing continuity with traditional labor relations, although it does constitute a more polarized form of hard bargaining. It is the most symmetrical influence option, in that it is similarly employed by management and labor, but the enforcement power of either party may wax and wane with changes in contextual factors.

Fostering Change

As a highly contrasting strategy, the parties can foster change so as to achieve their respective goals. Although some fostering initiatives occur as part of formal contract negotiations, the majority occur between contract discussions. Again, it is usually management that directs the fostering at both workers and their representatives, but unions also utilize fostering in response and as part of independent initiatives. This strategy, even more than the forcing strategy, relies on justification (for example, evidence of the competitive need for new practices to increase productivity and quality), and it seeks to promote voluntary change rather than mere compliance.

Management has traditionally used fostering activities in a limited and temporary way to soften labor's resistance to a planned change, such as the introduction of new technology, or to solicit labor's involvement in carefully delineated areas, such as a safety program. These fostering efforts by themselves do not disturb, nor are they intended to revise, the traditional social contracts.

During recent years, management has increasingly employed fostering for a strategic (rather than tactical) purpose and has therefore pursued it in a more dramatic and sustained way. The more sustained fostering is generally used to develop high commitment among employees and a more cooperative relationship between management and the union. Management attempts to negotiate a new relationship with workers based on mutual commitment rather than mutual compliance and seeks modifications in the traditional arm's-length union relationship leading toward a partnership, often embodied in a wide range of specific programs that require joint administration, such as training and quality.

The advantages management typically seeks from negotiating employee commitment are increased worker motivation, day-to-day participation in solving problems, improved quality and yield, and better equipment utilization. Management wants a more cooperative relationship with the union in order to produce an environment conducive to high employee commitment. It is also striving to increase the parties' reliance on problem-solving processes in place of legalistic approaches and power bargaining for resolving many matters of mutual interest.

The premise underlying most campaigns to foster cooperation is that by improving attitudes, they will produce substantive changes of benefit to all sides. These "proof of the pudding" results may be slow in coming, thereby posing dilemmas for management as to whether to introduce some measure of forcing into its approach.

In summary, in their more ambitious forms, forcing and fostering tend to place different priorities on achieving change in the substantive and social contracts. Strong forcing action is focused primarily on change in the substantive terms of employment, and management accepts whatever adjustment in the social contract is implied by these changes. In contrast, sustained fostering is usually guided by a desire for a revised social contract that management expects will provide long-term benefits for the business.

Putting All Three Strategies Together

The avenues by which the three change strategies—escaping, forcing, and fostering—enable management and labor to achieve their respective objectives are quite different. When management escapes to a greenfield site, it typically adopts practices in the new facility designed to enhance employee commitment and often attempts to avoid a union—a distinctive set of social contract objectives (individual commitment and institutional avoidance).

Forcing is a direct method for achieving objectives that can be realized by compliance. For example, once they are agreed to by union and management, wage-rate reductions are implemented automatically; they are, in effect, self-implementing. However, if management reduces the number of job classifications, the flexibility sought from the new system may or may not be achieved. Management still must obtain more than minimal compliance with this provision of the new labor agreement in order to achieve the anticipated flexibility.

By contrast, the strategy of fostering cooperation usually works via the indirect route of developing shared understandings and joint programs that over the long run may produce substantive changes in behavior and performance. Implicit in this approach is the premise that better working relationships with the union and workers will lead to substantive changes that benefit the bottom line.

Although, at any point, management or labor may choose to emphasize one of the three approaches, they are often used in combination or in sequence. For example, a forcing episode may precede an effort to foster change, or certain changes may be forced even after a history of fostering initiatives. Needless to say, initial strategies have great implications for subsequent shifts in strategy.

Case example of multiple change strategies: Cleveland Twist Drill. How do the substantive and social contract objectives combine with various strategy choices in a specific case? What are the dynamics that unfold over time?

The concurrence of all three change strategies can be observed in the relations between Cleveland Twist Drill (CTD) and its independent union during the early 1980s.[5] The second largest domestic manufacturer of cutting tools at the time, the company faced increasing competition from foreign and domestic sources, an industry recession, and a threatening decline in profit margins. The new president decided that among the problems requiring quick and drastic action were high-wage and benefit levels, which exceeded the industry average by more than 40 percent, and an extremely complex job classification system that seriously constrained flexibility. Management relations with workers and their union were generally within the traditional New Deal mode, although they were marked by unusually friendly attitudes. The president felt that management had been too indulgent of labor and that the relations between managers and labor were perhaps too cozy, contributing to noncompetitive labor terms. His actions to address these perceived problems involved all of the options just outlined.

In April 1982—18 months before the contract expiration date—the president and his staff began talks with the union bargaining committee, for the express purpose of securing immediate wage and work-rule concessions. He also began a series of communication meetings "on the state of our company," covering all hourly employees in 18 separate groups. In these sessions, he presented surveys showing that the company's wages and benefits were not competitive with the industry and outlined how inflexibility affected productivity. Management demanded a wage cut of $2.50 per hour, a benefits cut amounting to $1.50 an hour, a reduction in the number of job classifications, revisions of seniority provisions, and other concessions. Labor responded with anger and dismay. One machine tool worker expressed the sentiment of others when he rose to his feet during a presentation and commented: "Mr. Bartlett, if I understand what you are saying, the only difference between this meeting and the Jonestown massacre is that there is no Kool Aid in the corner."

Neither negotiations with the union nor direct appeals to the workforce made headway. In late June, the rank and file rejected the company's final proposal by a vote of 507 to 19.

Within a couple of months, CTD management began transferring equipment from its large Cleveland plant to its nonunion plants in Kentucky and Rhode Island. In addition to expanding these existing plants, it had purchased a new facility in North Carolina. During negotiations with labor officials, management had described in detail its contingent plans to transfer operations in the event that labor rejected its requests. Management even took union officials into its "war room," where the expansion plans and layouts for the other plants were spread out on drafting tables. However, at the time, neither union officials nor workers believed that management would carry out its threat to move.

When pieces of equipment were packed up and carted out of the Cleveland plant, hostility was sharpened and labor's self-confidence weakened. The local union president approached management asking to resume negotiations. Management accepted and talks proceeded while equipment continued to be moved out of the plant. In February 1983—after a third of the products, equipment, and jobs had been permanently relocated—the parties reached an agreement and halted the outflow.

The agreement provided for a larger cut in pay and benefits and more drastic concessions in work rules than had been requested in the earlier round of failed negotiations. Labor had suffered a big blow but had elected to preserve jobs. It was demoralized but compliant for a sustained period of time. Over the next several years, management introduced a gain-sharing scheme and participation mechanisms. Eventually, both morale and productivity recovered and reached new heights. Interestingly enough, because of the accumulated machining skills in the Cleveland workforce, the revitalized Cleveland plant was soon able to outperform the new plants by a wide margin, a possibility management had not appreciated when it formulated its move plans.

In this case, the three strategic options were interwoven in complex ways. Management first tried to employ forcing maneuvers aimed at both union leaders and workers to negotiate changes it felt to be critical for the company's survival. Unfortunately, management failed to create credibility for that survival rationale. Although the first forcing episode failed, it convinced managers, many of whom were genuinely friendly with labor, that the company had given labor a fair chance to influence its own fate. In the meantime, management was also preparing a contingency escape plan. It attempted to use the escape option as a threat in the service of forcing negotiations, but management's move plans—like its assessment of the need for change—simply were not credible to labor. They became credible only when they were executed, creating the conditions for labor to compromise. Unfortunately for labor, the fact that the move process had already begun and much of the expense associated with outfitting the outlying plants had already been committed increased the concessions management believed it needed from labor to warrant a decision to keep the remaining operations in Cleveland.

The consequences of the partial escape and the forcing negotiations were to demoralize CTD's Cleveland workforce and reduce the spontaneous cooperation management could expect from workers. However, over time, gain sharing and involvement mechanisms neutralized these antagonisms and eventually fostered good relations and relatively high performance.

PREVALENCE OF FUNDAMENTAL CHANGE IN COLLECTIVE BARGAINING

How representative is the Cleveland Twist Drill case? To what extent are employers—beyond the handful covered regularly in the business press—forcing and fostering change?

Analysis of Change Strategies across Firms

While the newspaper headlines, leading practitioners, and our own observations point toward a bipolarization trend around forcing and fostering change strategies in labor-management relations, it is difficult to ascertain just how representative newspapers, anecdotal, and other sources are. There is no systematic national-level data collection on bargaining process, and the outcome data that are collected (on strikes, wage settlements, and so forth) are centered on large firms (usually with bargaining units of 1,000 or more employees).

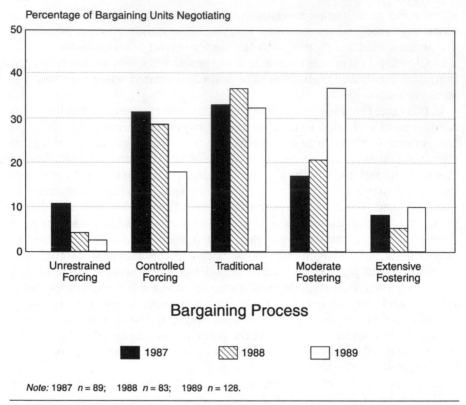

Percentage of Bargaining Units Negotiating

Bargaining Process

■ 1987   ▨ 1988   ☐ 1989

Note: 1987 *n* = 89;   1988 *n* = 83;   1989 *n* = 128.

Exhibit 2.1   Bargaining Process (1987–1989 Negotiations in Northeast Michigan)

In order to develop a more complete picture of collective bargaining as it currently operates, we have tabulated information from interviews with a federal mediator[6] who has classified all of the negotiations in his Michigan region based on a scheme that roughly matches the distinctions we make about negotiating strategy.[7] These data provide a unique window into nearly 300 separate collective-bargaining negotiations,[8] and they confirm our thesis that the traditional arm's-length model of collective bargaining has been declining in importance.[9]

Distribution of Change Strategies

As Exhibit 2.1 indicates, over the three-year period from 1987 to 1989, only one-third of the negotiations fell into the traditional collective-bargaining category, whereas about two-thirds of the negotiations involved some degree of forcing (31 percent) or fostering (33 percent). Interestingly, there is also a preliminary indication of a trend toward increased fostering, though this might also be a temporary effect. Although similar data from

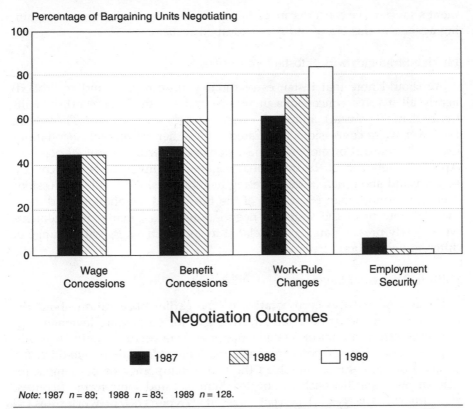

Percentage of Bargaining Units Negotiating

Negotiation Outcomes

■ 1987   ▨ 1988   ☐ 1989

Note: 1987 *n* = 89; 1988 *n* = 83; 1989 *n* = 128.

Exhibit 2.2 Selected Negotiation Outcomes (1987–1989 Negotiations in Northeast Michigan)

the same period at the end of the 1970s are not available, the current data indicate that the majority of labor negotiations can be categorized as either forcing or fostering—both of which probably involve a revision of social contracts.

Substantive Agenda

When we look at the nature of the agreements that were reached, we see that the substance of contracts is also shifting. As Exhibit 2.2 illustrates, approximately 40 percent of the negotiations during this three-year period involved wage concessions. Even more telling is the fact that more than 60 percent of the negotiations involved benefit concessions, and about 75 percent involved work-rule changes. In the latter two categories, there is a clear trend pointing toward an increase in the percentage of negotiations involving benefit and work-rule concessions. In contrast, less than 5 percent of the negotiations involved any measure of employment security. Thus, management's substantive concerns are certainly dominating the collective-bargaining agenda in this era of industrial competitiveness.

Linking Strategies with Substantive Contracts

We should note that instances of forcing (unrestrained and controlled) nearly all involve concessions in wages (more than 70 percent), benefits (more than 80 percent), and work rules (more than 90 percent). There were far fewer wage concessions associated with either traditional negotiations (about 30 percent) or moderate and extensive fostering (about 20 percent). Approximately half of the traditional negotiations involved benefit concessions, as did about half of the fostering negotiations. Work-rule concessions occurred in more than 60 percent of the traditional negotiations and more than 70 percent of the fostering negotiations. Thus, many managements were clearly pressing an agenda related to competitiveness with a range of different negotiation strategies.

Shifting Sources of Leverage

These data are also corroborative of the earlier observation about the unions' loss of the strike as an effective tool for bargaining leverage. Significantly, out of a total of 300 negotiations, there occurred only 16 strikes (representing about 5 percent of negotiations). More than one-third (38 percent) of these strikes involved the use of temporary or permanent replacements,[10] and the vast majority of them featured some form of concessions involving wages (81 percent), benefits (75 percent), or work rules (88 percent). Thus, nearly 90 percent of the workers in this sample came back from strikes to work under substantially revised contracts.

The data support another key point—namely, management's ability to unilaterally implement an agreement has become a key source of leverage. As Exhibit 2.3 illustrates, 19 percent of the negotiations involved the unilateral implementation of agreements by management. An additional 14 percent of the negotiations involved settlements that were reached on the basis of a final offer from management (with the threat of a unilateral contract implementation).[11] Nearly 90 percent of the forcing negotiations produced unilaterally implemented agreements or agreements reached under the threat of unilateral implementation.

One of a union leader's deepest fears is that forcing strategies are merely a prelude to escape. In fact, decertification of the bargaining unit (one form of escape) was nearly ten times more likely to occur in the context of an unrestrained forcing strategy. Of the 11 decertifications that occurred during this three-year period, 9 followed what we have termed unrestrained forcing strategies (1 followed traditional negotiations, and 1 followed an extensive fostering initiative that failed).[12] Forcing is not associated exclusively with dire consequences for the union, however. Ten firms went out of business

Percentage of Bargaining Units Negotiating

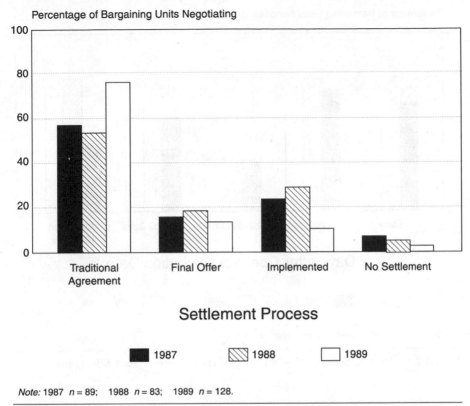

Settlement Process

█ 1987   ▨ 1988   ☐ 1989

Note: 1987 *n* = 89;   1988 *n* = 83;   1989 *n* = 128.

Exhibit 2.3   Contract Settlement Process (1987–1989 Negotiations in Northeast Michigan)

shortly after the completion of negotiations, seven of them in the context of forcing strategies (five unrestrained forcing and two controlled forcing).[13]

Given the ineffectiveness of the strike as a weapon, it should be no surprise that the contract expiration is less effective in driving settlements. Overall, Exhibit 2.4 indicates that more than half of the negotiations that reached a settlement (57 percent) did not do so until more than 25 days past the contract expiration date. In fact, one-quarter of the negotiations did not reach a settlement until more than 100 days past the contract expiration date. Interestingly, another 17 percent of the negotiations involved early settlements, leaving only one-quarter of the settlements that fell within what might be regarded as a more traditional range of settlements within 25 days of the contract expiration date.

While comparable data from other regions of the country are not available, much can be learned from this portrait of about 300 collective-bargaining negotiations over the 1987–1989 period in northeast and central

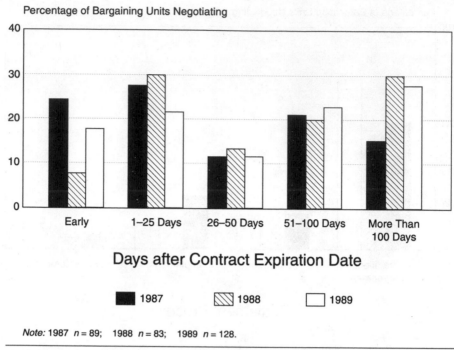

Percentage of Bargaining Units Negotiating

Days after Contract Expiration Date

■ 1987   ⬚ 1988   ☐ 1989

Note: 1987 *n* = 89;   1988 *n* = 83;   1989 *n* = 128.

Exhibit 2.4   Time to Settle (1987–1989 Negotiations in Northeast Michigan)

Michigan. Most important, even in this heavily unionized region of the country, we see that traditional negotiations represent a minority of about one-third of the negotiations, with the balance evenly divided between forcing and fostering strategies.

Moreover, many time-honored institutions of collective bargaining have been eroded. Negotiations have traditionally not involved labor concessions, yet the overwhelming majority of these negotiations involved some form of wage, benefit, or work-rule concessions. The strike has traditionally been an important weapon, but it has been undercut by the use of replacement workers. At the same time, management's threat of unilateral contract implementation is clearly a regular feature of the bargaining process. While unrestrained forcing does indeed carry an increased risk of decertification, it is also more strongly associated with the firm's going out of business. Finally, the contract deadline seems to have lost some of its potency in focusing negotiations toward a settlement. In sum, these data are a powerful indication that the traditional social contract around collective bargaining has eroded, setting the stage for the renegotiation of both social and substantive contracts.

SUMMARY AND CONCLUSIONS

Employers and unions rely on one or more of several change strategies. They may escape the relationship (e.g., by management's transferring operations), force change (e.g., by mobilizing bargaining power), or foster change (e.g., by attitude change and problem-solving initiatives). Forcing and fostering are broad direct negotiating strategies. Escape is an avoidance strategy, but it may also play a tactical role supporting the two engagement strategies.

Thus, in this and the preceding chapter, we have developed the following building blocks for a theory of strategic negotiations: a description of the present and prior eras in industrial relations in which the shift between the two is characterized as a negotiated process, a broad definition of negotiations that includes individual-level and institutional-level interactions, a set of substantive outcome objectives, a set of social contract outcome objectives, and a set of change strategies. In order to link these elements into a theory, we will now place them in a larger framework that features further detail and the introduction of additional key concepts.

NOTES

1. In other settings, such as Poland, escape has been a dominant and effective union strategy, as the Solidarity union has pressed to move from a centrally planned economy to a market economy.
2. This is what Fisher and Ury would term management's BATNA—"Best Alternative to a Negotiated Agreement." See Roger Fisher and William Ury, *Getting to Yes: Negotiating an Agreement without Giving In* (Boston: Houghton Mifflin, 1981).
3. The steel industry pressed for relief on customary practice in 1959 and was willing to take a strike for four months before accepting no change in the contract's key clause, 2B.
4. For example, in 1972, there were 443 strikes in bargaining units of 1,000 or more. In 1989, there were just 43.
5. This summary draws on "Cleveland Twist Drill" (A) and (B), Harvard Business School cases numbered, respectively, 385-082 and 385-083, 1989.
6. The mediator is Donald Power, who is responsible for the region that includes northeast and central Michigan. While this region is hardly representative of the nation as a whole, it is an area in which the collective-bargaining process would be expected to be fairly robust—given the high levels of unionization and the long traditions of collective bargaining in cities such as Flint, Saginaw, and Lansing. Thus, our findings on the erosion of traditional forms of collective bargaining are likely, if anything, to understate the degree of change nationwide.
7. Here is a mapping of the labels and definitions that Commissioner Power used (starting in 1987) to classify his cases and the concepts that we use in this volume. Both classification schemes use the same label and the same definition for traditional collective bargaining. What we have termed "unrestrained forcing," Commissioner Power has termed "nonproductive bargaining/total process destruction," which he defines as conflict to the point of a complete deterioration of the bargaining process. What we have termed "controlled forcing," Commis-

sioner Power has termed "nonproductive bargaining/internal difficulties," which he defines as conflict to the point that difficulties emerge internal to the bargaining process. What we would call "moderate fostering," Commissioner Power has termed "traditional with some problem-solving." What we would refer to as "extensive fostering," Commissioner Power has termed "target-specific bargaining," to refer to a full problem-solving process in which each issue is specifically targeted for joint problem solving. An additional category used by Commissioner Power is "nonproductive bargaining preceding employee involvement," which he uses to refer to target-specific bargaining that was preceded by some degree of forcing (we have included this in with extensive fostering). The rough match in the two classification schemes makes the following analysis possible and also serves as a valuable corroboration of the distinctions we have adopted.

Note, too, that we treat each negotiation as a separate event, even though approximately 10 percent of the negotiations in the second and third years involve parties who had previously negotiated one- or two-year agreements. While these negotiations are not independent in a formal sense, there is no *a priori* reason to expect that they would be any less subject to the same contextual forces as negotiations involving parties who are bargaining at the expiration of agreements lasting three years or longer.

8. This sample includes every collective-bargaining negotiation involving 25 or more workers in Commissioner Powers' region as well as selected cases involving fewer than 25 workers (where the parties asked for assistance or where Commissioner Power contacted the parties on his own initiative). A preliminary analysis of the cases involving fewer than 25 workers suggests that they are not any more likely to include instances of forcing and fostering than the rest of the sample.

As background to the sample, the distribution of firms by size is as follows: fewer than 25 employees (25 percent); between 25 and 50 employees (24 percent); between 51 and 100 employees (20 percent); between 101 and 250 employees (20 percent); between 251 and 500 employees (7 percent); between 501 and 1,000 employees (3 percent); and more than 1,000 employees (1 percent). Thus, this sample consists almost entirely of negotiations not normally tracked by the U.S. Bureau of Labor Statistics or any other source.

The distribution across industries (by number of negotiations, not number of employees involved in bargaining) is as follows: auto supply (20 percent); health care (16 percent); food service/distribution (14 percent); construction (10 percent); miscellaneous light industry (9 percent); miscellaneous services (6 percent); paper products (5 percent); finance/banking (3 percent); telecommunications (3 percent); transportation services (3 percent); retail/wholesale (2 percent); aerospace (2 percent); mining/extraction (2 percent); auto manufacturing (1 percent); public sector (by special request to the Federal Mediation and Conciliation Service—1 percent); chemicals (1 percent); and higher education (1 percent). This distribution reflects a higher percentage of auto supply negotiations than would be the case nationally and leaves out (for the most part) public-sector negotiations, both of which must be considered when generalizing beyond this sample.

9. Since we do not have comparable data on individual-level interactions in the same region, the institutional developments represent only a partial corroboration of our thesis.

10. These data on temporary or permanent replacements were corroborated by consultation of newspaper records.

11. An additional 3 percent of the agreements were never settled because the firms went out of business or transferred operations.

12. Moving to a nonunion location, a second form of escape, was less common in this sample (reflecting the smaller size of the firms). There were only two instances of this form of escape, one in the context of unrestrained forcing and one following traditional negotiations.
13. While these correlations with a forcing strategy are strong, it is important to note that they do not imply causality. Both types of destruction of the social contract (decertification and going out of business) may reflect underlying financial difficulties (which would also drive the forcing strategy). Still, there is a question as to whether an alternative strategy might have helped the parties avoid these outcomes, which are so destructive to one or both.

Chapter 3

A Theory of Strategic Negotiations

In reviewing the recent trends in industrial relations and the problems our theory addresses, the preceding chapters have also introduced two key elements of the theory. First, the theory is about revising both substantive agreements and social contracts. These contracts and the interactions that revise them occur both at the institutional level (between representatives) and at the individual level (for example, between individual employees and supervisors). Second, we specify three types of change strategies: escape, force, and foster.

Here, we set forth other elements and specify how all the elements fit together to form a systematic theory. The resulting theory builds on the central feature of *A Behavioral Theory of Labor Negotiations* and extends it in many respects.[1] The theoretical framework is intended to help analysts and negotiators make sense of the task of transforming labor-management relations.

We also take the theory an additional step, by deriving testable propositions about the behavior of actors engaged in negotiated change. These propositions address, for example, such issues as

- How certain factors influence a negotiator's strategic decision about whether to force, foster, or escape the relationship
- What tactical choices—regarding process and structure—will tend to be used to implement forcing and fostering strategies, respectively
- The dynamics commonly associated with each strategy, including the risks they pose for negotiators

The propositions are used in Part II to increase the rigor of our clinical case-by-case analyses of the 13 case histories. And in Parts III and IV, we use comparative analyses of the cases to "test" the theory. We advance these

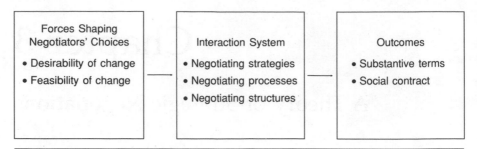

Exhibit 3-1   General Framework for Analyzing a Strategic Negotiation

propositions and present our preliminary empirical tests of them to encourage other scholars to subject them to further assessment and revision.

The theory has three major components: outcomes, the interaction system that produces the outcomes, and the driving and restraining forces that influence negotiators' actions (illustrated in Exhibit 3.1). We begin with *outcomes*, by reviewing and more formally defining two types of negotiation outcomes—substantive terms and the social contract. In outlining the *interaction system*, we identify three dimensions: the negotiating strategies, processes, and structures. These elements of the interaction system are then presented as subject to a range of *forces shaping negotiators' choices*, including those that determine the desirability of fundamental change and the anticipated feasibility of such change. In each section of this chapter, we will expand on the elements identified in Exhibit 3.1. As we do so, we will enlarge each box in the figure and include the subcomponents. At the conclusion of the chapter, we will present the full framework.

OUTCOMES

We are particularly interested in paradigm-breaking outcomes and the processes that produce them.[2] *Outcomes* are of two types: revisions of substantive terms and changes in social contracts. While the substantive terms are an outcome considered by nearly all scholars of negotiations, the social contract is rarely examined. Both forms of outcomes are listed in Exhibit 3.2, which is an expanded version of the outcomes box in Exhibit 3.1.

Substantive Outcomes

Substantive contracts set forth the rules, rights, and obligations of the parties. For example, Chapter 1 identified substantive issues with high priority for management in the industrial competitiveness era—payroll costs, flexibility, and worker effort. Labor's responses, we noted, included attention to employment security and influence at a strategic level of decision making. Management's proposals and labor's responses constitute a

```
┌─────────────────────────────────────┐
│              Outcomes               │
│                                     │
│  • Substantive terms                │
│                                     │
│    – Wages and benefits             │
│    – Work rules                     │
│    – Employment security            │
│    – Etc.                           │
│                                     │
│  • Social contract                  │
│                                     │
│    – Compliance/containment         │
│    – Commitment/cooperation         │
│    – Commitment/containment         │
│    – Etc.                           │
│                                     │
└─────────────────────────────────────┘
```

Exhibit 3.2   Negotiation Outcomes

significant shift relative to the last three or four decades and fit our idea of paradigm-breaking change.

While traditional collective-bargaining agreements are the archetypical example of a substantive contract, substantive outcomes are also reflected in personnel policies, well-established informal work rules, and other shared understandings about wages, hours, and conditions of work. Though negotiations over substantive contracts are usually formal and explicit, they can also take place on an informal, tacit basis.

Social Contract Outcomes

A social contract outlines in broad terms the nature of a relationship and prescribes broad quid pro quos among parties.[3] In the language of social theory, it is an ideology.[4] In the language of negotiations, it constitutes the metarules of the game.[5]

The several combinations of social contracts currently at play that were described in Chapter 1 (commitment/cooperation, compliance/containment, and commitment/containment) draw our interest since each represents a new paradigm, differing significantly from the traditional compliance/arm's-length accommodation.[6]

Where there is a clearly shared ideology among parties, the social contract is readily apparent.[7] Where one party seeks to initiate a change in the social contract, it becomes a subject of negotiations. The codification of a new social contract does not depend on formal, written agreement or even on willing cooperation, just on the clear establishment of a new ideology—a new set of rules—that serves as a guide to interactions.

Substantive provisions and social contracts are distinct, yet interrelated in complex ways. Substantive terms often can be renegotiated without a change in the social contract. However, a social contract usually cannot be changed without also implying changes in substantive terms. For example, the fostering of increased employee commitment usually requires changes in the reward system and in the mechanisms for employee participation.

INTERACTION SYSTEM

Substantive and social outcomes are a product of interactions among parties with a stake in the issues. The amount of influence exercised by stakeholders depends on the strength of their interests, the magnitude of their power resources, and how they interact to influence each other. These interactions take the form of negotiating strategies, processes, and structures—all of which are enhanced when they are aligned with each other. We examine these three elements of the interaction system (shown in the middle box in Exhibit 3.1) in turn. We begin with negotiating processes rather than strategies (which might be a more logical starting point) because these tactical processes are more concrete and help us operationally define the strategies.

Negotiating Processes

The three negotiating processes are: (1) bargaining (integrative and distributive) to reach agreements, (2) shaping the parties' attitudes toward each other (positively or negatively), and (3) influencing intraorganizational differences in one's own and the other's organization (toward greater consensus or discord). Negotiating processes are analytically distinct but highly interrelated in practice. Each has its own functions for the interacting parties, its own internal logic, and its own instrumental acts or tactics. The processes are listed in Exhibit 3.3.

Distributive and integrative bargaining. The negotiating process can take the form of either distributive or integrative bargaining. Each form of bargaining is distinct, with one or the other often tending to characterize the tone of the interactions.

Distributive bargaining has the function of resolving pure conflicts of interest. It serves to allocate fixed sums of resources ("dividing the pie") and hence often has a "win-lose" quality. Distributive tactics center on developing the negotiator's own relative power, convincing the other party of the first party's power and resolution, modifying the other party's expectations,

---

> • Negotiating processes
>
>   − Distributive and integrative bargaining
>   − Shaping intergroup attitudes
>   − Managing internal differences

Exhibit 3.3   Negotiating Processes: One Component of the Interaction System

closely guarding information, and preventing the other side from using the same tactics.[8] At the level of interpersonal communications, distributive bargaining typically involves strong assertions, selective responses, using the other side's statements tactically, and limited disclosure of feelings and underlying interests.

In contrast, *integrative bargaining* has the function of finding common or complementary interests and solving problems confronting both partners.[9] It serves to optimize the potential for joint gains ("expanding the pie") and hence often has a "win-win" quality. Tactics center on the exchange of accurate information, the exploration of underlying interests, and the use of structured problem-solving techniques. At the level of interpersonal communications, integrative bargaining typically involves paraphrasing, active listening, minimizing defensiveness, brainstorming, and disclosure of feelings and underlying interests.

Much research on labor-management relations focuses exclusively on just one or the other of these dimensions—seeking to explain either cooperative processes or workplace conflict.[10] Most theories of negotiations attend to the interactions between integrative and distributive bargaining, using labels such as "creating and claiming"[11] or "cooperating and contending." However, most theories of negotiations fail to give systematic treatment to the two additional negotiating processes that we believe are also important: the shaping of attitudes and the management of internal differences.

Shaping intergroup attitudes. The negotiating process we label "shaping intergroup attitudes" refers to the way the parties influence attitudes toward each other and the underlying norms and tone of their relationship. Attitude-shaping activities can promote either negative or positive attitudes between the parties.

Consider first the role of negative attitudes. A negotiator may intentionally generate fear and uncertainty in the other organization and hostility in his or her own organization in order to affect the parties' relative expectations, resolve, and bargaining power. The Eastern strike in 1989 illustrates this point well. The striking pilots and machinists used placards and slogans to characterize Frank Lorenzo (chairman of Texas Air, which owned Eastern) as an evil person, increasing intergroup hostility in order to strengthen solidarity among strikers and intimidate Lorenzo.

Although negotiators may cause negative interparty attitudes for tactical advantage, they sometimes sour the atmosphere inadvertently. Indeed, hostility often arises as an *unwanted by-product* of actions focused narrowly on one of the other two negotiating processes. Tactics instrumental to distributive bargaining (such as the use of deadlines and delays) can have this effect. So can tactics designed to build the organization's own internal solidarity (such as rallys and other public events). In either case, actions that create hostility, fear, and uncertainty usually are reciprocated and become mutual.

Positive attitudes are even more instrumental to integrative bargaining[12] than negative affect is to distributive bargaining. Negotiators often attempt to build positive bonds between their respective organizations to facilitate the open flow of information required by concurrent integrative bargaining. Over time, negotiators may promote these positive attitudes for more fundamental and enduring purposes—as integral components of a new social contract of commitment and cooperation.

Managing internal differences. The third negotiating process, *managing internal differences,* serves to either build consensus or encourage diversity of views within the interacting organizations.[13] We will make two distinctions with respect to the management of internal differences: (1) efforts directed within the negotiator's own organization as compared to efforts intended to influence the other side's internal differences and (2) building (or undermining) internal consensus about *goals* as compared to encouraging or discouraging internal diversity or dissent about proposed *means* to reach the goals. For example, negotiators may manage communications and decision making in their own organization to build support for both their own negotiating goals and the proposals that serve these goals. Alternatively, they may attempt to build consensus about goals and encourage diversity about proposed solutions. Also, they may direct communications to groups inside the *other* party's organization, either to promote divisions in the ranks about both goals and action proposals or to encourage goal consensus. The specific tactical requirements for managing internal differences depend partly on whether the negotiator wants to facilitate distributive or integrative bargaining.

We first consider the management of internal differences *within the negotiator's own organization.* Basically, consensus about goals is regarded as an asset for pursuing both distributive bargaining and integrative bargaining. In contrast, the management of one's own diversity or dissent about proposed solutions is very different under integrative and distributive bargaining. The problem-solving orientation of integrative bargaining benefits from the surfacing of internal diversity about proposals so as to achieve the highest-quality solutions. Under distributive bargaining, internal dissent may be seen as a source of vulnerability (since the other side may then use divide-and-conquer tactics). Hence, a distributive orientation will involve building internal consensus about both goals and solutions. An integrative orientation (once it is established) will involve both building internal consensus about goals and only allowing moderate internal diversity and dissent about means.

Additional subtleties or dilemmas associated with the management of internal differences can be seen in the ratification/approval process for a tentative agreement. A negotiator's task in selling a negotiated agreement to his or her constituents differs depending on whether the agreement derives primarily from distributive or integrative bargaining. After distributive bargaining, a negotiator may take an agreement to the constituents and say, "We may not like this, but it's the best we could get." If the agreement results from integrative bargaining, the negotiator must, in effect, acknowledge, "I believe this is in our best interests." In the latter case, the negotiator is more vulnerable politically since internal factions can challenge the extent to which the agreement really is in their interests. In effect, the integrative approach brings with it an implied understanding that internal diversity—once surfaced—will be addressed in the final agreement.

After a settlement is ratified, the nature of other intraorganizational challenges depends on whether the agreement was reached integratively or distributively. If the agreement was reached by integrative bargaining, both sides want subsequent implementation activities to succeed, and therefore, they prize consensus in their respective organizations. Equally, each side may value the surfacing and addressing of internal diversity about implementation methods in its own organization. However, when agreements are bargained distributively, the reluctant side has less at stake in effective implementation and therefore less interest in generating consensus about the value of the agreement.

In summary, negotiators generally value consensus within their own organization to support both distributive and integrative bargaining throughout the entire negotiation.

Negotiators' preferences for internal differences or consensus *in the other party's organization* are even more varied, depending on the choice of the form of bargaining and the stage of the bargaining process. As already discussed, to support integrative work, both negotiators want to promote internal goal consensus in both parties and recognize internal diversity regarding proposed solutions. This ensures the highest-quality problem solving while minimizing disruption by factional battles and avoiding resistance during implementation.

However, to support distributive bargaining, both negotiators may want to exploit divisions in the other side in order to weaken constituent support for tough positions their negotiators are taking at the bargaining table (a divide-and-conquer approach). But even in distributive bargaining, this interest changes during the final phase of negotiations, when a negotiator wants the other side to be able to sell the deal to its constituents. Now, the negotiators will help create at least sufficient consensus on the other side to support the deal.[14]

Negotiating Strategies: Tactical Requirements and Predictable Dilemmas

The concept of negotiating strategy characterizes a party's approach to the change task. We have already noted the interactions among the negotiating processes—how the actions intended to manage one process can also affect the other processes.

We propose that forcing and fostering strategies each impose a predictable set of tactical requirements on the three processes, which then lead to self-reinforcing dynamics. Further, mixed forcing-fostering strategies generate a predictable array of tactical dilemmas for negotiators. All three strate-

```
┌─────────────────────────────┐
│  • Negotiating strategies   │
│    – Forcing                │
│    – Fostering              │
│    – Escape                 │
└─────────────────────────────┘
```

Exhibit 3.4   Negotiating Strategies: One Component of the Interaction System

gies identified in Chapter 2 are listed in Exhibit 3.4. We will focus on just the two negotiating strategies: forcing and fostering.

Forcing strategies.   A forcing strategy emphasizes distributive bargaining. Management mobilizes coercive and persuasive power and attempts to convey strong tactical commitment to achieve the change. The union musters as much power as it can to resist the change. With respect to the management of internal differences, each party usually finds it advantageous to strengthen its own internal consensus, limit internal dissent, and highlight divisions within the other party. In this form of contentious bargaining, both parties often find it tactically advantageous to impugn the motives of the other party and display hostility toward it, the effect of which is to increase adversarial feelings on both sides. This promotes intragroup solidarity and intergroup hostility. As a result, still more intensity may be added to the forcing strategy, accompanied by both the potential advantage of successful change and the potential risk of escalating conflict. Thus, the forcing strategy links the negotiating processes together and may then be sustained by them—a self-reinforcing interaction between bargaining processes and bargaining strategies.[15] The triangle of forcing factors is presented in Exhibit 3.5.

We make an additional distinction between two types of forcing strategies. The first, which we refer to as "controlled forcing," or just "forcing," involves common forcing tactics, such as aggressive demands and strike threats. The second, which we have termed "unrestrained forcing," involves especially severe or harsh forcing tactics—such as hiring permanent replacements for striking workers.

Fostering strategies.   Fostering more cooperative relationships can give primary emphasis to either positive attitudinal change or integrative bargaining. In any event, they are mutually reinforcing processes: trust and respect facilitate the open exchange of information crucial to integrative bargaining, and integrative solutions give strong impetus to more positive attitudes.

To support and stabilize the integrative bargaining and attitude-forming processes, each party acts to promote goal consensus (and support diversity of perspectives) within both its own and the other party's organization. As a result, far-ranging forms of problem solving become possible, but there is a risk that a dominant focus on consensus may mask or discourage the

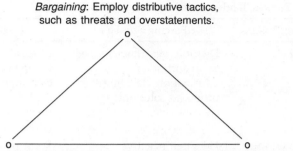

Bargaining: Employ distributive tactics, such as threats and overstatements.

Managing internal differences: Build internal consensus; exploit internal differences on the other side.

Shaping intergroup attitudes: Promote uncertainty and negative attitudes toward the other side.

Exhibit 3.5   Tactical Processes Associated with a Forcing Strategy

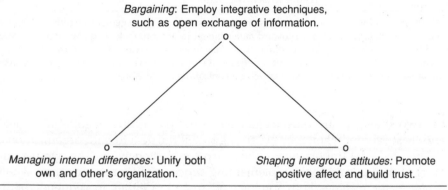

Bargaining: Employ integrative techniques, such as open exchange of information.

Managing internal differences: Unify both own and other's organization.

Shaping intergroup attitudes: Promote positive affect and build trust.

Exhibit 3.6   Tactical Processes Associated with a Fostering Strategy

surfacing and resolution of conflict. Thus, as was the case with forcing, the fostering strategy links the negotiating processes together and may then be sustained by them—a self-reinforcing interaction among negotiating processes.[16] Exhibit 3.6 illustrates the triangle of process requirements associated with a fostering strategy.

Tactical dilemmas in mixed forcing-fostering strategies. When the two sets of tactical requirements for forcing and fostering are juxtaposed, as in Table 3.1, the contrasts are apparent. The requirements for forcing and fostering are more than different; they are mainly opposites. This is most striking for two of the three negotiating processes: how the parties must manage information in the decision-making process and the type of emotions they would be inclined to encourage. The contrasts in building internal consensus under

Table 3.1 Tactical Tendencies of Forcing and Fostering

Negotiating Process	Forcing Strategy	Fostering Strategy
Bargaining	Distributive: Characterized by distortion of information, debating proposed solutions, coercion, etc.	Integrative: Characterized by open and accurate exchange of information, exploration of underlying interests, persuasion and education, etc.
Shaping intergroup attitudes	Heighten negative intergroup attitudes.*	Form positive intergroup attitudes.
Managing internal differences	Promote solidarity in own party and divisions within the other party during the phase of reaching agreement; seek consensus in both parties when trying to sell the deal.	Promote broad consensus and constructive use of differences in both own and other party.

*This applies more commonly to labor negotiators than to management negotiators. Labor negotiators often promote anger toward management in order to make bargaining tactics more credible and to increase union solidarity. Management may want to minimize intergroup tension because it is concerned about the effects on workplace performance and because, unlike the union leaders, it can exercise hierarchical control over its members.

the two strategies are most salient when the parties are negotiating a deal and least evident when they are trying to sell the deal to both organizations.

The predicted importance of the sharp contrasts between the two negotiating strategies and their implementing processes becomes apparent when a negotiator pursues both forcing and fostering either in sequence or in combination at the same time—and most change efforts involve some mixture of forcing and fostering. Chapter 11 explores in depth these contrasts and the dilemmas they create.

Negotiating Structures

The third element of the interaction system is its structure. We distinguish four structural elements in negotiations, each of which refers to a well-established area of research in the negotiation, industrial relations, and organizational literatures: (1) the periodic versus continuous nature of interactions and the extensiveness of the contacts between the organizations;[17] (2) the level or locus of negotiations—at the institutional or individual level;[18] (3) the degree of centralization of institutional negotiations—ranging in the United States from industry-level to plant-level;[19] and (4) the number of parties—bilateral or multilateral interactions.[20] All four elements are listed in Exhibit 3.7.[21]

- Negotiating structures
  - Frequency of interaction/number of channels
  - Individual and institutional levels
  - Degree of centralization
  - Number of parties

Exhibit 3.7 Negotiating Structures: One Component of the Interaction System

The structure of labor negotiations in the prior era was characterized by periodic and narrowly channeled interactions, conducted strictly between institutions, relatively centralized to either the industry or company levels, and largely bilateral in nature. In recent decades, labor negotiations have often departed from this classic structural form along each of these four dimensions.

Shift from periodic to more continuous interactions. In the present era, periodic contract bargaining (every two or three years) is increasingly supplemented by more frequent formal or informal interactions. This goes far beyond the traditional increase in the frequency of interaction as a contract expiration deadline nears or the use of informal "backdoor" meetings between chief negotiators in the early stages and again in the eleventh hour of a negotiation. We refer here to major shifts, such as the establishment of what are termed "living agreements" that feature brief statements of general principles, with the specific applications addressed on a continuous basis.[22] Similarly, the use of labor-management committees as standing forums to administer training, employee involvement, benefits, health and safety, quality improvement, communications, and so forth involves ongoing negotiations over issues that arise regarding the particular topic area.[23] As well, management efforts to force concessions in wages and work rules are no longer restricted to contract expirations. The increasing importance of individual-level negotiations, discussed next, also involves an increased frequency of interactions.

Increasing importance of individual-level negotiations. The institutional level continues to be important in this era, even if the structure of these interactions is shifting in several ways. A new development, however, has been the increased importance of individual-level negotiations, discussed briefly in Chapter 1. This importance arises particularly with respect to substantive agreements that are not what we have termed "self-implementing" but are instead dependent on individual initiative and cooperation. Further, the renegotiation of social contracts at the individual or institutional level surfaces issues of consistency across levels.[24] For example, an individual-level social contract oriented around high levels of employee commitment will typically create tensions if the institutional-level social contract remains oriented around arm's length accommodation since the union will feel threatened by the company's commitment initiatives.

Decentralization of negotiations. While formal labor negotiations in the United States have long been among the most decentralized relative to other nations, recent years have been characterized by a further devolution—from industry to company level and from company to plant level.[25] A reinforcing development has been the weakening of pattern bargaining.[26] Until recently, most negotiations in a given industry followed a pattern, usually set by one of the larger companies. Thus, even where the formal structure of bargaining was not centralized at the industry level, the practice of a key settlement followed by similar agreements created a high degree of coordination, if not centralization. The breakdown in such patterns, as well as in the formal bargaining arrangements, marks a structural shift with important tactical implications for labor and management.

Increasing number of parties exercising influence. Although traditionally conceived as bilateral in the United States, labor negotiations have always been subject to influence by third parties, especially government representatives. Today, additional third parties—such as customers, suppliers, communities, and various service providers—often become involved in labor-management negotiations and bring their own substantive agendas to the situation.[27] According to some negotiations theorists, this shift from a bilateral to a multilateral structure potentially represents a profound change.

Structures that shape strategies and strategies that shape structures. Some modifications in the structure of negotiations are exogenous, or imposed by forces outside the immediate labor-management relationship. Other structural changes are endogenous, or instituted by one or both parties to facilitate their current negotiating processes. Structures are important because they are so closely related to strategic choice and implementation.

If a structural characteristic is a given exogenous feature—for example, an industrywide master agreement that centralizes negotiations at that level—then it may serve as a constraint on the utility of certain process tactics (for example, it may complicate integrative bargaining) and hence bias strategic choice (for example, it may discourage fostering). In this case, the primary direction of influence among assessments and choices is as follows: the "given" structure → availability of process tactics → strategic choice.

On the other hand, if a structural feature is truly optional for a negotiator, then it will tend to be consciously aligned with previously formulated strategic preferences and tactical choices. For example, a negotiator who intends to use integrative bargaining and trust-development activities to foster changes may decide to create a structure characterized by more informal, continuous, and extensive contacts between the parties. In this case, the primary direction of influence is: strategic choice → tactical choice of processes → structural choice.

While we note that strategies influence structures and vice versa, we do *not* propose that these influences are simple and straightforward. Consider the level of negotiations. Individual-level negotiations can be associated with either a forcing or fostering strategy. For example, forcing campaigns to tighten management control over absenteeism or increase flexibility in worker assignments may involve daily negotiations between supervisors and workers—a shift toward increased negotiation at the individual level. Similarly, managers attempting to foster employee concern about quality may create a structure that includes the direct participation of workers—also resulting in increased negotiation at the individual level.

The implications of centralization are similarly complex. A party's efforts to change the degree of centralization in negotiations can be related to either forcing or fostering. For example, the initiatives of many steel companies to depart from industry bargaining in the early 1980s were based on distributive-bargaining considerations. Each company sought concessions tailored to its own precarious economic condition. However, this move toward decentralizing the structure also facilitated integrative bargaining in certain settings and the development of more cooperative attitudes.

The transformation of the structure from bilateral to multilateral can also have varied implications for the availability of forcing and fostering tactics. The addition of neutral third parties may facilitate integrative bargaining and mutual trust. On the other hand, some third parties are brought in as a coalition partner by either labor or management to bolster its own bargaining power at the expense of the other party.

FORCES SHAPING NEGOTIATORS' CHOICES

Thus far, we have highlighted alternative social and substantive outcomes that might be achieved via three distinct change strategies, two of which are negotiating strategies. The strategies are implemented tactically by coordinating actions in the three negotiating processes and by designing the negotiating structure. The question remains, however, as to why a party would choose a particular strategy, employ a particular set of process tactics, and select a particular structural option. What forces drive or constrain these negotiations choices?

We propose that choosing among various strategic options is influenced by two broad considerations:

1. The anticipated desirability of the particular change objectives most closely associated with the change strategy

2. The anticipated feasibility of successfully implementing the change strategy

We assume that negotiators will tend to adopt negotiating strategies and tactics that are better suited to the type of benefits on which they place higher priority (desirability). We assume that negotiators will also tend to select strategies and tactics that are more likely to succeed (feasibility). What, then, are the factors that influence negotiators' assessment of desirability and feasibility?

Exhibit 3.8 lists the key factors that we address here. Our analysis focuses on forces affecting choices among strategies, but these forces often exercise their influence on strategies by affecting the availability of the tactics used to implement a strategy.

Anticipated Desirability of Change

In Chapter 1, we identified several substantive objectives of management—reduced payroll costs, flexibility, and increased employee effort and attention to such matters as productivity and quality. We also identified a range of social contracts that management may want to create (or reinforce).

The negotiator's *substantive and social contract aspirations* will both drive and constrain his or her strategic choices. If management seeks change in issues about which the parties have strong conflicts of interest—for example, wages and benefits—it is more likely to formulate a forcing rather than fostering strategy. In turn, the labor union asked to make wage and benefits concessions is likely to force back. In contrast, when management seeks to make improvements in quality and machine utilization, which depend on voluntary actions by employees, management is more likely to adopt a fostering strategy. Similarly, when labor seeks increased company investment in training and career development for employees, a fostering approach is more likely.

Choosing between forcing and fostering is not always easy in the competitiveness era. A common pattern in this era is for management and labor to each place high priority on both types of objectives—those with inherent conflict potential and those that can best be realized by voluntary cooperation. Moreover, many other objectives (such as management's interest in increased flexibility or labor's interest in increased job security) may best be served by a combination of forcing and fostering. Therefore, while the

---

> - Desirability of change
>   - Substantive objectives
>   - Social contract objectives
> - Feasibility of change
>   - Expected responses
>   - Relative bargaining power
>   - Other enabling factors

Exhibit 3.8   Forces Shaping Negotiator Choices

nature of the agenda does exercise influence on actions, the typical agenda is sufficiently mixed and indeterminate in its implications that negotiators' choices are strongly influenced by other factors as well. Most of these factors involve the feasibility of implementing a particular strategy.

Anticipated Feasibility of Change

The factors that influence the ability of management or labor to successfully force or foster change include the receptivity or opposition of the other party, the relative power of the parties, and contextual factors that affect the availability of tactical maneuvers. Since management is often the initiating party in this era, we focus particularly on the assessment of feasibility from management's perspective. Where labor is the initiating party, the same logic would apply, but the sequence would be reversed.

Expected responses. How does management expect labor to respond to its proposals? Does management expect labor to be persuaded by the business rationale for company proposals to reduce, or constrain increases in, wages and benefits? If so, management is more likely to believe that it is feasible to achieve this objective through a fostering strategy. And if not, management will see forcing as the only feasible strategy.

Does management expect that labor would be receptive to initiatives to promote new social contracts based on commitment and cooperation? If not, management will assume that it has less to lose by forcing.

Thus, management's expectations about the feasibility of a strategy to achieve its priority objectives will influence its choice of strategy. However, management's expectations themselves and the union's actual response are complex and dynamic. They are intimately tied to the parties' interpretive frames.

To illustrate the role of frames in labor negotiations, consider a forcing action by management—a demand that, in effect, cuts the total wage and benefit package. The union can interpret this as an act of necessity driven by management's assessment of business conditions or as an act of greed timed to exploit a superior bargaining position. While unionists may choose to resist the concession in both cases, their tactics will vary depending on the interpretation, with differing potential for escalating the conflict and polarizing the relationship. Management, in turn, may interpret any union resistance as intransigence, which could then be taken as justification for shifting production to other locations—further strengthening the union resolve. In this unfolding dynamic, the union's frame shapes its response, just as management's frame guides its own actions.

Other types of actions may be susceptible to an even wider range of ascribed meanings. Management initiatives to promote quality circle programs or similar involvement activities are illustrative. Sometimes, it is unclear to labor whether the involvement activity is a forcing tactic or a fostering tactic or whether it is in fact insignificant and irrelevant. Union officials may regard it as a threatening bid to strengthen the bonds between employees and management at the expense of union solidarity. Alternatively, union leaders may accept it as a straightforward and serious attempt by managers to use employees' brains as well as their hands to improve the quality of both products and jobs. Finally, they may view the involvement program as an insincere but innocuous and temporary initiative by middle managers designed to impress their superiors.

In this example, the union's response will depend on which meaning it ascribes to management's actions. If the effort is viewed as an intentional threat to union solidarity, the union may feel compelled to block or undermine it. If accepted as a sincere effort to improve product quality and the workplace, the union may be receptive to joint sponsorship and comanagement of the program. However, if interpreted as an insincere effort that will sink of its own weight, the union can easily choose to ignore it.

Relative bargaining power. The role of power in shaping a negotiator's choices is readily apparent. A party is more likely to initiate change when it believes it has the coercive power to prevail. In the case of forcing, a direct application of power is anticipated. In the case of fostering, the availability of alternative coercive tactics may also serve as an important motivator, but the influence is less predictable.

Numerous factors may help determine the relative coercive power of management and labor. In the present era, these include: (1) management's ability to transfer equipment and other capital from one location to another, which makes escape a tactical tool that can powerfully influence forcing and fostering strategies; (2) management's ability to continue operations during a strike—for example, by using supervisors or replacement workers, a tactic that strengthens its hand in a forcing campaign; (3) unions' ability to invoke secondary boycotts and employ in-plant strategies, both of which are sources of tactical advantage in a forcing context.

In determining strategic choice or other negotiating actions, the *perceptions* of relative power are as important as actual power. This is because action choices are based on their expected feasibility, which may be very different from the actual interactions that follow. For example, management may believe that it has the power to force change, but labor may also believe that it has the power to resist change. Each may adopt a forcing strategy on the basis of power considerations, resulting in an escalating conflict that can leave both sides less powerful than when the negotiations began.

Other enabling factors. Some conditions not covered by the parties' expectations or their perceived power relations can also influence a negotiator's judgments about the expected feasibility of a given strategy. An example of a factor that enables management forcing is a contract expiration date because it creates an opening for substantive change proposals. Conditions that enable fostering include the availability of salient and credible common goals, such as safety, quality, and job preservation. Fostering choices are also

Table 3.2 Conditions That Affect Choices to Force and Foster: Some Propositions

	Conditions That Promote	
	Forcing	Fostering
Objectives of initiating party (management)		
Priority for and ambitiousness of substantive change?	High[*]	Low
Priority for improvement in social contract?	Low[*]	High
Expected responses (labor)		
Labor expected to be persuaded by business rationale?	Unpersuaded[*]	Persuaded
Labor believed to be receptive to social contract changes sought by management?	Unreceptive[*]	Receptive
Power equation		
Management confident it can force substantive change?	Confident[*,†]	—[‡]

[*]The more strongly these conditions are fulfilled, the more likely *unrestrained* forcing.
[†]When labor and management are both confident of their power, *unrestrained* forcing becomes even more likely.
[‡]No hypothesis for this power condition and fostering.

enabled when the leaders of both sides have experience and skills in joint problem-solving processes.

Summary of factors influencing negotiators' choices. The conditions that predispose negotiators' choices have been stated in extreme terms. In focusing on choices around strategy, we have highlighted, for example, "high-priority" versus "low-priority" substantive and social contract objectives. Table 3.2 summarizes the various factors in these extreme terms.

It is important to recognize, however, that parties always have the option of continuing the status quo. Compared to forcing and fostering, the status quo is an intermediate course of action. Thus, if the conditions are intermediate—for example, "medium priority" for modest substantive and social change objectives—we assume they promote a continuation of the status quo.

BROAD HYPOTHESES IN THE FRAMEWORK: A SUMMARY

This chapter has outlined a theory of negotiated change, containing three main components: (1) a set of outcomes produced by (2) an interaction

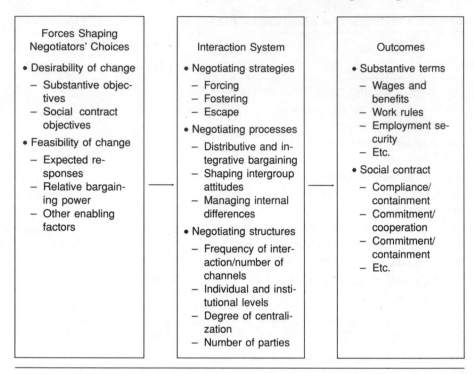

Forces Shaping Negotiators' Choices	Interaction System	Outcomes

• Desirability of change
  – Substantive objectives
  – Social contract objectives
• Feasibility of change
  – Expected responses
  – Relative bargaining power
  – Other enabling factors
	• Negotiating strategies
	  – Forcing
	  – Fostering
	  – Escape
	• Negotiating processes
	  – Distributive and integrative bargaining
	  – Shaping intergroup attitudes
	  – Managing internal differences
	• Negotiating structures
	  – Frequency of interaction/number of channels
	  – Individual and institutional levels
	  – Degree of centralization
	  – Number of parties
		• Substantive terms
		  – Wages and benefits
		  – Work rules
		  – Employment security
		  – Etc.
		• Social contract
		  – Compliance/ containment
		  – Commitment/ cooperation
		  – Commitment/ containment
		  – Etc.

Exhibit 3.9   Detailed Framework for Analyzing a Strategic Negotiation

system, which is, in turn, subject to (3) various driving and restraining forces. The numerous elements of these three main components are assembled in Exhibit 3.9.

The relationship between interdependent parties such as labor and management can be defined in terms of the web of rules (substance) or in terms of the underlying ideology (social contract). We are particularly interested in change processes intended to bring about *major* revisions in the substantive terms and/or social contracts between labor and management.

Substantive and social contract outcomes are produced by a system of interactions between the parties. At the heart of the interactions are three critical negotiating processes—bargaining (distributive and integrative), shaping attitudes between the parties, and managing differences within the parties. The three processes are highly interrelated: acts instrumental to one can affect the others as well.

A party's actions in each of these processes are guided by an explicit or implicit strategy. We propose two general negotiating strategies (forcing and fostering) and a strategy of avoidance (escape). Each of the two negotiating

strategies imposes a predictable set of tactical requirements on every negotiating process. Because the tactical requirements differ radically between
forcing and fostering, actual strategies that mix forcing and fostering produce action dilemmas for negotiators—dilemmas that are also predictable.

Structural features—for example, the degree of centralization—can
influence the three negotiating processes. They exercise their influence on
outcomes by either complicating or enabling the tactical management of the
bargaining task, the modification of attitudes, or the management of internal
differences.

The structures within which negotiations are conducted and the tactics
the parties employ are to a large extent a matter of choice, but they are also
influenced by various driving and restraining forces. The degree of choice
can range widely. One structural feature or tactical action may be wholly a
matter of choice while another is imposed by forces outside the parties'
control. Ultimately, a negotiator's choices—about strategies, processes, and
structure—are a function of both the desirability of a given approach and
the feasibility.

Based on the desirability of various substantive and social contract objectives, a party may pursue either a forcing or fostering strategy. Where the
objectives are many and complex, however, desirability alone will not explain a negotiator's initial choices.

The anticipated feasibility of a given strategy or tactic is based on expectations or perceptions prior to the interaction. The first relevant management expectation focuses on whether labor is likely to respond positively
or negatively to a management proposal. The second factor is management's
perception of its relative bargaining power. Finally, economic, technological,
social, and legal contextual factors, as well as other factors, shape a negotiator's judgment about the expected availability of tactics.

Thus, negotiators seeking fundamental changes in social and substantive
contracts may make broad strategic choices and select from a range of
tactics. Some of these choices are shaped in part by certain factors one can
identify in advance. We have formalized testable propositions covering
several choices in Table 3.3. However, because of a multitude of potential
misperceptions, changing expectations, self-reinforcing dynamics, and formidable dilemmas, both choices and final outcomes are indeterminate.
This combination of predictable and unpredictable aspects of negotiated
change makes it an especially interesting process to study and challenging
to guide.

Part II presents an overview of strategic negotiations in three industries
and synopses of 4 or 5 instructive case histories drawn from each industry.
In subsequent parts, we apply our theoretical framework and its propositions to systematically compare and contrast the three industries, the 13 case
histories, and the 20 discrete historical periods that make up these case
histories.

Table 3.3 Propositions Derived from the Theory

Strategy and Process Tactics

Forcing/process proposition: Within the context of a forcing strategy, negotiators will tend to emphasize distributive bargaining, promote the formation of adversarial attitudes toward the other party, and build solidarity in their own party while encouraging internal differences in the other party.

Fostering/process proposition: Within the context of a fostering strategy, negotiators will tend to emphasize integrative bargaining, promote positive attitudes toward the other party, and encourage internal consensus in the other party as well as within their own party.

Mixed strategies/tactical dilemmas proposition: When negotiators attempt to employ a combination of forcing and fostering in the same time period or in close sequence, they will encounter dilemmas regarding each of the subprocesses—for example, whether or not to share information in bargaining, promote antagonism toward the other party, and help build internal consensus in the other party.

Structure and Strategy

Structure/strategy proposition: The structures within which negotiations occur and the strategies that parties adopt tend over time to become aligned. The alignment of structure and strategy occurs because a structural feature can assist or interfere with the implementation of tactical processes associated with a strategy. Thus, when structural features are "givens" in the situation, they influence negotiators' tactical process choices and strategic choices. Conversely, when structural features can be altered by the negotiators, they are shaped to serve strategic choices that have been based on other considerations.

Desirability

Forcing/desirability proposition: Management is more likely to decide to force and to employ more severe forcing tactics when its objectives include:

- High priority for an "ambitious" agenda for substantive changes in work rules and the economic package
- Low priority for (or no interest in) moving toward a new social contract based on commitment and cooperation

Fostering/desirability proposition: Management is more likely to foster when its objectives are the converse of those encouraging forcing—specifically, when it places:

- Low priority on substantive changes in work rules and the economic package
- High priority on moving toward a new social contract based on commitment and cooperation

---

Feasibility

Forcing/feasibility propositions:

1. Management is more likely to decide to force and to employ more vigorous forcing tactics when it not only has the objectives specified in the forcing/desirability proposition presented above but also expects labor to:

Table 3.3 (continued)

- Remain *un*persuaded that there is a strong business performance rationale for management's substantive agenda

- Oppose a move toward commitment and cooperation, should management have such an objective

2. Management is more likely to decide to force when it believes it has superior distributive-bargaining power. The forcing tactics are more likely to escalate to a severe, even unrestrained, form when management believes it has the power to force the changes it seeks *and* labor believes it has the power to resist those changes.

Fostering/feasibility proposition: Management is more likely to foster when labor is expected to be relatively receptive to its substantive agenda and social contract objectives. This is the opposite extreme of the profile of expectations supporting a decision to force.

NOTES

1. The earlier book by Walton and McKersie, *A Behavioral Theory of Labor Negotiations* (Ithaca, N.Y.: ILR Press, 1991), addresses negotiating processes (integrative, distributive, attitudinal, and intraorganizational) in order to explain the choices negotiating parties must make, the probable consequences of their actions, the contingent nature of their choices and consequences, and the dilemmas inherent in the process.

   Core elements of *Behavioral Theory* are still at the heart of our analysis of current developments in industrial relations, but we have also found it necessary to make key additions. First, as our analysis in Chapter 1 suggests, the concept of negotiations outcomes has been refined to incorporate the distinction between substantive outcomes and social contract outcomes. Second, as is indicated in Chapter 2, we have introduced the idea of primary negotiating strategies. Third, we have formalized the concepts of negotiating structure. Fourth, we have given more formal attention to forces that shape negotiators' choices. In addition, we have changed our organization of the negotiating processes that were featured in *Behavioral Theory*. We collapsed the two types of bargaining into one of three processes labeled "bargaining." The other two processes—attitudinal structuring and intraorganizational bargaining—have been renamed, and each plays a more important role in the present theory, but they each continue to refer to the same general phenomenon.

   The result is a relatively comprehensive theory of negotiations associated with fundamental change. We believe that in the present era, the theory will be applicable not only to labor-management negotiations but also to other interactions involving the renegotiation of substantive and social contracts, such as strategic alliances among competing firms; greater integration between suppliers and customers; and the formation of community, regional, and cross-national coalitions.

2. Our usage of the term *paradigm* is similar to the usage popularized by Thomas Kuhn, *The Structure of Scientific Revolution*, 2d ed. (Chicago: University of Chicago Press, 1970)—that is, fundamental shifts premised on new assumptions, in contrast to incremental changes that stay within the rubric of existing assumptions.

3. The concept of a social contract has a long history, of course. While the usage of the term by political theorists may seem far removed from the current labor relations context, there are important parallels. In both cases, the concept stands as an alternative to a hypothetical state of nature in which there is an absence of explicit rules or implicit understandings. See John Locke, *Second Treatise of Government* (Arlington Heights, Ill.: Harlan Davidson, 1982).

   As we noted earlier, the presence of a social contract does not require affirmative concurrence. In the labor relations context, for example, a social contract oriented around union containment would be present where an employer is engaged in union avoidance activities and the union is responding with various forms of resistance. While neither side would have explicitly agreed to such an arrangement, it nevertheless represents a common understanding about the nature of the relationship—with clear implications for the behavior of all parties—and can thus be thought of as a social contract.

4. Our use of the term *ideology* is similar to the usage in Dunlop's *"industrial relations systems"* framework set forth in his book *Industrial Relations Systems*, rev. ed. (Boston: Harvard Business School Press, 1993).

5. There is relatively little research on negotiations over the rules of the game (or metabargaining). The concept is addressed by Roy J. Lewicki and Joseph A. Litterer, *Negotiation* (Homewood, Ill.: Irwin, 1985), 294, and it underlies negotiations-related scholarship in the social-construction-of-reality tradition, such as Deborah Kolb, *The Mediators* (Cambridge, Mass.: MIT Press, 1985). Still, this represents a fertile area for future research.

6. Industrial relations scholarship is often focused on just one of these social contract combinations or even on just one part of these combinations.

   For example, research focused primarily on the labor-management cooperation dimension includes Clinton Golden and Valerie Parker, *The Causes of Industrial Peace under Collective Bargaining* (Washington, D.C.: National Planning Association, 1955); Irving Siegel and Edgar Weinberg, *Labor-Management Cooperation: The American Experience* (Kalamazoo, Mich.: W. E. Upjohn Institute, 1982); and William Cooke, *Labor-Management Cooperation* (Kalamazoo, Mich.: W. E. Upjohn Institute, 1990).

   Examples of research focused just on the containment dimension include Janice A. Klein and David Wagner, "The Legal Setting for the Emergence of the Union Avoidance Strategy," in *Challenges and Choices Facing American Labor*, ed. Thomas A. Kochan (Cambridge, Mass.: MIT Press, 1985); and Anil Verma and Thomas A. Kochan, "The Growth and Nature of the Nonunion Sector within a Firm," in *Challenges and Choices Facing American Labor.*

   Examples of scholarship focused primarily on the compliance dimension begin with Marx and extend through Robert Blauner, *Alienation and Freedom* (Chicago: University of Chicago Press, 1964); Harry Braverman, *Labor and Monopoly Capital: The Degradation of Work in the Twentieth Century* (New York: Monthly Review Press, 1974); Stephen A. Marglin, "What Do the Bosses Do? The Origins and Functions of Hierarchy in Capitalist Production," in *Class, Power, and Conflict*, ed. Anthony Giddens and David Held (Berkeley: University of California Press, 1982); and numerous current scholarly works in this tradition.

   Research that spans the commitment/cooperation combination includes Thomas A. Kochan, Harry C. Katz, and Robert B. McKersie, *The Transformation of American Industrial Relations* (Ithaca, N.Y.: ILR Press, 1993); Edward Cohen-Rosenthal and Cynthia Burton, *Mutual Gains: A Guide to Union-Management Cooperation* (New York: Praeger, 1987); Charles C. Heckscher, *The New Unionism: Employee Involvement in the Changing Corporation* (New York: Basic Books, 1988), 114–152; and Rosabeth Moss Kanter and Erika Morgan, "First Report on the

Pacific Bell/Communication Workers of America Business Partnership," working paper, Harvard Business School, March 1987.

Research that spans the compliance/containment and/or the commitment/containment pattern is more rare, but examples include Kochan, Katz, and McKersie, *The Transformation of American Industrial Relations;* and Heckscher, *The New Unionism,* 85–113.

7. Elements of the social contract may be taken for granted by the parties, but its broad contours will be visible in established patterns of interaction, published statements, role definitions, shared myths, and other such indicators. For example, the traditional compliance/arm's-length social contract in U.S. labor relations was visible in the form of regular rounds of collective bargaining (usually every three years), the primary focus of a union steward's role on contract administration, countless statements in union and company newsletters, myths around the accomplishments or mistakes of past leaders during collective bargaining, and other such indicators.

8. See, for example, Barry O'Neill, "Conflictful Moves in Bargaining: Warnings, Threats, Escalations, and Ultimatums," in *Negotiation Analysis,* ed. H. Peyton Young (Ann Arbor: University of Michigan Press, 1991), 87–108; and Dean G. Pruitt and Jeffrey Z. Rubin, *Social Conflict: Escalation, Stalemate, and Settlement* (New York: Random House, 1986).

9. Many scholars have helped advance the theory and practice of this particular component of negotiation. Several of their works are cited below.

R. B. Peterson, L. N. Tracy, and A. Cabelly, "Problem Solving in Labor Negotiations: Retest of a Mode," *Relations Industrielles* 36 (1981): 87–105; and Dean G. Pruitt, "Creative Conflict Management: How Bargainers Develop Integrative Agreements," in *Conflict Management and Industrial Relations,* ed. Gerard B. Bomers and Richard B. Peterson (Boston: Kluwer Nijhoff Publishing, 1982), have conducted systematic research to identify the conditions and operations that promote effective integrative bargaining.

In addition, Roger Fisher and William Ury, *Getting to Yes: Negotiating an Agreement without Giving In* (Boston: Houghton Mifflin, 1981); and Lawrence Susskind and Jeffrey Cruikshank, *Breaking the Impasse: Consensual Approaches to Resolving Public Disputes* (New York: Basic Books, 1987), have drawn upon their own experience as third-party consultants to outline the principles and procedures for integrative, or *mutual-gains,* bargaining.

10. Examples of each were given earlier in note 6.

11. See David A. Lax and James K. Sebenius, *The Manager as Negotiator: Bargaining for Cooperation and Competitive Gain* (New York: Free Press, 1986).

12. The role of positive attitudes in promoting integrative bargaining has been confirmed in many studies. See, for example, the 1981 study by Peterson, Tracy, and Cabelly cited in note 9.

13. The importance of intraparty differences is frequently recognized by students of negotiation. For example, see Thomas Kochan and J. Baderschneider, "Dependence on Impasse Procedures: Policy and Fire Fighters in New York State," *Industrial and Labor Relations Review* 31 (1978): 431–449, who show how intraorganizational conflict affects distributive bargaining—by increasing the cost of agreement and, in turn, the probability of an impasse. Also see Charles C. Heckscher, "Searching for Mutual Gains in Labor Relations," in *Negotiation: Strategies for Mutual Gain,* ed. Lavinia Hall (Newbury Park, Calif.: Sage, 1993), 86–104. Heckscher notes the effects of intraorganizational differences on integrative bargaining and concludes that the fact that both sides are pushed around by their constituents is the fundamental barrier to creative bargaining, restricting the scope of invention. A few negotiation theorists go still further and give

intraside bargaining formal treatment, including Lax and Sebenius, *The Manager as Negotiator;* and Robert D. Putnam, "Diplomacy and Domestic Politics: The Logic of Two-Level Games," *International Organization* 42 (1988): 427–460.

14. The shift in this final phase of negotiations and its relation to group processes is analyzed in Deborah G. Ancona, Raymond A. Friedman, and Deborah M. Kolb, "The Group and What Happened on the Way to 'Yes,'" *Negotiation Journal* 7 (1991): 155–173.

15. These self-reinforcing dynamics are a staple of the negotiations literature; they are variously captured in the study of the following topics: threats and commitments, Thomas Schelling, *The Strategy of Conflict* (Cambridge, Mass.: Harvard University Press, 1980); destructive conflict, M. Deutsch, *The Resolution of Conflict: Constructive and Destructive Processes* (New Haven, Conn.: Yale University Press, 1973); the conflict-spiral model, Pruitt and Rubin, *Social Conflict;* the conflict escalation process, Mark Anstey, *Negotiating Conflict: Insights and Skills for Negotiators and Peacemakers* (Cape Town: Juta and Co., 1991); and deep-rooted conflict, John W. Burton, *Resolving Deep-Rooted Conflict* (Lanham, Md.: University Press of America, 1987).

Some of these analyses emphasize psychological processes, and others focus on distributive power dynamics or structural changes. While some—such as Pruitt and Rubin's *Social Conflict,* 88 ff, and Anstey's *Negotiating Conflict,* 51 ff—bring together literature on all three subprocesses, there has been little new research on the full set of interacting subprocesses since the idea was set forth in the 1965 edition of *A Behavioral Theory of Labor Negotiations.*

16. This sort of virtuous cycle is at the heart of the literature on labor-management cooperation. See Cohen-Rosenthal and Burton, *Mutual Gains;* and Cooke, *Labor-Management Cooperation,* which places special emphasis on attitudinal trust issues or the joint gains that can accrue from cooperation. The concept is also integral to the game theory literature, in which special attention is given to issues of reciprocity and cooperation. See Robert Axelrod, *The Evolution of Cooperation* (New York: Basic Books, 1984). The emphasis of the theory presented here is the interaction of all three elements of strategy.

17. In their 1981 study cited in note 9, Peterson, Tracy, and Cabelly found that frequency of contact promoted problem solving.

18. In the negotiations literature, there is little work that bridges the individual and institutional levels of analysis, though both have been studied extensively as separate areas. In the industrial relations literature, the focus has historically been at the institutional level, though current scholarship on workplace practices does encompass what we term individual-level interactions. In the organizational literature, there is a vast body of work concerning individual-level interactions, and there is a growing, but still largely separate, body of work known as the new institutionalism, which bears directly on issues surfaced here (such as self-reinforcing dynamics). A seminal piece in this area is Paul DiMaggio and Walter Power, "The Iron Cage Revisited: Institutional Isomorphism and Collective Rationality in Organizational Fields," *American Sociological Review* 48 (1985): 147–160.

19. The negotiations literature has dealt with issues of centralization and decentralization, though not at great length. In contrast, this was a key issue in research on collective bargaining in earlier eras and has been subject to research more recently given the changes along this dimension. Harry. C. Katz, "The Decentralization of Collective Bargaining: A Literature Review and Comparative Analysis," *Industrial and Labor Relations Review* 47 (1993): 3–22, documents a trend toward decentralization in Western European countries as well as in the United States. He finds that the trend is driven primarily by a more basic movement toward redesign of work organization tailored to local conditions but is also

influenced in some cases by management's gaining the upper hand in power relations and insisting on local negotiation.

20. The negotiations literature has focused extensively on the impact of the number of parties to a negotiation, with a core finding that there are major differences in the character of bilateral negotiations as opposed to multilateral negotiations. We find the work of David A. Lax and James K. Sebenius especially promising. See, for example, Lax and Sebenius, "Thinking Coalitionally: Party Arithmetic, Process Opportunism, and Strategic Sequencing," in *Negotiation Analysis*, 153–193.

21. Although structural issues were discussed at various points in Walton and McKersie, *A Behavioral Theory of Labor Negotiations*, current developments have heightened their salience and led to a more formal treatment.

22. For example, the full Memorandum of Agreement between the UAW and the Saturn Corporation is 28 pages long, in contrast with the UAW-GM National Agreement, which is 527 pages long—even though both documents cover core issues such as compensation, job classifications, work rules, benefits, decision making, training, vacations, holidays, and the like. For a detailed discussion of the operation of a living agreement, see Heckscher, *The New Unionism*.

23. Early research on labor-management committees assumed that they would largely be characterized by joint problem solving around common concerns. In fact, it has consistently been observed that joint committees just as often serve as a forum for surfacing and addressing conflicts of interests. See Thomas A. Kochan, Lee Dyer, and David Lipsky, *The Effectiveness of Union-Management Safety and Health Committees* (Kalamazoo, Mich.: W. E. Upjohn Institute, 1976); and Cohen-Rosenthal and Burton, *Mutual Gains*.

24. This issue of linkage or consistency across levels is a core thesis in the research in Kochan, Katz, and McKersie, *The Transformation of American Industrial Relations*.

25. And some experts are calling for further decentralization of collective bargaining. Barry Bluestone and Irving Bluestone advocate a form of enterprise industrial relations that would ground labor-management relations in the economics of the business and make possible productive partnerships at the local level. See Bluestone and Bluestone, *Negotiating the Future* (New York: Basic Books, 1992).

26. See Daniel J. B. Mitchell, "Shifting Norms in Wage Determination," *Brookings Papers on Economic Activity* 2 (1985): 575–599; and Audrey Freedman, "How the 1980s Have Changed Industrial Relations," *Monthly Labor Review* 111 (1988): 35–38. We join these two authors and others in arguing that the decline of pattern bargaining is a lasting and significant shift. It is important to note that a few scholars see the change as a temporary artifact of the current economic downturn. See John Dunlop, "Have the 1980s Changed U.S. Industrial Relations?" *Monthly Labor Review* 111 (1988): 29–34. See also Kathryn J. Ready, "Is Pattern Bargaining Dead? An Exchange," *Industrial and Labor Relations Review* 44, no. 1 (October 1990): 152–155; Daniel J. Mitchell, comment in "Is Pattern Bargaining Dead? An Exchange," *Industrial and Labor Relations Review* 44, no. 1 (October 1990): 156–159; and Kathryn J. Ready, "Is Pattern Bargaining Dead? An Exchange," *Industrial and Labor Relations Review* 44, no. 1 (October 1990): 160–165.

27. See also Charles Heckscher, "Multilateral Negotiation and the Future of American Labor," *Negotiation Journal* 2, no. 2 (April 1986): 141.

Part II

Thirteen Cases of Negotiated Change in Three U.S. Industries

We have advanced a general theory of strategic negotiations. Now we will put it to work.

Part II describes negotiated change in 13 case histories. Our purposes are both descriptive (to ground the concepts of our framework) and analytical (to apply the framework in the interpretation of specific change episodes). We are also laying the groundwork for Parts III and IV, where we analyze the common themes and contrasting dynamics across the cases.

Our cases are drawn from three industries: Chapter 4 presents four cases from pulp and paper; Chapter 5, five cases from auto supply; and Chapter 6, four cases from railroads. Because we believe that change negotiated between a company (or plant) and its union and workforce can only be correctly understood in context, each of these chapters begins with a description and analysis of the industry context shared by the four or five case histories that follow.

We selected cases with the intention of achieving a rough balance of forcing and fostering examples from each industry. However, when we analyzed each case in detail, we discovered that the strategies illustrated were often more complex than expected. In some instances, the company (or plant) history covered by our study included a sequence of two or three relatively distinct periods, each marked by the predominance of a different negotiating strategy. We identified 20 strategic periods in total.

Table II.1 shows the three industries, 13 cases, and 20 strategic periods. In effect, we have three units of analysis—industries, company (or plant) case histories, and strategic periods—each unit relevant for a different comparative analysis.

First, the description and analysis of the paper, auto supply, and railroad industries will permit a comparative analysis at the *industry level* of the conditions that may predispose negotiators toward escape, forcing, or fostering strategies.

Second, the description and analysis of case histories will permit a comparative analysis at the *company (or plant) level* of the factors that can help explain negotiated outcomes.

Third, the identification of periods, each marked by a distinct management strategy—forcing, fostering, or combined forcing/fostering—will permit a comparative analysis at the *strategic period level* of the factors that shape negotiators' actual choices about strategies and tactics and of the dynamics associated with particular strategies.

Thus, the chapters in Part II provide the raw material for these several comparative analyses, which we present in Parts III and IV. Fortunately, our research sites provided sufficient diversity ("variance" in research parlance) to make these comparative analyses instructive.

Shortly, we will present our systematic judgments about various aspects of the three industries and 13 case studies, including, for example, the extent to which each industry has relied on each of the three change strategies and the amount of substantive and social change that occurred in each of our case studies. These and other judgments presented throughout the chapters in Part II are arrived at through case-by-case clinical analyses. We comment further on these judgments—including acknowledging their subjectivity—in Appendix B, which outlines our study methods.

We preview first the variation in industry contexts and then the diversity among the company cases themselves.

DIFFERING INDUSTRY CONTEXTS

In each American industry, management's change agenda, its pattern of reliance on the several change strategies, and the union's responses all follow a particular pattern, shaped by the industry's own unique combination of economic, social, and technological forces. These several forces determine not only the parties' interests but also their relative capacity to promote or resist change affecting their interests.

All three industries we have selected for analysis—pulp and paper, auto supply, and railroads—were intensively organized by unions and experienced substantial pressures for change, but they offer instructive variations in several other respects: the pressures for change derived from different sources; the parties' negotiating agendas emphasized different issues; the overall amounts of observed change ranged from low to high; and the relative emphases given to escape, forcing, and fostering initiatives differed significantly.

The pressures for change in our sample derived from stronger domestic competition, new foreign competitors, increasing availability of substitute materials or services, escalating customer requirements, and heightened demands for economic performance from the financial community. Each industry was subjected to a unique combination of these factors, yielding a different amount of overall pressure on management for change.

Table II.1 Thirteen Cases and the Strategic Periods That Comprise Them

Industry	Case Histories	Strategic Periods		
		Forcing	Fostering	Combined Forcing/Fostering
Paper	Jay (International Paper)	Period 1		
	De Ridder (Boise Cascade)	Period 1	Period 2	
	Bidwell (disguised name)		Period 1	
	Pensacola (Champion Paper)	Period 1	Period 2	Period 3
Auto supply	AP Parts	Period 1		
	Adrian Fabricators	Period 1	Period 2	
	Packard Electric		Period 2	Period 1
	Budd		Period 2	Period 1
	Anderson Pattern		Period 1	
Railroads	Guilford	Period 1		
	Union Pacific		Period 1	
	Conrail		Period 2	Period 1
	CSX		Period 1	
Total	13 case histories	6 forcing periods	10 fostering periods	4 periods combining forcing and fostering

As Table II.2 illustrates, we assessed the overall pressure in the paper industry during the 1980s to be "moderate," composed of pressure from domestic competition and from the financial community for improved rates of return on the large amounts of invested capital the industry requires. Auto supply experienced "high" pressure, based on strong pressure from domestic and foreign competitors and from the Big Three automakers as customers. In railroads, which were judged to be under "moderate to high" pressure during the 1980s, deregulation had intensified competition not

Table II.2 Pressure for Improved Performance in Three Industries during the 1980s

Industry	Sources of Pressure					
	Domestic Producers in Same Product Market	Foreign Competitors	Substitute Products or Services	Customers' Escalating Requirements	Financial Community's Expectations for Increased Returns	Overall Pressure
Paper	Moderate to high	Moderate to low	Moderate to low	Moderate to low	Moderate to high	Moderate
Auto supply	High	High	Low	High	Moderate	High
Railroads	Moderate to low	Low	High	Moderate	High	Moderate to high

Table II.3 Management Utilization of Change Strategies during the 1980s

Industry	Escape Unionization	Force Change	Foster Change	Overall Change Effort
Paper	Low	High	Moderate	Moderate
Auto supply	High	High	Moderate	High
Railroads	Low	Low	Low to moderate	Low

only within the railroad industry but also between railroad companies and alternative modes of transportation that served the same region.

Managements emphasized different change priorities in the three industries (see Table II.3). In paper, management gave high priority to slowing the rate of increase in payroll costs and expanding contractual flexibility in the assignment of work during the first half of the 1980s and paid increased attention to changing workplace attitudes and relations during the latter half. In the auto supply industry, management placed priority first on lowering compensation costs and second on increasing workforce flexibility. In railroads, management's dominant objective was to decrease employment levels as rapidly as possible, with somewhat less concern about compensation levels.

Finally, the three industries varied in the amount of change effort by managements as well as in the strategies they relied on to produce this change. Paper, which experienced an overall moderate change effort, manifested heavy reliance on forcing. Auto supply, which experienced a high change effort, was marked by frequent resort to all three strategies. And railroads, which experienced the least change effort, relied on fostering slightly more than on escape or forcing; but even here, in fostering, the railroad industry's change efforts were less frequent than in paper and auto supply.

The preceding statement characterizing the change strategies implemented in these three industries is accurate for the period of our study, but will need to be modified with the passage of time. For example, during the 1991–1992 negotiations in the railroad industry, management gained the right to reduce crew sizes much more rapidly than had been possible in the past, possibly setting the stage for an increased level of forcing by the carriers during the rest of the 1990s.

Thus, the three industries provide sufficient diversity to explore many aspects of the proposed theory. Within each industry, however, there was a

Table II.4   Outcomes

Case History	Substantive Terms
Paper industry	
Jay	Major economic and work-rule concessions
De Ridder	Work-rule concessions; many mutual benefits
Bidwell	No change
Pensacola	Economic and work-rule concessions; various changes for mutual benefit
Auto supply industry	
AP Parts	Economic and work-rule concessions
Adrian Fabricators	Economic concessions; various changes for mutual benefit
Packard Electric	Economic concessions; many changes for mutual benefit
Budd	Economic and work-rule concessions; various changes for mutual benefit
Anderson Pattern	Economic and work-rule concessions; many changes for mutual benefit
Railroad industry	
Guilford	Economic and work-rule concessions
UP	No change
Conrail	Many changes for benefit of business
CSX	No change via task force; some changes craft by craft

Social Contract with Employees	Social Contract with Union	Other Benefits and Costs
Stronger compliance	Containment	Costly strike and aftermath
Commitment	Arm's-length (no net change)	Costly strike; improved performance
Compliance (no change)	Arm's-length (no net change)	Little performance effect
Commitment	Cooperation	Improved performance
Compliance (no net change)	Arm's-length (no net change)	Costly strike
Commitment	Cooperation	Costly strike; improved performance
Commitment	Cooperation	Improved performance and job security
Commitment (modest change)	Cooperation (modest change)	Performance improvement (modest)
Commitment	Cooperation	Performance improvement (modest)
Stronger compliance	Avoidance of craft unions; arm's-length with UTU	Costly strike
Compliance (improved attitude)	Improved attitudes in arm's-length relations	No improvement
Commitment (modest change)	Cooperation (modest change)	Performance improvement (strong)
Compliance (no change)	Improved attitudes in arm's-length relations	Performance improvement at local level (modest)

Table II.5 Social Contract Outcomes at the End of Our Case Histories

Employee Relations	Union-Management Relations		
	Containment	Arm's-Length Accommodation	Cooperation
Compliance	Jay Guilford	AP Parts Bidwell CSX UP	
Commitment		De Ridder	Adrian Anderson Budd Conrail Pensacola Packard

Note: All of the labor-management relationships were in the arm's-length accommodation/compliance cell at the beginning of the periods we studied. The one possible exception is Packard Electric, where one could judge the relationship to have already begun moving toward cooperation/commitment at the time our study began.

range of choices available to labor and management at individual locations. The range is well illustrated by the cases we selected from each industry.

A DIVERSE SET OF CASE HISTORIES

Table II.1 shows the diversity of our company cases in terms of the negotiating strategies they employed: six forcing periods, ten fostering periods, and four periods combining forcing and fostering. Note that some cases began with periods of forcing (a subset of which were followed by periods of fostering); some cases began with periods of fostering; and some cases began with periods of mixed forcing and fostering (and were followed by periods of fostering).

Table II.4 shows the diversity of outcomes. The relationships in some companies (plants) were marked by changes in the social contract intended by management; other relationships showed no change; and a few moved in a direction unintended and perhaps unwanted by management, the initiating party. In most cases, but not all, the negotiations yielded changes in substantive terms favorable to management. In roughly half the cases, labor realized no substantive benefits. Performance improvements attributable to changed relationships, where we could assess them, varied widely. Finally, two types of costs that we could associate with change efforts—strikes and soured attitudes—also varied widely. Five of our cases involved mutually costly strikes, and in a couple of these, we believe bitterness continued to be a liability.

All the relationships, except perhaps Packard Electric's, were of the arm's-length accommodation/compliance type at the beginning of the periods covered by our study. Table II.5 portrays the diversity in social contract outcomes mentioned above: four cases involving no change in management's traditional relationship with labor, two cases involving a movement toward a more adversarial containment relationship with the unions, one case involving a commitment relationship with employees, and five or six cases involving movement toward a cooperative relationship with unions and a commitment relationship with employees.

Each summary case study presented in Part II contains an overview of developments, an explanation of the strategies employed, and a brief description and explanation of the outcomes. These summaries are intended to familiarize the reader with each situation and suggest how it can be instructive. In subsequent parts, we introduce further details about negotiating behavior in these cases as we attempt to deepen our understanding of the tactics and dynamics of negotiated change.

Chapter 4

The Pulp and Paper Industry: Shifts in Power and Agendas

This chapter begins with a description and an analysis of the pattern of negotiated change in labor relations in the paper industry, identifying the contextual conditions common to the four case studies of paper mill negotiations that follow. The cases themselves illustrate the diversity of negotiated change experiences in this industry.

Labor negotiations in unionized paper mills departed from a traditional and stable pattern in the early 1980s, when managements began to force work-rule and economic concessions using more potent power bargaining tactics. As a result of this forcing, the social contracts with unions in several major paper companies moved from arm's-length accommodation toward a more adversarial mode of containment.

In the latter half of the 1980s, another shift in the pattern of labor negotiations gained momentum: management was increasingly fostering cooperation and commitment. By the end of the decade, a growing number of managers were trying to develop a blend of forcing and fostering tactics in a mixed strategy that they hoped would yield a competitive cost structure, a high-commitment workforce, and a viable relationship with the union.

Labor's responses to management initiatives in this industry have been in line with general American experience in the competitiveness era. Unions have vigorously contested management's efforts to contain payroll costs and repeal existing work rules and have responded in varied ways to management's efforts to foster commitment and cooperation, ranging from opposition to enthusiasm. However, by 1991, the national leaders of the major union, the United Papermakers International Union (UPIU), were showing an increased receptivity to fostering.

The net effect of management initiatives and labor responses was a diverse pattern of changes during the period studied, with the diversity existing within companies as well as among them—as illustrated by the four cases we present.

The experience at International Paper's mill in Jay, Maine, provides an example of unrestrained forcing. In Boise Cascade's mill in De Ridder, Louisiana, management first forced substantive change and then fostered a new relationship with employees. In the mill we call Bidwell, management's strategy consisted almost exclusively of fostering. In the fourth case, involving Champion's mill at Pensacola, Florida, management forced substantive change during the 1985 contract negotiations, then fostered for several years, and finally pursued a delicate combination of forcing and fostering during the 1988 contract negotiations.

PRESSURE FOR CHANGE

The paper industry comprises mills producing three types of output— pulp, paper, and paperboard. During the late 1970s and 1980s, approximately 150 companies operated paper mills. About 25 of these companies also operated pulp mills. A total of about 100 companies, including many paper companies, operated paperboard mills. The industry was moderately concentrated, with 15 to 25 percent of the companies in each category accounting for 70 percent of total shipments.

From 1976 to 1986, employment of production workers in pulp and paper remained constant at about 110,000, while employment in paperboard mills declined from 50,000 to 40,000.[1] This pattern of relatively stable employment continued through the end of the decade.

Paper manufacturers have not been vulnerable to the kind of large-scale international competition that has threatened to overwhelm the American automobile and steel industries as well as other manufacturing industries. North America is still a low-cost paper producer because of the timber-growing advantages of a temperate climate and large forested areas, but industry observers see on the horizon threats familiar in other industries: substitute materials and foreign competition.

In addition, papermakers face stiffer domestic competition and a more demanding financial community. Declining returns on invested capital contributed to a flurry of mergers, acquisitions, takeover battles, and divestitures in the late 1970s and early 1980s and to a new corporate focus on profitability. Some old, respected companies disappeared, and survivor companies realized in very direct ways that recent industry standards of adequate performance would no longer suffice in a climate of heightened investor expectations.

Like their counterparts in other industries, a number of executives became conscious of the complacency of their corporations. In the late 1970s and 1980s, these managers set out to transform their organizations so that they could achieve continuous improvements. Their efforts often included changing labor relations strategies to support manufacturing flexibility, cost reduction, and stringent quality standards.

PAPER INDUSTRY UNIONS

The paper industry was unionized early and thoroughly, and paper remains a relatively heavily unionized industry, with two-thirds of employees represented by unions in 1980.[2] The dominant union in the industry is the UPIU. In addition, approximately 15,000 Pacific Coast workers are represented by the Association of Western Pulp and Paper Workers (AWPPW). Membership in both major pulp and paper unions declined slightly during the 1980s.

The UPIU is a descendent of several AFL craft unions whose history mirrors the clear distinction still felt between papermakers (who operate the paper machines per se) and other paper mill employees (who operate wood-handling and pulping equipment, work with chemicals, and so forth). These "classes" of workers did not amalgamate their unions until 1972, and the UPIU still exhibits a degree of direct democracy and decentralized control that contrasts with many old industrial unions such as the Steelworkers and the UAW. In some mills, the maintenance workers are represented by other international unions, such as the International Brotherhood of Electrical Workers (IBEW), and as a result, bitter jurisdictional disputes have been known to arise. The UPIU also contrasts with other industrial unions in terms of its rural roots; neither the UPIU nor its predecessors have exhibited the militancy associated with the urban-based unions concentrated in large manufacturing centers in the East and the Midwest, and its history is unmarked by the celebrated and violent confrontations with management that occurred, for example, in the steel and auto industries. The UPIU, however, represented its members firmly through the 1970s in negotiating—chiefly through the threat of strikes—steady increases in income and other protections.

This union has, in fact, derived power advantages from several factors: its members represent a relatively small cost of production, many have highly specialized skills, new technology has not replaced existing jobs on a large scale, and (with pattern bargaining taking wages out of competition) wage cost increases have been passed along to customers. However, as we discuss below, in the most recent decade, several trends have weakened the unions' strong bargaining position, including management's increased ability to operate mills with supervisors during strikes, the company's legal right to permanently replace striking workers, and the breakdown of pattern bargaining.

MANAGEMENT'S AGENDA

During the most recent decade, management developed an ambitious negotiating agenda—to reverse a pattern of above-average economic settlements, to roll back restrictive work rules, and to promote cooperative practices in the workplace.

Changes in the Pattern of Economic Settlements

Labor negotiations traditionally occurred on a mill-by-mill basis, but by the 1970s, a pattern had evolved wherein many companies followed the lead of International Paper (IP). Under this pattern bargaining, paper industry wages rose rapidly between 1970 and 1985, with annual increases reaching 10 percent by the late 1970s. By 1980, other companies started to reject the IP lead, but the average wage increases continued to be large until the mid-1980s. Meanwhile, the major companies and the UPIU attempted to formulate companywide coordinated strategies within which individual mill negotiations would take place.

Once cost-of-living allowances (COLAs) were granted in other industries, paper companies apparently agreed to sharp increases in base wages in order to obviate union demands for COLAs. Company and union negotiators also gradually agreed to an improvement in overtime and premium pay provisions, uncapped medical benefits, nonoperating holidays, and special payment practices that yielded real wages comparable to the oil and chemical, auto, and steel industries and well above prevailing rates in the rural areas in which most paper mills are located. These labor costs looked excessive to most paper company managers by the early 1980s.

Pulp and paper mills are characterized by high fixed costs and capital intensity. For example, in 1985, pulp and paper mills averaged more than $300,000 in assets per employee, compared to about $50,000 in assets per employee in manufacturing overall. Conversely, labor costs as a percentage of total costs were lower in pulp and paper (25.5 percent) compared to all manufacturing (28 percent).[3] Thus, paper companies, faced with a need to maintain operating ratios higher than approximately 95 percent of capacity to stay in the black, have traditionally felt vulnerable to strike threats—despite the fact that the industry has not experienced strikes with either the frequency or the militancy seen in industries organized by the more centralized industrial unions such as the UAW. The combined prospects of the costly shutdown and restart of a continuous manufacturing process and of the loss of business associated with a strike caused managements to agree to annual increases higher than the national average. Despite this accommodation over substance, relations between union locals and managers were not always, or even usually, cordial; paper companies and their UPIU locals tended to maintain a traditional adversarial relationship.

The strikes that did occur resulted in complete mill shutdowns until 1979, when Crown Zellerbach refused to agree to an Association of Western Pulp and Paper Workers proposal for pattern-bargained contracts. Crown Zellerbach shut down its affected mills and then brought them back into operation with replacement workers. The development of computer-based process controls made it increasingly easier for replacements to run pulp and paper equipment. Weyerhaeuser followed suit later that year. When Champion International and Scott Paper mills in Alabama were struck in 1980, they

Table 4.1 First-Year Negotiated Wage Increases in the Pulp, Paper, and Paperboard Industry and in Major Agreements in Other Areas of Manufacturing

	Percentage Increases									
	1980	1981	1982	1983	1984	1985	1986	1987	1988	1989
Pulp, paper, and paperboard industry	9.2	8.7	6.9	5.6	3.3	2.1	0.4	0.4	0.1	1.1
Major agreements in manufac- turing		7.2	2.8	0.4	2.8	0.8	−1.2	2.1	2.2	2.9

Source: Adapted from a presentation by Richard P. Klinzing, based on Paper Industry Association data. (Presentation to a meeting of the Pulp and Paper Manufacturers Association, Milwaukee, Wisconsin, April 15, 1990.)

were also run with salaried replacements. In these and other strikes during
the early 1980s, however, replacement workers were used only on a temporary basis, and striking employees eventually returned to their jobs.

The realization that paper mills could be kept running—albeit with reduced production—even in the face of a strike gave paper industry managers a new sense of possibilities. Then, in 1981, President Ronald Reagan's
successful termination of illegally striking air traffic controllers and the
subsequent decertification of their union signaled to many employers the
end of the era of union power in American life. In the paper industry, this
move by the president coincided with the early experimentation with replacement workers, resulting in a reexamination of the practices that had
supported the accelerating rise in wages. What had been a normal part of
the landscape began to look avoidable to managers and at risk to union
leaders.

And indeed, in the mid-1980s, the landscape did change. Table 4.1—in
effect, a box score of the 1980s—shows first-year negotiated wage increases
in the paper industry and in major agreements in other industries for each
year between 1980 and 1989.[4] The data indicate that labor was successful in
negotiating more favorable settlements during the first half of the decade
and management was more successful during the second half.

The biggest pay increase in paper came during the early part of this
period. For example, the size of first-year negotiated pay increases in paper
declined each year between 1980 and 1986, reflecting the increasingly tough
bargaining stance adopted by paper companies. However, because this
decline in the size of pay increases in paper initially lagged a similar decline
in other major manufacturing industries, wage increases in paper continued
to be relatively high each year through 1986.

Table 4.2   Average Hourly Earnings in Selected Industries

			Increase	
Industry	1977 ($)	1987 ($)	($)	(%)
Paper	6.80	14.06	7.26	107
Manufacturing	5.68	9.86	4.18	74
Steel	8.36	13.63	5.27	63
Autos	8.22	15.38	7.16	87
Chemicals	6.99	13.69	6.70	96
Petroleum	8.48	15.71	7.23	85

Source: Adapted from the American Paper Institute, based on BLS data. (Richard P. Klinzing, presentation based on Bureau of Labor Statistics data [given to the Bargaining Forum, Senior Executive Meeting, New York, October 14, 1987].)

Then, in 1987, 1988, and 1989, wage increases in paper fell below the average negotiated increases in other major agreements in manufacturing. In fact, paper management was able to use lump sums totally in lieu of general increases in two-thirds of the settlements. These settlements in the latter years of the decade reflected the fact that paper companies had succeeded in breaking the traditional pattern of economic settlements—clearly, paperworker unions had reluctantly accepted a new reality in union-management power relations.

Between 1977 and 1987, before the effects of this power shift were fully reflected in new settlement patterns, labor in the paper industry enjoyed increases in hourly average earnings that exceeded the increases in manufacturing as a whole and in the major industries with which paper was usually compared—steel, autos, chemicals, and petroleum (see Table 4.2).[5]

Management gained a number of provisions during the last half of the 1980s, the benefits of which would continue to accrue over time. Several provisions would continue to slow the rates of increase in average hourly earnings. For example, the use of lump-sum increases in base rates and the elimination of "Sunday premium as such" (for work that was still within a 40-hour workweek and an 8-hour day) would have this effect. Other management gains, including the elimination of certain restrictions on work assignments, would potentially be reflected in increased operating flexibility. A growing number of early negotiations, extensions, and longer-term contracts promised to yield a more stable environment both for operations and for efforts to improve relations in the mill.

Recognizing the Need for Other Changes

While paper managers' perceptions of their ability to control wage levels were changing, another set of changed attitudes and practices was in the air in American industrial circles. Managements were pressing for more flexibility in making work assignments and offering employees more involvement.

Paper managers felt especially frustrated by contract language that assigned specific tasks to specific crafts and that required specific complements of employee classifications to be on duty at all times. Reestablishing managerial control over hourly employee work assignments came to be called *flexibility* or *team concept* in this industry. These terms have many meanings, ranging from high levels of employee teamwork to a relaxation of work rules to provide management with flexibility in assigning labor.

Paper industry managers also began to recognize new possibilities for tapping the potential of their workforce. Although they were not new, either in the United States or in the industrialized world, work systems that encouraged workers to cooperate, both with each other and with their managers, to find more efficient and intelligent ways of doing things were increasingly being described and touted in business publications. Papermaking had been deskilled in some ways—certain process variations once dependent on the physical senses of veteran machine tenders were now computer-controlled—but the skills of trained hourly workers were still essential to effective operations. Even beyond this, operating managers thought that their highly structured systems used only a portion of their employees' skills, and they knew that most employees were discouraged from pooling their skills and ideas both by work rules and by long traditions of managerial control and adversarial relations.

DEVELOPMENTS IN SOCIAL CONTRACTS BEFORE 1980

The pioneering efforts to create a more committed workforce and productive work organization occurred in many new mills (with nonunion workforces) as early as the 1960s. Procter & Gamble's Charmin Paper Division, as it was then known, started a new mill in 1966 in Mahoopany, Pennsylvania, with a work structure it called the "technician system"—featuring a new pay-and-advancement scheme that encouraged and rewarded the acquisition of multiple skills, flexible assignment patterns, and progressively more delegated responsibility from supervision to operators. Over the succeeding ten years, P&G built many new paper mills, all of which remained nonunion. Its experience helped advance the concepts and techniques for managing high-commitment work systems. By 1980, several other companies had implemented similar flexible, team-based work systems in greenfield plants that remained nonunion, including Mead Paper in Stevenson, Alabama; Weyerhaeuser in Columbus, Mississippi; and International Paper in Mansfield, Ohio.

These new approaches to organizing and managing work were generally judged successful, and although some companies tried to avoid publicity about their new work systems, managers in other pulp and paper companies and UPIU officials were generally aware of the approaches taken in these new mills and of their general achievements. Consequently, these new mill work systems served as models for the start-up of additional new facilities in the industry. They also encouraged managements to explore ways of transferring the approach to their unionized mills.

Again, P&G was first among the pioneers. During the 1970s, the company began a long process of transforming the unionized mills it had acquired when it bought the Charmin Paper Company—one located in Sheboygan, and two in Green Bay, Wisconsin. The Sheboygan mill's workforce was particularly militant, and its labor relations were highly adversarial. Nevertheless, the company's efforts to promote high employee commitment and cooperative union relations, and to introduce the technician system policies, met with success during the 1970s and then (to get ahead of our story) achieved work practices and employee commitment in all three union mills by the end of the 1980s that were comparable to those at the company's nonunion facilities.

P&G's primary change strategy in its unionized mills emphasized initiatives aimed directly at workers in order to change the basic employee-employer social contract. These bottom-up fostering initiatives were supplemented by communication and consultation with local union officials and the UPIU international representatives—which also signaled management's acceptance of the union as an institution.

P&G's relatively early success in its unionized mills, achieved before similar changes had occurred on a wide scale in American industry and in the absence of any sharp competitive threat, was facilitated by a number of factors. First, the company had a strong reputation among its employees for fair and relatively generous treatment—in wages, employment security, and day-to-day practices. Therefore, even in its Sheboygan mill (which was characterized by adversarial relations), management could draw on a reservoir of company credibility and goodwill. Second, what management saw as its unambiguously positive experience with the technician system in its nonunion mills resulted in a strong resolve to negotiate similar policies and practices in the unionized mills—a resolve that was readily sensed by workers, union leaders, and lower-level managers. Further, many managers had been transferred to Green Bay and Sheboygan from the nonunion mills, and therefore, their determination was based on direct experience rather than on written reports or visits to technician mills. Third, management posted head-to-head performances comparisons for paper machines and converting equipment at the nonunion (technician) mills and the union mills, creating a feeling in the Green Bay and Sheboygan mills that it was in the workforce's long-term interest to be competitive with the nonunion technician mills. Indeed, the workforces in these mills proceeded to help make them fully competitive.

LABOR RELATIONS DIVERSITY DURING THE 1980S AND EARLY 1990S

Concerted efforts to renegotiate the social contract in unionized paper mills during the 1970s were confined to a few companies and to a relatively small number of mills. Taking advantage of their more favorable power balance, described earlier, companies began in the 1980s to negotiate contractual rights to exercise greater control in assigning work—generically termed "flexibility" in most companies. They also prevailed in securing unprecedentedly small increases in the overall economic package, actually eliminating certain pay practices, such as premium pay for Sunday as such. Examples of these changes are described later in more detail, and it will suffice to note here that both of these contractual changes were vigorously opposed by the unions in most companies and often conceded only after strikes and/or after engendering bitterness. Labor's resentment was heightened because, in almost all cases, the companies forced these changes in the absence of evidence of any pressing business need credible to the union.

In many mills, resentment translated into behaviors ranging from the type of inattention that accompanies disaffection to deliberate tactics to depress performance. These behaviors adversely affected machine utilization and yields, often resulting in significant reductions in profits. Although the costs of disaffection gave management an incentive to improve relations, it is unclear whether they also provided the union with any tactical advantage in resisting the changes.

Based on comparisons of eight of the larger companies provided by UPIU officials and labor relations executives in the industry as well as on our own observations, we judge that as of 1991, several of the companies were largely characterized by a heightened adversarial version of traditional relationships. Included in this group are International Paper and Georgia Pacific. Boise Cascade was clearly in this group during the 1980s but revised its labor relations policy in 1990 and 1991. A few companies, including James River and Champion Paper Corporation, presented a relatively mixed picture during the late 1980s. Champion's relations with the UPIU improved significantly in the early 1990s. Finally, a few companies, including Kimberly Clark and Scott Paper, made substantial progress in negotiating change at both the employee and institutional levels. James River made a major bid to join this pattern with an agreement with the UPIU that it signed in 1989. In the summer of 1989, both James River and Scott reached formal agreements with the UPIU to work jointly toward commitment and cooperation. In the following subsections, we illustrate these several patterns by discussing some of the companies just mentioned.

Adversarial Relations: International Paper and Boise Cascade

Two companies at the leading edge of tougher bargaining by management during the 1980s were International Paper (IP) and Boise Cascade. And both experienced major strikes that produced severely strained labor relations.

IP began to take an especially tough bargaining position during the mid-1980s. Although the union resisted, it did not draw the line on the reduced settlement pattern during this period. The major mismatch in expectations developed with the round of bargaining that started in 1987. Management wanted to translate its perceived advantage into changes in economic and noneconomic provisions. The UPIU observed that whereas IP's settlement pattern had first been initiated during a period of depressed profits, business was booming in 1987, and therefore, it was not prepared to go along with concessions in the additional mills coming up for negotiation.

The result was a lockout at IP's Mobile, Alabama, mill and strikes at three of its other facilities: Jay, Maine; Lock Haven, Pennsylvania; and De Pere, Wisconsin. The latter three involved especially harsh tactics on both sides (permanent replacement of striking workers by the company and decertification drives by procompany workers, OSHA complaints and "corporate campaign" tactics by the union). The strikes ended in 1988. The climate in the Jay mill remained tense, and the local union was decertified in July 1992. (We discuss this episode at IP in more detail later in this chapter.) IP's relations with UPIU leaders remained bitter into 1993.

The IP disputes arose over company demands to cut out various premium pay mechanisms, change work rules to achieve increased operating flexibility, and eliminate jobs. These demands had become part of a pattern many other managements also sought when their own labor agreements came up for renegotiation.

Boise Cascade was regarded as another "bad guy" by the UPIU until about 1991. Hard distributive bargaining by management resulted in bitter strikes at its mills in De Ridder, Louisiana, in 1983 and Rumford, Maine, in 1986. Although De Ridder relations improved in the poststrike period, for reasons we analyze in a case study below, both strikes remained a negative factor in the minds of international officials of the UPIU.

In 1989, Boise Cascade created a corporatewide task force to work on a plan for creating positive employee relations as well as for improving institutional relations with the UPIU. The task force presented its recommendations to management in November 1990 and then shared its report with UPIU and AWPPW officials during the spring of 1991. Significantly, the report concluded that the company had been too confrontational with its unions. It recommended steps to create more positive institutional relationships with unions in order to provide a more constructive context for the development of a committed workforce and the implementation of a total quality program. The steps included sharing information with local unions at the mill level, dialogues with international union representatives on business issues, and somewhat greater latitude to negotiate arrangements appropriate to a mill's circumstances. The report also cautioned that, of course, the company needed to be prepared to manage work stoppages. Considered against the backdrop of the company's labor relations of the 1980s, this report was a significant step toward thawing its union relations. By 1993, both Boise Cascade managers and UPIU officials confirmed that a more cooperative relationship was developing.

Mixed Patterns: Champion Paper Corporation

Champion illustrates a mixed picture in terms of the framework used in this study. Beginning about 1985, management became increasingly active in promoting employee commitment and in planning how to promote union-management cooperation. The company's business strategy emphasized continuous improvement in the utilization of its capital-intensive production facilities, and flexibility and participation in all of its mills were seen as instrumental to achieving this improvement.

Encouraged by its experience with a high-commitment work system in a new nonunion mill in Quinnesec, Michigan, started up in 1982, management undertook to promote participative management in its other ten union mills. It used the company's mill in Pensacola, Florida—featured in one of four case studies—to pioneer this effort in unionized mills. By 1988, Champion executives had created a top-level steering committee to guide the effort, employed consultants to assist each of the company's mills, and provided abundant resources and reinforcement to keep the change effort on track. It encouraged mill managers to engage their union counterparts in dialogue, enlist the union's support for the changes in work practices, and work jointly to plan the change in the union-management relationship.

By early 1989, before a new round of contract negotiations got under way, the responses of workers and union officials to these various initiatives fell across a wide range among Champion's ten unionized mills. In the forerunning Pensacola mill, labor strongly supported the evolving labor-management partnership. In several mills, labor's response was one of cautious but positive interest; labor permitted increased employee involvement, revision of some work practices, and new forms of joint union-management activity. In a few other mills, no meaningful change had occurred. The remaining mills fell somewhere between the moderate-change and no-change mills. Although modest in absolute terms, the company's progress between 1985 and 1989 was a positive achievement given the time usually required for change to occur in other companies elsewhere in this industry and in other industries.

Champion's progress in negotiating a new social contract was dealt a setback in 1989 and 1990. Labor contracts in 7 of its 11 mills expired during 1989. The company was committed to following through on a pattern of substantive changes that IP, Georgia Pacific, Stone, Union Camp, and Boise Cascade were pursuing and that Champion had already achieved in 3 of its mills during the previous two years. An especially controversial element of this pattern was the elimination of premium pay for Sunday as such.

The union was determined to exercise all the economic power at its command to prevent Champion from continuing this settlement pattern. The international union's strategy was to continue working after the expiration of a particular mill contract but also to refuse to agree to the company's proposals. Over time, as other contracts expired, they were to be pooled so that eventually the union would be in a position to threaten to strike all seven of the mills at once. The union reasoned that a strike affecting a large fraction of the mills would be more difficult for the company to counter by continuing operations with supervisory personnel and/or replacement workers.

In three mills, management reached settlements with local union officials, and the agreements were ratified by local members. However, the UPIU succeeded in keeping the other four mills with expired contracts in the pool into 1990, creating impasses in these locations, whereupon management implemented the terms in its final proposal that were favorable to itself (but not those favorable to labor).

In early June 1990, the members of the locals at these four mills voted to authorize a strike by majorities ranging from 82 percent to 95 percent. However, the UPIU soon accepted the company's proposals with minor modifications. Both sides were undoubtedly relieved to have concluded a long and acrimonious struggle, but neither celebrated its achievements. Labor had succeeded in making its feelings felt and in demonstrating that it could coordinate bargaining across many mills, but it had not denied the company the major proposed changes that were in contention. Management had achieved its major substantive objectives, including the elimination of premium pay for Sundays as such, but the struggle had delayed for one to two years its efforts to move toward commitment and cooperation in most of its mills and had adversely affected performance in these mills for more than a year.

Over the next several years, relations improved dramatically between Champion and the UPIU at both the corporate and mill levels. One marker of this improvement was the formation in March 1992 of a joint leadership body called the UPIU-Champion Forum.

Our cases presented later in the chapter include Champion's Pensacola, Florida, mill—its most advanced mill in terms of renegotiating the social contracts toward commitment and cooperation.

Cooperative Relations: Scott Paper and James River

Scott and James River illustrate the end of the spectrum at which more change had occurred by 1991 in negotiating a new institutional relationship with the UPIU.

In the summer and fall of 1989, both Scott Paper and James River reached agreements with the UPIU that committed management and labor to develop cooperative institutional relations and to involve employees in performance improvement activities. Both agreements committed the parties to promote not only performance improvements but also employment security and better jobs. The James River agreement, signed and dated October 29, 1989, also specifically provided the UPIU with the following assurance: "[T]o the extent [that] the Union and management at any specific locations are working cooperatively and achieving the above improvements [in performance and working relationships], the Company will not demand reductions in job rates or Sunday/Holiday premium, unless the viability of the operation is threatened."

Thus, explicitly in the James River case and implicitly in the Scott case, the international officials of the UPIU decided to support and join management's aspirations for a new social contract, provided that management was, in turn, willing to accept the continuation of certain substantive provisions that the union and its members felt were sacrosanct. Although the formal agreements committed the parties to cooperative activities, they were hammered out by a process that included both distributive and integrative bargaining. In each case, the corporate-level agreements between union and managers followed cooperative efforts in several of the companies' mills.

We have already noted that P&G continued in the 1980s to transform its unionized mills into high-commitment/cooperative relations. This cooperative route yielded the company much more flexibility than was achieved through contract negotiations at other mills. P&G also conformed to the industry pattern of granting only smaller annual pay increases but did so with less negotiating difficulty than characterized most of the rest of the industry.

FACTORS INFLUENCING THE USE OF ESCAPE, FORCING, AND FOSTERING IN PAPER: 1980S AND EARLY 1990S

We have noted the trends first from traditional patterns to forcing and then to fostering (usually accompanied by some continued forcing). We conclude that overall, during the period studied, paper management relied least on escaping unionization and most on a forcing negotiating strategy; it utilized fostering to an intermediate extent. What factors influenced the relative frequency with which the strategies were used?

The Escape Option: Not Available on a Wide Scale

Perhaps the most straightforward aspect of the explanation for the pattern of change strategies relates to the escape option—specifically, the relatively minor role played by transferring operations to settings with labor relations situations more favorable to management, such as greenfield mills and offshore locations. To be sure, some additional capacity has been built in greenfield sites and has been used by management to explore and demonstrate the efficacy of new labor practices. These mills, which typically have remained nonunion, may theoretically influence the unions in the paper industry to be more accepting of new practices in the mills they represent. But except for the P&G case, discussed earlier, there is little evidence of this tendency.

While some of the additional capacity built during the last two decades has been located in greenfield sites, a far larger fraction of it has been located at sites already unionized. The economic case for maintaining capacity in existing mills is compelling. Pulp and paper mills are highly capital intensive; they have long productive lives, given the stable nature of the technology and its physical durability. Moreover, the mills are sited for their access to timber and water, which is used in the process and for the disposal of waste. Once the mill infrastructure is embedded in a site, it is extremely difficult to justify shutting down the mill's capacity, even in part, except when the mill's market is lost, raw materials dry up, or insurmountable environmental problems develop.

The Forcing Option: Conditions Were Right for Management

Paper industry managers evidently saw considerable promise in forcing substantive change in their contractual agreements with unions and in their day-to-day relations with employees. For many of them, this negotiating strategy combined a traditional sense of management rights and a new-found sense of management bargaining power, described earlier.

The union tide—in terms of both numerical strength and political clout—that had risen through the 1950s was clearly on the ebb by the 1980s. In paper, companies now increasingly considered the strike threat an acceptable risk as they discovered that it was feasible to take a strike, run a mill, and even hire permanent replacements for striking workers. In addition, the high level of industry wages made it easy for companies to argue that compensation had gone beyond reasonable levels. This was especially true in regions dominated by troubled manufacturing industries, where well-paid paper workers and their supervisors drove past shuttered auto and steel plants. The UPIU seemed to industry observers to lack the strength to resist a broad-based move toward wage and benefit containment. Once a few companies had successfully bargained significant changes in labor agreements, this window of opportunity looked even wider to other companies. Moreover, in the absence of the real possibility of wholesale extinction, offshore construction, and other extreme measures, it seemed clear to company managers that it would be difficult, if not impossible, to convince union members to accept change without some degree of coercive pressure.

The Fostering Option: Cooperation Offered Long-Term Advantages

The logical rationale for fostering commitment and cooperation is especially strong in pulp and paper manufacturing because of its capital intensity and the crucial importance of efficient utilization of equipment and raw materials. Moreover, because of the "art" that remains in papermaking, machine utilization and yields are especially sensitive to employee attitudes and skills, which can be shaped by fostering. Despite this logic, the fostering trend developed later than the forcing trend. Many factors explain both the fostering trend itself and the reason it developed more slowly than the forcing pattern in the 1980s.

As outlined above, managers in paper companies also started to realize in the early to mid-1980s that optimal manufacturing performance might require not only contractual changes (in wages, benefits, and work rules) but also a new kind of employee relations that would encourage both shop-floor-level teamwork and institutional-level understanding and cooperation between managers and UPIU officials. The new progressive commitment policies that were appearing in the business press tapped into mythologies about an earlier, golden age when "people worked together" and workers and their supervisors were "like a family." Wasn't it almost self-evident that involved workers would produce more, move more quickly to end outages, pay more attention to safety considerations, and file fewer time-consuming grievances? Wasn't it obvious to everyone, even to the union, that the industry's handful of greenfield mills—mostly organized along "team" rather than "classification" lines—were running well and were likely to garner increasing shares of corporate capital investment dollars?

The UPIU did not respond in a unified way to corporate proposals for cooperation as unions tended to do in textiles and steel, for several obvious reasons. First, the dire economic threat was not there. Second, as noted above, the UPIU could not bring to bear the centralized, controlling force available to other unions such as the Steelworkers. Thus, local histories and local relations strongly influenced mill-level responses. In specific cases, some international representatives of the UPIU did embrace cooperation early on—but others remained strongly opposed to what they termed "collaboration" with corporate and mill executives. Third, to foreshadow the dilemmas and dynamics inherent in combined forcing/fostering strategies, to be described later, some companies introduced forcing tactics and cooperative concepts during the same time period. This made union suspicion of the motivation behind managerial overtures not only inevitable but also understandable, given the historical context of paper industry labor relations.

In addition, although the joint committees proposed by companies might have presaged an unprecedented level of union oversight and influence (and UPIU officials knew that union officers in other industries had even taken board seats in some American companies), such proposals also posed a threat to union solidarity. Union officers might move closer to their management counterparts than to either their union superiors or their rank-and-file members. Coupled as they were with teamwork and fluid assignment proposals, cooperative notions also seemed like threats to hard-fought union achievements, especially seniority principles and craft classifications.

Finally, by the late 1980s, most paper company executives had concluded that they would have to achieve *both* substantive contractual change *and* a cooperative spirit in order to accomplish their broader corporate goals. Some managements that had already won both work-rule and economic concessions concluded that fostering cooperation now took priority over forcing any further revisions of substantive terms. And the trend toward longer-term contracts would facilitate mixed strategies emphasizing foster-

ing over forcing. The interaction between these change agendas and negotiating strategies will develop as we discuss examples of each strategy and
of the mixed strategies we have seen in the experience of specific companies.

Our industry review shows that faced with growing pressure for improved performance, paper industry managements actively attempted to
revise both substantive and social contracts with labor—and they enjoyed
some successes. Overall, during the period studied, paper managements
made the most use of forcing, followed by fostering. Within that broad
pattern, the mix was shifting, as of the late 1980s and early 1990s. We have
described the trends and analyzed the forces influencing them. The four
cases that follow provide an in-depth look at situations exemplifying these
trends.[6]

The first trend, toward forcing, started in the early 1980s and has continued in a somewhat moderated form into the 1990s. The first two cases, on
the Jay mill (International Paper) and De Ridder mill (Boise Cascade),
illustrate major forcing campaigns and the dynamics associated with them.
The Jay case illustrates an episode of unrestrained forcing with costly outcomes for both parties, but especially labor. The De Ridder case presents a
successful example of controlled forcing followed by effective fostering. This
sequence—forcing followed by fostering—provides some particularly instructive lessons.

The second trend, which began to emerge in the mid-1980s, was growing
in importance by the early 1990s. The brief and disguised Bidwell case
illustrates a relatively halfhearted and temporary management effort to
foster change and is typical of many such management initiatives in paper
and elsewhere, especially during the earlier years of the period studied. By
the early 1990s, managements were more likely to combine forcing and
fostering, but within an overall context that emphasized a fostering orientation. Our final case, on the Pensacola mill (Champion), portrays in micro-
cosm the overall industry trends—from strong forcing in the 1985 contract
negotiations to concerted fostering during 1985–1988 to a delicate combination of forcing and fostering in the 1988 contract negotiations. More important, it provides an in-depth look at the issues involved in combining forcing
and fostering during the same negotiating period.

INTERNATIONAL PAPER, JAY, MAINE, MILL:
A MUTUALLY COSTLY DISPUTE

This case focuses on a publicized and influential labor dispute at several
International Paper (IP) mills, including one at Jay, Maine, during 1987 and
1988. The Jay mill is located on the Androscoggin River in western Maine.[7]
In 1987, the mill employed 1,200 people in a town with a population of
5,000.

The negotiations in this dispute illustrate vigorous forcing by management to obtain ambitious changes in economic and work-rule provisions,
efforts that met determined opposition from labor and escalated into unre-

strained forcing. A 17-month strike ensued. Management won—and the union lost—regarding the substantive changes at stake, but the dispute was costly in other respects to both parties.

Escalation of Conflict

In 1985, after a few years of poor earnings, IP management initiated a major cost-reduction effort and advised top UPIU officials that the effort included bargaining the elimination of premium pay for Sundays and holidays over the next two years. IP successfully negotiated the elimination of these premiums in 37 consecutive local negotiations. As of mid-1987, IP had only 10 remaining contracts with the UPIU in which they had not yet negotiated this issue.

Meanwhile, during 1986, the UPIU successfully employed a new "pooling" strategy in its negotiations with another paper company in order to get the company to back off its demands for the elimination of similar premium pay provisions. IP management learned that the union intended to use the same strategy against IP, withholding ratification at successive local bargainings in order to be able to call a strike involving a pool of multiple locations.

The parties appeared to be on a collision course. Management was committed to following through with the pattern of settlements already negotiated in 75 percent of its locations and the union believed it could stem the tide of concessions. Moreover, the union noted that IP, along with other paper companies, was now enjoying higher profits. The first test of wills was at IP's Mobile, Alabama, mill, where in March 1987 the dispute precipitated a lockout.

In April, IP presented the Jay locals with demands similar to those negotiated earlier in many IP mills; it included the elimination of Sunday premium pay and 178 jobs. In June, the company made its final offer, softening its demands only slightly. The UPIU local refused the offer, and a strike began June 16. The UPIU conducted coordinated strikes against IP in De Pere, Wisconsin (300 workers), and Lock Haven, Pennsylvania (720 workers). Thus, these three UPIU plants plus the locked-out Mobile plant, had formed a "pool."

IP hired replacement workers recruited throughout Maine soon after the strike started. The scale of the simultaneous strikes against several IP mills would have made it difficult to employ alternative strategies (chiefly, moving in supervisory personnel from other company mills).

The dispute drew the prolabor attention of Democratic presidential candidates Jesse Jackson and Michael Dukakis, triggered a corporate campaign against IP, and involved a variety of maneuvers by labor to bring local and state government pressure to bear on the company. It was led by Ray Rogers, who had won recognition in some labor circles by orchestrating a similar campaign against Hormel's meat-packing operations.

In November 1987, the company implemented a "best and final offer" contract incorporating the changes it had sought. IP also announced that

988 permanent replacements had been hired, that there would be only 12 more jobs open to returning strikers, and that there had been 200 applicants for those positions. By now, almost 3,500 UPIU workers were out at the four IP mills in dispute.

Resolution Efforts

The parties, which had met in December 1987 for four hours in the Federal Mediation Services offices in a failed attempt to get talks restarted, met again in March 1988 in Louisville, Kentucky. Negotiations lasted for two and a half weeks, resulting in a proposed agreement that the UPIU insisted must be ratified by pooling votes from all strike locations. For the paperworkers, the major features of the IP proposal were provisions for early retirement and a guarantee of work within one year somewhere in the IP system for all striking workers. The contract was rejected overwhelmingly by the pooled votes of the four locals.

At the union convention in August 1988, there was strong support for continuing the strike, and it was assumed that as other plants came up for contract negotiations, they would join the pool. However, in October, when UPIU President Wayne Glenn called local IP union presidents together and tested the idea that plants with upcoming negotiations "join the pool," he failed to elicit much support among delegations from the affected plants. Some delegates expressed concern that IP might attempt to replace all 12,000 workers. Jay local union leaders were also growing more fearful that some junior workers would decide to cross the picket line.

End of the Strike

The union agreed to call off the strike as of October 9, 1988. The workers accepted less favorable terms than they had rejected months earlier. Under the National Labor Relations Act, returning strikers were entitled to return to the job they held at the start of the strike, but only when vacancies occurred. Some strikers chose to return to positions several rungs down the job ladder; and others opted to return only when their former jobs became available. IP fared better: the fact that only a small percentage of its capacity had been affected minimized the strike's financial strain on the company.

Some of the dispute's costs to IP, however, continued after the strike ended. The replacement workers often lacked the depth of experience, knowledge, and skills of those they replaced. Moreover, as replacement workers left the Jay mill and their positions were filled by strikers, there was inevitably some tension between the strikers and those remaining replacement workers whom strikers called "scabs." In addition, union members directed special animosity toward the 50 strikers who had crossed the picket line. They were referred to as "superscabs." Union and management spokesman disagree in their reports to us about the extent and effects of this tension—the union reporting severe tension and adverse effects on performance, and management discounting this view.

Aftereffects persisted in the union as well. For example, many unionists with upcoming negotiations who declined to join the pool of striking IP mills felt shame as well as anger at IP for causing them to go back on their "brothers" out of fear of losing their jobs. The strike also had a temporizing effect on subsequent negotiations within the system. Some locals conceded the Sunday premium without also engaging in in-plant tactics to show their displeasure.

Still later, in July 1992, the employees in the Jay mill voted to decertify the union. However, because individual workers who had been replaced during the strike were still entitled to reinstatement when positions became available, there was a steadily growing fraction of former strikers in the mill. The UPIU was hopeful about the prospects for a successful organizing drive in the future.

Outcomes

In summary, the outcomes for management were mixed and for labor clearly negative. Management prevailed in negotiating the terms of employment it wanted and apparently strengthened its own confidence and power for entering into subsequent contract negotiations at other IP mills. Eventually, it was able to operate the Jay mill without a union. At the same time, it incurred costs: the loss of profits during the strike and the loss of skills which continued after the strike. The international union not only conceded the substantive changes it had opposed but also appeared to be weakened and divided in the aftermath of the strike. IP management and the UPIU had moved from arm's-length accommodation toward a more adversarial mode of containment.

Explaining Management's Strategic Choice

The Jay negotiations resulted in poor outcomes for both parties because they escalated into an unrestrained form of forcing. Why the choice to force, and why did forcing become unrestrained?

Many factors must be taken into account in explaining why Jay management employed this strategy of unrestrained forcing. IP management approached the 1987 negotiations with a desire to continue to break the pattern of above-national-average economic settlements that had characterized the paper industry in the 1980s through 1985. It also wanted to continue the momentum to revise work rules. Moreover, it had reason to believe it could probably achieve these results without a strike because of earlier settlements in its own southern mills and recent UPIU settlements at two other mills in Maine. However, the UPIU local at Jay was more resolved to resist the proposed changes than management had expected. For its part, the union regarded the proposed changes as particularly unjustified given IP's record profit levels. It decided to take a stand. Therefore, management was faced with a situation in which it had to either back away from its objectives and expectations or escalate its power tactics—from controlled forcing to unrestrained forcing. In making this choice, it was not inhibited by any ongoing effort to negotiate employee commitment.

IP management's confidence that it could sustain a strike or lockout, even affecting four mills, was bolstered by the fact that it had a large system of mills and by an assumption that it could recruit permanent replacements and operate the targeted mills at satisfactory levels of efficiency. Management judged that it could not operate several mills with supervisory personnel. The union decided to sustain its position, escalate its tactics, and pool four mills. Management may have miscalculated the degree of union resistance. We can be more confident that the union decision makers underestimated management's power and resolve because, in the end, the union lost the forcing contest.

In summary, the negotiating pattern that emerged at Jay appears to be accompanied by the conditions we hypothesized in Chapter 3 to predispose the parties to unrestrained forcing: (1) management's ambitious substantive agenda and the absence of any inhibiting objectives to revise the social contract; (2) the local union's apparent distaste for management's proposals and its rejection of IP's business rationale for the changes; and (3) management's confidence in its power to prevail in a showdown of economic power. In addition, the fact that *both* parties were confident of their respective bargaining positions helped explain the escalation into unrestrained forcing.

The case provides grist for many of the questions about negotiated change that we address in Parts III and IV, including: Why does forcing sometimes escalate to an unrestrained form? Why does distributive bargaining often leave a legacy of attitudes that can frustrate integrative bargaining? How do negotiators attempt to strengthen the internal solidarity of their own organizations during forcing? We will provide additional details about the Jay case when we discuss it in relation to these and other analytical questions.

BOISE CASCADE, DE RIDDER, LOUISIANA, MILL:
SUCCESS IN FORCING—AND THEN FOSTERING FLEXIBILITY

Boise Cascade Corporation succeeded first in forcing major change in the labor contract covering its De Ridder, Louisiana, mill by prevailing in a two-and-a-half-month strike during 1983 and 1984 (period 1) and then in fostering and forcing related changes over the rest of the decade (period 2). This account is based in part on a report by Casey Ichniowski[8] and in part on our own fieldwork.

Forcing Campaign: 1983–1984

The forcing phase of this change effort began during preparations for the 1983 negotiations, intensified during the strike, and continued into the first year of the new contract as management's fostering effort gained momentum.

Rationale for drastic change. Built in 1969, the De Ridder mill was the company's newest and largest operation, but it had performed poorly. Between 1976 and 1980, hourly employment had increased from 385 to 490, without commensurate increases in production, and return on total capital employed declined both absolutely and relative to other Boise Cascade mills. In 1982, the mill's accident and grievance rates were high compared to those of other company mills. Coincidentally, its management turnover rate was also high: seven different mill managers had rotated through De Ridder in less than 14 years.

Management attributed the mill's poor performance to the increasingly restrictive work rules negotiated during the 1970s. The rules constrained operational flexibility, generated grievance activity, and sustained an adversarial climate.

The parties had evolved this elaborate set of work rules by dynamics common to many American industries. The mill was marked by bitter strikes of more than two months' duration twice during the 1970s. Throughout this period, management agreed to restrictive provisions that were embedded not only in explicit work rules but also in a proliferation of work practices recorded in memoranda of understanding between supervisors and workers. After the turnover of a number of mill managers and personnel directors, the union ended up with the only complete set of these memoranda—a decided advantage in grievance administration and arbitration.

Ichniowski analyzed grievance activity and productivity rates in Boise Cascade's 11 mills. He found that the 2 mills with the highest grievance rates—one of which was De Ridder—were 10 percent less productive than the mills with the company average mill grievance rate.

Decision to force. Management decided to use the 1983 contract negotiations to eliminate many work rules in the contract as well as all sidebar agreements and to secure the authority to make decisions based on business needs. While it also sought containment of health care costs, it chose not to seek wage concessions. It expected opposition, and it planned for a possible strike.

When contract negotiations commenced, the union committee reacted strongly to management proposals and effectively refused to consider them. A strike began in September 1983 and lasted two and a half months. The mill was operated at two-thirds capacity by management personnel and temporary workers. Management had threatened to hire permanent replacements for the striking workers, but it never did so.

Language of the 1983 contract. Returning workers were subject to a company-implemented contract containing management's original proposals. Especially important changes were the introduction of the "team concept" (assignment flexibility) and the insertion of a "zipper clause" explicitly overturning all previous side agreements. Ninety-four separate job classifications were telescoped into a small number of "clusters" of related jobs to be performed interchangeably. The contract expanded management's right to contract work out and to fill temporary vacancies, and it restricted seniority-based bumping rights in layoffs of less than 30 days. It also provided for a new performance evaluation system that would increase the role of merit in decisions to fill permanent vacancies.

The economic terms were quite favorable. First, the three-year contract provided wage increases of 6 percent, 6 percent, and 5 percent, in line with other industry settlements. Moreover, under the new classification system, each worker was paid at the rate of the highest old-progressions job subsumed in his or her cluster, yielding immediate additional base pay raises for more than half of De Ridder's hourly employees. The 1983 contract also included a groundbreaking employment security provision.

Phased Transition to Fostering—at the Individual Level

After the 1983 strike and throughout the remainder of the 1980s, management fostered a new relationship with mill employees, one based on mutual commitment.

New mill management. A new mill manager, David Spence, took over shortly after the strike. He had previously worked at the mill and was therefore familiar with its history but not associated with recent events. Corporate also assigned a new human resources manager to De Ridder.

Spence acted promptly to demonstrate concern for quality and productivity, safety, and other issues that were important to hourly workers. He recalled later:

> I started right away emphasizing safety, quality, productivity, and management on the people side. Then we just tried to sell it. [The mill human resources manager] and I had meetings with all the natural work groups and their supervision, and they really unloaded on us. . . . Our whole thrust has been that the people are going to be the difference. . . . We put our whole emphasis on people. They had the feeling we would sacrifice one of them for a ton of paper [in the past], and sometimes they were right.

Spence took many other steps to signal to employees his new priorities and to ensure that supervisors were supporting these priorities by their own actions. After a while, the initial wave of employee anger and frustration had begun to recede, and some promised changes were starting to take hold.

Union-management relationship. The change effort at De Ridder was confined to the individual level; it did not include initiatives at the institutional level. It worked on improving managers' relationships with hourly employees. Managers were trained, disciplined, and rewarded for pursuit of millwide objectives: safety, productivity, and efficiency in the use of material and human resources. Mill managers did not extend any public gestures of rapport to union leadership, and for the first two years of the new contract, the officers of the two UPIU locals refused to sit on joint committees.

During subsequent contract negotiations, the company firmly declined to renegotiate issues other than wages and benefits, but these negotiations were consummated in an integrative rather than a distributive mode.

Team concept effects. An analysis by Ichniowski confirmed that by early 1986, the team concept was yielding the performance advantages management had sought. And by early 1990, De Ridder's managers reported further improvements in productivity, yields, safety, and grievance rates. In addition, the De Ridder mill became the first Boise Cascade mill to entirely eliminate the Sunday premium.

In 1990, De Ridder managers reported that the size of annual increases and the clustered pay system had made De Ridder workers' average straight-time pay the highest in the paper industry. However, productivity increases continued to more than match that rise.

De Ridder and Boise Cascade. The De Ridder strike and a subsequent strike at Boise Cascade's Rumford, Maine, mill soured the company's relationship with the UPIU during the 1980s. Nevertheless, the union's international officers grudgingly approved of what they heard about the "people-oriented" management of the De Ridder mill. Then, late in 1990, as reported earlier in this chapter, Boise Cascade top management abruptly and explicitly revised corporate policy about union relations, calling for major efforts to replace adversarialism with cooperation. The UPIU responded favorably to the initiative. These developments led to fostering initiatives targeted at union officials at De Ridder, but this occurred after the conclusion of our field study of this mill.

Outcomes

Thus, in summary, the successful forcing episode targeted work-rule changes but *not* a diminution of the economic package. The predominant pattern of fostering that followed the watershed contract negotiations in 1983–1984 achieved an impressive move toward mutual commitment with workers but did not transform institutional relations with the local union. Management merely restored the basic arm's-length accommodation— which is all it had sought.

By 1990, the plant had been transformed from one of the more poorly performing mills in the Boise Cascade system to the top performer—in terms of productivity, safety, and grievance rates. The workers, who had always been well paid, had become some of the highest-paid paper mill workers in America, according to the company. A turnover of union officials occurred over the half decade following the strike. Reportedly, by 1990, both

UPIU international officials and local officers approved, if grudgingly, the policies employed by mill management to elicit employee commitment.

Explaining Management's Strategic Choices

The favorable results for De Ridder management (as well as the neutral to positive outcomes for De Ridder labor) over the period covered by our study resulted from management's successful forcing campaign in 1983–1984, followed by effective fostering during the rest of the decade. Why did De Ridder management pursue these negotiating strategies when it did?

Mill management decided to force change in the 1983 negotiations because it was under mounting pressure to improve performance, and its diagnosis of performance shortfalls centered on poor labor relations. In particular, the diagnosis targeted grievance activities and inflexibility, both of which related to a set of constraining work rules agreed to over the past two decades. Management therefore sought to negotiate the elimination of a large number of work rules. It realized that the union would vigorously resist these changes and prepared for the strike that ensued.

The reasons management did *not* escalate its forcing strategy to unrestrained forcing include the following: (1) since management had only one of its dozen or so mills on strike and could operate it with supervisory personnel from other mills, it didn't have an immediate need to use the permanent replacements who had been recruited and trained; (2) the union ended the strike before management felt the need to bring in the permanent replacements; (3) the union was more willing to settle after two and a half months because management confined its tough demands to work rules and was prepared to offer generous economic terms and employment security; and (4) management apparently anticipated that it would need plenty of goodwill in the workforce after the strike in order to reap the benefits from the contractual right to use the workforce more flexibly.

Having successfully forced the revision of all the work rules it found constraining, management could focus on changes in the social contract that would promote the implementation of the new flexibility provisions. The plant manager aimed fostering at employees and not union officials both because the new contract minimized the union's daily role regarding operations and because the plant manager did not believe the union officials were gatekeepers to the attitudinal change he sought among employees.

The beliefs, credibility, and skills of the new mill manager, who played a key leadership role during the poststrike period and through the rest of the decade, help explain why the fostering strategy was pursued so systematically and persistently. His philosophy also helps explain why he focused fostering on employees and not on union officials. In addition, contrary to general trade union practice, union leaders *allowed* management to generate employee commitment without insisting that the institutional relationship between management and labor also be changed. Several factors help explain the union's acceptance of management's individual-level initiatives: (1) the union had lost some credibility with workers during the strike; (2) labor officials were not full-time union employees and thus were less invested in preserving traditional union roles; (3) union officials probably decided that the positive response from their fellow workers made it difficult politically to sustain their opposition to fostering activities; and (4) the UPIU, especially in the South, had generated less union solidarity than other unions such as the autoworkers, steelworkers, and machinists unions.

It may also be significant that De Ridder management did not advance any new vision or ideology of commitment capable of stimulating great anxiety on the part of union officials. Instead, it emphasized noncontroversial people-oriented policies, such as safety and training. Management treated participation by workers merely as a means to implement these policies, not as a stated goal in and of itself.

Finally, the fostering strategy was sustained over a long period simply because it was working—paying off for the company in record performance and for workers in high wages. The reasons for the success of the forcing and fostering sequence can be found largely in the choices of appropriate tactics and their skillful implementation. These tactics are discussed in greater detail in Part IV.

BIDWELL MILL: AN ABORTIVE BID TO FOSTER COOPERATION

The Bidwell paper mill case is about a QWL program initiated in mid-1981 and aborted in early 1984. It is based on the facts contained in a published account of this episode by Susan Albers Mohrman,[9] but the interpretation of events presented here is ours. The case is a mirror image of the Jay case (in which management focused totally on changing the substantive contract and used only forcing tactics). Bidwell management focused exclusively on the social terms of its relationship with labor and employed only fostering tactics. The Bidwell case illustrates how our concept of negotiations applies to the QWL genre of change efforts.

Developing Internal Management Agreement for a QWL Program

Corporate management provided the impetus for the QWL program at the Bidwell mill, which employed 500. It sponsored a three-day workshop for mill managers, including a team from Bidwell, designed to "encourage" mills to undertake QWL change efforts. Although Bidwell managers had little spontaneous enthusiasm for the idea, they nevertheless agreed to start a QWL effort.

In September 1981, the mill manager hired a consultant and began a series of meetings with his own staff. These early meetings surfaced many issues, including managers' doubts about the merits of the QWL effort. The mill manager and consultant used these meetings to develop internal consensus about the QWL effort in particular and greater cohesion within management in general. The consultant noted that they agreed to proceed on QWL "with a cool, dispassionate resolution."

Negotiating Union Support and Employee Involvement

The change effort entered a second phase when management sought to actively involve the four unions that represented workers in the mill. The mill manager had kept the local union presidents informed about the preparatory work with management personnel and his intention to approach them formally about sponsoring a QWL effort.

In the spring of 1982, the mill manager debated when to schedule preliminary discussions with the unions and when to establish a steering committee. The mill manager was aware that Bidwell's sister mills already had their unions "on board," but he also knew that summer vacations made it difficult to schedule meetings. His staff was divided on the timing issue. Some were prepared to form the steering committee soon, whereas others felt that September was the earliest practical option. The mill manager finally decided to proceed with the preliminary meetings before summer but to start up the steering committee meetings in September.

In the first meeting, management agreed with a request by the union officials for the same orientation workshop that the consultant had provided managers. During the workshop, union officers expressed doubt about the seriousness of management's interest in QWL, but in the end, officers from three of the four unions wanted to proceed. The officers of the fourth union—representing the highly skilled paper-machine operators—remained opposed to the program, but they decided to participate in another meeting with management.

In this next meeting, managers and union officials agreed to establish a mill QWL steering committee and three substeering committees in parts of the plant represented by the three interested unions. The officers of the fourth union agreed to sit on the mill committee but not to initiate any activities in their area of the mill.

The parties reached an agreement to proceed during the summer with the steering committees and three-day joint training sessions. Although managers had expressed their reasons for preferring a September start, they agreed to go along with a summer launch in response to the union's urgings. In addition, they perceived that the consultant had tilted the discussion toward the unions' preference.

The QWL activities got off to a fast start that summer. The mill steering committee agreed on how it would guide the QWL process. The training was soon generating considerable enthusiasm in the mill. By fall, problem-solving teams were active in two of the mill's four areas, tackling shop-floor problems such as scrap rates, maintenance backlogs, and cleanup procedures.

QWL structures, procedures, and activities became the vehicles for a more or less continuous pattern of attitude change and integrative-bargaining activities. An increasing number of managers, union officials, and employees became directly involved in these efforts, making labor-management negotiations a two-tiered and multiple-channeled process. These negotiations produced more cooperative relationships in specific departments—relationships that in some cases, were self-sustaining. We don't know about the changes in work roles made at the mill-floor level, but we can assume that some workers and union officials in these units accepted broader responsibility for performance and that managers, in return, shared more information and power with them. Although limited in organizational scope (as will become apparent below), these renegotiations of work roles apparently were successful and mutually beneficial.

Cooperative Work Undermined by Internal Divisions

Two factors broke the momentum of the summer's change process—one affecting management's internal consensus and commitment to the process, the other impinging upon the unions'. First, the Bidwell mill was put up for sale, diverting management attention and creating uncertainty in the organization about future management's commitment to the change effort. In the context of this uncertainty, some individual managers and supervisors who had felt that QWL was unwise began to express their doubts more publicly. Second, the paper-machine operators' union withdrew from the mill steering committee, attacking management for discrepancies between its QWL rhetoric and its actions, claiming that officers of the other unions were being brainwashed, and predicting that QWL would undermine the unions. Officers of the other unions vigorously defended their involvement in QWL, but the papermakers union succeeded in raising doubt elsewhere in the mill.

The QWL change effort lost further momentum in the fall, when new corporate owners installed a new mill manager. Although he expressed support for QWL, he soon discovered that his staff was internally divided on many issues and decided that he had to give highest priority to development of this group.

The divisions among his staff included their views of QWL. In February 1983, when mill managers reviewed the status of QWL, they confirmed that some areas were doing well but others were bogged down. In the latter areas, union members had asked for visible signs of management commitment to cooperation, such as the removal of time clocks. All of this discussion, including its implications for how management might proceed to negotiate more employee commitment and union cooperation, was overshadowed by an emotional outpouring that followed. One manager expressed concern about the stresses top management was creating for supervisors and managers by asking them to change their behavior so dramatically and by seemingly being concerned only with "making the union employees happy." Other managers joined in complaining that too much time was spent in meetings, that the unions were pressing for faster progress and asking for additional "proof" of management's commitment to QWL, and that union employees were becoming increasingly emboldened to criticize supervisors and accuse them of blocking productivity improvement.

In the months that followed, the new mill manager redoubled his attention to team development, while the papermakers union stepped up its attack on the QWL effort. Two additional unions withdrew from the QWL effort, citing management's failure to change its ways and to support QWL. By now, only a few of the union officers who had originally been involved in establishing QWL were still in office: some had lost elections, and others were either too worn down by the effort or too discouraged by the results to run for reelection. One local union continued the cooperative efforts in its area of the mill.

The participative processes on the mill floor were not all dead, but the effort by management and labor to renegotiate their institutional relationship and the mill's overall work environment had been aborted.

Outcomes

At management's initiative, mill managers and officials of three of the four local unions successfully negotiated an agreement to jointly sponsor a QWL program. The fourth local opposed the program but allowed QWL activities to proceed elsewhere in the mill. Activities took root firmly among employees and their supervisors in some parts of the mill, allowing them to renegotiate their daily work roles and responsibilities. Thus, labor and management had taken steps that on their face could have been the beginning of a journey toward new social contracts at both the institutional and individual levels. Then the apparent agreement between management and the unions unraveled, and in the absence of institutional support, QWL activities on the mill floor declined.

Explaining Bidwell Management's Decision to Foster

The explanation for Bidwell management's halfhearted fostering strategy is relatively simple. Bidwell mill management in this case was not guided by a diagnosis of the general need for either substantive changes or a change in the social contract. Rather, it was presented with a corporate mandate to engage in a particular change effort—i.e., QWL—and supplied with a facilitating consultant. Underlying the QWL change program, which had become fashionable among progressive managers in many American industries by the 1980s, was an implicit assumption of the desirability of revising the social contract with labor. However, the original motivation of Bidwell management to foster change was based not so much on a clear desire to produce commitment and cooperation as on a perceived need to conform to a corporate mandate. The fact that its labor relations were not marked by strong adversarialism encouraged management to assume it would be relatively easy to engage the unions in the fostering process.

CHAMPION PAPER, PENSACOLA, FLORIDA, MILL: ALTERNATING EPISODES OF FORCING AND FOSTERING CHANGE

By the end of the decade of the 1980s, a large fraction of managements in the paper industry concluded that to stay competitive, they must be prepared to bargain forcefully for the types of substantive changes reflected in the economic package obtained by IP at Jay, Maine, and in the contractual flexibility achieved by Boise Cascade at the De Ridder mill, and they must learn how to foster the type of employee commitment and union cooperation that had begun to develop with Bidwell's quality of work life efforts before the program unraveled. The efforts of Champion Paper International's Pensacola mill management over the 1985–1988 period provide us with a case in point.[10]

Management forced major changes in the Pensacola mill contract during the 1985 negotiations (period 1), developed a strongly supported effort to foster commitment and cooperation over the next several years (period 2), and returned to the 1988 negotiations with a major wage provision objective it could not sell by persuasion and therefore needed to force (period 3).

Hard Bargaining: 1985 Contract Negotiations

The Pensacola mill, which came to Champion through a merger with St. Regis in 1984, had begun to decline as the market for kraft paper products shrank in the 1970s. Champion continued a downsizing process at Pensacola already started by St. Regis—shutting down several paper machines and closing an adjacent bag plant. It also converted a huge state-of-the-art kraft-paper machine to white-paper production.

In 1985, with the three-year labor agreement (negotiated by the previous owner) due to expire, Champion management analyzed the changes in the current labor contract that would help assure profitable mill operations. It saw in the uncertainty about the mill's fate a unique opportunity to regain control over staffing patterns and work rules. The final company agenda included far greater flexibility and control of the workforce, medical care cost containment, the end of cold (shutdown) holidays, elimination of restrictive work rules, and adoption of a "zipper clause" that would overturn all previous side agreements and past practices.

Contract negotiations at Pensacola had followed the periodic and formal patterns of "traditional" New Deal era labor relations. Hourly workers were represented by three UPIU locals and an IBEW local. The UPIU international representative and the corporate regional negotiator dominated the discussions, with major input from union local committees and mill human resources managers. Operating managers were excluded from the table.

The 1985 negotiations were traditional in both structure and process, but the company's proposals—an extensive 49-item agenda—violated the expectations of union negotiators, who were still accustomed to regular annual increases. The union's own agenda was a relatively short "wish list." The company's aggressive agenda coupled with the fact that the corporation had the fate of the mill in its hands permitted the management team to dominate the talks. One company participant recalls: "We knew going in [that] this was going to be a flabbergasting experience for the union: they were frustrated, irritated, felt we were taking advantage of them. Correctly, I might add."

The company argued that the large investment needed to return the mill to profitability required substantial union concessions in return, while the union committee argued that the contract language management proposed was unnecessary in view of a local tradition of accommodative labor relations and furthermore that the proposed changes would lead to the very kinds of abuse that work rules arose to prevent. The UPIU international representative, who said he was philosophically sympathetic to flexible staffing and worker participation, expressed doubt that some Pensacola managers could actually implement the proposed new language. When the union team continued to refuse to propose any language modifications or substitutions, company negotiators finally included Champion's staffing proposal to be voted up or down with the rest of the contract provisions.

In September 1985, the union committee presented to local members on a "nonrecommended" basis a contract embodying nearly all the company's initial proposals. It was rejected by the locals. After a federal mediator extended the talks, the union achieved a few minor economic gains but no substantive changes on flexible staffing or other noneconomic issues. In November, the union committee recommended, and the membership ratified, the slightly modified contract.

New Cooperative Initiatives: 1985–1988

In December 1985, corporate officers decided to promote "participative" management at the Pensacola mill. They had formulated a policy to move all of their mills toward a more participative model that would encourage workers' commitment to productivity, quality, full utilization of workers' time and knowledge, and the success of the corporation. Pensacola would pioneer these changes in the corporation's unionized mills.

Over the next two and a half years, mill management engaged in a series of initiatives intended to (1) implement the flexibility and supervisory discretion provided by the new contract and (2) negotiate social contracts based on cooperation with its four unions and commitment on the part of its workers. From an operational standpoint, the changes management sought involved forming self-managing teams, broadening job classifications and task responsibilities, and revising pay where appropriate. The techniques for guiding this type of work redesign were introduced by consultants and called sociotechnical systems analysis.

Although one local president was strongly opposed to revising the traditional arm's-length relationship and to the work redesign contemplated by management, other union leaders and most workers were more amenable philosophically to the types of changes proposed. They were, however, appropriately skeptical of mill managers' intentions at first and only gradually became more optimistic that the parties could achieve changes that were in the interests of all stakeholders.

The early initiatives by management included a joint trip by managers and union officials to conferences on labor-management cooperation, a workshop meeting for mill managers to develop understanding of and support for the cooperation and commitment objectives, a series of in-plant meetings with union officials, and an off-site meeting of managers and union leaders.

Work redesign efforts were pioneered in six departments volunteered by their managers. In each department, joint union-management teams were formed to redesign how work was to be organized and compensated. Some teams proceeded more effectively than others, influenced in part by the amount of internal cohesion that had existed in the units prior to the change effort.

A major focus of attention was the determination of wage rates for redesigned jobs. An expectation developed that all wages in redesigned departments would go up—an expectation that strongly encouraged cooperation by the redesign team and by other departmental members. But differences arose around two compensation issues. First, should pay increases go to the top jobs in a redesigned unit even when these particular jobs were not broadened? Second, what size pay increases are warranted for the jobs whose responsibility has been broadened?

As important as these pay issues themselves was the question of how they were to be decided. Corporate management and the UPIU international representative handled the wage proposals from the first departmental design team in a traditional pattern of high demands and low offers, and the result was an impasse. Then the parties devised a new process more in keeping with the new relationship they were trying to establish. They began with a day's integrative problem solving, moving into economics only on the second day of talks. They also provided larger roles for those closer to the shop floor than was normally allowed by the company and union representatives who had traditionally handled such matters.

Mixed Bargaining: 1988 Contract Negotiations

Management approached the 1988 contract negotiations with two major objectives. One objective, insisted upon by corporate, was to eliminate Sunday premium pay and a miscellaneous complex of other pay provisions, such as meal allowances and shift differentials. Corporate management had already negotiated similar reforms in pay provisions at a few mills, and it was resolved to follow through with this pattern in all its mills. A second objective, shared by both mill managers and corporate managers, was to preserve, or indeed further, the mill's movement toward a new social contract. As a part of this latter objective, management hoped the parties would adopt language committing them to promote participation and work redesign and to form a joint committee to oversee these activities.

Talks began in May 1988. Management's primary substantive agenda item—revising the pay package—provided management negotiators with a major challenge. Pensacola employees and their unions were adamantly opposed to the elimination of Sunday premiums—not only because of the monetary value involved but also because, for labor in this industry, the issue had come to symbolize the ability of companies to force changes favorable to themselves regardless of their current economic requirements. Labor was chagrined by the idea that Pensacola management would insist on this change in 1988—after several years in which labor had responded positively to management's change initiatives and during a year in which mill performance was improving.

Management negotiators did not manifest a clear sense of how best to deal with this potentially corrosive issue. Although they communicated accurately their resolve to eliminate Sunday premiums, they also attempted to offer reasoning and data to support the proposal as if they were expecting to persuade union negotiators of the correctness of the company's position. This treatment only served to heighten union negotiators' anger. In the end, management representatives stopped attempting persuasion and treated the item like what it was—an unpopular demand that the company had the power to impose. They did protect the local labor-management relationship from the full adverse effect of this agenda item by making it clear that this was a corporate issue, not one to be ascribed to local mill managers' aspirations.

Management negotiators also initially misjudged how the union would want to handle the language related to cooperation and participation. Managers assumed the parties would develop the language by cooperative dialogue, whereas union representatives preferred to treat any such language as a management proposal in return for which labor might obtain some benefit. And in any event, union officials wanted to portray this aspect of the agreement to their members as a management request to which they had acceded. Eventually, management and union negotiators agreed on how to handle the issue and produced a letter of agreement that met the needs of both parties. Despite the difficulties management experienced in finding an appropriate mix of distributive and integrative bargaining to deal with the Sunday premium issue and develop cooperation language, most of its actions reflected new attention to relationship effects and new sensitivity to the intraorganizational issues faced by union negotiators. Although company negotiators continued, successfully, to depend on the dominant and moderating presence of the UPIU international representative, they also took local union politics into account in many of their proposals and reactions.

Leaders of both committees acknowledged changed expectations for negotiations. They no longer saw formal contract and informal midcontract negotiations as different species. The international representative said later, "The point was not just getting a contract, it was getting a contract *and* maintaining a relationship." A management observer pointed to disposition of one union agenda item as an illustration of a new approach. The union had proposed one-day-at-a-time (ODAAT) use of vacation time, which management resisted on the grounds of administrative difficulties with scheduling. The union finally proposed a side agreement that would permit a one-year experiment with ODAAT vacations—and an assessment of logistics after one year. The company committee accepted the union proposal both as a reasonable compromise and as a way of reinforcing the union's role as a deviser of integrative language sensitive to both union and management concerns.

The final economic proposals were negotiated in traditional fashion, with offer and counteroffer accompanied by many feints and threats. The union finally did accept a buyout of the Sunday premium, which was, however, to be phased out over a one-year period.

The contract was ratified by 80 percent of the members of the four Pensacola locals. The contract-signing ceremony was businesslike—neither the bitter event of 1985 nor a celebration of renewed community.

Outcomes

Over the next several years, management continued to make impressive progress negotiating employee commitment and union-management cooperation. Participation continued to broaden in scope and deepen its penetration into the management of operations. Union officials became more trusting of participation in particular and of mill management's intentions in general. The union officials who had staked out an entrenched position in opposition to participation activities became less active and more neutral in their positions. The mill's operating performance continued to improve in ways that drew high praise from corporate executives.

Thus, over the 1985–1991 period, company managers succeeded in renegotiating the basic terms of employment and the social contract with labor. They had, in the process, made the mill more competitive in the marketplace and more secure as a corporate asset and had achieved a considerable amount of integration of the interests of the parties.

Explaining Management's Strategic Choices

Pensacola's management employed a series of strategies: controlled forcing, fostering, and mixed forcing and fostering. Its success was due in part to the appropriateness of each strategy to the circumstances under which it was pursued and in part to the efficacy of the tactics employed.

Mill management's decision to vigorously force concessions from the union in the first period—the 1985 contract negotiations—emerged from several factors. While management's substantive agenda was ambitious, it was only moderately disagreeable to labor (compared to Jay and De Ridder). Moreover, management had no social contract objectives that would inhibit forcing tactics. Finally, the power balance favored management because labor felt threatened by the recent change of corporate ownership, especially given a corporate decision to exit the kraft-paper business to which the mill's equipment had been devoted. In this circumstance, new mill management could readily consider making a sharp break with the past.

Management's fostering during the second period—between the 1985 and 1988 contract negotiations—can be explained by reference to several factors. Corporate management was providing growing support and encouragement for participation in the mills and had targeted Pensacola to take a lead role in this movement, based on the fact that management had already achieved important contractual changes there and the workers and union officials were viewed as potentially receptive.

The third period—the 1988 contract negotiations—was marked by a combination of forcing and fostering because management had two compelling objectives. First, corporate management was committed to pursuing certain unpopular changes in the economic package already achieved in other corporate mills; second, mill and corporate managements were also committed to making further progress toward the new social contract based on commitment and cooperation. The combination of forcing and fostering was thought to be workable because mill management's relations with both workers and union officials had already improved and because corporate management more than mill-level managers could "take the heat" for the unpopular economic demands. The relative weakness of the minority union faction opposing the new social contract made fostering feasible, and the absence of any close linkage with other Champion mills made the forcing component of the strategy less risky.

SUMMARY AND CONCLUSIONS

The paper industry was marked by a great deal of change in labor-management relations during the 1980s and the early 1990s. Here we summarize these changes in terms of the theory of strategic negotiations outlined in Part I.

The Pulp and Paper Industry

Our review of the pulp and paper industry underscored several facets of the context it provided for labor-management relations during the 1980s (see Table 4.3).

Table 4.3   Potential Benefits, Feasibility of Implementation, and Observed Frequency of Strategic Options in the Pulp and Paper Industry

	Strategic Options		
	Escape	Forcing	Fostering
Potential benefits	High	Moderate (Pay is not a major fraction of total cost.)	High (Yields and equipment utilization, which are sensitive to attitudes, are very important.)
Feasibility of implementation	Low (Paper mills involve embedded infrastructure.)	High (Supervisors or replacements can operate mills.)	Moderate (Rural areas create a more receptive workforce. The UPIU was not receptive until the late 1980s.)
Observed frequency during the 1980s	Low (There were relatively few greenfield mills.)	High (Most companies participated in a pattern of forcing economic and work changes.)	Moderate (A growing number of companies attempted to foster improved relations, especially during the latter years of the decade.)

We observed that despite the high benefits for management experienced by companies that built new greenfield paper mills, there was relatively little of this type of escape activity in this industry during the 1980s, primarily because the deeply embedded infrastructure made it so difficult to walk away from existing mill sites and because environmental concerns made it extremely difficult to find new mill sites in the United States.

Forcing activity dominated management change efforts in the mid-1980s and, overall, was the most prevalent change strategy during the period studied. Interestingly, this occurred more because of the development of a climate conducive to forcing (following the air traffic controllers' strike) and techniques for forcing (enabling companies to operate during a strike) than because revising the pay package and formal work rules was critically important to mill performance.

Fostering activity became more prevalent in the late 1980s and early 1990s. The potential benefits of fostering are especially high given the importance of yields and equipment utilization and the sensitivity of these performance factors to employee attitudes and union-management relations. The question is why fostering did not occur earlier. While the rural employees whom paper mills employ tend to be more potentially receptive to commitment and cooperation, the international union was generally

Table 4.4   Strategic Periods and the Factors Proposed to Influence Strategic Choice

| | Factors Proposed to Influence Strategic Choice | | |
Strategic Periods	Management's Priorities	Management's Expectations of Labor's Responses	Management's Perceptions of the Labor-Management Power Balance
Jay			
Period 1: unrestrained forcing	Management sought ambitious work-rule and economic concessions. It had no social contract objectives.	IP's rationale was not tailored to Jay and was undermined in labor's eyes by the company's strong profit performance.	Management was confident and had the corporate resources to sustain work stoppages. It probably underestimated the union's forcing tactics.
De Ridder			
Period 1: forcing	Management sought ambitious work-rule changes but no economic concessions. It wished to build positive attitudes *after* the strike.	Management regarded its mill-specific rationale as clear and persuasive, but labor did not. Labor was unaware of any management desire to revise the social contract.	Management was confident and prepared for a strike. De Ridder had the resources of Boise Cascade.
Period 2: fostering	The new mill management's objectives included revising the social contract and the need to implement the new contractual flexibility.	Labor was initially viewed as antagonistic to cooperation and commitment overtures.	(Power balance not applicable to fostering)*

*Note that in Chapter 3 we did not propose a hypothesis relating power and fostering (see Table 3.2).

Table 4.4   (continued)

| | Factors Proposed to Influence Strategic Choice | | |
| | | | |
Strategic Periods	Management's Priorities	Management's Expectations of Labor's Responses	Management's Perceptions of the Labor-Management Power Balance
Bidwell			
Period 1: fostering	Management was acting in response to a corporate request, but underlying support at the mill management level was weak.	Labor was seen as initially skeptical but not antagonistic to cooperation and commitment overtures.	(Power balance not applicable to fostering)*
Pensacola			
Period 1: forcing	Management sought ambitious work-rule and economic concessions. It had no social contract objectives.	Labor found management's business rationale plausible but not persuasive.	Management was confident that it could force changes.
Period 2: fostering	Management's new objective was to revise the social contract. It also felt a need to implement the new contractual flexibility.	Labor was initially viewed as antagonistic to cooperation and commitment overtures.	(Power balance not applicable to fostering)*
Period 3: forcing and fostering	Management had both a moderately ambitious, substantive agenda and a strong resolve to preserve momentum toward cooperation and commitment.	Labor was not persuaded by the business rationale for eliminating the Sunday premium. Labor seen as supporting move toward commitment and cooperation.	Management was confident that it could force changes.

*Note that in Chapter 3 we did not propose a hypothesis relating power and fostering (see Table 3.2).

opposed to such developments until the late 1980s. In addition, of course, the forcing activity, once it was under way and until it had run its course, tended to make fostering difficult.

Negotiating Strategies at the Mill Level

The four situations in the paper industry were selected to enable us to investigate two broad, contrasting negotiating strategies—forcing (at Jay and De Ridder) and fostering (at Bidwell and Pensacola). Our subsequent analysis of these cases revealed several additional interesting contrasts among the strategies employed by management.

First, two cases illustrated more complex change strategies. De Ridder, initially selected as an example of forcing, contained an equally instructive fostering effort. Similarly, Pensacola, identified primarily to illustrate fostering, also involved a highly significant forcing episode as a backdrop to the subsequent fostering and mixed forcing/fostering negotiations. Thus, both De Ridder and Pensacola were more mixed than we initially understood, and the combinations of forcing and fostering—whether combined simultaneously or sequentially—were especially instructive.

Second, the paper cases illustrated another strategic distinction—whether forcing was restrained or unrestrained. Whereas Jay and De Ridder both used vigorous forcing tactics and sustained major work stoppages, they differed critically in the degree of restraint involved. Jay exemplified "unrestrained forcing," whereas De Ridder illustrated a more controlled form of forcing. Two other episodes illustrated more refined differences in the severity of forcing. Pensacola's forcing campaign in 1985 was even more controlled than De Ridder's, and the forcing component of its 1988 contract negotiations was the most carefully moderated forcing activity.

Thus, our four cases included a total of seven time periods, each characterized by a particular strategy for negotiating change: three periods of forcing, three periods of fostering, and one period in which management pursued a combination of forcing and fostering.

How do we explain the strategies management employed in each of these periods? We have already presented on a case-by-case and period-by-period basis a clinical analysis of the factors that appear to have influenced these strategic choices. Table 4.4 summarizes these explanations in terms of our formal propositions about the influence of several factors—management's priorities, its expectations of labor's response, and its perception of power relations—on strategic choice.

Outcomes in Paper Cases

The outcomes in the four paper cases varied dramatically (see Table 4.5).

At both Pensacola and De Ridder, management first negotiated work-rule changes in the formal contract and then secured their effective implementation in practice. In both cases, management generated sustained move-

Table 4.5 Changes in Substantive and Social Contracts Favorable to Management

Net Change in Social Contract	Net Change in Substantive Contract		
	Small or None	Intermediate	Large
Toward containment and compliance			*Jay:* Major economic and work-rule concessions; hostility in the plant and with the UPIU after the strike.
No change from compliance and arm's-length accommodation	*Bidwell:* Effort aborted after a few years, with the situation reverting to the traditional pattern.		
Toward *employee* commitment only			*De Ridder:* Major work-rule concessions; impressive commitment developed in the six years following the strike.
Toward employee commitment and union-management co-operation		*Pensacola:* Some work-rule and economic concessions; major revision of the social contract.	

ment toward employee commitment over time. The cases differed in several respects. Pensacola management sought and gained moderate economic and work-rule concessions, whereas De Ridder management negotiated extraordinary flexibility but allowed pay to rise to among the highest in the industry and provided employment security; Pensacola's union relations moved toward cooperation, whereas De Ridder's were merely restored to a traditional pattern of accommodation; and finally, Pensacola's negotiations did not involve a strike, whereas De Ridder's did. On the whole, we judge the outcomes at both mills to have been in the interests of management, the union, and workers.

The outcomes at Bidwell netted no change or minimal change. The moderate first-step movement toward millwide commitment and cooperation was largely reversed, with a few pockets of QWL activity continuing. There were no changes in substantive terms. In general, we regard the abortive effort as a missed or wasted opportunity to make changes in the interests of the company, workers, and unions.

In our judgment, Jay's outcomes were very mixed. Although IP management achieved the economic and work-rule changes it had sought, the strike was moderately costly in lost production and produced a difficult operating environment in the Jay mill after the strike. The union lost in its bid to avoid economic and work-rule concessions, paid the economic price of a strike, lost mill jobs to nonunion workers, ended up in a weakened power position for purposes of future bargaining, and eventually saw itself decertified at the plant. The social contract at Jay moved from compliance/accommodation toward tightened employee compliance and a more adversarial containment mode with respect to union relations.

NOTES

1. U.S. Department of Commerce, *U.S. Industrial Outlook*, (Washington, D.C.: International Trade Administration, 1988, 1989.
2. Edward C. Kokkelenberg and Donna R. Sockell, "Union Membership in the United States: 1973–1981," *Industrial and Labor Relations Review* 38, no. 4 (July 1985): 497–543); and Census Industry Classification 328.
3. *Annual Survey of Manufacturers* (Washington, D.C.: U.S. Department of Commerce, Bureau of the Census, 1985–1986).
4. Richard P. Klinzing, presentation based on Paper Industry Association data (given to a meeting of the Pulp and Paper Manufacturers Association, Milwaukee, Wisconsin, April 15, 1990).
5. Richard P. Klinzing, presentation based on Bureau of Labor Statistics data (given to the Bargaining Forum, Senior Executives Meeting, New York, October 14, 1987).
6. We are fortunate that the four cases cover all the trends. At the time we selected the four cases for study, we were clear about neither the general industry trends themselves nor the complex sequence of strategies the cases included.
7. The account of this dispute is based on newspaper reports over the years and on discussions with labor, management, and third-party participants and observers. The facts are consistent with those contained in other published analyses. See, for example, Adrienne M. Birecree, "Capital Restructuring and Labour Relations: The International Paper Company Strike," *International Contribution to Labour Studies* 1 (1991): 59–86.
8. We have relied heavily on unpublished materials of Casey Ichniowski ("The Impact of Team Concept," 1986) for a description of De Ridder change processes and an analysis of selected performance results through 1985. Our discussions in 1989 with mill and corporate managers provided us with additional details on the period before 1985 as well as with the data to construct our account of subsequent events.
9. We have based this account primarily on an article by Susan Albers Mohrman, "A Case of Union-Management Cooperation: A Contextual Presentation," *Consultation* 6, no. 1 (spring 1987): 43–62. We also discussed the Bidwell events with an industry observer familiar with the mill.
10. The Pensacola mill case is based wholly on our field research.

Chapter 5

The Automobile Supply Industry:
A Fiercely Competitive Context

Labor relations in the U.S. auto supply industry is a study in contrasts. On the one hand, some auto suppliers and their unions have forged joint labor-management partnerships that are among the most advanced in the nation. On the other hand, many auto suppliers have pressed for deep concessions from their employees, and some have challenged the very legitimacy of unions representing these workers. This diversity of practice is driven by fierce economic competition, rapid technological change, relatively mobile capital, and tightly coupled relations with customers.

The changes currently occurring in labor-management relations stand in sharp contrast to the stability that emerged in this industry during the 1960s and early 1970s. In those years, pattern agreements reached between the UAW (United Automobile Workers) and the original equipment manufacturers (OEMs)—General Motors, Ford, Chrysler, and others—flowed through to the first tier of suppliers within a year or two and thereafter (at least in part) to the subtier of suppliers. Thus, the auto supply sector embodied a traditional model of arm's-length contract negotiations and highly formal contract administration, in which very predictable incremental changes followed the OEM/UAW pattern.

Today, the auto supply industry typifies the transformation thesis presented by Kochan, Katz, and McKersie,[1] featuring vivid examples of corporate strategies linked directly to labor-relations choices—around either union avoidance or union-management cooperation.

In this chapter, we trace the negotiations associated with these highly divergent strategic initiatives. To understand the choices and the related negotiations, however, it is important to first define what we mean by the auto supply industry. There is no prototypical auto supply firm. Rather, the industry is characterized by heterogeneity among firms, extending across at least half a dozen standard industry classification (SIC) codes and ranging from the large auto supply divisions of Ford, General Motors, Chrysler, and other auto manufacturers to hundreds of small "job shops" with fewer than 50 employees. Because of the difficulty of assigning precise boundaries to the industry, estimates of its size range from 4,000 to 15,000 firms.[2] Still, similarities can be found among auto supply firms, including the common influence of the OEMs as customers and a historic orientation toward mass-production technologies. In our analysis, we focus on firms that reflect the broad diversity of this sector.

INDUSTRY STRUCTURE AND PRESSURES FOR CHANGE

Negotiations in the auto supply industry are directly affected by five structural characteristics of a firm: (1) its customers (OEMs or the motor vehicle "aftermarket"), (2) competitors, (3) size and ownership structure, (4) dominant product and technology, and (5) location. There are important pressures for change associated with each of these structural circumstances.

Two Distinct Market Segments

The market structure of the auto supply industry reflects a dichotomy between the production of original equipment parts (for OEMs) and replacement parts (for the aftermarket), which has a direct impact on a firm's objectives and on the sources of leverage available to labor and management. In the OEM market, strong customer pressure directly shapes the content and process of negotiations, while in the aftermarket, local economic conditions and competition (domestic and foreign) dominate. Although some firms are producers in only one segment, many firms are involved in production for both market segments, which increases their tactical options.

OEM market segment. The tone for labor relations in the industry is set by the suppliers to the OEMs, and it is almost impossible to overstate the depth of the OEMs' influence—as customers—on labor relations within these supplier firms. Historically, collective bargaining between the UAW and the OEMs has always served as an important frame of reference for supplier negotiations. The bargaining pattern was for UAW gains with OEMs to be passed along, with a lag of one or a few years, to a first tier of supplier firms (firms supplying finished components) and then, with a further lag, to the second- and third-tier suppliers of subassemblies and raw materials.[3] Even the rise of concessionary bargaining in the early 1980s followed the pattern, with Chrysler (an OEM) leading the way by negotiating more than $200 million in wage and benefit concessions from its UAW workforce. Today, however, the influence of OEMs on supplier labor negotiations reaches far beyond the historic pattern negotiations.

Some of the increased OEM influence stems from excess productive capacity in the industry, which is predicted in North America to be at around 2 million units by the mid-1990s.[4] *Auto supplier consolidation* is a polite term for the implications of this excess capacity; industry observers also use the term *bloodbath* to describe the current and anticipated implications. For example, Ford reduced the number of suppliers in its North American operations by 34 percent, from about 3,200 in 1980 to 2,100 in 1987,[5] and that trend has continued into the 1990s. In this competitive climate, OEMs have successfully demanded constant prices or even annual *reductions* in product cost of 1 to 3 percent—with most suppliers now having faced this steady pressure on product prices for more than a decade. As a result, successive rounds of wage and benefit concession demands were a standard feature of auto supply labor relations throughout the 1980s and into the early 1990s.

A further driving force in the consolidation of suppliers can be found in the growing utilization of lean production,[6] with its orientation around just-in-time delivery, high quality, and tight engineering and design links between supplier and customer. Firms that can meet these criteria and supply these additional services have a chance of being in the first tier of suppliers—those that directly supply assembly operations.[7] To enter the first tier, a supplier firm must pass the OEM's extensive certification audit annually or even more frequently. GM's program is termed "Targets for Excellence"; Ford has two levels of certification, "Q1" and "Total Quality Excellence"; Chrysler has its "Pentastar" program. The most stringent programs are found at the Japanese-owned assembly facilities in North America, which are modeled on programs established in Japan.

Each program involves a comprehensive audit by a team of inspectors that generally lasts for three to five days. For example, when GM auditors visited Simpson Industries, an engine parts maker, they examined the company's research and design capabilities, checked its financial stability (including medical cost-containment efforts), and even conducted private focus group meetings with groups of workers to assess the labor relations climate.[8] While each company has its own term for its program, one auto supply plant manager offered a single term for all the programs: he referred to them as "death programs" since "the most you can hope to do at the end of an audit is stay alive until the next one."

Among the key items in an OEM audit are issues that have a direct bearing on labor-management relations, including the utilization of worker-administered statistical process control (SPC) techniques, employee involvement (EI), and other forms of worker participation; flexibility in job assignments (reflected in reduced numbers of job classifications) and team-based work systems; the negotiation of long-term contracts with unions; and evidence of wage and benefit cost containment. Needless to say, management in this industry has pursued all these issues with great vigor in collective bargaining, providing an example of customers' directly shaping the negotiations agenda for supplier firms and unions.

From a negotiations point of view, however, there are deep contradictions inherent in the OEM demands. The direct pressures on product cost and the close inspection of wage and benefit administration all lend themselves to forcing strategies. Yet the OEMs' emphasis on employee involvement, SPC, team-based work systems, and long-term contracts calls for a significant measure of fostering in order to produce meaningful results. Consequently, the auto supply industry—at least among suppliers to the OEMs—is a case in which there is explicit customer pressure for firms to move to social contracts based on union cooperation and employee commitment at precisely the time that these same customers are demanding cost cutting that points toward forcing strategies likely to undermine cooperation and commitment.

Aftermarket suppliers. Among suppliers to the automotive aftermarket, there is less direct pressure from the OEMs. Historically, labor negotiations have been subject to much greater influence from local labor market conditions and economic cycles (this is a countercyclical segment of the industry). Today, some large customers (such as Sears, Kmart, and Montgomery Ward) are setting increasingly higher quality standards, but their role in shaping the bargaining agenda is in no way comparable to the influence of OEMs on their suppliers since they do not utilize the same audit procedures. For firms that sell to both OEMs and the aftermarket, there is the possibility of using lower community wage levels as a basis for pay and still citing pressure from OEMs as justification for cost-containment demands—a tactic that we will see used in the case of AP Parts, highlighted later in this chapter.

Foreign and Domestic Nonunion Competitors

A growing number of domestic nonunion auto supply firms and foreign (mostly Japanese) suppliers have made innovative employment relations systems a central feature of their competitive business strategies.[9] These firms provide highly visible examples of successful systems that can serve as a form of leverage for the unionized employers with which they compete.

Foreign competitors. In public and private debate, great attention is given to foreign competition, but the issue is quite complex in this industry. Until 1983, the United States had a positive trade balance in automotive parts; since then, there has been a growing deficit.[10] Much of the deficit is attributable to new production capacity built by OEMs in lower-wage nations such as Mexico and Brazil or OEM outsourcing to foreign suppliers in Brazil, Mexico, Singapore, South Korea, Taiwan, and elsewhere. In Mexico, for example, employment in the auto supply industry has risen from fewer than 10,000 in 1978 to close to 100,000 in 1989.[11] In some cases, auto supply firms are themselves moving abroad. For example, Champion has opened new production facilities in India and South Korea.[12] While the actual dollar volume of imports is still relatively small (13 percent) in comparison with the scale of domestic production,[13] the presence of these low-wage production facilities serves as a powerful form of leverage for managers, which we will see vividly illustrated in the Packard Electric case, presented later in this chapter.

Equally significant, however, is the competition from foreign manufacturers via production facilities here in North America. As Japanese auto assembly plants have opened in the United States and Canada (there are now nine independent assembly plants or joint ventures with U.S. OEMs), Japanese suppliers have established nearby facilities to maintain just-in-time supply arrangements. There were fewer that 50 Japanese-affiliated suppliers in the United States in 1984, and it is estimated that there were as many as 200 five years later.[14] Leading suppliers, such as Nippondenso and Ogihara, have established team-based work systems that involve extensive worker control over quality and utilization of "kaizen" techniques for continuous improvement in production operations. These firms have also generated exceptionally high levels of employee commitment while keeping wage costs relatively low (through location in low-wage rural settings and the absence of accumulated pension costs). For unionized U.S. auto supply firms seeking to establish new work systems, the Japanese-owned North American facilities provide palpable evidence that such systems do not depend on a Japanese workforce and that they represent a powerful alternative approach to manufacturing operations.[15]

Domestic nonunion competitors. Nonunion domestically owned facilities provide a similar counterpoint, both in terms of a comparison on the basis of lower costs and as an illustration of alternative work systems. Although we do not have an exact count, nearly every major domestic auto supplier with which we are familiar owns at least one nonunion facility, typically located in a "right-to-work" state. Many of these facilities use production process and work systems comparable to those in the unionized operations (though with fewer work rules); thus, their primary impact on negotiations is as lower-cost alternative locations for manufacturing work. In some cases, the facilities have been established with team-based work systems—typically utilizing sociotechnical design principles (a contrast with the Japanese lean production system). Toronto-based Magna International is perhaps the most visible among the nonunion firms employing alternative work systems. In a time of retrenchment and consolidation in the industry, this firm has grown to include more than 80 production facilities—and was estimated in 1986 to be adding a new facility on the average of one every three weeks.[16] Each new plant is designed to be small (never exceeding 200 employees), dedicated to a nearby customer, and structured around flexible team-based work systems.

Where one company owns both unionized and nonunion facilities, there is great potential for management to pit one plant against another regarding investment dollars and the location of new work. Thus, the nonunion competition comes not only from other firms: it may come from sister plants owned by the same company. In our discussion of escape strategies later in this chapter, we will present the example of TRW, a corporation that has utilized this source of leverage (combined with the sale of union facilities and the acquisition of new nonunion ones) to wrest deep concessions from its unions and concurrently to transform itself from an almost entirely unionized manufacturing firm to an almost entirely nonunion firm.

Size and Ownership Structure

Auto supply firms fall into one of the following three broad organizational types, based on their firm size and ownership structure: (1) large supply divisions or subsidiaries within the OEMs, (2) large independent suppliers, and (3) small independent suppliers. Labor-management relations vary considerably across these three groups.

Supply subsidiaries at the OEMs. The largest producers in the U.S. automotive supply industry are the parts subsidiaries of General Motors, Ford, and Chrysler. Most of these producers are separate operating units within the automotive manufacturing firms. In the case of Nissan, Honda, and other Japanese OEMs with North American production facilities, most supply operations are separate firms—though they are highly enmeshed via ownership, financing, and long-term contracts.

Collective bargaining in the U.S. OEM supply operations has generally fallen under the broad umbrella of the national agreements between the OEMs and the UAW. There are some exceptions, however, that date back to the acquisition of formerly independent suppliers, such as General Motor's Packard Electric Division, which bargains with the IUE (International Union of Electrical, Radio, and Machine Workers). Within the OEMs, the supply operations have been under the greatest pressure to cut costs and innovate in work operations, given the potential to shift production overseas or to outsource some or all of the work. In the cases of Ford and Chrysler, there was extensive outsourcing during the early and mid-1980s, with the same process occurring primarily in the late 1980s and early 1990s at General Motors. The outsourcing pressure is vividly illustrated by a classification system developed at General Motors in which world-class facilities were designated with a "green light," facilities with clear potential for improvement were designated with a "yellow light," and noncompetitive facilities were designated with a "red light," indicating they were slated to be sold or closed.[17] This system is a source of great controversy within the labor movement by virtue of the way it "pits plant against plant" in creating pressure for work-rule flexibility and other changes.[18]

Ownership by the OEMs and coverage under the UAW national agreements serve as both constraints and drivers for forcing and fostering strategies. The UAW negotiations and common OEM ownership are constraints on management forcing in that wages and benefits are reserved for national negotiations—where concessions have been tempered by the bargaining power associated with the assembly facilities. In contrast, for example, the IUE, which represents workers at GM's Packard Electric Division, agreed to a multitier wage structure (tied to a no-layoff pledge). The OEM ownership can also aid in management forcing around work-rule issues, which are subject to local negotiations, given the above options regarding outsourcing and the shifting of work across locations.

Fostering is enhanced by the negotiations structure in that many suppor- tive institutions have been created under the terms of the national UAW agreements. These include the establishment of national joint training cen- ters (the UAW-GM National Human Resource Center is funded at a rate of more than $200 million per year, for example), extensive job and income security protections, procedures for designating joint union and manage- ment appointees to address issues such as employee involvement and safety, and numerous other innovative initiatives. Joint strategic planning is en- couraged at GM, for example, under Attachment C of the national agree- ment, in which labor and management agree to "focus on cooperative efforts toward our common goal to improve the effectiveness of operations and remove barriers to improvements, increase job opportunities and fully util- ize the work-force. The local committees will jointly develop a plan through an exhaustive analysis of the location's operational efficiency."

At the same time, fostering is constrained by the large scale of these organizations and the attendant difficulties of organizational change efforts. For example, local labor and management leaders in the Rochester, New York, facility of GM's AC/Rochester Division (formerly Rochester Products) were unable to expand a key line of their business because corporate accounting procedures did not fully take into account the costs of having workers assigned to a job bank system (as an alternative to layoffs) or the potential savings if these workers were reallocated to the proposed new work.

Large independent suppliers. In addition to the OEM subsidiaries, there are several large independent diversified suppliers. The top four independent suppliers—Borg Warner, Budd, Rockwell International, and TRW—together accounted for, during the early 1990s, almost 10 percent of the sales in motor vehicle parts and accessories.[19] Other large independent suppliers include Bendix, Dana, Eaton, Kelsey-Hayes, Lear-Siegler, Magna International, Nip- pondenso, Ogihara, and Sheller Globe.

Many of the large independent suppliers have been organized for dec- ades, with collective-bargaining relationships that in some cases predate the UAW's recognition by the OEMs. For example, Kelsey-Hayes in Detroit was the site of the UAW's first successful sit-down strike.[20] Historically, there has been a "connective bargaining structure"[21] in place wherein (as we noted earlier) wage and benefit gains that the UAW achieved with the OEMs would be passed along in negotiations at these firms after a one- or two-year lag.

Since the rise of concession bargaining in the 1980s, however, the link to OEM gains in wages, benefits, and other areas has been almost completely eroded. National negotiations still occur in some of these firms, such as at Budd, but they are driven less by the comparison with OEM contracts and more by pressures regarding cost savings and a need for increased cooperation and commitment.

Among the large independent firms, there is a great controversy regarding "double-breasting" strategies—in which similar work is conducted in union and nonunion facilities owned by the same company. TRW, Eaton, and Dana have all been aggressive in utilizing this structural arrangement as a source of leverage in negotiations. As well, TRW, Borg Warner, and other multidivision firms have effectively used wages, benefits, and conditions in non-auto-related parts of their business as a point of comparison. Even in this context, however, they have also sought to build positive relations with many of the union locals in their unionized facilities—again reflecting the pressure from OEMs in this area and the capacity of some local union and management leaders to work together amid the seemingly contradictory signals.[22]

One factor that facilitates fostering strategies among the large independent supplier firms—even given the cost pressures—is the movement by OEMs to establish long-term contracts with a smaller number of suppliers, which, in turn, become much closer business partners. For example, one of the first moves announced by Roger Stempel upon assuming the position of CEO of General Motors was the formation of a "GM Supplier Policy Forum" to improve communications between the corporation and its suppliers. It is these large independent firms that are most likely to achieve partnership status with the OEMs, which then creates at least the potential for greater employment security and stability in labor relations.[23]

Small independent suppliers. While the 8 largest auto parts suppliers account for about 70 percent of shipments in the industry (SIC 3714), the next largest 50 firms account for only about an additional 15 percent of shipments.[24] Given that, as noted earlier, the industry comprises anywhere from 4,000 to 15,000 firms, it should be clear that auto supply includes a vast number of small firms. This is confirmed by Department of Commerce estimates that about 34 percent of the firms in SIC 3714 have fewer than ten employees (with a similar distribution in other relevant SIC sectors).[25]

These smaller suppliers are at the greatest risk in this industry. They are mostly in a subtier (supplying larger, first-tier auto suppliers) and are first called upon to absorb fluctuations in volume. There is anecdotal evidence from federal mediators to suggest that union density is much higher among these small firms in comparison with other small manufacturers. Few of these small firms have the resources needed to contemplate the escape or double-breasting strategies available to large independent suppliers. Consequently, most of these firms are engaged in deep forcing around wage and benefit concessions while simultaneously fostering at least enough to maintain productive relations within a small community of workers and managers.

In some cases, the fostering in these settings can be quite far-reaching, by virtue of the small size. For example, in a case study of one small unionized firm (with 17 employees), a customer demand for a price reduction led management to assemble all the employees in a room and brainstorm around the immediate response and the future direction of the business.[26]

Where the small suppliers are in a subtier supplying larger suppliers, they are not directly subject to the agenda-setting influence of the OEMs. However, some large independent suppliers are adopting the same certification approach in dealing with the smaller suppliers. Local labor market conditions and the practices of major area employers (even though they may be in other industries) are still more likely to influence the agenda for collective bargaining among unionized smaller employers.

Changes in Technology, Products, and Materials

Changes in customer requirements around materials and components raise fundamental questions for a supply firm. For example, Champion has faced a shrinking market for spark plugs at a time when automotive shipments in general were rising due to the use of smaller modern engines, which have fewer cylinders and require fewer tune-ups.[27] Similarly, Rochester Products produced nearly every carburetor used by GM and was among the world's highest-quality producers of this product, but it lost its competitive advantage and faced massive retooling costs when the industry shifted to fuel injection. As the industry has turned increasingly to the use of plastic components, the Budd Company has even created a separate corporate division dedicated to plastics.

The consequences of adjustments in materials and products include worker displacement and retraining. At one extreme, an auto supplier may respond to changes in material or component requirements by opening a new facility (a form of escape), with negotiations being highly restricted. At the other extreme, the technological shift can become a focal point for joint collaboration, which is what occurred at Rochester Products (with the benefit of the job and income security protections of the national UAW-GM contract).

In addition to changes in materials and products, this industry (like most of manufacturing) has made extensive use of programmable manufacturing technologies. These include robots for operations such as welding, painting, and movement of materials or products; programmable machine tools; and computer-aided design technologies.

Collective-bargaining negotiations over changes in manufacturing technology in auto supply firms are especially intense among skilled trades operations, in which there are long-established work rules concerning equipment utilization. For example, negotiations of this sort are the focal point in the Anderson Pattern case, presented later in this chapter.

In the case of robots and other programmable equipment for manufacturing and assembly, there are well-established traditions around the upgrading of operations. When these new technologies are introduced unilaterally, the equipment may end up in place more quickly, but extensive informal negotiations are subsequently required before it will be "up and running."

As such, new manufacturing and assembly technologies provide a clear managerial strategic choice in which forcing is an option (but subsequent fostering is likely to be required), while fostering involves ceding managerial autonomy and incurring potential initial delays.

Tactical Implications of Location

Geographically, the industry is concentrated in a handful of states—especially Michigan, Ohio, Indiana, and New York.[28] Geographic concentration of the auto supply industry is consistent with the location of automotive assembly plants, which until recently have been concentrated in the same states. The construction of new nonunion supply facilities has included some southern states, with the construction of new assembly plants (BMW, Nissan, Saturn) in the South likely to further spur development outside the Midwest.

For large independent suppliers, geographic location has been used as a tactical lever, with the construction of new nonunion facilities in the southern United States and abroad representing alternative productive capacity. This locational leverage is available due to the relative mobility of capital. Although total assets per employee are higher than the national average ($60,000 in auto supply versus an average for all manufacturing of $47,000), the percentage of fixed assets in buildings (as opposed to machinery) is lower in auto supply (16 percent) than the national average (23 percent).

However, given the growing attention to just-in-time delivery systems, automotive parts suppliers are experiencing new pressures around geographic location. The increased emphasis on delivery performance accords some bargaining leverage to unions in older facilities that would otherwise be less competitive.

UNIONS IN THE AUTO SUPPLY INDUSTRY

Historically, the auto supply industry has been highly unionized, with the United Automobile Workers (UAW) being the dominant union. Other significant unions include the Allied Industrial Workers (AIW); the International Brotherhood of Teamsters (IBT); the International Brotherhood of Electrical Workers (IBEW); the International Union of Electrical, Radio, and Machine Workers (IUE); and the International Association of Machinists (IAM).

Among the auto supply subsidiaries of the OEMs, the union structure includes both a national level (for national negotiations, arbitration, and national joint activities) and a local level (for local negotiations, most grievance administration, and local joint activities). This same structure is matched at some of the large independent suppliers, such as the Budd Company. Otherwise, suppliers negotiate on a local or plant basis with their respective unions. As was noted earlier, the pattern bargaining that previously linked these various negotiations has eroded considerably.

In fact, the very presence of unions in this industry has eroded—with a

Table 5.1   Union Coverage in the U.S. Auto Parts Industry

	Percentage Organized		
	1969	1974	1983
Estimates for independent parts firms in BLS industry data[*]	80.0	80.0	58.0
	1976–1978	1982–1984	1987–1988
Estimates using UAW membership data and SIC employment figures[*]			
Including Big Three parts plants	82.0	68.0	58.0
Excluding Big Three parts plants	59.0	37.0	24.0

	1976	1980	1984	1988
Independent auto parts suppliers whose workers belong to unions[†]	62.0	50.0	30.0	22.0

[*]Source: S. Herzenberg and H. Shaiken, "Labor Market Segmentation in the North American Auto Industry" (paper presented at the annual meeting of the Canadian Industrial Relations Research Association, Victoria, British Columbia, 1990).
[†]Source: Greg Gardner and Nunzio Lupo, "UAW Reeling from Big Defeat at Smyrna," Detroit Free Press, July 28, 1989, 1a, 14A.

rate of decline that is even faster than that in the U.S. economy generally. Table 5.1 presents three different estimates of changes in auto supply union density, all of which point to a dramatic decline (though the bases for the individual estimates differ in various ways). This decline contrasts with the high and stable unionization rate in the paper and railroad industries.

The decline in union density reflects the utilization of escape strategies by existing employers, the entry of new nonunion (foreign and domestic) competitors, and the loss of older unionized employers that have gone out of business. While all of the UAW's internal departments have faced difficult times in recent years, the dominant experience of the international staff who service independent parts suppliers is one of having spent the better part of a decade in concession bargaining or presiding over plant closings.

MANAGEMENT'S AGENDA

There are many sources of bargaining leverage available to management in the auto supply industry, but how are they utilized? What does management want? As we noted earlier, many of management's priorities have been dictated by OEM pressures for a combination of cost savings and demonstrated gains in flexibility, efficiency, and stability.

Wage and Benefit Cost Containment

Nearly every major form of wage and benefit cost containment that emerged in the 1980s has diffused broadly in the auto supply sector, including reduced wage increases, wage freezes, wage reductions, lump-sum payments, freezing or eliminating cost-of-living increases, two-tier and multitier wage systems, co-payments on health care benefits, and reductions in or elimination of other benefits. In addition, many auto supply firms and their unions have experimented with various forms of contingent compensation, including gain sharing, bonus payments, profit sharing, and pay-for-knowledge systems. In some cases, employee stock ownership plans (ESOPs) have been established—especially as part of bailout plans for economically troubled firms. This is what occurred in the Adrian Fabricators case, presented later in this chapter.

During the past decade, the UAW has developed considerable expertise in assessing the financial pressures facing firms and weighing the validity of concession demands. It has retained leading accounting firms in response to company offers to "open the books" in order to demonstrate the need for cost and benefit savings. Still, the threat of outsourcing or plant closure has generated concessions from unions not otherwise persuaded of the need.

Flexible Work Rules and Work Restructuring

Full work restructuring has come relatively late to the auto supply industry. Quality of work life (QWL) and other participative programs do date back to the late 1970s in this industry—especially in supplier divisions of the OEMs (such as Packard Electric) and large first-tier independent suppliers. In fact, one of the most celebrated early QWL efforts involved the UAW workforce in Harmon's Bolivar, Tennessee plant. Still, most of the experiments in the late 1970s and early 1980s with QWL programs and quality circles were short-lived and rarely fully integrated into regular business operations.[29] Furthermore, there have been few cases of unionized auto supply firms utilizing the sort of sociotechnical redesign principles that are emphasized in paper and other continuous-process industries.

By the late 1980s, however, employers were increasingly demanding "modern operating agreements" (MOAs) in collective bargaining, which featured dramatic reductions in job classifications and reorganization of work around "work cells" or teams. In part, these demands reflected the priority being given to such innovations by the OEMs, but they also were given increased emphasis as a result of the success of Japanese suppliers that operated with flexible systems of this sort. While unions have often been pressured to agree to such arrangements (typically under threat that the contract will be implemented anyway), they frequently complain that managements do not know how to effectively utilize the flexibility that they have insisted on. One international representative from the UAW, for example, dismissed the utilization of most job classification reductions as little more than a means for coping with high absenteeism.

Individual Commitment and Worker Participation

At the same time that managements have aggressively sought to cut costs, they have been instituting statistical process control (SPC) programs, total quality management (TQM), and other changes in work systems that rely on individual worker commitment and participation in decisions. In contrast to the worker-participation efforts noted earlier, SPC, TQM, and similar initiatives are designed to be directly integrated into business operations. Relatively little of the negotiations regarding such initiatives occurs at an institutional level (in collective bargaining). Rather, most of the negotiations occur at the individual level, between the employee and the supervisor.

In smaller firms, these negotiations around individual effort have long been central to relations between entrepreneurs/owners and their employees. Now, however, OEM pressure and competitive realities have forced large independent suppliers and OEM supply subsidiaries to adopt formal programs aimed at producing the same result. A key constraint on the effectiveness of such programs is a firm's utilization of double-breasted strategies, which can prompt workers to restrict their effort out of resentment (fueled by union "in-plant" strategies centering on individual worker actions). The importance of individual worker effort under the new workplace systems affords the unions some leverage against the double-breasted strategies and the hard forcing on economic issues.

LABOR'S AGENDA

Although management has increasingly set the agenda for negotiations in the auto supply industry, labor leaders have been working to establish their own independent agenda. All the potential elements of the labor agenda are, however, controversial within labor. Thus, there is no single unified labor response, and the responses that do emerge are frequently second-guessed by others in the labor movement for ideological, practical, or political reasons.

Employee Involvement and Joint Activities

There is a long history of joint union-management activity in the auto supply industry in the areas of skilled trades apprenticeship and health-and-safety committees. Although the issue of the quality of work life was first raised by the UAW in its negotiations with the OEMs, it marks the beginning of a sharp split within the labor movement around issues of union-management cooperation and employee commitment. When the idea of contract language on QWL was first proposed, its sponsor, then UAW Vice President Irving Bluestone, reports that there was only one positive vote on the UAW executive committee—his own.

It was fashionable in the early 1980s to report that, despite internal disagreement on the issue, no union leaders had lost an election on the basis of the QWL issue, but a highly visible election loss at UAW Local 599 in 1982 elevated the political significance of the issue. The politics further intensified with the emergence within the UAW of the "new directions" faction, which characterizes most forms of joint activity as sophisticated vehicles for pitting workers against workers and locals against locals. At the same time, some local leaders have been elected on explicit platforms of working with management to "grow the business." The internal UAW tensions around joint activities directly affect social contract discussions within the OEM supply subsidiaries and are also replicated in internal factional splits (and election challenges) within bargaining units at many independent suppliers.

As a result of the internal union divisions on these issues, there is a wide variation in the scope of joint activities across plants in the OEMs and in the large independent suppliers. Within the same company, some local union leaders will have staked their political careers on constructing viable social contracts centered on union-management cooperation and employee commitment, while others will have staked their careers on opposing these developments.

Employment Security

The issue of employment security is a union priority—despite its elusive nature among independent suppliers—given the fear of job loss among union members and the potential of this issue for tempering internal splits regarding joint activities. The OEM contracts with the UAW are noted for long-standing income security protection (via the supplemental unemployment benefits [SUB]) and more recent employment security protections via the job bank programs at GM and Ford. GM's contract with the IUE at Packard Electric goes even further by providing lifetime job security to bargaining unit members (linked to a multitier wage system, work-rule flexibility, and provisions for the use of temporary employees). However, the UAW's income security protections at GM have recently come under fire, given the spate of announced plant closings.

For most of the independent suppliers, even these debates seem a luxury. The difficulty of establishing such protections, in view of the scarcity of resources in this highly competitive industry, is illustrated by the Anderson Pattern case, presented later in this chapter, in which the parties fashioned a complex guarantee for bounded periods of layoff linked to local labor market conditions. In the absence of direct job security guarantees, some local unions have successfully negotiated explicit increases in capital spending, often in exchange for long-term (four- to seven-year) contracts (which then enable the supplier to seek longer-term contracts with the OEMs).

Information Sharing and Institutional Survival

The U.S. auto supply industry's relationship with unions features extremes of both cooperation and containment/escape. Further, employers seem able to move from cooperation to containment relatively quickly. As a result, unions closely study the actions of employers. There is always some ambiguity as to whether an ostensibly cooperative action can be accepted at face value or whether it is a ploy in the course of a broader forcing strategy. As one senior staff member at the UAW commented, "I'm still a believer in joint decision making, but I'm getting hung up on the word *competitive* these days. What I see has nothing to do with competition and everything to do with maximizing profit—with greed." The doubts and ambiguity experienced by union leaders are heightened by the fact that many employers like to keep their options open.

At stake are basic issues of business success for management and institutional survival for unions. Though the issue has not been fully articulated in the form of international union policy at the UAW or other major unions in this industry, many local union leaders in the auto supply industry are increasingly pressing management for detailed information on strategic business-planning decisions.

FACTORS INFLUENCING THE USE OF ESCAPE, FORCING, AND FOSTERING IN AUTO SUPPLY: 1980–1991

All three strategies highlighted in this book—forcing, fostering, and escape—figure prominently in the U.S. auto supply industry. Here, we identify the factors that account for the high frequency with which each is employed. Also, at the conclusion of the discussion on escape, we offer an illustration of a corporate escape strategy. Though escape is, in effect, a nonnegotiating strategy, it is important to identify this option as a backdrop to forcing and fostering in the auto supply industry.

Forcing Change: A Dominant Feature of Auto Supply Labor Relations

The utilization of forcing strategies in the auto supply industry is driven by the severe competitive pressures on firms, which come from other U.S. firms (unionized, nonunion, and foreign-owned in the United States), from firms in other nations, and from customers that are themselves facing severe competitive pressures. Key enabling factors include the relative mobility of capital (which lends credibility to escape threats), management's ability to operate many supply plants during a strike through the use of replacement workers, and growing awareness that new forms of work organization (which require contractual changes) are integral to the success of leading firms in this sector.

Forcing is tempered, however, in most supply divisions of the OEMs by their inclusion with assembly plants under the national contracts with the UAW. It is also tempered in the independent suppliers by the OEM inspection processes, which emphasize cooperative employment relations as one of the criteria for certification.

Fostering Change: A Core Element of Successful Employment Relations Systems

The utilization of fostering strategies in the auto supply industry builds on a long tradition of union-management cooperation on selected issues and the leading role of the overall auto industry in the areas of QWL and employee involvement. Fostering is greatly facilitated in the OEM supply operations by the provisions of the national contracts with the UAW, which support joint activities through direct funds, the allocation of appointee positions, the creation of various labor-management committees, and explicit identification of topic areas subject to joint governance. Among large independent suppliers, many of these provisions have been adopted via pattern bargaining. Further, the certification processes established by the OEMs provide a business-related driver for many fostering activities.

The fostering is constrained, however, by the scarce resources and deep cost pressures characteristic of this sector—especially among smaller independent suppliers. A further constraint on fostering is the relative ease with which employers can utilize forcing strategies and the contradictory signals sent when they do utilize such strategies.

The Escape Option: A Backdrop for Fostering and Forcing

There are many forms of escape, including closing a facility, moving some of the work out of a facility, selling a facility, cutting off capital investment in a facility, and seeking to decertify the union(s) in a facility. All of these forms of escape can be found in the auto supply industry (though we don't have exact data on their distribution). The prevalence of escape strategies primarily reflects the relative mobility of capital equipment in this sector, combined with the extensive cost pressures that businesses face. Employers also utilize the movement of work tactically to make credible larger forcing initiatives. Similarly, past episodes involving escape often serve as powerful learning experiences that sustain many fostering initiatives.

While the threat of escape (implied or explicit) often serves a tactical role in forcing or fostering negotiations, the actual movement of work usually takes place after negotiations have collapsed. In this sense, escape itself is a nonnegotiating strategy. Our case examples, presented later in this chapter, focus on forcing or fostering strategies. However, since escape provides a key backdrop for these cases and for the industry as a whole, we will first review one example of a corporation that has systematically utilized the escape strategy—TRW.

TRW: Escape as a corporate strategic choice. TRW has been in operation since 1901.[30] It was founded in Cleveland as Thompson Products, a small manufacturer of screws. Since then, the company, which in the 1950s became known as TRW, has grown into a larger conglomerate with more than 75,000 employees worldwide.

In the 1920s and 1930s the company developed a philosophy of close and direct contact with its employees. Thus, management bitterly opposed the third-party influence of unions. However, because of increased organizing pressure from national unions in the late 1930s and early 1940s and perceptions among several top management leaders concerning the inevitability of unionization, the company decided to initiate employee representation plans ("independent" unions) in several of its facilities.[31] These independent unions would maintain a decentralized human resource/industrial relations structure, consistent with the philosophy of direct employee-employer contact. By the late 1950s, half of TRW's plants were organized by independent unions, while a quarter were organized by national unions and the rest remained nonunion.

As TRW moved into a period of expansion beginning in the late 1950s, it gave increasing emphasis to the nonunion operations. Growth at TRW has occurred in two ways: acquisitions and opening new plants. In terms of acquisitions, from 1958 to 1970, the company acquired 30 plants, of which half were already unionized. Between 1970 and 1980, TRW secured 10 new plants, all nonunion. With respect to new facilities, TRW's nonunion strategy is even more pronounced. The company opened 17 new plants between 1970 and 1982, and all but 1 has remained nonunion. Furthermore, in 1984, TRW sold 2 plants in Cleveland that were represented by the Aircraft Workers Alliance.

Although TRW has sold several unionized facilities, unlike other firms in the industry (e.g., Eaton), it has not attempted to dislodge existing unions through decertification drives.[32] Nonetheless, evidence does suggest that management has been more generous, in terms of capital expenditure, toward both newer and older nonunion facilities than toward unionized facilities. In a sample of eight TRW plants, three unionized and five nonunion, Verma[33] found that from 1971 to 1981, the average annual capital expenditure per employee in the unionized plants was $538; while in older nonunion facilities, it was $1,220; and in newer nonunion plants, it was $2,220.

Through investment and acquisition, TRW has assumed a much more proactive nonunion stance. TRW's movement toward a nonunion industrial relations strategy is consistent with the company's philosophical opposition to unionization. Moreover, the move has been prompted by TRW's interest in pursuing issues cited in Chapter 1 as being part of management's substantive agenda. For example, TRW saw a possibility of reducing payroll costs by using nonunion labor since, in TRW's unionized plants, the wage and benefit levels are higher than those in TRW's comparable nonunion facilities.[34]

In addition, in the late 1960s and early 1970s, the company experimented with innovations in human resource management and attempted to restructure work using semiautonomous work teams and contingent pay systems. These early efforts were successful in nonunion plants but were largely abandoned in unionized facilities because of union opposition. While the early efforts to increase flexibility and employee commitment in the unionized settings likely involved elements of both fostering and forcing, it is clear that neither strategy has been pursued with much vigor at a corporate level relative to the escape option. Indeed, by the mid-1970s, TRW's innovative human resource practices became a strategy both to enhance productivity and to deter unionization.

It is of note, however, that some of the remaining unionized facilities have, in the late 1980s, experienced a revival of team-based work organizations now being implemented on a joint basis with the unions. This probably reflects the extent to which the escape option is perceived as a highly credible threat.

As discussed earlier, TRW recently has not only been shifting investment away from its unionized facilities but has also sold several of its plants that were organized by independent unions. Management was "willing to shoulder the burdens" of the inflexibility associated with collective bargaining with independent unions as long as "national unions posed a clear and present threat."[35] However, the innovative human resource practices associated with the nonunion workplace model, which combined dispute resolution mechanisms and employee involvement processes, are seen by management as having reduced the distinctive claims made by union organizers.

Thus, the social contract between TRW and its employees—always important to the firm—has been systematically reinforced, while the social contract between TRW and the union has been undermined. This is, in many ways, a classic escape story, and it provides an important backdrop to our examination of both forcing and fostering strategies.

Summing Up the Analysis of Forcing, Fostering, and Escape

The auto supply industry emerges from this analysis as a highly volatile context for labor-management negotiations. As Table 5.2 illustrates, this is an industry in which all three strategic options are desirable (from management's perspective). As was seen above, all three are also feasible in this industry, and all are observed in practice. Our cases center on forcing and fostering strategies and further illustrate the availability and utilization of multiple strategies.

Table 5.2   Potential Benefits, Feasibility of Implementation, and Observed Frequency of Strategic Options in the Auto Supply Industry

	Strategic Options		
	Escape	Forcing	Fostering
Potential benefits	High	High	High
Feasibility of implementation	High	High	Moderate to high
Observed frequency	High	High	Moderate

The five cases presented here were selected both as vivid illustrations of forcing and fostering strategies *and* as illustrations of the range of ownership and size within this industry.

First, we examine the microdynamics associated with a highly publicized example of a forcing strategy—the case of the AP Parts plant in Toledo, Ohio, and UAW Local 14. The case begins with a contentious strike in 1984 featuring hard forcing by management and some effective counterforcing by the union. It concludes with the reestablishment of traditional arm's-length relations in the years following the strike.

Second, we consider Adrian Fabricators, a very small firm in which an employee stock ownership plan provides a powerful frame of reference through which employees view the employment relationship. In this setting, we see a management forcing response to union activities, followed by a shift to an alternative fostering strategy.

The third case involves a division of an OEM—the Packard Electric Division of General Motors—and the IUE. This relationship is one of the oldest and most far-reaching examples of fostering activity in the auto supply industry, and we focus on a series of events that led up to a lifetime employment security pledge for employees as well as some subsequent contract administration issues.

Fourth is the case of a large independent manufacturer—the Budd Company—and the UAW, which in many ways typifies the full range of labor-management developments in this industry. We highlight the negotiations processes associated with movement to a team structure for changing dies on stamping presses, an instance of individual-level forcing within a fostering context, and other developments.

The final case involves a small, skilled trades setting—Anderson Pattern and the Pattern Makers' Association—in which distinctive issues emerged around new technology and skilled trades workers. In particular, a progression of fostering discussions enabled the parties to move from a one-time experiment with flexible staffing on new equipment to a complete revision of past work rules.

COLLAPSE AND RECONSTRUCTION OF A SOCIAL CONTRACT:
THE CASE OF AP PARTS AND UAW LOCAL 14

AP Parts has been producing mufflers in the Toledo, Ohio, area since it
was founded in 1927.[36] Led by its founder, John Goerlich, for half a century,
the firm has had three different owners over the past decade. In addition to
manufacturing operations in Toledo, there are AP plants in Michigan, North
Carolina, and Indiana. AP derives its competitive advantage through a
stamped muffler that contains only 4 separate pieces (in contrast to 17 in a
typical muffler), which allows great flexibility in developing new products
or modifying the product for customers. UAW Local 14, established in 1938,
is an amalgamated local incorporating the AP Parts bargaining unit and
three other units, the largest of which is a General Motors drivetrain plant.

The facility came under increasing economic pressure in the years immediately preceding the 1984 strike due to the loss of a major customer (Sears)
and management's subsequent decision to shift production for the aftermarket to the company's Goldsboro, North Carolina, plant—leaving the Toledo
plant as a supplier to the OEMs (with consequent pressures on cost, quality,
and delivery). In this context, management initiated a round of concession
bargaining that resulted in a wage reduction of 50 cents per hour. As well,
a quality of work life process was initiated in 1982. These two initiatives—
one distributive and one integrative—both represented incremental (if contrasting) adjustments within the rubric of the existing labor-management
relationship. However, the Toledo facility experienced further financial
losses in 1983, creating pressure for deeper financial and work-rule concessions.

Management-Initiated Forcing Strategy

In the 1984 negotiations, management departed from past negotiating
patterns—in both process and content. Procedurally, the company broke
from traditional bargaining norms by opening negotiations with its own
extensive set of demands and concurrently passing out handbills in the
plant stating that "we are committed to staying in Toledo." Substantively,
the company sought $5.84 in wage and benefit concessions, replacement of
the individual incentive system with a measured workday system, elimination of the 30-and-out provision, freedom to subcontract, redefinition of job
classifications, and the reorganization of the plant around work cells—all of
which were controversial demands. In addition, the company installed a
chain-link fence around the property, began taking employment applications from potential replacement workers, and hired a private security firm
that specialized in helping to maintain operations during a strike.

The union interpreted the company's actions as a direct threat to its
institutional security and began a set of parallel responses. For example, it
countered company letters to its members with letters of its own. By the
contract expiration date of March 1, 1984, a tit-for-tat dynamic was well

established. At expiration, the company's final offer was rejected by a vote of 425 to 30.

Union Forcing Response and the Escalation of Tension

The union, which suspected that the company was expecting a strike, did not walk off the job when the contract expired. Instead, the union instructed the workforce to show up and continue working under the terms of the company's final offer. The tactic apparently caught the firm by surprise. Workers reportedly arrived to find security guards hurriedly packing up food, cots, and other supplies presumably intended to sustain a replacement workforce stuck overnight in the factory.

Relations in the plant were tense, with security guards videotaping workers and workers offering predictable physical and verbal responses. Under the company's final offer, the workers took a $5.84-per-hour cut in wages and benefits and were subject to new shop rules. More than 150 workers were laid off during the first month (bringing plant employment to 232), and 80 employees received a total of 200 disciplinary notices for violations of the new work rules and other infractions.

The union filed an unfair labor practice (ULP) charge with the National Labor Relations Board (NLRB) on March 22, 1984. Although local NLRB hearing officers were reportedly supportive of the union's charges, the NLRB Region 8 director rejected the union's ULP charge on April 30, 1984.

Collapse of Relations

Once the NLRB had rejected the ULP charge, the union indicated it was on strike, and the employer then began bringing in workers to maintain production. The first 40 replacement workers encountered a boisterous group of about 125 picketing employees as they arrived at the plant. The next day, in response to punctured tires and broken windshields, a court order was issued limiting union picketing.

There were initial attempts by federal mediators to work with the parties, but no progress was reported in negotiations. In the plant, conflicts among picketing strikers, security guards, and replacement workers intensified. There was also a series of public demonstrations, the largest of which was on May 22, 1984. Three thousand people attended the demonstration, which became violent as an 18-wheel semi truck was used to break the plant gate. The police responded with tear gas canisters. One union official characterized the ensuing conflict as worse than his combat experiences in Vietnam.

Inability to Reconstruct Social Relations

Secret talks began in mid-June, at the company's urging. Despite a new location (Ann Arbor, Michigan), casual dress, and a stated desire for openness, the talks collapsed with little progress having been made. As relations deteriorated, the community became increasingly vocal in expressing its concern about the negotiations. In response, the company advertised in the paper that it was committed to Toledo and indicated its current negotiating position. The union responded with its own advertisements promising to offer "The Truth about the AP Negotiations." The company rejected an early call from Toledo's mayor to convene a labor-management citizens committee to assist in settling the dispute.

After the mass demonstration on May 22, 1984, the mayor appointed a five-member community committee, which included representatives from the Toledo Area Labor-Management Committee. This committee recommended a settlement package, which the union immediately agreed to accept and which the company then rejected.

Management of Internal Differences during the Strike

Within management, the strike apparently led at least one of the company's principal owners to sell his shares. Some supervisors also quit during the strike. Further, members of the broader management community in Toledo increasingly separated themselves from the management of this firm.

Management attempted to divide the union with return-to-work offers for striking workers and other tactics. In order to build solidarity in response, the UAW's regional director made the case to the international union and the larger labor movement that the AP Parts strike would be a harbinger of things to come in the region. Union members from elsewhere in the UAW and from other unions all over the United States responded by sending food and money to help the striking workers. In addition, the UAW vice presidents responsible for negotiations with General Motors and Ford joined in one set of demonstrations in Toledo—sending a signal to these customers of AP Parts.

Resolution of the 1984 Strike

In September, the company again rebuffed mediation efforts by the mayor. Talks did resume at the end of October with union movement on the company's demand for a work-cell concept, but amnesty for striking workers emerged as a key point of contention.

Talks were on and off throughout the months of November and December. A company offer that included amnesty for all but 21 union members was rejected by the union in mid-December by a vote of 225 to 5. The company called the vote "a terrible breach of faith," and negotiations were again broken off.

Despite continued production efforts during the strike, inventories were shrinking and customer pressure was mounting. Apparently, however, the event that brought the strike to an end was a representation challenge petition filed on January 31, 1985, by the Maritime Engineers Beneficial

Association. Under those circumstances, the replacement workers would be time-barred from filing for a decertification election. Shortly afterward, the company agreed to a settlement with the union that included some wage and benefit concessions, the addition of a plant productivity bonus system, a two-year freeze on cost-of-living increases, some work-rule changes giving the company more flexibility in temporary job transfers, language regarding the use of a team-based work-cell structure for welding, retention of holidays and retirement benefits, and an agreement that no worker would be fired for any picket line activity. By a vote of 254 to 72, the contract was ratified.

Reconstruction of the Traditional Social Contract

Following the strike, both sides were faced with the difficult task of resuming regular plant operations. Shop-floor relations were tense for more than a year after people had returned to work. Some workers and many of the supervisors left the firm for employment elsewhere. Faces also changed in key higher-level management positions, including the plant manager and the personnel director.

A new slate of union leaders was elected to office on a platform oriented around rebuilding labor-management relations. Thus, within two years of the strike, the leadership on both sides of the table had changed—setting the stage for reconstruction of a relationship.

Successful, Traditional Negotiations

The 1987 negotiations were a turning point in this process. Management opened bargaining with relatively few demands—a sharp contrast to its opening position back in 1984. The union responded in kind, and both sides reportedly conducted a set of negotiations characterized by the give-and-take associated with traditional approaches to collective bargaining. In a relatively short period of time, an agreement was reached and ratified.

In daily relations, however, management continued to take an arm's-length approach to employment relations. One top manager stated that "we take a Theory X approach." In an apparent response, the union leadership that had been elected following the strike was replaced by a slate of union leaders advocating an arm's-length relationship with the company. This slate included a number of individuals who had served on the bargaining committee during the 1984 strike.

Consequently, by 1990, many indicators suggested that the relationship had reverted back to a traditional pattern of compliance at the individual level and arm's-length relations at the institutional level. Two concurrent developments stand as potential threats to the stability of this reestablished traditional pattern. First, the same customer pressures on cost, quality, and delivery that precipitated the 1984 strike have continued and, if anything, intensified. Second, at the end of the time period that we examined, the company had just purchased and completed restoration of a facility in Indiana capable of producing mufflers and other auto parts. This represented an important new source of leverage in the relationship.

The strike illustrates the deterioration and collapse of a labor-management relationship. Because each side had fundamental interests at stake, initial tactical moves took on great significance, and an escalation of conflict ensued. The escalation was further fueled as each side sought to derive power by breaking from traditional negotiating norms. The union's decision to strike and management's use of replacement workers both afforded tactical advantage but also served to erode any foundation of a social contract upon which a settlement might have been constructed.

While tensions followed the settlement, the parties reverted back to a traditional mode of operations with surprising speed. Instrumental in this reconstruction of the relationship were new faces at the table and customer pressure for labor stability. Since the reconstruction has been around a traditional social contract, however, it remains to be seen whether this will be sufficient to meet management's long-term needs regarding cost and flexibility and labor's long-term needs regarding employment security and institutional stability.

Outcomes

The strike at AP Parts was costly for both sides. The direct costs to management included reduced production and other expenses associated with maintaining production during a strike. These costs are perhaps minor compared to the long-term implications around low employee morale, supervisor turnover, and a negative reputation in the community and with customers. The firm did gain a contract that included substantial wage, benefit, and work-rule concessions, though it had not taken full advantage of the work-rule flexibility that it won in negotiations.

The union and its members suffered the costs associated with a long strike, including reduced income and emotional travail. In addition, the union experienced some internal turmoil, with the turnover of two sets of local leaders. The union did gain in demonstrating its tactical ability to match management's forcing strategy with its own counterforcing strategy.

For both sides, a traditional, arm's-length social contract has been reestablished. It remains to be seen whether this will prove viable for each side as the firm faces increased customer pressure on costs at the same time that it is being pressured to demonstrate positive labor-management relations.

RECONCILING FRAMES OF REFERENCE: THE CASE OF
ADRIAN FABRICATORS AND UAW LOCAL 963

Adrian Fabricators is an independent manufacturer of wire mesh industrial containers used in the warehouse operations of manufacturing facilities.[37] Located in Adrian, Michigan, the company is close to numerous automotive production facilities. With total employment of 141 in 1989, Adrian Fabricators is a relatively small supplier.

Adrian Fabricators began operations in 1966 under the ownership of the Tri-State Engineering Corporation and was organized by the UAW in its first year of operation. Over the following 25 years, the company's fortunes rose and fell cyclically with those of the automobile industry (which accounted for more than 75 percent of its business). The collective-bargaining arrangements followed the general automotive pattern.

Though the company was used to cyclical shifts in the economy, it was unprepared for the drop from a record sales volume of $26 million in 1979 to only $6 million in 1982. Layoffs at this time left a small, high-seniority workforce. The financial situation deteriorated—at one point, several employees voluntarily worked without pay in hopes of keeping the operation afloat. By February 1983, the company filed for bankruptcy.

Development of the Employee Stock Ownership Plan

As part of an effort led by several senior employees, state government agencies and private consultants were called in to help formulate an employee stock ownership plan, which was established by the fall of 1983. Despite the union's active role in establishing the ESOP, the workforce decided to discontinue holding union meetings—reflecting a belief that union representation was no longer required now that they were owners of the business.

Tensions began to build, however, because the company president's unilateral style now seemed inconsistent with the ESOP structure. As well, management announced that earnings were not sufficient for a wage increase, which directly contradicted worker expectations of greater wealth now that they were owners. The many tensions provided the impetus for a 1985 UAW reorganizing drive, which was met with resistance by management.

Workers Striking against Themselves

Over half the workforce walked off the job on February 5, 1986, in protest over management's having fired the chair of the bargaining committee for leaving work early to attend a union meeting. Management continued operations during the strike, using those employees who were willing to cross the picket line. The remaining worker-owners were, in effect, striking against the very company that they owned.

The strike was a highly emotional experience for everyone involved. In some cases, one brother or cousin was working while another was on the picket line. Windows at the factory were broken by rocks. The negotiations at the bargaining table were highly acrimonious. Management and the union finally reached agreement in May 1986. The three-year package included a one-and-a-half-year freeze on wages, recognition of union stewards, creation of a union shop, and implementation of a grievance procedure and a seniority system. .

Constructing a New Frame of Reference

Following the strike, the company's financial situation remained precarious, and labor-management relations remained tense. The fall of 1987 brought a change in top management leadership: the company president left for another job and was replaced by the chief financial officer. The new president was more open in sharing information with the union and more participatory in his style.

Also in the fall of 1987, state officials from the Michigan Governor's Office for Job Training (who had been involved in formulating the initial ESOP) recommended the creation of a joint labor-management problem-solving committee, which was formally established via a negotiated letter of agreement. This committee forum addressed substantive issues, such as changes in the absenteeism policy, production problems, and safety concerns. In subsequent collective bargaining, the parties even agreed to use the committee as an additional step in the grievance procedure.

The workforce had always perceived the profit-sharing component of the ESOP formula as more favorable to the firm's managers. In fact, workers received payments earlier as part of their wage package, but the differential in the checks surfaced deep equity issues. The resolution of this situation involved agreement on a uniform system for profit-sharing payments.

Some further developments were driven by external events. In 1989, the plant was cited for safety violations by federal OSHA inspectors and state MIOSHA inspectors. In response, a joint safety committee was established outside the formal structure of collective bargaining. Subsequently, a second joint committee was established to address equipment issues, including overseeing the installation and training needs for a major new capital investment.

Although the Adrian Fabricators case began with harsh forcing, the joint committees are pointing the way toward a social contract based on labor-management cooperation. At the end of the time period we examined, the fostering was being extended to encompass the use of a team concept and group leaders as well. The contrast between the last two negotiations reflects a further shift in frames of reference. In the 1986 negotiations, management challenged the legitimacy of the union; in the 1989 negotiations, the company opened its books for inspection by UAW experts.

Economic Stability and a New Social Contract

In the fall of 1988, the company's financial picture began to improve, which greatly facilitated the change efforts. The value of shares has increased 247 percent since the strike, accompanied by a 145 percent rise in employment. The first profit-sharing payments were made in 1989. At the bargaining table, the good fortunes were reflected in wage increases that averaged more than 25 percent. Most managers and union officials give the improved labor-management relationship significant credit for the improved economic performance.

One interesting twist on the case involves Adrian Fabricators' adoption of a business strategy designed to insulate the company from the cyclical automotive supply industry. This includes efforts to establish long-term contracts with large customers and an explicit effort to diversify the customer mix. In 1986, more than 75 percent of the company's business was with automotive customers, whereas by 1990, that figure had fallen to less than 15 percent. The firm was acting on a clear strategy of removing the labor-management relationship from the volatile context associated with the automotive supply industry. Ironically, this case, which began as an example of forcing within the auto supply industry, concludes as a case of fostering that is increasingly outside the industry.

Outcomes

Both labor and management suffered significant costs during the strike, including lost production for management and great tensions—not only between management and labor but also within the bargaining unit. The repair of relations following the strike has, however, led to positive outcomes for all parties. Economic performance has improved, and the business has a new strategic direction; the workforce now holds increasingly valuable stock in this enterprise; and the union is playing a central role in business operations.

THE CASE OF PACKARD ELECTRIC AND THE IUE, LOCAL 717

The Packard Electric Division of General Motors produces most of GM's wiring harnesses and related components.[38] About half of the division's 25,000 employees work in Warren, Ohio, which is where the firm began. The International Union of Electrical, Radio, and Machine Workers (IUE), Local 717, represents all the production workers in Warren. Historically, a low ebb in relations was reached in the mid-1970s, when morale was low, absenteeism was high, and economic performance declined. Just during the summer of 1977, there were three work stoppages, and for the full year, 97.9 grievances were filed for every 100 hourly employees.

Constructing a Cooperative Labor-Management Relationship

Contract language on improving the quality of work life was first agreed to in 1973, modeled on language negotiated by General Motors and the UAW in the same year. The initial focus was on issues clearly of common concern, such as a toys-for-tots program, a joint safety communications program, a joint United Way drive, voter registration, and credit counseling.

In May 1978, a joint Jobs Committee was established after the union insisted on joining a management task force to increase productivity. The purpose of the committee was to "develop an ongoing union-management approach that will maintain job security and identify opportunities for hiring in the Warren operations." Among the ground rules of the Jobs Committee was an agreement that "No employee will lose his or her job as a direct result of a project," an issue that was to have great significance for the parties.

In February 1979, the Jobs Committee agreed on a plan to hire 100 new employees to work in new "branch" plants. This was the first new hiring in the Warren plants since 1973 and was based on evidence that the new facilities could be competitively placed in Warren rather than near Packard Electric facilities in Mississippi or Juárez, Mexico. The new branch plants featured reduced job classifications, job rotation, and an emphasis on team-work.

The Jobs Committee then addressed ways to retain some plastic moulding business and other related issues. Altogether, by June 1981, the Jobs Committee had helped in the addition of 850,000 square feet of new floor space, $100 million of new investment, and 379 new jobs. In the 1980 model year alone, Packard Electric distributed $454,000 in awards to Warren for employee suggestions that resulted in savings of $2.36 million.

Continued Competitive Pressures

Despite the successful union-management efforts, management determined in late 1981 that the viability of the Warren operations was threatened by declining auto sales and the cost advantage of doing business abroad—particularly in Mexico.[39] The wage gap in the late 1970s was between approximately $2.50 per hour and more than $19.00 per hour, which grew as the Mexican peso was devalued in the early 1980s.

The company's executive committee and the union's bargaining committee met in December 1981 for a two-day off-site session at which the company indicated that only 64 percent of the business would be cost-competitive in five years (leaving 3,800 jobs at risk). In response, the parties developed a five-year business plan entitled "Plan to Compete." Under the plan, the most labor-intensive work was to be moved to Mexico, the more technologically intensive lead wire preparation would be brought back from Mexico to Warren, and early-retirement options would be developed, with an attrition goal of 1,650 direct labor jobs.

During the 1982 local IUE-GM collective-bargaining negotiations, management suggested that the parties bargain early, using brainstorming and other problem-solving processes. The union agreed, and the parties explored a final assembly option (FAO), which would involve deep wage reductions (to about $6.00 per hour) for new employees hired for any final assembly work that was to remain in Warren. Although the union resisted the idea, it complied with a management request for a membership vote, where it was rejected by nearly a 3-to-1 majority.

Packard continued to expand labor-intensive work in Mexico (as was discussed in the "Plan to Compete"), but it was not expanding the number of jobs in Warren. By the end of 1982, about 2,400 employees were on permanent layoff, and about as many were on temporary layoff. In local union elections during the fall of 1983, there was great debate over the layoffs, QWL, and perceived job security guarantees. Ultimately, the entire union bargaining committee was voted out of office—with the exception of one zone committeeman, Nick Nichols, who had led the challenge around the job security issue and who was voted in as chairman of the bargaining committee.

Crossroad in the Relationship

The internal union debate and local elections were a pivotal precursor to the 1984 negotiations. Many of the newly elected officials argued that the union should withdraw from all cooperative activities, but Nichols took a unique stance. He urged continued support for cooperation and attention to improving the company's competitive situation, but he also pressed for attention to job security. A series of informal meetings was then held involving about a dozen top union and management leaders, who called themselves the Resource Group. These sessions focused on two core interests—job security and competitiveness.

Procedurally, the 1984 negotiations were traditional (with opening positions, offers and counteroffers, and so forth), but the content built on the Resource Group discussions and sharply departed from the concurrent 1984 negotiations between the UAW and GM. A lower starting wage was established for new employees (at 55 percent of the base wage and at 55 percent of the COLA), which would increase over ten years to parity with the rest of the workforce. The quid pro quo for this wage flexibility was an agreement to provide a "Lifetime Job and Income Security Agreement for the Warren Operations." This included the following language:

> A. No employee will lose his/her job due to a shift of work from Warren Operations to other locations or because of technological change.
>
> B. The parties will manage the Warren Operations work-force so that a layoff of protected employees for other than temporary reasons will not occur. . . .
>
> C. Opportunities to maximize employment for employees will be provided by training employees and reassigning employees and/or work

within the Warren Operations and pursuing new business so that income security will be provided.

The contract was a pioneer "living agreement" in that it also included the phrase "This agreement will remain in full force and effect forever."

Outcomes

In the next eight years after signing the 1984 contract, GM invested more than $300 million in the Warren operations. The system was characterized by extensive joint problem solving at the shop floor (via employee participation groups) and regular higher-level union-management dialogue. Employees hired at the lower starting wage were progressing toward parity, and there were no longer any employees on layoff. The process was aided by growing orders due to the increased use of electronics in automobiles.

Of course, difficult issues continued to arise in the context of this farreaching combination of social and substantive agreements. For example, the 1984 contract featured language allowing management the flexibility to utilize temporary workers, which it first exercised in February 1985. When the first round of temporary assignments was complete, however, there was an unexpectedly high level of dissentation over the temporary employees' departure (many of the temporaries wanted to stay, and many of the permanent workers didn't think it was fair to make them leave).

Another three years passed before management again exercised this option under the contract. When it did, there was a pressing need (the additional workers would help keep a partially utilized facility open, and high levels of overtime were being worked). Attempts were made to clarify expectations all around, yet the same difficulties still arose when it was time for the temporary employees to leave. One union leader discussed the subsequent pressure that he received on the issue and concluded that "there are certain things that you just shouldn't ask a friend to do, and this is one of them."

Ultimately, management did not realize the full advantages of the contractual quid pro quo it had negotiated, and the union found the language more costly (in terms of internal dissention) than it had anticipated. The temporaries were never utilized frequently enough to establish a new social contract around this group of workers. Instead, resentment arose as they were apparently viewed through a lens that involved lifetime job security. Thus, even with the many gains that emerged from the joint efforts of the IUE and Packard Electric, difficult challenges continued to face the parties.

Altogether, the past decade and a half brought management at Packard Electric substantial flexibility in work operations, a multitier wage system, a chance to conduct redesign experiments in the branch facilities, and an underlying partnership relationship with the union. For the union, the same time period produced a lifetime job security guarantee and extensive experience in joint dialogue with management over core strategic decisions. Areas of tension and complexity still faced both parties, such as we saw in the utilization of temporary workers, but the case stands as one of the most enduring and far-reaching examples of the building of a new social contract.

THE BUDD COMPANY, THE UAW, AND THE CAW

Founded by Edward G. Budd in 1912, the Budd Company currently employs 14,000 people worldwide and has sales of $1.3 billion.[40] Now owned by the German conglomerate Thyssen AG, Budd is organized into three main divisions: Stamping and Frame, Wheel and Brake, and Plastics. Production operations are concentrated in Michigan and Ohio, but Budd also has facilities in Pennsylvania, Wisconsin, California, and Kentucky, as well as in Canada, Argentina, and Germany. This analysis focuses on plant-level interactions in Detroit, Michigan; Kitchner, Ontario; and Philadelphia, Pennsylvania, as well as national negotiations between Budd and the UAW.

Budd workers were organized by the UAW in the 1940s, and the majority of Budd manufacturing facilities became unionized. In Canada, the Canadian Automobile Workers Union (CAW) represented Budd workers. Historically, labor relations followed the UAW pattern set with the original equipment manufacturers, including arm's-length collective bargaining, high levels of wages and benefits, and adversarial contract administration.

Early Forcing at the Plant Level

There were massive layoffs throughout the Budd Company in the early 1980s. Union membership in the Detroit plant, for example, declined from 2,800 to 1,200 between 1979 and 1982. Before the largest of the layoffs, in 1981, the company pressed for substantial concessions. Local union leaders, persuaded that adjustment was needed, presented a concessionary agreement to the membership, with the stated alternative being the loss of more than half the jobs in the plant. Although local union president Norm Tunessi recommended ratification, 95 percent of the membership voted against the proposed contract—precipitating Tunessi's resignation. Following the rejection, the business was indeed shifted out of the Detroit plant, resulting in a layoff of more than 900 employees. As one union leader recalled the situation, the membership "never believed it until the machines were disassembled."

Employee Involvement and Statistical Process Control as Customer-Driven Changes

Joint initiatives in the areas of employee involvement (EI) and statistical process control (SPC) began around 1982 in many Budd facilities. Both initiatives were customer-driven, but in different ways. General Motors and

Ford had pioneered QWL and EI programs (respectively), and Budd joined many other auto suppliers in voluntarily adopting similar contract language in its agreements during the early 1980s. In contrast, SPC represented one of the first domains in which the OEMs explicitly pressured suppliers to implement new work practices.

The EI and SPC efforts vividly illustrate the individual-level negotiations that often accompany institutional-level agreements. These negotiations, which were over workers' voluntary participation and commitment to the new initiatives, occurred between supervisors and employees, between QWL or SPC coordinators and employees, and among groups of workers. By the mid-1980s, the EI effort had expanded to include approximately one-quarter of the workforce in many Budd plants, but there was a plateau in the number of additional volunteers interested in joining the EI process.[41] As well, despite the broad range of work environment improvements from EI, there were only incremental gains in economic performance.

Tensions in the Shop-Floor Negotiations over Worker Commitment

Distributive tactics and even forcing initiatives may occur at the same time that a fostering initiative is under way—a dynamic that is well illustrated by a series of disputes in Budd's Kitchner, Ontario, plant.[42] The Kitchner plant began operations in 1967. It's contentious history of labor relations reached a low ebb in 1978, when it experienced 68 work stoppages (an average of more than 1 per week). In 1979, with governmental assistance, the parties embarked on a relationships by objectives (RBO) process, which was followed by a reduction in the level of overt conflict (27 work stoppages in 1979 and none in 1980). However, those years also saw a dramatic series of layoffs (total employment went from 2,499 in 1978 to 2,148 in 1979 to 819 in 1980). By March 1981, the union formally withdrew from the RBO program, stating that it had lost its momentum, and the parties also rejected a proposed sociotechnical redesign of the facility.

In 1982, a joint safety program was begun at the facility; in 1983, an SPC program was established with hourly trainers; and in 1984, the parties established an employee involvement program. Each of these fostering initiatives was preceded by joint discussion and off-site planning sessions and involved extensive training of joint steering committees, appointed facilitators, and hourly workers.

All three fostering programs were in place when management pressed to increase the portion of the day that workers were at their machines and to prohibit them from spending breaks in the cafeteria. The program to increase the fraction of the day spent on the job achieved compliance from all but a handful of workers. However, when one of the workers who had resisted the bell-to-bell program was disciplined for inappropriately being in the cafeteria, a group of about 50 workers gathered in an impromptu protest—recalling the history of wildcat strikes in this location. It was only after a series of meetings and confrontations that the disciplinary action was set aside and the formal pressure to work from bell to bell was replaced by the informal injunction for everyone to "use a little common sense."

The Phoenix Project

At Budd's Philadelphia plant, the possibility arose for the corporation to make a substantial investment in an expansion of the facility—but management indicated that it would only do so if certain changes were made in work rules and other matters. A round of special local negotiations ensued involving the two Philadelphia UAW locals (757 and 813).

In 1986, the parties reached an agreement to establish a greenfield "plant within the plant." Entitled the "Phoenix Project," the effort involved an investment of about $17 million to refurbish a portion of the Philadelphia facility and a newly purchased industrial site next door. At the time of the local negotiations, the main facility had 174 job classifications, but the new Phoenix operations—which were to be a separate division within the Budd Company (much like Saturn at GM)—were designed to operate with 9. Moreover, the subcommittee responsible for designing plant operations consisted of four hourly employees and three management employees. In this way, the Phoenix Project represented a bold step toward a new social contract around commitment and cooperation, but the question remained whether similar changes could be negotiated in existing facilities.

Negotiating Flexibility and Autonomy in Detroit

Negotiations over the 1987 contract began early at the Detroit facility, paralleling early national negotiations. The local negotiations focused on die changes—a key aspect of economic performance in the stamping plant since production is lost while these dies (some weighing as much as 50 tons) are changed for new product runs. The discussions centered on establishing a "hit-to-hit" labor-management committee that would provide oversight to autonomous "die transition" teams of approximately 20 craft employees. The teams' goal was to reduce the time between the last good stamping, or "hit," in one production run and the first good hit in the next run.

Local negotiations, which lasted about four months, faltered when it came time to draft a letter regarding the establishment of such a committee and an autonomous work team structure. Members of the labor relations department were unable to generate language that was satisfactory to themselves or to the union. Finally, the production manager turned to the union, which came up with acceptable language. In the process, however, it became clear that the production manager and other line managers were much more deeply engaged in this issue than was the industrial relations staff. As a result, the union began to speak primarily to line management in discussing the innovative work structure—with industrial relations playing an increasingly marginal role.

Shifting Patterns of Interaction at the Level of the Company and the
International Union

In the 1987 national negotiations between the Budd Company and the UAW, Budd stepped out of the traditional cycle of building inventory prior to contract expiration (in order to assure customers of continued deliveries) and then laying off workers after an agreement is reached. Management began the process by offering to sweeten an early agreement with the savings from avoiding the inventory buildup, which helped provide the union with an incentive and internal legitimacy for departing from arm's-length bargaining.

The formal negotiations began in early fall of 1987, continued for three months, and then broke off in mid-December. Even with the incentive of sharing the gains from not building inventory and the recognition of legitimate competitive pressures, the union was uncomfortable with the discussions. The bargaining process was directly contrary to the established practice, in which the union makes most of the opening demands in bargaining. Here, the company had a set of concrete proposals designed to improve its competitive posture—a shift that was difficult for union leaders.

Following the holidays, the company began a campaign to educate the union leadership and the workforce on the economic pressures that it was facing. The information sharing was designed not just to shape the attitudes of union leaders; rather, based on the experiences of the early 1980s, the company also chose to educate the union membership directly.

Management began the communications process by meeting with the union bargaining committee, followed by plant meetings at which the division president spoke to all employees. The plant newsletter became more business-data-oriented, and "Budd Bulletins" at the corporate level brought further economic information. UAW Vice President Odessa Komer spoke to management and helped to increase understanding regarding the UAW's interests. State-of-the-plant meetings were held, and there were issue-specific meetings with high-level Budd labor relations staff and UAW-Budd department officers. Management's emphasis on education and open information sharing brought the union back to the bargaining table.

The parties settled in early 1988, more than six months prior to the scheduled contract expiration. One key element of the agreement, beyond the early settlement, was the four-year term, which helped Budd secure a long-term contract for business with Ford. Given the extended contract length, the parties also established quarterly quality improvement meetings of the principals from both bargaining teams—a significant departure from the approach among the major auto manufacturers.

In many respects, the parties also departed from the pattern of the OEMs. In fact, since the settlement was early (only Ford had reached an agreement at that point), the terms of two or three different OEM settlements were not on the table (which would usually have been the case). In the contract, the union won a wage increase in the first year, but it agreed to have wage increases in the second, third, and fourth years of the agreement paid as lump sums (which would not be added to the base wage). While a holiday was added to the third year, there was a diversion of COLA benefits, and below-pattern settlements were reached on certain retiree benefits (reflecting the cost implications for a company that has more retirees than active workers). These economic features of the settlement were designed to provide value to the membership while also enhancing the company's ability to bid on new business. One last element of the agreement was that, for the first time, all of the local agreements were settled on the same day as the master agreement. The settlement was ratified by favorable votes from 82 percent of the membership.

In this one round of national negotiations, the parties departed from past negotiating norms in terms of the timing of bargaining, the length of the agreement, the substance of the settlement, the relationship between local and national negotiations, the approach toward ratification, and the structure of subsequent relations. The agreement between Budd and the UAW to hold quarterly meetings of the bargaining committee throughout the four-year contract was not part of the initial proposals from either side. Rather, it was an emergent solution to the challenge of administering a long-term agreement.

The parties have since used the forum of these quarterly meetings of the labor-management committee not just for quality issues but also for discussion of outsourcing issues, health insurance cost containment, and job security concerns. Thus, these meetings address some issues that are potentially very contentious. Given the scope of the issues addressed and the continuing nature of preparations to address these issues, the meetings are a significant move toward a more continuous form of collective bargaining—though the parties have maintained the issue-by-issue focus.

The stability of this new forum was tested when Budd opened a new facility in Shelbyville, Kentucky, and the union status of the workforce in this facility came up for discussion during a quarterly meeting. Budd was unwilling to grant the union automatic recognition if it meant including the location under the national Budd-UAW master agreement. The union was unwilling to accept what it viewed as a substandard agreement. A union recognition election was held in which local company officials campaigned strongly against union representation (reportedly contrary to corporate wishes). When a majority of the workforce did indeed vote "no," the leadership from the international union took personal offense at the perceived inconsistency within management. While hard feelings about the election persisted for some time at the national level, the parties did not abandon the quarterly meetings. Work still moved forward, for example, in the area of health care cost containment.

Outcomes

The relationship between Budd and the UAW continues to evolve and shift as the parties face ongoing pressures from customers, competitors, and internal dynamics. Still, management has benefited from negotiating a long-term contract, working with the union on key issues (such as health care) in a task force structure, and implementing a number of successful plant-level experiments with new forms of work organization. Labor has built tighter links to manufacturing operations management at the plant level, and it has begun to craft a stronger role in business planning and develop an internal understanding of what it takes for a union to survive in the context of what may become a living agreement.

IDENTIFYING PIVOTAL EVENTS WITHIN A FOSTERING
FRAMEWORK: THE CASE OF ANDERSON PATTERN AND
THE PATTERN MAKERS' ASSOCIATION OF MUSKEGON

Founded in 1931, Anderson Pattern manufactures permanent molds, dies, and patterns and also provides related design and machining operations.[43] By 1990, it had become a leading North American firm in a marketplace dominated by small firms. Anderson Pattern had 110 employees and annual sales of $12 million. It was the flagship plant for a company that included two plants in Michigan and one each in Ohio, Arizona, and Ontario (for a total of 200 employees and total sales of $20 million), supplemented by production arrangements with shops in Mexico.

John McIntyre, the president and chief executive officer, was at one time a journeyman pattern maker. McIntyre joined the firm as general manager in 1980 and purchased the firm in 1982 along with a partner. Since Anderson Pattern is a small firm, negotiations were strongly influenced by McIntyre's values and personality.

The Pattern Makers' Association of Muskegon, an affiliate of the Pattern Makers' League of North America, represented most of the workforce (about 85 employees), with the balance including supervisors, managers, the sales force, and office staff. Unionization was historically high in the pattern-making industry, with similar wages across firms. With wages similar and their skills in demand, workers would often switch employers just to get more overtime or more interesting work—a process that was becoming less common with the growing number of nonunion operations. For example, in Muskegon, only half of the pattern-making industry shops (four out of eight) were still unionized.

Jim Howard, the business manager of the Pattern Makers' Association of Muskegon, worked at Anderson Pattern. The workforce at all four unionized operations in Muskegon belonged to the association, with areawide collective bargaining. Aspects of employment relations (such as wage levels and benefits administration) were still governed on an areawide basis, but recent initiatives at Anderson Pattern raised issues of consistency and coordination for the union.

Managerial Initiative to Offer Profit Sharing

The collective-bargaining agreement between Anderson Pattern, three other unionized pattern-making firms, and the Pattern Makers' Association of Muskegon expired in 1984—about two years after McIntyre became co-owner. Most of the negotiations were conducted on an areawide basis, but McIntyre was the only employer to propose a profit-sharing plan. Bilateral discussions on this issue then proceeded between the union and Anderson Pattern.

At first, the union rejected the proposal, indicating that it had higher priorities and that it did not want to break from the area compensation pattern. McIntyre, who sought to more tightly align the interests of the employees and the firm, indicated that he was prepared to "give" the union profit sharing without seeking anything in return. On this basis, the union agreed to the proposal.

Over the years, the plan became a regular part of operations. Profit-sharing checks were distributed at a special dinner in August, with featured speakers and door prizes. In its first five years, the profit-sharing plan paid out $260,000 to a workforce of approximately 110 employees.

Bargaining over the Introduction of New Technology

A second major managerial initiative—this time on new technology—followed about one year after the profit-sharing language was negotiated. Anderson Pattern periodically replaced lathes and drill presses or added computer numerical controls (CNC)—all of which improved machine tolerances and consistency but did not fundamentally change most jobs. Much more fundamental change was at stake in 1985 when the president of Anderson Pattern approached the union with an offer to purchase a state-of-the-art machine center and coordinate measuring machine in exchange for flexibility to run the equipment with fewer workers.

Under the contract, operators could only run more than one "automatic" machine if no workers were laid off at the time and, even then, only for certain combinations of machines—which resulted in additional downtime and constrained the firm in bidding on new work. This was a key issue for the union. Challenges to this language at another area firm had prompted a two-year strike that ultimately ended in the decertification of the union in that location. Thus, issues of forcing and escape underlaid the discussions at Anderson Pattern.

In addition to union-management dialogue on the matter, there were extensive debates among the workforce. In order to address workforce concerns, the company president offered to let any interested employees travel to a trade show in Chicago that was featuring the proposed equipment. Although only 25 machine shop employees would be directly affected by this new technology, almost the entire workforce chose to go to the trade show. According to the union's business manager, the workers returned with a vivid understanding of how the computer-controlled equipment could operate with fewer workers and why the equipment was important in terms of staying competitive.

The fostering approach was successful. On May 10, 1985, the parties signed two letters of understanding—one for a programmable coordinate measuring machine and one for a vertical CNC milling machine. The wording of the letters was similar, with each waiving the "one-employee, one-machine" rule and guaranteeing that programming and related work would be in the bargaining unit.

Making Flexibility the Rule Rather Than the Exception

When the collective-bargaining agreement expired in 1987, so did the letters of understanding regarding the new equipment. The parties had to decide whether to abandon their experiment or continue to expand it. Management again took the lead in this dialogue, by proposing to eliminate the entire article in the contract on machine operations (Article XIX). Further, management proposed reorganizing jobs around work cells, where the operator's work would be defined relative to multiple machines.

Although the two new pieces of equipment purchased under the 1985 letters of agreement had generated the anticipated increase in work, it was much harder for the union to assess the potential impact of completely eliminating the contract language. This issue was a direct concern to most employees since layoffs within the pattern-making profession are generally made not on the basis of seniority but rather on the basis of work requirements and worker skills.

Though job security is an especially difficult issue to address for a small firm in a cyclical industry, the union took a hard distributive stance and indicated that management had to address job security before it would agree to the work cells or the elimination of Article XIX. After extensive discussions, the parties agreed that in the event of a downturn, a worker could not be laid off for longer than two months unless 75 percent of the workers in that work area had been laid off for more than two months. With this degree of job security, the workers agreed to eliminate Article XIX.

By 1990, new technology at Anderson Pattern included three work cells with two machining centers, one work cell with turning centers, two machining centers for model work, and two additional automated machines in a cell—with additional automation planned. What began as a special exception for two pieces of equipment had become a dominant characteristic of the facility. In the five years following the initial investment, the agreement with the union enabled the firm to spend more than $3 million, which was accompanied by a tripling in sales to more than $11 million (including $1.5 million in exports).

Training for New Technology

While apprenticeship programs have long been the primary mode for training the highly skilled pattern makers, the introduction of new technology surfaced the need for continuing training for journeymen pattern makers. Even before the investments in new technology, Anderson Pattern's policy was to pay 100 percent of the costs of continuing education for its employees.

Once the initial letters of agreement were signed for the purchase of the first two pieces of equipment, Anderson Pattern approached Muskegon Community College about designing training in the area of computer-aided design and computer-aided manufacturing (CAD/CAM). In turn, the community college successfully applied for funding for course development under the Michigan Department of Education's Quick Start Program. Anderson Pattern made this training available to all employees, many of whom expressed interest in additional training. As the employees' requirements were assessed, however, it become apparent to the community college that some needed basic training in shop math and other topics, while others were prepared for more than a single course.

A set of negotiations then unfolded between Anderson Pattern and Muskegon Community College, the result of which was that the community college established a custom-designed two-year associate's degree program. The firm paid the full cost for all courses, with the exception of a few courses in English and other topics. On the basis of this experience, Muskegon Community College approached other area employers about establishing similar customized degree programs. Further, Western Michigan University developed a customized four-year degree program that was specially designed for Anderson Pattern employees who had completed the two-year program.

The expanded worker training illustrates the increasingly multilateral nature of the employment relationship. Although the union was not a direct participant in the negotiations between Anderson Pattern and either Muskegon Community College or Western Michigan University, it was still a stakeholder with respect to training issues. Indeed, the training opportunities that became available for Anderson Pattern employees raised a set of internal dilemmas for the union.

Although the firm did not limit the number of employees who could enroll in the two- and four-year programs, it limited the number who were given a chance to work in the new work cell areas. The employer was reluctant to have all employees operate the new equipment for two reasons.

First, in each case, there would be a learning curve, with consequently lower productivity. Second, once employees had operated the CNC equipment, their labor market value would rise substantially compared to their just having had the coursework—especially considering that Anderson Pattern was one of the first shops in the area to have such equipment on site. From the union's perspective, here was a training arrangement developed by the employer, in conjunction with the local community college, that was ostensibly in the interests of all employees. Yet equity issues arose in its implementation.

Negotiations over the Structure and Delivery of Health Care

For many decades, there was an areawide union-management structure in place for the administration of health and pension benefits among workers in Muskegon's pattern-making industry. The arrangement arose from the pattern makers' high degree of mobility and the staffing flexibility desired by employers. Skilled workers were able to move from shop to shop, depending on the availability of overtime or particularly interesting work, without compromising their health and pension benefit coverage. Area firms were able to expand or contract staff rapidly in response to customer orders, which were highly variable in the auto supply industry. The administration of the fund was in the hands of a committee of representatives from each of the area firms and the Pattern Makers' Association of Muskegon. Traditionally, the joint administration of the fund was highly cooperative—with most decisions reached on a consensus basis.

While this areawide structure was still in place in 1990, it had become a source of great tension in union-management relations because of a series of changes that were (or were not) made in the structure of the health care component of the plan. The tensions dated back to the 1984 negotiation of the master agreement for the area, when the union successfully pushed for the employers to fund the total cost of medical care rather than contribute a fixed amount to a fund. This marked a pivotal event because it changed incentives that had reinforced the cooperative social contract. Subsequently, the cooperative administration of the fund deteriorated as employers sought to control their liability for medical costs while the union focused on whether the quality of care was being compromised.

Three years later, in recognition of the negative consequences of the arrangement, the union sought to return to the prior fixed-contribution system—a second pivotal event. This time, the employers resisted because their health care payments had proved lower than the prior fixed payments. Now, however, the escalation of health care costs posed a third pivotal event, and employers were having second thoughts. The union then became fearful of a shift back to set contributions. What had been a highly stable and cooperative arrangement had become a complex and contentious feature of labor-management relations.

The experience with health care helps illustrate how the substantive arrangements (fixed contributions versus defined benefits) can have a dramatic impact on the extent of labor-management cooperation. Once the union sought to move to a structure that emphasized separate gains, a source of instability was introduced into the relationship. The focus of subsequent interactions centered on a sequence of positions, each premised on the gains or losses of one side or the other. Thus, the health care negotiations represent a series of pivotal events that have had the effect of increasingly reinforcing the distributive elements of the social contract between the employer and the union.

Outcomes

Management at Anderson Pattern has succeeded in introducing new technology and increasing operational flexibility while still maintaining high levels of worker commitment and productive ongoing dialogue with the union. The union has broken from the area pattern and, as a result, helped assure a high level of investment in this business and a degree of job security.

SUMMARY AND CONCLUSIONS

Escape tactics as well as forcing and fostering strategies can be observed across the auto supply industry. Two and sometimes all three strategies can even be found interacting within the five cases presented. For example, both Budd and Packard are cases in which tactical escape was utilized via outsourcing, forcing played a part in concessionary negotiations, and fostering occurred both at the bargaining table and in daily relations. Even the Anderson Pattern case, which we have classified as solely involving fostering, can only be understood in the context of escape and forcing occurring at other area pattern-making firms. Also, the Anderson case includes plenty of distributive as well as integrative bargaining.

Two of the cases—AP Parts and Adrian Fabricators—were marked by unrestrained forcing. But it is instructive to consider which factors help to account for the fact that Adrian followed the contentious strike with fostering and AP Parts did not. In part, the contrasting experiences can be traced to tactical moves after the strike by both sides at Adrian Fabricators that helped to smooth tensions. Also, the ESOP structure, which had been a source of tension, became part of the solution as it was linked to mechanisms for employee participation and union-management dialogue. AP Parts, on the other hand, did not fully implement the flexible contract language that it had won—so there was no backdrop of subsequent continuous improvement in work operations.

Looking across the five auto supply cases, there are eight distinct time periods, two of which involved forcing, two of which involved a mixture of forcing and fostering, and four of which involved fostering. These eight

Table 5.3   Strategies Employed, by Periods, in Each Case Study

Case Study	Periods	Strategies
AP Parts (1984–1989)	1 (1984–1989)	Unrestrained forcing
Adrian Fabricators (1985–1990)	1 (1985–1986)	Unrestrained forcing
	2 (1987–1990)	Fostering
Anderson Pattern (1984–1989)	1 (1984–1989)	Fostering
Budd Company (1981–1989)	1 (1981–1987)	Forcing and fostering
	2 (1987–1989)	Fostering
Packard Electric (1977–1990)	1 (1977–1980)	Forcing and fostering
	2 (1980–1990)	Fostering

periods are listed in Table 5.3, which then becomes the framework for the analysis offered in Table 5.4 of the factors that influenced the choice to force or foster.

In examining management's priorities, it is clear that all of the auto supply cases involved some priority for work-rule and economic changes, but the forcing time periods were distinct in that the social contract objectives were limited or nonexistent. In all cases, management anticipated strong responses from labor, but the fostering cases were distinct in that management was prepared to include consideration of job security issues as it negotiated with labor. Alternative production facilities were key parts of the power equation in the forcing and mixed time periods. Although these options were often still present during the fostering time periods, the union's role as a gatekeeper with respect to its members became more salient in the fostering context.

Table 5.5 reviews the substantive changes. Since management was the moving party, we examine the changes from management's perspective. All of the cases feature at least intermediate changes in substantive agreements, and two cases—Packard Electric and Anderson Pattern—show evidence of large substantive changes. Four of the five cases also indicate movement toward employee commitment and union-management cooperation, with just one—AP Parts—having reverted back to an arm's-length relationship. It is important to note that this set of outcomes does not match the industrywide distribution of outcomes. Competitive pressures have led a large percentage of firms to embrace containment social contracts (and even to seek escape from union relations) or to focus just on employee commitment. We illustrated these dynamics in our earlier discussion of the TRW case. Nevertheless, the picture that emerges from our analysis of auto supply cases is that of an industry that is experiencing dramatic changes in social and substantive contracts in the context of substantial competitive pressures.

Table 5.4 Strategic Periods and the Factors Proposed to Influence Strategic Choice

| | Factors Proposed to Influence Strategic Choice | | |
Strategic Periods	Management's Priorities	Management's Expectations of Labor's Responses	Management's Perceptions of the Labor-Management Power Balance
AP Parts			
Period 1: unrestrained forcing	Management had a very ambitious agenda for work-rule and economic concessions. It had no social contract objectives.	The proposed changes were very unpopular with labor, which did not fully accept their business necessity. They were seen as union busting.	Management was confident and prepared for a strike, with alternative production capacity available. It underestimated the union's forcing ability.
Adrian Fabricators			
Period 1: unrestrained forcing	Management had a moderately ambitious agenda for work-rule and economic concessions. It had no social contract objectives.	The proposed changes were very unpopular with labor and seen as inconsistent with ESOP.	Management was confident. Workers were divided in their response.
Period 2: fostering	Management had a moderately ambitious work-rule flexibility agenda as well as a strong resolve to move toward cooperation and commitment.	Labor was insistent on employee participation in decision making and receptive to the need for change after a mutually costly strike. The union was seen as willing to work jointly.	(Power balance not applicable to fostering)*

*Note that in Chapter 3 we did not propose a hypothesis relating power and fostering (see Table 3.2).

Table 5.4 (Continued)

	Factors Proposed to Influence Strategic Choice		
Strategic Periods	Management's Priorities	Management's Expectations of Labor's Responses	Management's Perceptions of the Labor-Management Power Balance
Anderson Pattern			
Period 1: fostering	Management had an ambitious work-rule flexibility agenda as well as a strong resolve to move toward cooperation and commitment.	Labor was seen as insistent on employment security, receptive to the need for change, and willing to work jointly.	(Power balance not applicable to fostering)*
Budd Company			
Period 1: mixture of controlled forcing and fostering	Management had a moderately ambitious agenda for work-rule and economic concessions as well as a moderate resolve to move toward cooperation and commitment.	Proposals were very unpopular with labor, which doubted their business necessity and saw as inconsistent with the EI program. Labor was seen as neutral to social change.	Management was moderately confident. Multiple production facilities were available. The union was seen as a gatekeeper, and union contracts had historically been strong.

*Note that in Chapter 3 we did not propose a hypothesis relating power and fostering (see Table 3.2).

Table 5.4 (Continued)

	Factors Proposed to Influence Strategic Choice		
Strategic Periods	Management's Priorities	Management's Expectations of Labor's Responses	Management's Perceptions of the Labor-Management Power Balance
Period 2: fostering	Management had a moderately ambitious work-rule flexibility and quality agenda as well as a strong resolve to move toward cooperation and commitment.	Labor was seen as insistent on certain issues of its own, guardedly receptive to the need for change, willing to work jointly.	(Power balance not applicable to fostering)*
Packard Electric			
Period 1: mixture of controlled forcing and fostering	Management had an ambitious agenda for work-rule and economic concessions as well as a moderately strong resolve to move toward cooperation and commitment.	The proposed changes were unpopular with labor, which did not fully accept their business necessity. They were seen as inconsistent with past actions and with the QWL program.	Management was moderately confident. Multiple production facilities were available. The union was seen as a gatekeeper and was less subject to the UAW pattern.

*Note that in Chapter 3 we did not propose a hypothesis relating power and fostering (see Table 3.2).

Table 5.4   (Continued)

	Factors Proposed to Influence Strategic Choice		
Strategic Periods	Management's Priorities	Management's Expectations of Labor's Responses	Management's Perceptions of the Labor-Management Power Balance
Period 2: fostering	Management had an ambitious work-rule flexibility and quality agenda as well as a strong resolve to move toward cooperation and commitment.	Labor was insistent on employment security and input in HRM planning and was receptive to the need for change after past subcontracting of jobs. The union was seen as willing to work jointly.	(Power balance not applicable to fostering)*

*Note that in Chapter 3 we did not propose a hypothesis relating power and fostering (see Table 3.2).

Table 5.5 Changes in Substantive and Social Contracts Favorable to Management

Net Change in Social Contract	Net Change in Substantive Contract		
	Small	Intermediate	Large
No change from compliance and arm's-length accommodation		*AP Parts:* Major economic and work-rule concessions but not a coherent package; return to traditional pattern with new managers.	
Toward employee commitment and union-management cooperation		*Adrian Fabricators:* Some work-rule and economic concessions; moving toward business partnership with the union in ESOP context.	*Packard Electric:* Extensive work-rule flexibility and multitier wage system; partnership with the union rooted in lifetime job security.
		Budd Company: Work-rule and economic concessions at the plant and national levels; building a partnership with the union, also at the plant and national levels.	*Anderson Pattern:* Extensive work-rule flexibility regarding new technology; step-by-step construction of cooperative relations between union and management.

NOTES

1. Thomas A. Kochan, Harry C. Katz, and Robert B. McKersie, *The Transformation of American Industrial Relations* (Ithaca, N.Y.: ILR Press, 1993).
2. U.S. Senate Investigation Report to the Committee on Finance, "U.S. Global Competitiveness in the U.S. Automotive Parts Industry," Senate investigation no. 332–232, Publication 2037 (Washington, D.C.: VSITC, December 1987); U.S. Department of Commerce, *County Business Patterns* (Washington, D.C.: Bureau of the Census, 1986).
3. Robert McCaffery, *Employee Benefit Programs: A Total Compensation Perspective* (Boston: PWS-Kent, 1988); Harry C. Katz, *Shifting Gears: Changing Labor Relations in the U.S. Automobile Industry* (Cambridge, Mass.: MIT Press, 1985).
4. U.S. General Accounting Office, "Foreign Investment: Growing Japanese Presence in the U.S. Automotive Industry," GAO/NSIAD-88-111 (Washington, D.C.: U.S. General Accounting Office, 1988); Michael S. Flynn and Robert E. Cole, "Automotive Suppliers: Customer Relationships, Technology, and Global Competition," in *Is There Enough Business to Go Around? Overcapacity in the Auto Industry,* ed. Peter Arnesen (Ann Arbor: University of Michigan, Center for Japanese Studies, 1988).
5. Brian S. Moskal, "Fearing Darwin Was Right," *Industry Week,* June 29, 1987, 28–30.
6. James P. Womack, Daniel T. Jones, and Daniel Roos, *The Machine That Changed the World* (New York: Rawson Associates, 1990).
7. David Versical, "Adjust or Rust, Analysts Advise Auto Parts Makers," *Automotive News* (May 11, 1987), 40.
8. James B. Treece, "U.S. Parts Makers Just Won't Say Uncle," *Business Week,* August 10, 1987, 76–77.
9. Joel E. Cutcher-Gershenfeld, Michio Nitta, Betty Barrett, Nejib Belhedi, Cheryl Coutchie, Takashi Inaba, Iwao Ishino, Seepa Lee, Wen-Jeng Lin, William Mothersell, Jennifer Mulder, Stacia Rabine, Shobha Ramanand, Mark Strolle, and Arther Wheaton, "*Japanese Team-Based Work Systems in the United States: Explaining the Diversity,*" manuscript under review.
10. U.S. Department of Commerce, *U.S. Industrial Outlook* (Washington, D.C.: International Trade Administration, 1988, 1989).
11. S. Herzenberg and H. Shaiken, "Labor Market Segmentation in the North American Auto Industry" (*paper presented at the annual meeting of the Canadian Industrial Relations Research Association,* Victoria, British Columbia, June 2–5, 1990).
12. Stephen Phillips, "Champion Is Starting to Show a Little Spark," *Business Week,* March 21, 1988, 87.
13. *U.S. Industrial Outlook,* 1988, 1989.
14. *GAO,* 1988; Herzenberg and Shaiken, 1990.
15. H. Shimada and John Paul MacDuffie, "Industrial Relations and Humanware: Japanese Investments in Automobile Manufacturing in the United States" (working paper, Sloan School of Management, MIT, 1986).
16. Lynn Adkins, "Auto Suppliers Race into the Future," *Duns Business Month,* October 1986, 58–59.
17. Michelle Krebs, "GM Products to Die If They Can't Compete," *Automotive News,* March 30, 1987, 56.
18. Eric Mann, *Taking on General Motors* (Los Angeles: Institute of Industrial Relations, 1987).
19. U.S. *Senate Investigation* Report to the Committee on Finance, "U.S. Global Competitiveness in the U.S. Automotive Parts Industry."
20. Steve Babson, *Working Detroit: The Making of a Union Town* (Detroit: Wayne State University Press, 1986).

21. Katz, *Shifting Gears.*
22. Susan Helper, "Comparative Supplier Relations in the U.S. and Japanese Auto Industries: An Exit/Voice Approach," *Business and Economic History* 19 (1990): 153–162 Susan Helper, "How Much Has Really Changed between U.S. Automakers and Their Suppliers?" *Sloan Management Review* (summer 1991): 15–28; Susan Helper, "Strategy and Irreversibility in Supplier Relations: The Case of the U.S. Automobile Industry," *Business History Review* 65 (1991): 781–824.
23. Note the contrast with GM's experience with Ignacio Lopez. Al Fleming, "Suppliers Buzz over 100 Days of Lopez," *Automotive News* (August 3, 1992), 35; Al Fleming, "Call to Arms: Lopez Shows Charisma in Role as General of GM's Cost War," *Automotive News* (August 31, 1992), 33; Al Fleming, "GM Insider's Notes Outline Lopez Cost-cutting Meeting," *Automotive News* (September 28, 1992), 34.
24. U.S. Department of Commerce, *U.S. Census of Manufacturers* (Washington, D.C.: Bureau of the Census, 1987).
25. U.S. Department of Commerce, *County Business Patterns.*
26. Richard Block, Joel E. Cutcher-Gershenfeld, Ellen Kossek, Michael Moore, Debra Gash, Patrick McHugh, and Almira Gilles, "Research Report on Innovative Labor-Management Practices in Small Firms" (Washington, D.C.: U.S. Department of Labor, 1991).
27. Phillips, "Champion Is Starting to Show a Little Spark."
28. U.S. Department of Commerce, *U.S. Census of Manufacturers* (1982).
29. Joel E. Cutcher-Gershenfeld, Thomas A. Kochan, and Anil Verma, "Recent Developments in U.S. Employee Involvement Initiatives: Erosion or Transformation?," in *Advances in Industrial Relations*, ed. Donna Sockell, David Lewis, and David B. Lipsky (Greenwich, Conn.: JAI Press, 1987), 1–32.
30. Our analysis in this subsection draws on research conducted independently by Anil Verma as well as on later research conducted by Anil Verma with Thomas Kochan, Sandy Jacoby, and Robert McKersie.
31. Sandy Jacoby and Anil Verma,"Enterprise Unions in the United States," *Industrial Relations*, 31, no. 1 (Winter 1992), 137–158.
32. Anil Verma, "Relative Flow of Capital to Union and Nonunion Plants within a Firm," *Industrial Relations* 24, no. 3 (1985): 395–405.
33. Ibid.
34. Anil Verma and Thomas A. Kochan, "The Growth of the Nonunion Sector within a Firm," in *Challenges and Choices Facing American Labor*, ed. Thomas A. Kochan (Cambridge, Mass.: MIT Press, 1985), 89–117.
35. Jacoby and Verma, "Enterprise Unions in the United States."
36. We thank Professor Bevars Mabry, of Bowling Green State University, who facilitated access to this location.
37. This case draws on research reported in Block et al., "Innovative Labor-Management Practices in Small Firms."
38. The material presented on this case draws on "Packard Electric" (A) and (B), written by Elisabeth Ament Lipton under the supervision of D. Quinn Mills, Harvard Business School case no. 484–109, 1984, as well as other secondary materials and interviews with current and former local union and management leaders.
39. The southern U.S. locations no longer served as lower-cost alternatives since the IUE had joined the UAW in successfully challenging what became termed GM's "southern strategy" of building new, nonunion facilities in the South. Attempts to organize these facilities, which featured autonomous work groups and other sociotechnical innovations, had not been successful in the mid-1970s. However, GM's agreement to a neutrality pledge in the late 1970s set the stage for the successful organization of most of these facilities—including the Packard Electric operations—and the achievement of wage parity.

40. The majority of the material on the relations between the Budd Company, the UAW, and the CAW has been derived from field interviews. Also helpful were the following two publications: Stephen Herzenberg (with Joel Cutcher-Gershenfeld and John Chalykoff), "Labor-Management Conflict and Cooperation: The Role of Shop Floor Leaders," BLMR 131 (Washington, D.C.: U.S. Department of Labor, 1988); and Thomas P. Murphy, "Partners in Progress: Employee Involvement between the Budd Company and Local 757 and Local 813 of the United Auto Workers in Philadelphia, PA" (Harrisburg: Pennsylvania Department of Labor and Industry, 1988).

41. Joel E. Cutcher-Gershenfeld, Thomas A. Kochan, and Anil Verma, "Recent Developments in U.S. Employee Involvement Initiatives."

42. This portion of the case is drawn directly from Herzenberg et al., "Labor-Management Conflict and Cooperation."

43. This case represents a reinterpretation of material developed for a study of labor-management innovations in small firms, which was sponsored by the U.S. Department of Labor and Michigan's Labor-Management Partnership Project. The research team on this study included Richard Block, Joel E. Cutcher-Gershenfeld, Ellen Kossek, Michael Moore, Debra Gash, Patrick McHugh, and Almira Gilles—all of Michigan State University.

Chapter 6

The Railroad Industry: A Clash of Traditions and Pressures to Change

The pattern of change that characterizes the railroad industry differs significantly from that of the paper and auto supply industries.[1]

First, there is the rate of change, especially in work rules and staffing, which for most of the 1960s, 1970s, and 1980s was slow even compared to paper. However, when aggregated over several decades (1960–1990), the *amount* of change was large, even compared to auto supply.

Second, there is the *locus* of change. Until the 1980s, with only a few exceptions, virtually all the changes of any consequence resulted from industry-level negotiations and were applied equally by all the major carriers. To understand the story of change in this industry, it is therefore necessary to analyze the factors that have contributed to the national handling of key agenda items.

As the pressures for change increased, a number of carriers during the 1980s sought to make breakthroughs outside of national negotiations. We have chosen two as illustrations: Conrail, which negotiated dramatic changes in work rules and staffing against a backdrop of bankruptcy, and CSX, which sought (unsuccessfully) to fashion a comprehensive program of change with its operating and nonoperating unions.

Two other cases have been singled out for separate attention because they illustrate other generic attempts undertaken by individual carriers to pursue distinctive change strategies during the 1980s. Guilford pursued a strategy of unrestrained forcing reminiscent of a historically significant approach initiated by Florida East Coast (FEC) in the 1960s. Similarly, the institution of local task forces by Union Pacific (UP) with its operating unions resembled a series of yard-level labor-management committees that first emerged during the early 1970s.

Before turning to an explanation for the pattern of change that characterized most of the past three decades and an examination of four company-level strategies that were instituted during the 1980s, it is important to note that toward the end of the 1980s and continuing into the 1990s reductions in staffing levels across the industry accelerated, largely as a result of the national settlements reached in 1986 and 1991. We will return to this important development after we have examined the four cases. We need to compare the strategy of relying heavily on national settlements to provide the impetus for change with those strategies that involve taking the initiative and seeking to realize change by the negotiation and implementation of carrier-level programs.

PROFILE OF STEADY CHANGE

What changes characterized the industry, especially during the 1970s (the decade just prior to deregulation) and the 1980s (the decade of deregulation since the enactment of the Staggers Act in 1980)? Table 6.1 portrays several dramatic changes. The number of class I railroads dropped precipitously, in large part because of mergers. Consolidation of parallel systems may have run its course, however, since in 1989, the Interstate Commerce Commission disallowed the proposed merger between Southern Pacific, the nation's sixth largest system, and Santa Fe, the seventh largest.

The overall rate of employment decline since the 1950s, when employment exceeded 1 million workers, has been significant, with the workforce being cut by half every 20 years. Basically, this large workforce reduction has resulted from several policies pursued by the carriers. On the operating side they have slowly and steadily forced reductions in crew size, and increased the number of cars per freight train.

Significantly, the nonoperating groups, which account for about two-thirds of rail workers, have experienced as great or greater reductions. The number of clerks has been reduced by the wide-spread adoption of computers, improved tele-processing, mergers, and the centralization of work. For example, UP has reduced the number of clerical workers from 4,000 to 900 by consolidating its offices in one location. The shop crafts have been heavily impacted by reductions in the locomotive fleet (down 35% since 1980) and in the railroad-owned car fleet (down 42% since 1980). The latter changes have come through the improved utilization of equipment and by the acquisition of more powerful locomotives and larger cars.

Table 6.1   Structures of the Railroad Industry, 1970–1990

	Carriers	Track (miles)	Employment	Tonnage (billions)	Ton-Miles (billions)
1970	71	206,265	566,282	1.5	765
1980*	42	174,000	448,000	1.5	819
1990	17	144,000	248,526	1.4	943

*Year of the Staggers Act.

The reductions, however, were not uniform across the different segments of railroad operations. Existing labor agreements and safety regulations made it more difficult to effect deep cuts in some of the operating crafts. Where management was able to introduce computers and subcontract work, for example, larger reductions occurred. Historically, most of the important changes in the industry were driven by new technologies. For example, the diesel locomotive revamped maintenance practices, which, in turn, decimated many of the shop crafts, and advances in maintenance-of-way equipment heavily influenced the use of outside workers.

While employment declined steadily between 1970 and 1990, tonnage remained approximately constant at 1.5 billion annually. Ton-miles increased from 765 billion to almost 1,000 billion, as railroads steadily concentrated their activities on bulk shipments over increasingly long distances.[2] For example, coal, chemicals, lumber and paper, and agricultural products accounted for 65 percent of overall revenue in 1989.

Significantly, the seven large regional rail systems accounted for more than 85 percent of all freight moved by rail. They were Conrail in the Northeast, the CSX Corporation and Norfolk Southern in the South and mid-Atlantic, Burlington Northern in the Midwest and northwest, Union Pacific in the Midwest and West, and Santa Fe and Southern Pacific in the West and Southwest.

Staying Power of the Traditional System

The decline in employment generally occurred via attrition. The resulting slow pace of adjustment can be seen in some data presented to the emergency board convened in the late 1980s to deal with a crew size dispute involving the Chicago and Northwestern (CNW) and the United Transportation Union. The carrier sought the right to operate all its trains with three-person crews. At the time of the hearing, the carrier was operating 35 percent of its trains with three people. It was estimated that on an attrition basis, it would take almost 20 years before all trains could operate at this level. Given the number of workers on furlough and various recall agreements, the carrier judged it needed three "attritions" for every position it could eliminate.

While some change had occurred, payroll costs per worker did not decrease. Indeed, the industry has remained in the top decile in the ranking of pay for major industries, exceeding the compensation paid to blue-collar workers in manufacturing.

Increased flexibility, a key agenda item in many industries and referred to as "craft consolidation" in railroads, was also rare. Similarly, few of the innovations occurring in manufacturing (such as extensive communication programs and quality of work life programs) were installed in the railroad industry. Several carriers—such as CSX, Conrail, and UP—have initiated QWL-type programs, but by comparison to other industries, the scale of such efforts in railroads was quite limited. In general, relations between supervisors and workers still reflected the dominance of rules and regulations developed over a century of railroad history.

Union-management relations remained at arm's length—neither acrimonious nor especially cooperative. Most railroads dealt with the unions on "their property" by carefully processing grievances with an emphasis on precedent and procedure.

Dominant Strategy: Traditional Collective Bargaining

Until the late 1980s, management strategy generally followed in the railroad industry could be characterized as conventional collective bargaining. In terms of our framework, management neither forced, fostered, nor escaped. Typically, the collective-bargaining sequence involved the employers pressing proposals, with the unions, for their part, resisting changes. Armed with the possibility of a secondary boycott, lawful under the Railway Labor Act (RLA), unions presented management with a united front and escalated impasses to the point where third-party intervention was almost always necessary. The structure of bargaining in the industry and the government's ability to modify settlements toward a compromise meant that the power equation remained balanced. For an individual carrier seeking to go it alone, the deck was stacked in favor of the unions.

The industry's approach of following conventional procedures preserved a degree of working accommodation among the parties. One important contribution of the National Mediation Board (NMB) was to help the parties communicate and to sustain satisfactory working relationships. Indeed, blame for the loss of jobs and changes in work rules could often be placed on the federal government. Since all major carriers implemented changes at about the same speed, individual union leaders could not be singled out as having been too "soft" in negotiations with employers. The incremental nature of the changes enabled union leaders during the 1960s and 1970s to preside over a steadily shrinking membership base without facing political upheaval. The political realities facing union leaders changed in the 1980s— a development we will discuss later in the chapter.

Explaining the Baseline

The inertia in both the content and the tone of labor-management relations, even in the face of dramatic declines in employment, invites explanation. The general expectation was that when employment shrinks, labor-management contracts would change considerably, as they did in many manufacturing industries, such as autos and steel.

Craft-based unionism. The distinctive nature of unionism in this industry was pivotal. Unlike the paper and auto supply industries, where there was one dominant union, railroads had a multitude of craft unions. This fact alone explains much of the work-rule and demarcation complexity.

Most carriers dealt with 13 to 15 unions. The three main operating crews were road, local, and yard service, with two major unions: the United Transportation Union (UTU) for conductors and trainmen and the Brotherhood of Locomotive Engineers (BLE) for engineers. Track work was performed by members of the Brotherhood of Maintenance of Way Employees (BMWE). There were six traditional crafts in the shops: machinists (IAM), electricians (IBEW), carmen (Brotherhood of Railway Carmen, which had become part of the Transportation Communications Union [TCU]), firemen and oilers (IBF&O), boilermakers and blacksmiths (IBB&B), and sheet metal workers (SMWIA). In addition, lower-ranking shop foremen were often represented by the American Railway and Airline Supervisors Association (ARASA), which was a division of the TCU. Employees—called hostlers—who shuttle locomotives in and around shops were represented by either the BLE or the UTU. Finally, clerical employees working in or around shops were represented by the TCU.

Thus, unions were a dominant force in this industry, and management found it difficult to deal directly with employees. Programs designed to enhance worker commitment were seen as an "end run" by the unions. And in several instances unions pulled away from quality-type programs that they initially supported. In addition, most middle managers came up through the ranks, having been union members and in some cases union leaders themselves. Therefore, the craft traditions, combined with worker solidarity, meant that in railroads, the unions were able to exercise a high degree of job control.

Strength of tradition. The current work system—including the mileage payment system, different rules for different classes of workers, explicit seniority rights, and extensive regulations governing overtime and delays—was a result of the very special nature of operations in the industry. Railroad employees travel away from their homes, often working under very difficult weather conditions and without direct supervision. The industry has been likened to a military culture, with a command structure and elaborate rules and regulations that are thought to be essential when resources are deployed at great distances under a wide range of circumstances. Company regulations and the work rules contained in the labor agreements in effect represented the "supervisor in the hip pocket."

Special legislation. Railroads were one of the first industries in the United States to undergo unionization, with industrial relations taking form in the late 1800s. The fact that the Railway Labor Act was passed in 1926, a decade prior to the National Labor Relations Act (NLRA), indicates the early attention given to labor unrest and industrial conflict in the industry. Whereas we use the term *New Deal* to describe the *traditional* system of industrial relations in paper and auto supply, in the railroad industry, the appropriate term would be *turn of the century* industrial relations. In fact, many of the work rules that have been in contention for the past 40 years were instituted during World War I—a period during which the railroads were nationalized.

Given an early history of strikes with considerable disruption in service (which quickly affect customers, especially those shipping perishable products), government intervened frequently to bring about a degree of order and dependability in the industry. Without reviewing all the emergency boards that dealt with such issues as the removal of firemen on diesel locomotives and the reduction of operating crew size from four to three and, prospectively, to two members, changes in contract language occurred only under the auspices of government commissions and studies—often quite literally requiring acts of Congress—and only after the passage of many years.

One emergency board convened to deal with the crew size issue reported: "This same dispute has been in one or more stages of handling for more than 9 years without any lasting results. Three Presidents, the Congress, the Courts, a Presidential Railroad Commission, various Boards and other Tribunals have been drawn into the controversy."[3]

One of the major effects of the RLA, therefore, was to reduce the exercise of economic power available to parties under the NLRA. The National Mediation Board guided the course of negotiations, requiring the parties to use lengthy mediation procedures before releasing them to "self-help"—i.e., strike action and even lock out, as used by some carriers in the 1991 negotiations. Given the public policy objective of avoiding nationwide rail strikes, the results were settlements representing political rather than economic compromises.

Structure of collective bargaining. A very centralized structure of bargaining in the industry—called industrywide "handling"—was the norm for many decades. From the union side, centralized bargaining facilitated the standardization of wages. And until the late 1980s, the major carriers preferred to deal with the unions in concert, largely as a defensive arrangement to avoid being singled out and struck separately. Thus, in national negotiations, as long as some degree of adjustment was taking place, the pace of change might be acceptable for most of the industry, especially for large carriers.

The continued centralization of collective bargaining at the industry level in railroads—in *contrast* to airlines, another major transportation sector governed by the RLA and NMB—requires some explanation. What accounts for the company-by-company bargaining in airlines that enabled most airlines to more readily achieve substantial changes in contracts and industrial relations (e.g., reductions in crew size and two-tier wage agreements) during a comparable period of deregulation?

First, it was easier for a new carrier to enter the airline industry and use its entry status to organize operations on a basis different from traditional practices in the industry. Second, it was possible for airline management to play one craft union off against another and to push forward with basic changes in industrial relations. With only a few exceptions, this did not happen in railroads—largely because of the coalitions formed by various unions and their willingness to observe the picket lines of any striking union.

Increasing Pressures for Change

During the late 1980s, the pressures for change mounted steadily. These pressures stemmed from intermodal competition, escalating customer requirements, and expectations of the financial community.

Intermodal competition. The decline in the railroad share of ton-miles traffic in transportation accelerated between 1980 and 1990, especially after the deregulation of over-the-road trucking. Certain types of shipments and certain corridors of traffic came under severe intermodal competition. And as we will note in our case analysis, it was in precisely these markets that railroad management was able to negotiate breakthrough agreements.

The railroads' version of deregulation, the Staggers Act, enabled carriers to set rates without the approval of the ICC. The result was that carriers were able to couple a bid for new business with proposals to the unions to revise related work rules.

Customer requirements. Customers increasingly insisted on better performance and lower rates from their carriers. Since a growing fraction of railroad tonnage fell into the commodity and major shipment categories, large customers could exert considerable leverage on the railroads. With new operating requirements such as just-in-time (a development that trucking companies responded to quickly), quality service became the norm.

Expectations of the financial community. While rates of return on shareholders' equity moved up slightly (to the range of 6 percent to 10 percent) during the mid-1980s, by the end of the decade, financial results were again back in the range of 2 percent to 3 percent. One expert concluded that this poor financial performance explained "the unprecedented change in corporate structure. Specifically, pressure on railroad boards of directors to find new management teams and new corporate structures capable of improving the yield from an industry whose net property investment has been estimated at $45.3 billion."[4]

Emerging Objectives and Strategies

A number of indications suggest that key officials, especially on the management side, became more interested in exploring new options for dealing with the challenges they faced. Certainly, a growing frustration was evident on management's part. In our interviews during the mid-1980s with executives of most of the major carriers in the industry, they identified high labor costs and the carriers' inability to realize any significant relief as the central challenges. Most CEOs pointed out that labor costs as a percentage of revenue had remained in the range of 40 percent to 50 percent despite substantial increases in productivity.

A new breed of top management was pressing for the fashioning of new strategies. Many of these new CEOs emphasized standards and objectives for operations and industrial relations that evolved from their own experience in other industries that had undergone transformations in the late 1970s and early 1980s. For example, Mike Walsh, who served a major stint as CEO of Union Pacific, spent a large part of his career working for Cummins, the diesel engine manufacturer—a company that pioneered reform in work organization and the development of high-commitment systems. Significantly, he promulgated some very ambitious goals for improving operating performance at UP.

At two other railroads, key executives entered the industry from the ranks of government economists—in fact, from agencies where the ideas for deregulation were formulated. Both John Snow, CEO of CSX, and Darius Gaskins, CEO during the 1980s at Burlington Northern, hold Ph.D.'s, and it is significant that they attempted to chart new strategies for their respective companies.

A strong indication of top management's willingness to try new options can be seen in the new and very complex bargaining structure that emerged in the early 1990s. Instead of a very consolidated structure for negotiations, considerable fragmentation occurred, with some carriers participating in national handling with some unions but not others, and with some subjects on the main-table agenda (like health and welfare) and others discussed locally. The matrix of craft unions versus agenda items presents a different profile for each of the major carriers.

Management's Agenda

While compensation costs stand high in the league tables of major U.S. industries (railroad workers' wages averaged approximately $40,000 per year in 1990), reduction in payroll costs per worker was *not* a priority. (One executive commented that he would willingly pay $60,000 if work rules could be substantially revised.) Rather, management's main objectives were to reduce personnel, achieve flexibility in the deployment of personnel, and gradually revise the industry's elaborate fringe benefits programs.

A related priority was the revamping of work rules and the annulment of arbitration decisions that required the continued employment of workers considered unnecessary by management. Unlike experiences in other industries, in which the staffing of new equipment was done to the specifications of the supplier, until the 1980s railroads found it necessary to continue to employ "full crews" on new equipment because of work-rule requirements.

Turning to the social agenda, most carriers did not seek to change the traditional compliance relationship between management and workers. With respect to the social contract with unions, the picture contains sharp contrasts. A few carriers were pursuing objectives that diverged from the arm's-length pattern, either by seeking to weaken or eliminate their unions or, contrastingly, by developing cooperative working relationships with them. Case examples of these different "choices" will be presented shortly.

Labor's Agenda and Approach

In the railroad industry, the unions' primary objective was to preserve as many jobs as possible by ensuring that employment reductions took place on a voluntary basis. A secondary consideration was to preserve (insofar as possible) work rules and special payment provisions that typically accounted for 40 percent of the compensation package for operating personnel.

The steady decline in membership exerted pressure on the financial viability of many railroad unions. As a result, a number of union mergers took place, and others were imminent. Several unions sought to represent craft workers in situations in which representation rights were unclear. For example, the BLE represented all workers on several new branch lines. For its part, the UTU moved aggressively during the 1980s to be the "industry union" for railroads and, as a result, was considered for a time a "pariah" by the other brotherhoods: indeed, for several years the UTU chose not to be a part of the Railway Labor Executives Association. Significantly, the BLE, which for many years had remained outside the house of labor, has rejoined the AFL-CIO.

Most railroad unions appeared to tolerate management's long-standing strategy of gaining incremental changes in each new contract, primarily because this approach allowed union leadership to manage the inevitable discontent of the rank and file, who saw employment losing more ground each year. Union leaders in the railroad industry believed that they had done more than their share in accommodating to economic pressures and that additional changes should continue to be implemented gradually and not "by convulsion." When such expectations were violated—e.g., through management efforts to escape collective bargaining or drastically revamp the contract—then union leaders exhibited strong and sustained resistance (as we will see in several case examples). Such responses ranged from nationwide secondary picketing of the freight of a carrier that was struck (e.g., Guilford) to delaying the renegotiation of a new contract as a pressure tactic to punish a railroad that had subcontracted portions of its operations (e.g., Burlington Northern).

However, not all unions reacted negatively to carrier initiatives. In the early 1990s, several unions agreed to "deals," leading to dramatic changes in work rules and operating arrangements. For example, the BLE stepped forward to be the sole representative (at least for operating employees) for a regional carrier, the Montana Rail Link spun off from BN.

Generally, the unions' response to a management strategy of fostering was one of cautious support. For example, the union representing clerks, the Transportation Communications Union, worked collaboratively with a number of companies to negotiate contracts for new computer facilities. And more significantly, the BMWE during the 1980s, under the leadership of Jeff Zeh, hired a quality consultant and advanced proposals for reducing the seasonality of employment and increasing the operating flexibility of repair gangs. All of these examples evidenced a growing willingness on the part of several railroad unions to address economic issues facing the industry or, viewed from a pragmatic perspective, to take the initiative in an environment of intense union rivalry.

With respect to the social contract at the local level, the picture has remained generally arm's-length. An important factor perpetuating the status quo was that the jurisdictions of some local chairmen cut across several carriers, especially where small carriers were involved, making it difficult to respond to an overture for more cooperation from an individual carrier. Certainly, the many levels within the union structure (RLEA, national union, regional and local leadership) tended to impede positive responses to the fostering initiatives of individual carriers. While certain subjects, such as health and safety and substance abuse, had been handled jointly for some time, the emergence of other forms of labor-management cooperation were extremely limited.

EMERGENCE OF DISTINCTIVE STRATEGIES

The key factor motivating individual carriers' efforts to realize change during the 1980s was the less-than-desired pace of national negotiations. While a few carriers continued to rely exclusively on industrywide handling, many resorted to strategies that could be initiated at the company level and would supplement any changes realized at the industry level.

We have grouped the various examples into the broad categories of escape, partial escape, forcing, fostering, and a mixed strategy.

The escape option was, for the most part, not available to railroads, which were largely bound to existing track and facilities. Even more than the paper industry (in which companies are site-committed due to their large investments), the railroad industry is very much "embedded," with its capital fixed in place. However, if escape is defined as moving out from under collective bargaining with a particular union, as was done in the 1960s by Florida East Coast (FEC) and more recently by Guilford, then the escape option was available for railroads, albeit difficult to execute.

Guilford, one of our four cases, will be examined in detail shortly. In terms of strategy, it can be classified as either unrestrained forcing or escape, to the extent that the company has been successful in sustaining its desire to deal with the UTU for all its unionized employees.

Florida East Coast. This case provides one of the earliest and most dramatic examples of the use of an escape strategy to force change, especially at the system level. After having operated for decades in receivership, FEC was recapitalized in 1960 and began operating under new management on January 1, 1961. One year later, the FEC withdrew from national handling of negotiations for its nonoperating employee unions.

Eventually, negotiations between FEC and its nonoperating unions broke down when FEC refused to follow the wage-increase pattern that had been established in national negotiations. Picket lines set up by the nonoperating unions were honored by the operating unions. One week later, FEC staffed trains with supervisors and former strikers. By late summer 1963, FEC had hired sufficient replacements to restore full freight service. Passenger service was eventually restored two years after the strike but was then permanently discontinued a few years later.

Although FEC managed to restore operations relatively quickly, its battle with the unions was long and acrimonious. The Justice Department and the affected unions took the dispute through the federal court system in a process that lasted three years. Shippers, civic groups, and business organizations filed numerous complaints, alleging service problems on FEC's part. The Florida Public Utilities Commission, the Department of Defense, the Department of Labor, and NASA all conducted inquiries and issued special reports. A December 1963 presidential emergency board report found FEC's claims about its financial position and inability to pay to be inconclusive and recommended that the parties adopt the national wage pattern. FEC management refused to comply.

Subsequently, in 1984 FEC reported its first profit in 30 years. One account noted that in 1987, FEC "had the lowest operating ratio [ratio of expenses to revenues], lowest labor cost percentage, and highest profit percentage of any Class I American railroad. After the onset of the strike, FEC used a two-person crew for most of its runs and was the first railroad in the United States to eliminate cabooses from main line service."[5]

The pattern of union representation that eventually emerged was quite different from that existing prior to the strike. An independent union, the Florida Federation of Railway Employees (FFRE), represented all workers except trainmen, who remained unorganized. The FFRE resembled an enterprise union with separate representatives for the various crafts.

What are the implications of the FEC experience—a story that goes back almost 30 years—to the crucial management decision to continue operations in the face of strike? We can summarize the broad outlines. After the strike started and management continued to operate the railroad with replacement personnel, a long period ensued during which the atmosphere could be described as very tumultuous. By 1990, other railroads looking at Florida East Coast saw a railroad that was operating with a single union and with streamlined "crew consist" arrangements. They also saw a railroad that was continuing to improve in profitability. What these onlookers might not recognize was the size of the investment required to bring about the operating benefits that eventually emerged. The costs were large in terms of operating problems, turmoil, and the emotional drain inherent in a situation of potential violence and community polarization.

In our research, we encountered railroad executives who held strong views about the FEC story. The comment of a vice president of industrial relations of a large national carrier is typical of one perspective: "The FEC story is irrelevant. There is no applicability of their strategy to the rest of the industry when you realize that this is a small, 300-mile railroad in one corner of the country." On the other hand, a top official at Guilford Industries, who clearly saw FEC as a pioneer and in some ways a model that Guilford management has found instructive, observed: "Only now [1989], over 25 years after the FEC strike, has the railroad press finally begun to recognize the accomplishments of this railroad [FEC]. The industry is both clubby and conservative and looks with extreme skepticism on any company that breaks out of the mold."

Partial Escape

The steps taken by many railroads to subcontract various functions and to spin off feeder lines to third parties can be seen as a *partial* form of escape. Given the low rate of return in the railroad industry and the deeply held belief that industrial relations arrangements have been "locked up," it is not surprising that top management of the holding companies cast a critical eye on those parts of the business that might be sold off or contracted out as separate business entities.

Some companies pursued the contracting-out mode. For example, Burlington Northern (BN), in constructing a new terminal in Seattle, chose to have it operated by a separate company with BN purchasing the services. The same railroad contracted with General Electric and General Motors to supply "power by the hour": the locomotives were supplied by these two manufacturers, using BN operating crews, with the maintenance work being supervised by personnel from GE and GM.

Short lines. By far the most commonly used form of partial escape occurred in the sale of peripheral parts of the business. Based on AAR's surveys, it appears that short or regional railroads employed slightly more than 10,000 workers and operated more than approximately 25,000 miles of track.[6] The Illinois Central Railroad was one of the largest users of this strategy, having spun off a large percentage of its track to new companies formed to operate these branch lines.

The restructuring opportunity presented by subcontracting a portion of the operations or by selling off a piece of the business enabled the prospective buyer to exert considerable leverage over the terms and conditions of employment. Many of the new branch lines operated without unions, and consequently, managements of these lines were free to establish pay and work arrangements in line with what they considered "market arrangements." Usually, this meant simplifying the classifications, compensating on a salary basis, cross-utilizing personnel to a considerable extent, and instituting new payment plans such as profit sharing and gain sharing.

Faced with the prospect of the sale of part of the business, railroad unions pursued several options. Some allowed it to happen and sought to represent the employees under new ownership arrangements. Unions such as UTU and BLE responded to branch lines opportunistically and were willing to negotiate new contracts in order to continue existing representation rights or secure new ones. Other unions fought the railroads' presumed right to conduct the sales with petitions before the National Mediation Board, various courts, and even Congress itself. As of the late 1980s, the legal status of branch line divestment was somewhat in doubt. Railroad labor agreements did not prevent contracting out work or selling parts of the business, although under some interpretations, such a reorganization could be deemed a merger, making the affected workers eligible to receive protection of pay and benefits for six years.[7]

Significantly, in only a few instances did the threatened sale of a portion of the business produce sufficient concessions for the divestment to be called off. If a union agreed to a change in the contract because of the threatened sale of part of the business, internal differences were generally intensified. When the quid pro quo for the proposed concessions was the preservation of jobs that many believe would *not* be lost ("The company is only bluffing") or would be lost regardless ("We are on a slippery slope"), then union leadership faced a difficult task in developing consensus and support for concessions that could help avoid the restructuring. In our interviews, several labor leaders confided that their roles would be made easier if management were to act more aggressively in educating the workforce about the economic imperatives that required divestment.

This version of the escape strategy can be seen as an integral part of more general forcing and fostering strategies that many companies were pursuing to transform operations that heretofore had resisted change. The partial escape maneuver sent a signal to workers and unions that management was determined to become more profitable and served as a powerful object lesson. Certainly, 10,000 workers (employed on short lines) out of an industry of approximately 300,000 is not a large proportion. And even with the best estimates that the extent of branch lines might double or even triple, the proportion of the industry that could ultimately be affected amounted to 10 percent or, at most, 20 percent. However, this "edge" could exert considerable leverage on the core of the industry.

Forcing

Given the amount of excess personnel (as perceived by management), the benefits from continuing (and accelerating) the reduction of the workforce appeared substantial. However, if management sought to align existing personnel to the "ideal" more rapidly by insisting on work-rule and crew size changes, then negotiations could easily become confrontational.

The feasibility of management's "staying the course" with a company-level strategy of forcing change depended on a power equation that included management's ability to operate the system with supervisors and possibly with replacements; union countermoves, including a secondary boycott, with the possible escalation of the dispute to a nationwide emergency; and federal officials' response to such a development.

Most carriers, however, did not want to embark on a change strategy involving such high stakes. For most carriers, it was preferable to remain in national handling as a means of securing some of the relief they might have sought by pursuing an individual forcing strategy. Consequently, the forcing strategy—to the extent that it was employed at the carrier level—more often involved the use of lower-level threats rather than replacement of the workforce and included the possibility of selling a piece of the business or using the offices of a third party to dictate a settlement that could then be accepted as a *fait accompli.*

Conrail, a case study that will be examined in some detail, successfully executed a strategy with significant elements of forcing because it found itself in the compelling circumstances of bankruptcy, with the government dictating the conditions under which a bailout would be available.

Implementation of new technology. In this variant of the use of negative inducements, employers in effect say to the unions and workers: "We need your cooperation, but if we don't get it, we will have to move ahead with these changes in order to ensure the survival of the business." Such a proposition can put considerable pressure on the workers and unions. The tactical challenge is to keep the pressure on and to escalate matters to a point at which the carrier makes credible its rationale for, and intention to implement, the specified changes but at the same time does not allow the dispute to escalate systemwide.

For example, the Santa Fe Railroad, like several other railroads (especially the Norfolk Southern), experimented in the 1980s with the use of road railers, containers with two sets of wheels, one for highway and the other for railroad operations. Santa Fe thought it had agreement from the unions to conduct a test with General Motors, the equipment supplier, but it became apparent that two regional UTU chairmen were not supportive. Consequently, when management commenced the test, picket lines went up at various locations. For the next three days, management personnel operated the entire railroad system (not just the road railer experiment). Management reasoned that it was important to see the episode through. Eventually, both sides found a "face saver" via the mediation efforts of a judge who granted an injunction.

Fostering

Most of the change strategies initiated by carriers during the 1980s could be classified as fostering. Generally, carriers perceived efforts aimed at improving social relations to be low risk. Not much might be gained, but not much would be lost either. While the agenda items of primary interest to the carriers (reduction in crew sizes and revision of pay systems) did not necessarily correlate with the possibilities of fostering, the improvement in attitudes that could accompany task forces and communication programs could nevertheless be valuable in its own right.

The one fostering effort to emerge during the 1980s that represented an ambitious attempt (and in this sense an exception) to restructure the contract and employment relations was the problem-solving process entered into by CSX and its craft unions. We will analyze this important exercise shortly.

Historically, fostering-type activity at the carrier level appeared periodically. For example, as far back as the 1920s, the B&O and Canadian National Railroads were involved in extensive labor-management cooperation with an emphasis on tapping worker know-how through suggestion systems.[8]

During the 1970s and 1980s, cooperation often took the form of local task forces created on a yard-by-yard basis to bring together representatives from all the relevant unions to discuss common problems outside the confines of collective bargaining. In the late 1980s, most carriers instituted communication programs focusing on attitudinal change.

Task forces. Over the years, many railroads instituted programs that involved workers in addressing major problems facing the business. These local programs placed considerable emphasis on sharing information with key workers and union representatives.

The first generation of fostering change on a project-by-project basis emerged in the 1970s. A good example of this early approach was the task force formed between the UTU and the Missouri Pacific to examine practices in the East St. Louis freight yards. Dan Collins, a UTU official, took the lead on the union side and traveled the country publicizing the design and approach of this program. Basically, the concept was "to find a terminal, take it as it is, change people's attitudes and do things without spending dollars on capital improvements."[9]

Two important ground rules were adopted: (1) separation of the task force activities from collective bargaining and (2) implementation on an experimental basis so that participants had the protection of being able to return to earlier methods if desired. After a trial period, a report was prepared, and the parties then decided whether to stay with the changes or return to the status quo ante.

The results for East St. Louis, for example, were impressive: time spent in the terminal on a boxcar decreased from 18 hours to 12 hours. In terms of cost-benefit analysis, the parties estimated that for every dollar spent on the program, the railroad had saved three dollars. And the East St. Louis terminal division ended up in first place in safety in 1976.

Given the importance, historically, of the task force approach in the railroad industry, we selected UP as a case study. A joint undertaking, called Labor Management Process (LMP), that emerged during the 1980s was typical of the many efforts made by labor and management (often referred to as "quality of work life" in manufacturing) to improve relationships on a yard-by-yard basis.

Communication programs. Several examples illustrate how carriers initiated a series of meetings with key union personnel to acquaint them with the business outlook and to engage key people in general discussions about areas of mutual concern. The Long Island Railroad (LIRR) instituted regular monthly meetings involving the president, other top executives, and interested union representatives. Union Pacific held regular work environment committee meetings as well as annual business update sessions that were attended by national presidents and other leaders of the major unions. Southern Pacific implemented a communications program that included periodic letters from senior management, open letters to employees on both general and specific subjects, and during negotiations, weekly updates distributed to all employees.

Customer relations presents another opportunity for cultivating greater employee commitment. Union Pacific and Southern Pacific instituted programs that recruited conductors and trainmen to call on customers, with each of the emissaries receiving extensive training in how to talk with customers and how best to present the company's services.

Our field research also uncovered one example of a communication program aimed directly at employees. Bangor and Aroostock Railroad (BAR) sent letters to employees' homes outlining in very clear terms the economic situation facing the company. Management reported that this communication program was instituted in large part out of frustration over negative results from its efforts to present economic information to union leaders.

Mixed Strategy

Several additional approaches could not be clearly classified into either predominantly forcing or predominantly fostering. The two examples that we present contain elements of forcing (in that the unions and workers involved were presented with hard choices), but the choices themselves emerged from a process that resembled integrative bargaining.

Inducements to reduce crew size. Starting in the mid-1980s, most of the carriers initiated buyout programs aimed at reducing the size of the work-force via voluntary separations. In situations in which workers were on the Furlough Reserve board (i.e., in layoff status), inducing senior workers to retire might not immediately reduce the size of operating crews, but it would bring the railroad closer to the point when it could leave positions "blank"—when all furloughed personnel had been recalled. At the start of the 1980s, the "price" for early retirement was around $25,000; then, it rose to $40,000; and by the early 1990s, it was in the vicinity of $75,000.

Another variant of the inducement aimed at reducing crew size was an *ex gratia* payment similar to the following. In late 1989, Santa Fe reached agreement with the Brotherhood of Locomotive Engineers regarding incentives to encourage engineers to work with reduced crews (without firemen). This agreement included an up-front payment of $10,000, with an additional $15,000 paid when the engineer retired. Moreover, for every mile traveled without a fireman, the engineer received an additional 4-cents-per-mile bonus.

Expediter agreements. During the 1980s, a number of carriers approached their unions with the following proposition: "If you will agree to reduced crew sizes, then we can go after some business that the trucking companies have taken away from us and bring it back to the railroads for everyone's benefit." Consider these examples:

- Santa Fe worked out an arrangement for the run between Chicago and Kansas City that provided for the following: if the parties were able to increase the volume of traffic above the baseline of 20 crews (with four workers each), then additional crews would be added with a two-person complement.

- Norfolk Southern owned a subsidiary, North American Van Lines, and made extensive use of piggybacking. Concomitant to establishing a corridor for fast service between Atlanta and Chicago, agreement was reached that when traffic exceeded 50 truckloads per day, then the crew size would be two persons.

- Other railroads reached agreement with their operating unions for reduced crews to handle special products and runs, such as a unit train from a quarry, "sprint service" from Seattle to San Francisco, and CSX's Orange Blossom Special.

- Southern Pacific reached agreement with its operating crafts for reduced crew operations on cabooseless trains for sprint service in Texas. Quite significantly, this concept began to be expanded on a systemwide basis.

This approach required considerable discussion and communication of information about the anticipated new business that would be forthcoming if the carriers could operate with lower labor costs. While, in some cases, discussions took place at the national level, for most of these agreements, the carriers engaged the local chairmen.

In fact, there were cases in which local chairmen were prepared to enter into these expediter agreements, only to find that the national headquarters of their respective unions were opposed. For example, one large railroad negotiated a package deal with a general chairman and then discovered that the national union would not hold the local chairman "harmless" if rank-and-file members raised any objections. At the time of our interviews, management was trying to decide how to proceed with an agreement that seemed to be to everyone's advantage while at the same time protecting the local chairman from political challenges.

The approach of "growing the business" had considerable appeal because existing crew size and work-rule arrangements for the core were left intact and the changes were instituted only for the new pieces of business. Expediter agreements were more successful in bringing about changes than the proposed sale of branch lines, for example, precisely because they were framed in positive terms.

Nevertheless, difficulties could surface with respect to implementation. Over time, the dividing line between existing business and new business would become blurred and make it difficult for the company and the union representatives to determine whether a given run should be staffed at the traditional or new levels. Since such agreements represented a "foot in the door," management might use them to set in motion other changes consistent with a step-by-step forcing strategy.

Staffing arrangements on unit coal trains for BN and UP illustrate these worst fears of national union leaders. For the particular piece of business in question, the BN route was shorter and required 150 crews, while UP required 200 crews per month. In the beginning, BN had the contract and operated with an engineer and two UTU personnel (a conductor and a brakeman). To keep the business, BN proposed to its local chairmen a reduction to "1 + 1." The answer was negative, and the contract went to UP, where local officials had agreed to 1 + 1 in order to bid for the coal business. Several years later, when the contract was up for renewal, BN convinced local union officials to approve the 1 + 1 arrangement, and subsequently, the business came back. So the employment numbers went from 450 to 400 to 300 in this "whipsaw." Naturally, many national union leaders viewed expediter agreements as high risk, with a potential for undermining prevailing practice.

Internal differences over the wisdom of exchanging work-rule concessions for prospective enhancement of employment also occurred across unions at the local level. For example, in an effort to keep a repair shop open, Santa Fe proposed a program whereby it would take over the work of several utility companies that owned their own railroad cars. The plan would have made it possible to get the cars into and out of the maintenance shop in substantially less time, given the proposed changes in work rules and craft jurisdictions. Management went to the unions and obtained acceptance from the International Association of Machinists (IAM) and the carmen's groups. However, the International Brotherhood of Electrical Workers (IBEW) refused to go along. Management then took the issue to the employees via communications to their homes. The deal was not accepted, and as a result, the company closed down a large portion of one of its maintenance shops. (The aftermath of the story, according to a company report, saw employees affected by the shutdown visiting other shops in the system to convince fellow workers of the need to accept revised work rules.)

Incidence of Strategic Options across the Industry

Table 6.2 summarizes the benefits, feasibility, and frequency of the various approaches that have emerged in the railroad industry during the 1980s.

The escape strategy shows high gains, but only over the long run, since implementing new terms and conditions, hiring replacements, and fashioning new employment relationships all require a substantial amount of time. As we will see in our analysis of the Guilford story, it was not clear in the early 1990s whether this carrier could weather the turmoil and realize the long-run benefits from reduced crew size, a revamped union structure (one major union), and the elimination of "arbitraries." While the escape strategy may be a theoretical option, it was not feasible for most carriers. Most CEOs were unwilling to assume the risk involved in pursuing the escape strategy: they were not about to embroil their companies in a long showdown with the unions.

Forcing can produce significant benefits, but the circumstances in which it can be used without creating an escalating dynamic tend to be limited. When Santa Fe operated with supervisors during the dispute over road railers, it did not cross the divide of hiring replacements. Rather, it sought to settle the systemwide strike as quickly as possible. Consequently, resort to this strategy was rather limited during the 1980s and early 1990s.

Theoretically, the benefits from fostering were potentially large, but in practice, the gains remained rather limited. The feasibility of executing these approaches that emphasize the improvement of relationships and "win-win" solutions was limited by the multicraft nature of union representation and an entrenched adversarial system.

Before considering our four cases, it is useful to compare them to the other approaches to change that have emerged during the 1980s and early 1990s. Significantly, all of these approaches were employed at the company (system) or local level, reflecting a desire to bring about change

Table 6.2   Potential Benefits, Feasibility of Implementation, and Observed
Frequency of Strategic Options in the Railroad Industry

	Strategic Options			
	Escape	Forcing	Fostering	Mixed
	(divestment of branch lines, subcontracting, hiring of replacements)	(avoidance of bankruptcy, introduction of new technology)	(joint planning, task forces, communication programs)	(expediter agreements, buyouts)
Potential benefits	High	High	Moderate	Moderate/high
Feasibility of implementation	Low	Low	Low/moderate	Moderate
Observed frequency during the 1980s	Low	Low	Low/moderate	Moderate

more quickly—i.e., on a faster timetable than was occurring through national negotiations.

These many approaches to change can be distinguished by the emphasis chosen for getting under way, whether the agenda was limited or comprehensive, and whether the scope was local or systemwide (see Table 6.3). Regardless of the starting point, the ultimate objective, in most cases, was to move to the lower-right-hand corner of the matrix in Table 6.3.

The strategic approaches summarized in the table do not represent the same degree of effort. Aside from the important distinction that a number of the strategies are peripheral and do not deal with the core parts of the business (e.g., divestment and expediter agreements), some of the strategies only deal with a limited agenda (e.g., new technology).

The table also indicates which of the approaches we have decided to illustrate in some detail via separate case studies. Three of the cases represent some combination of a comprehensive agenda at the system level: Conrail, with its negotiations to avoid bankruptcy; Guilford, with escalation into unrestrained forcing; and CSX, with intensive efforts to reach a breakthrough agreement via joint planning. The fourth case, UP, illustrates the task force approach to change.

Table 6.3   Approaches to Change

	Agenda	
Scope of Change	Limited	Comprehensive
Local business affected	Task force (UP)	Divestment (branch) New business (expediter)
System affected	Communication New technology	Bankruptcy negotiation (Conrail)
		Implementation of new contract (Guilford)
		Joint planning (CSX)

THE GUILFORD STORY: UNRESTRAINED FORCING

Guilford is the clearest example of unrestrained forcing in the railroad industry during the 1980s. What is not so clear is whether the parties actually intended to engage in unrestrained forcing. Nevertheless, after the company and the BMWE reached an impasse in negotiations, escalation quickly occurred, causing federal government intervention. Eventually, the dispute was settled, and shortly thereafter, Guilford responded with several reorganizations that allowed significant contract and union representation revisions. While some important changes in work rules were obtained, the overall social contracts were demolished. Even by the early 1990s, it was unclear whether healing would evolve or whether the parties would ever be able to reconstruct a semblance of working relations.

This is a complex story. We have highlighted the key elements of the approach taken by Guilford, which fall into four phases:

Phase 1: acquisition and expansion (1981–1985)

Phase 2: the BMWE strike (1986)

Phase 3: the Springfield Terminal concept (1987)

Phase 4: The UTU work stoppage and its aftereffects 1987 to the early 1990s).

Phase 1—Acquisition and Expansion: The Quest for Viability through Controlled Forcing

In phase 1, three railroads were consolidated: the marginally profitable Maine Central; the Boston and Maine, which had been in bankruptcy since 1970; and the Delaware and Hudson, which was teetering on the brink of bankruptcy. During this period, shops, offices, and other facilities were revitalized, and investment was made in labor-saving technology such as track repair equipment.

In late 1984, the clerks' union agreed to a series of changes that allowed the company to consolidate clerical work, thereby giving Guilford greater flexibility. For its part, the carrier agreed to severance payment benefits for employees who were affected by the changes. With this success in hand, Guilford continued throughout 1985 and early 1986 to negotiate similar exchanges: a supplemental unemployment benefits (SUB) plan with the machinists (IAM) in exchange for flexible transfer and consolidation.

Simultaneously with these negotiations, the BMWE began seeking, among other things, lifetime protection benefits for its members while, at the same time, Guilford sought to cap severance pay for redundant workers. In addition, it sought to create a single seniority district for the Maine Central, replacing the existing two separate districts. This meant that if additional crews were needed, members could be drawn from a statewide seniority district, subject to overtime limits. Clearly, such a composite district would reduce the amount of personnel needed, so Guilford offered a $26,000 severance program for redundant individuals.

In September 1984, mediation was initiated, and in September 1985, the NMB became involved. The company suggested a 90-day moratorium on any unilateral action, a plan that the BMWE accepted, and during this period, negotiations continued. Beyond the $26,000-per-person severance, the company agreed to match wage increases that emerged from national negotiations. However, the BMWE insisted on retroactive severance payments for already-furloughed employees, which the company promptly refused to grant. As a result, the BMWE went on strike on March 3, 1986.

In most respects, the positions and responses of both sides were in line with past behavior and with settlements elsewhere in the industry. At this stage of the story, the company was not seeking change that could be termed ambitious. Nor was the onset of the strike unusual. What followed, however, was unprecedented.

Phase 2—The BMWE Strike: The Shift to Unrestrained Forcing

At the start of the strike action, Guilford took steps to continue operations at reduced levels. In addition to using managerial employees, it hired permanent replacement workers to keep the system running. Two weeks later, the BMWE asked Guilford to reconsider its prestrike offer as a basis for agreement. However, the strike had changed everything for Guilford, including its decision-making basis, and it was no longer interested in the prestrike offer.

In May, the union started picketing at various interline points in the Northeast as well as at points in the Midwest and on the West Coast. Within weeks, the dispute began to threaten the operations of most of the major carriers, causing the White House to appoint an emergency board, which recommended that Guilford settle along the lines of its last offer. That recommendation was accepted by all parties. However, replacement workers remained employed, and as operating levels increased, the strikers themselves began to be called back on a seniority basis.

Phase 3—The Springfield Terminal Concept: Continuing the Strategy of Unrestrained Forcing

As a result of the strike, however, relations between labor and management became much different from those existing prior to the strike. In the fall of 1986, Guilford began implementing another aspect of its forcing strategy via an incremental transfer of some of its railroad subsidiaries to its Springfield Terminal (ST).

For some time, Guilford had maintained a small transfer line in Springfield, Vermont, with one union, the UTU, whose contract covered all the workers involved. As the result of several reorganizations, Guilford began a "paper" transfer of the Boston and Maine, the Delaware and Hudson, and the Maine Central operations into the Springfield Terminal jurisdiction. When questioned, Guilford insisted that because of the reorganizations, the ST was free to apply its existing UTU agreement, which permitted substantial flexibility, to the transferred operations.

However, management and the UTU were unable to reach a new agreement for the transferred operations until February 1989. The new agreement covered a number of issues: wage increases, new administrative bidding procedures, and displacements and reductions in force. One of the most important settlements included a mutual agreement to dovetail employee seniority in a way that covered all the various railroads that had been placed under the ST umbrella. The agreement also contained a moratorium on any changes through December 31, 1994.

Phase 4—UTU Work Stoppage and Its Aftereffects: Consolidation and Union Representation Struggles

In this most recent phase, the unions[10] (all of which had been "derecognized" except for the UTU) went on strike in November 1987. Their strike was based on the claim that safety was not being maintained under the Springfield Terminal arrangements. With 1,200 workers affected by the strike, Guilford management again responded by operating the system with supervisors and replacements—an arrangement that continued until June 1988, when the NMB ordered the parties into arbitration.

Numerous threats, legal suits, and countersuits have arisen out of the ST reorganization. Various federal agencies and arbitrators have had to deal with issues ranging from transferred workers' seniority and appropriate pay levels to furloughed workers' protection.

As of the early 1990s, many of the issues created by the various restructuring moves of Guilford continued to be contested by the unions before arbitrators and in the courts. The general pattern that appeared to have emerged represented gains for both sides. The unions gained a restoration of wage scales to prior labor agreements and the company retained the flexibility it had created with the Springfield Terminal agreement. Indeed, almost all of its trains operated with two-person crews.

Outcomes

From management's point of view, the gains included an approximately 30 percent reduction in break-even volume. A 20 percent decline in compensation costs was realized as a result of implementing contracts with lower wage scales and reduced crew sizes. Such dramatic reductions in labor costs enabled management to schedule shorter, more frequent trains—thus providing better service to its customers. In the past, it had been forced to hold up traffic in order to build longer trains as a means of gaining greater economies of scale—thus not providing the best service to its customers.

The potential downside was that unions might eventually prevail and restore the status quo ante, and thereby eliminate most of the savings. Indeed, the benefits expected from many of the new arrangements materialized very slowly. While flexibility and cross-utilization of personnel were emphasized (in fact, the signed agreement provided for salary enhancement as workers learned other skills), few changes occurred initially, primarily because middle management failed to take advantage of many new opportunities for cross-utilization of personnel.

By the early 1990s, the "bottom line" was still negative in terms of revenue and employment but the trend line was positive. Tonnage was still below levels existing prior to early 1986, and while profitability had improved somewhat, revenue was 25 percent lower overall, and employment was down by about 1,500.

Relations between the two sides remained very acrimonious. Of the current workforce, approximately one-third were hired as replacements over the course of the two strikes. Relations were marked by allegations of safety problems and harassment.

Initially, many managers in the industry quietly hoped that Guilford would succeed. To the extent that significant changes could be put in place, then they could be leveraged as models that unions would be asked to accept across the industry. It was reported, for example, that top management at Burlington Northern was watching the Guilford situation very closely. Indeed, BN had indicated in the mid-1980s that it was going to insist on changes and that it would be dealing with the unions outside of industrywide collective bargaining.

However, as it gradually became clear that the Guilford program for bringing about fundamental changes was bogging down in a series of arbitration decisions and commission rulings, the industry's attitude reverted to noninterest. The main outcome that other carriers perceived in the Guilford imbroglio was embittered relations. Given the high risks involved in the Guilford approach, most companies said, in effect, "More power to them if they succeed, but not for us."

Eventually, the rest of the industry (including BN) decided to steer clear of the Guilford strategy. Top management at Guilford confided that as the saga wore on, telephone calls from other railroads dropped off dramatically. In fact, as one of the top executives commented in an interview: "We feel like we have some social disease."

The Guilford story underscores the dilemma of adopting a forcing approach to achieve substantive changes without at the same time implying anti-union attitudes. If the desired practices are in place elsewhere, then management can focus on the need to match these changes for competitive reasons. But if the rest of the industry holds to a set of work practices that one company is intent on revising, then this company will be seen as abrogating the existing social contracts with its unions and employees.

In interviews, Guilford management asserted that it did not enter the negotiations with the BMWE with any plan of confrontation in mind. The unions maintain otherwise. But regardless of the company's true intent, when the union rejected what the company negotiators thought was a fair package, top management adopted a very different stance.

In effect, the concerned parties evaluated the initial strike from sharply contrasting perspectives. Going on strike was a normal course of action for the unions whenever the RLA procedures had been exhausted. For the company, however, the strike represented a pivotal event—"the last straw." When the union rejected management's offer, the relationship moved beyond the point of no return.

Certainly, a strike was the expected outcome of the union's refusal. So why did it push Guilford management to a new level? The union expected management to change its offer in small ways, which would allow the strike to be called off and the contract signed. If management stuck to its position, then an emergency board would undoubtedly be appointed, and a recommendation would be forthcoming that would "sweeten" management's last offer. But when management chose to continue operations, especially by hiring replacements, management signaled that it had decided on a very new course. What can explain this crucial development?

When management made its aggressive moves, it was, in effect, releasing decades of pent-up frustration over its inability (from its point of view) to deal adequately with the "labor problem." Although the settlement did not involve large financial stakes, management had reached its limit. The decision to move from traditional distributive bargaining to a strategy of unrestrained forcing also reflected the thinking of the CEO, Tim Mellon. The combination of privately held company and a small regional carrier operating primarily in New England coalesced to make management feel that the new strategy was both necessary and feasible.

Choice of Strategy

But why did Guilford management persist with a hard forcing strategy and implement the ST concept? When the emergency board recommended that the dispute with the BMWE be settled on the basis of the company's last offer, it might have been expected that the social contract would return to arm's-length—i.e., the businesslike dealings that had existed for several decades. After all, the company had obtained the changes that it wanted, and the workers had received acceptable levels of compensation. Why, then, was the company proceeding with additional forcing tactics by using the shell[11] of the ST to rewrite existing labor agreements?

Guilford's campaign to force changes in work practices and pay levels is explained by the fact that the company saw little value in preserving the labor-management relationship. Under normal circumstances, the labor-management relationship remains intact, and the need and/or desire to preserve it serves as a restraint on the behavior of all parties. But in Guilford's case, the social contract was already ruptured prior to management's decision to begin replacing workers when the BMWE struck. Since it had nothing to lose and was already perceived as the "bad guy" of the industry, Guilford continued with other forcing tactics, such as using the ST subsidiary as a way to revise all its labor contracts.

THE CONRAIL STORY: FORCING AND FOSTERING AT THE SYSTEM LEVEL

Another of our core cases, Conrail, also embodied some elements of forcing, although since "circumstances dictated the outcome," the approach followed by the parties remained very controlled. At the same time, distinctive elements of fostering were also present as key leaders constructed a solution that would prevent the railroad's breakup. In this regard, the skill and values of top management were critical in creating the climate necessary for fostering. After Conrail regained economic viability and was spun out from under government ownership, cooperative social relations continued and the parties began engaging in other joint activities.

Pursuing Mixed Strategy in the Throes of Bankruptcy

Conrail emerged out of the Regional Rail Reorganization Act of 1973 (known as "3R"). As a new entity, it consisted of the railroads formerly known as the Penn Central, Erie Lackawanna, Central Railroad of New Jersey, and several other smaller lines. Conrail began operations in early

1976. Over the next several years, large losses developed, and by 1981, with Conrail still losing money, its management developed a plan to make the railroad profitable once again.

After substantial analysis, management produced a plan that it felt was realistic, although, at existing compensation levels, a gap of $200 million existed. The idea evolved of bridging the gap through a wage freeze that would allow a 12.5 percent deferral of national wage increases. Concurrently, management also developed a plan for reducing crew size on trains— one that involved a separation payment of $25,000 per individual and required federal funding. With the federal government's decision to accept this funding requirement—and taking into account the massive rehabilitation efforts that would be entailed, the labor protection costs, and financial settlements with Conrail's various predecessors—the total price tag came to more than $8 billion. The buyouts alone amounted to $630 million in direct federal grants.

Several structural changes were implemented as well. Continuing its original consolidation plans, Conrail eliminated many facilities. The number of maintenance shops for diesel locomotives was reduced from 50 to 9, and those 9 shops went to three-shift operations as a way to make better use of plant and equipment.

As a result of these steps being incorporated into the Northeast Rail Service Act of 1981, Conrail could expedite its procedures for abandoning unprofitable lines. In addition, the number of local labor agreements was reduced, and most arbitraries were eliminated. For example, when Conrail commenced operations in 1976, there were 285 separate agreements; by the early 1980s, there were 23.

While negotiating and then implementing the consolidation program, management continued to emphasize the importance of maintaining rapport with union leaders and made strong efforts to handle the changes in an open and participative manner. This fostering strategy was supported by the values and style of the CEO and other top executives. The vice president for labor relations played a critical role in formulating the business strategy, and key executives focused on achieving constructive labor-management relations. Employees were kept informed of progress via extensive communication programs. Management looked for alternatives that would provide continued employment for redundant workers. For example, when there developed a shortage of skilled signal personnel who could work with new electronic technologies, approximately 300 individuals were recruited from other crafts and given both classroom and on-the-job training in order to qualify as signalmen—in keeping with the company's policy of affording employment opportunities to employees who had been furloughed from other lines of work.

A key player in the fostering process was William Usury, former secretary of labor, who helped the parties reach consensus on major portions of the labor relations program—involving such issues as severance payments, reductions in crew size, and consolidation of local agreements—and also encouraged them to approach change in a spirit of accommodation.

Intensification of Fostering

By 1987, Conrail had regained profitability, and the decision was made to return ownership to private control. This potential shift raised the question of whether the increased working accommodation forged during the throes of bankruptcy would continue. Several pieces of evidence suggest an affirmative answer. A labor-management program inaugurated in 1982 was expanded substantially. And in 1988, the parties instituted a joint labor-management safety program. Both these initiatives were guided by a joint labor-management committee, with the union representatives on this committee being full-time Conrail employees.

As of 1991, joint labor-management projects numbered 265, involving 1,700 employees. Facilitators were available to work with the groups, and different methodologies were used, such as quality circles and concept teams. A project usually lasted for a year. An illustrative project was the removal of electric meters from abandoned poles in Michigan, which resulted in a savings of $400,000.

Outcomes

Conrail eventually returned to profitability, but with it came a decline in employment from more than 90,000 to approximately 25,000 by 1992. All through freight trains and a number of yard and local trains operated with two-person crews. An interesting contrast is illustrated in the run between Chicago and Boston: previously, 9 crews and 53 individuals were used; by 1992, 5 crews and 10 individuals. Labor costs had declined from 62 percent to 36 percent of total costs. Although wage increases were deferred for some time, eventually they were restored, at an average of approximately $6,000 per employee, enabling most Conrail workers to more than recoup their losses, especially considering that they received Conrail stock when the company went public.

The picture is more mixed when we look at the social contracts. UTU officials gave Conrail high marks as one of the best railroads with which to deal. On the other hand, several unions pulled out of the joint labor-management program. In the case of the BMWE, relations became strained; for example, during the 1992 negotiations the BMWE pressed for strike action in an effort to avoid the industrywide pattern.

Choice of Strategy

The fundamental approach taken by the parties was not really a choice since the situation spoke for itself: "Agree to the proposed changes or face the uncertainty inherent in a drastic reorganization of the railroad." While this point helps explain much of the story, it does not suffice to explain the actions that began with the return of the railroad to private control in 1987. Instead of reverting to a more arm's-length relationship, the parties continued to strengthen their cooperative relationship. Having realized the benefits from fostering, the parties decided to continue this strategy.

UNION PACIFIC: FOSTERING AT THE LOCAL LEVEL

The Union Pacific (UP) story illustrates a type of bottom-up fostering. By proposing joint programs in areas where the ground was fertile, management hoped to fashion a systemwide change effort. The process took place outside of collective bargaining and was developed on a location-by-location basis.

The first terminal chosen by the parties for the labor-management process (LMP) approach was Kansas City, where substantial problems existed because of an earlier merger between the Missouri Pacific and the Union Pacific. The freight yards found themselves with multiple seniority units and a bifurcation of cultures due to the separate and distinct histories of the two organizations.

Specifically, in 1986, a group of managers from the Kansas City terminal met with local chairs from all the craft unions. The group agreed to experiment with LMP, adopting the goals of improving customer satisfaction, job security, safety, and overall communication. Like the earlier efforts in the industry during the 1970s, the approach was experimental and nonbinding. The idea was to see how well such a process would work at one location and then, if successful, export the concept to other Union Pacific facilities.

The next yard to embrace the concept was Fort Worth, where a key operating manager, who had observed the benefits of the Kansas City approach, insisted that the same idea be tried at his location. At the third site, San Antonio, the impetus developed differently: during a talk with employees at San Antonio, the CEO touted the benefits of the Kansas City and Fort Worth LMPs. Soon thereafter, management and union leaders inaugurated the LMP approach at San Antonio.

While the process was locally based and varied somewhat across locations, the structure was essentially the same. A general committee was formed consisting of all local chairmen, along with representatives from terminal operations, sales, and labor relations. Policies and project priorities were discussed at quarterly meetings of the general committee. A steering committee, cochaired by representatives from both labor and management, served as the implementation arm of LMP. Task forces coordinated projects in specific areas, such as customer satisfaction, terminal efficiency, and safety and health. Finally, ad hoc groups, involving a cross section of employees on a project-by-project basis, worked to develop and implement solutions for particular problems.

In 1989, Union Pacific developed a new, broader strategy for employee involvement. Building on the lessons from LMP, management launched a total quality management (TQM) system in which employee involvement played an integral and substantial role. The LMP process was de-emphasized and incorporated into the larger quality program. Attention was focused on providing financial and training support to quality improvement teams, which were structured either around particular tasks or along functional work group lines.

Outcomes

In appraising the overall impact of task force programs such as LMP at UP, it is clear that the benefits almost always exceeded the dollar costs. In addition, communications and working relations across craft lines were enhanced. However, these projects were not generally diffused systemwide, and in many instances, even the pilots were not sustained. In short, these projects achieved their (limited) objectives, but no incentives or "drivers" existed to extend such initiatives.

Participants in LMPs successfully identified issues that needed to be addressed and proposed possible solutions. However, implementing these suggestions proved more problematic. The LMPs operated at the margins of everyday terminal operations and outside the larger system. Without direct access to financial resources and decision-making structures, LMP participants found it difficult to effect change—and consequently, a degree of frustration developed over the lack of identifiable and tangible results.

In the case of UP, some new business accrued as a result of the Customer Action Program—an effort that mobilized off-duty operating personnel to call on shippers to better understand their needs and to enhance service delivery. Handling times also improved in the freight yards as a result of better coordination. But for the most part, the main effect of the task forces was to "clear the air" by fostering communication among key local leaders and setting the stage for the company's total quality management program.

LMP-type projects often follow a kind of life cycle, with momentum steadily eroding. For example, at Union Pacific, participation by some of the unions in the Kansas City and Fort Worth sites gradually waned. A "honeymoon" period initially existed, and during the first couple of months, substantial enthusiasm was evidenced as participants met and discussed a wide range of topics. Then a plateau developed, and interest slackened. While the parties attempted to meet this challenge by expanding the agenda and extending the process to additional terminals as well as to system gangs, LMP's momentum could not be sustained.

In comparing the TQM system to the LMP initiative at UP, a couple of differences are worth noting. First, the work of the quality improvement teams was more tightly linked to business objectives and customer satisfaction than the work of the LMPs. Second, the TQM effort was systemwide and integrated into all aspects of the organization's performance. It was therefore less likely to encounter the issues of organizational isolation with which LMP participants struggled. Finally, while managers at UP were committed to involving union leaders in the development and implementation of the quality system, the structure was designed primarily to foster employee involvement around quality issues. The LMP structure, on the other hand, was designed to emphasize and facilitate cross-craft communication and coordination.

Before we leave the assessment of outcomes at UP, it is significant to note that the economic performance of this railroad was among the best in the industry during the late 1980s and early 1990s. By avoiding the semblance of a forcing strategy at the local level, UP positioned itself to take advantage of opportunities provided by new national settlements, especially the 1992 agreement. By contrast, BN was unable to reach agreement with the UTU for its northern division regarding the principles embodied in the new national pattern until long after the industry settlement had been reached, primarily as a result of union resentment over the carrier's earlier attempts to spin off branch lines and divest other facilities.

Choice of the Task Force Approach

Union Pacific adopted the LMP largely because of encouragement from its CEO, who had seen the success of worker involvement–type programs in manufacturing. Management reasoned that there was nothing to lose by launching a series of task forces and perhaps the stage would be set for bigger initiatives.

In general, the choice of the task force approach as a change strategy (a moderate form of fostering) hinges on the importance that the parties give to the social relationship. Since task forces are necessarily implemented on a local level, an opportunistic quality tends to characterize their use. Where the parties perceive that the climate is right, then a joint working group is created.

In some cases, a particularly difficult or troublesome local situation may motivate management to propose such a vehicle for improving relations, and some general chairmen are more likely to respond than others. It is out of this chemistry of need and feasibility that the parties fashion this project-by-project approach.

In general, task forces in railroads did not grapple with agenda items of fundamental importance to the parties. Those subjects were, for the most part, addressed in collective bargaining, usually at the national level. The task force approach was chosen primarily for one reason: it has inherently low risk for the parties involved.

THE CSX STORY: AN AMBITIOUS EFFORT TO FOSTER

The most dramatic example of fostering via integrative bargaining is the joint planning project undertaken by CSX and its unions during the late 1980s. This case stands out during the past two decades as the most ambitious effort by a major railroad carrier to engage in a process with all its operating and nonoperating unions to design a comprehensive package of new work rules, employment protection, and gain sharing.

The main points of the story can be summarized briefly. As national negotiations ended in 1987, CSX management asked top union leaders from all the crafts whether they would consider a different approach to resolving the many long-standing issues. The company reasoned that if the parties began a planning and negotiation process before the 1988 start of national negotiations, perhaps they could achieve substantial and mutually beneficial breakthroughs.

The concept was jointly conceived by John Snow, CSX president, and John Sweeney, vice president of industrial relations, both of whom had extensive railroad negotiating experience. They were convinced that the parties could establish something more workable than the arm's-length atmosphere that characterized national negotiations and the drawn-out procedures of the National Mediation Board. The unions agreed, and so began an 18-month, very intense, and complex venture involving many meetings at every level of the system.

The first meeting was held at Greenbriar, West Virginia with almost every union being represented by its president. During the meeting, CSX presented a scenario that clearly defined its financial situation as well as its long-term goal of concentrating on railroading. Of particular concern to the company was the issue of overstaffing. CSX offered several potential solutions, for example, gain sharing, and expressed a willingness to explore various forms of employee ownership. The unions were given substantial time to question top executives, including those representing finance, operations, and labor relations.

One outcome of the Greenbriar meeting was a meeting of the executive board of the Railway Labor Executives Association (RLEA), at which CSX representatives were asked to make a follow-up presentation. As a result of the meeting, the RLEA established a task force for the purpose of considering the CSX ideas that were beginning to take shape in specific recommendations. A consultant, Brian Freeman, was hired to represent the unions' interests. Meetings were held between CSX officials, Freeman, and union representatives. During this time, the idea of worker ownership was discarded in favor of developing a gain-sharing proposal.

In February 1988, a meeting took place in Florida at which CSX presented the parties with an expanded proposal, and the unions were asked whether they wanted to consider the plan formally. Each union was allowed to frame a response, with the understanding that the company needed participation from unions representing a minimum of 80 percent of the workforce before it could proceed with a final proposal.

The plan embodied a completely different approach, on the part of CSX and its unions, to institutional and work arrangements. CSX workforce reductions of approximately 10,000 employees were suggested, with a concomitant separation pay schedule ranging from $30,000 to $50,000 per indi-

vidual. The realized savings would then be shared among remaining workers on a 50-50 basis after separation costs were amortized. Crew sizes would
generally be reduced to 2 people per train, and there would be considerable
flexibility among crafts in the repair shops. All the myriad details would be
worked out union by union.

Each union approached the deliberations differently. For instance, in the
negotiations with the BMWE, all the general chairmen were involved, subcommittees were formed, and progress was communicated to the membership via the union's journal. At the other extreme was the UTU, which
assigned to the sessions several vice presidents who communicated very
little to the general chairmen or the membership.

The BMWE went to work on the plan immediately, and in the ensuing
discussions, progress was evident as it sought to refine the proposal. Suggestions were put forth for a mutually beneficial arrangement that involved
a reduction in the number of seasonal work gangs, along with corresponding plans to stabilize the workforce by generating alternative maintenance
shop opportunities during the winter months.

In contrast, when the draft was presented to the UTU general chairmen—
at a meeting during which both Brian Freeman and CSX representatives
made presentations—the chairmen decided not to act. They responded by
saying, in effect: "This is the first time we have heard about this plan, and
we are not convinced that it is a good deal." After the UTU general chairmen
voted against the plan, CSX responded by sending a letter to all employees
outlining the plan's features. A number of labor leaders criticized CSX for
withholding information, while others saw the communication as an attempted "end run."

UTU officials opposed the plan because, of the 10,000 workers who would
be severed, 4,000 would come from UTU ranks. UTU officials calculated that
given the lopsidedness of the reduction, the savings shared by remaining
UTU members would amount to only 25 percent.

Another explanation for the rejection was unease at the sharp drop in
membership contemplated in the plan. CSX management later commented,
"If we could only have made resources available to the unions, we would
have been able to get over the rough spots." At one stage of the deliberations, it was reported that management offered to pay the union the equivalent of lost dues for a period of 15 years. This idea was later dropped when
it was determined that such a plan was probably illegal.

In a final-hour effort to salvage the negotiations, BMWE president Jeff
Zeh proposed that gain-sharing plans be developed on a union-by-union
basis. CSX declined the offer, indicating that it needed all the unions on
board before a gain-sharing proposal would be feasible.

Outcomes

On the positive side, it should be noted that the process introduced by
CSX brought about provisional agreements from several unions as well as

an imaginative plan for handling many of the industry's main problems. Greater levels of trust developed between many officials. Union leaders praised CSX management for its efforts to consider labor's interests. Richard Kilroy, chairman of the RLEA, noted that CSX produced complete financial information so that the unions could judge the "facts of the current and long-term picture." He noted that CSX's proposal did not claim there was a financial crisis. Instead, the company emphasized that even though it was still profitable, its present profit levels ($400 million in 1985) were not sufficient for the long term. Kilroy concluded by saying: "The first ingredient of a project of this magnitude is trust. I know there will be employment declines, whether I sit at the table or not."

The positive attitudes and improved relationships that emerged from this plan were apparent during ensuing local discussions over the issue of reduced staffing. CSX successfully reached agreements with several unions regarding separation programs that encouraged surplus workers to accept buyouts. For example, on the system's Louisville and Nashville line, crew sizes were reduced to 3, and the parties agreed to consider further reductions in the future. As a result of these buyout programs, over the 1987–1990 period, CSX was able to reduce its workforce by 4,000 employees.

Although the union agreements are voluntary, the company benefited because there was no gain sharing of the savings that resulted from reduced personnel levels. The downside was that the arbitraries and special pay rules remained in place, typically adding 40 percent to base pay. Under the proposed plan, these would have been eliminated.

Cooperation emerged on a limited basis. In 1990, an employee involvement program was begun in Florida. When a new computer subsidiary was opened, CSX agreed to recognize the TCU and train redundant personnel from other craft areas for the new information center.

Nevertheless, disappointment was also apparent, and there were those who felt that the parties had missed a golden opportunity to implement a comprehensive program. The UTU was the focus of some ill will because it did not ratify the agreement, thus forcing the overall package to be set aside. It was thought that other interested unions might pressure the UTU to reconsider, but this did not happen. Instead, the UTU distanced itself from the other craft unions, especially the Brotherhood of Locomotive Engineers, and pressed onward with the intention of becoming the "industry union" of railroads.

Choice of Strategy

In many ways, the situation facing CSX was propitious for the utilization of a fostering strategy. Working relations among top officials were good, and an opportunity presented itself to try for a breakthrough before the next round of national negotiations commenced. Certainly, the complexity of the agenda argued for a problem-solving approach.

Basically, the CSX strategy represented an ambitious experiment to determine whether an innovative package could be formulated outside the framework of national negotiations. Key leaders reasoned that they would be no worse off if discussions failed, and they might create a better basis or social contract for proceeding with change on a more limited scale. Others, however, felt that it was "crass" for a union to "sell jobs" and to allow those who remained (as a result of possessing sufficient seniority) to benefit handsomely from the deal. When this perceived inequality was combined with the realization that the union's size would shrink rapidly (with a consequent diminution in dues income), then a profound difference in paradigms was established. If the financial crisis had been severe enough (as in the case of Conrail) and the primary challenge had been survival, then misgivings about such matters as exchanging money for employment rights would undoubtedly have been less pivotal.

CSX succeeded in convincing top union leadership of the need for change; unfortunately, this conviction did not carry into the ratification process among the lower levels of the organization, especially within the UTU. The top-down approach almost succeeded, but ultimately, the leaders were unable to produce a change of attitude profound enough to convince members and their local representatives to accept a whole new approach to industrial relations.

The CSX story also highlights challenges the parties faced in coping with internal differences. CSX employees were represented by 13 different unions, involving approximately 140 general chairmen. Achieving majority support was a formidable task. Compounding the problem was the history of craft union rivalries. Company officials were simply unable to keep key union representatives in the same room and thus missed opportunities to use group pressure to work out differences. In fact, most of the discussions occurred within union subsets, and in the case of UTU, key regional representatives were not even present for these critical discussions.

From CSX's viewpoint, it seemed logical to design a program for reducing the workforce rapidly, thereby gaining more flexibility in deploying personnel and sharing the savings with the remaining workers. In formulating its approach to fostering, the company faced the challenge of both achieving as much participation as possible on the part of the various interest groups (as a way of managing all the differences on the union side) and at the same time proceeding with dispatch and concreteness. CSX leaned in the latter direction by choosing to crystallize a plan rather early as a way of focusing the negotiations. Tactically, it chose to work closely with a consultant who had been selected by several of the unions and to meet separately with the major unions.

While some unions leaders criticized CSX management for moving too quickly and not using a multi-union task force that might have achieved more buy-in both across and within the unions, the reality was that the unions were at odds. The company concluded that a specific proposal had to be put forward to test the feasibility of implementing a new plan. The prospect of constructing a proposal through arduous working group processes, only to discover that a major union was opposed, did not appeal to CSX. A cautious approach might have helped a more ambitious plan to succeed, but the rapid test of feasibility allowed the company to learn "sooner rather than later" that a multi-union program was out of the question.

From the outset, good working relations were required in order for the union leaders to agree that it was worth their time to engage in a "Let's see whether it works" process. While the overall relationship remained arm's length and while the effort did not achieve the substantive breakthroughs originally envisioned, the stage had been set for a series of breakthroughs. Subsequently a number of integrative agreements were reached on a union-by-union basis—agreements that contained many of the principles first proposed in the package that had to be set aside.

Having presented the essence of the change experiences at Guilford, Conrail, UP, and CSX, we now turn to the pattern of strategies chosen as well as a comparison of these local initiatives to developments that have occurred as a result of industry-level collective bargaining.

Negotiating Strategies at the Carrier Level

Several new perspectives have emerged as a result of examining these four cases. The long, drawn-out, acrimonious story of Guilford echoed the earlier FEC saga, which unfolded over a score of years before anything approaching normalcy returned. While negotiations initially resembled the traditional approach of industry-level collective bargaining—in other words, protracted discussions, supervised by staff from the National Mediation Board, concluding with impasse—once this stage was reached, the carrier embarked on a distinctly different strategy. The parties engaged in an escalation of power tactics that, as of the writing of this study, six years later, still had not run their course.

Another of the core cases, Conrail, also embodied some elements of forcing. However, in this case, "circumstances dictated the outcome," and the approach followed by the parties remained very restrained. Indeed, distinctive elements of fostering were also present, and the key leaders improved relationships as they fashioned a solution to prevent the railroad's breakup. After Conrail regained economic viability and was spun out from under government ownership, cooperative social relations continued as the parties moved to engage in other joint activities.

Conrail illustrates a very intricate blending of the two strategies. Indeed, the more we probe, the more evidence accumulates that both strategies were inextricably involved. The first phase, during which the breakthrough agreements were signed, contained much more attitudinal structuring than just the compulsion to save the company and acquiesce to governmental initiatives. On the other hand, the observation that positive working relations developed during the recovery and then continued when Conrail was privatized should be qualified in light of evidence found in 1993 that, for some employees and for some unions on the property, working relations had again deteriorated.

The other two cases fell distinctly on the fostering end of the spectrum. CSX opted to get a head start on the 1988 contract negotiations by engaging in a joint planning process with the craft unions in an effort to construct a package that would reduce the workforce more rapidly, with the resulting gains shared among the workers who remained. When this ambitious effort at integrative bargaining failed, the company shifted to a local focus for its fostering strategy. While many of these "deals" for reducing the workforce (via large severance payments) paralleled what has been taking place generally in the industry, CSX has been able to negotiate these arrangements more quickly and on a wider scale as a result of the improved social relations that developed during the deliberations of the joint working group.

Union Pacific's task force approach serves as an example of a bottom-up approach tried by a number of carriers over the past several decades. The emphasis was on improving attitudes in order to set the stage for eventually undertaking a CSX-type joint planning exercise or negotiating local "deals." The UP experience demonstrates the lesson widely learned from certain quality of work life programs—namely, that these experiments will atrophy if they do not evolve into mainstream efforts that tackle agenda items of real importance to the parties. In the case of UP, the LMP was superseded by a management-driven quality initiative program. The effects of these various programs at UP can only be fully evaluated with the benefit of a longer time frame than is currently available.

Profile of Outcomes

Table 6.4 portrays, from management's perspective, the range of outcomes for the four cases.

There are no systematic data across the four cases that capture the outcomes of unique interest to union members and their leaders. It is clear, however, that virtually all the national leaders who were associated with major fostering strategies, such as at CSX, have been defeated for reelection. The telling message is that any semblance of endorsing change in the industry has been detrimental to the political health of union leaders.

Choice of Strategy

Table 6.5 presents, in summary form, the evidence for the three key factors presumed to be related to the choice of a particular strategy.

Management priorities. Since all railroads embrace the objective of reducing staffing as rapidly as possible by eliminating historic work rules, we cannot compare those carriers that opted for forcing with those that opted

Table 6.4 Changes in Substantive and Social Contracts Favorable to Management

Net Change in Social Contract	Net Change in Substantive Contract		
	Small	Intermediate	Large
Toward containment and compliance			*Guilford:* Work rules revamped and more favorable union representation achieved, but at a considerable cost in terms of social relations.
No change from compliance and arm's-length accommodation	*UP:* Program superseded by management-initiated quality program.	*CSX:* Many of the gains sought via national negotiations ultimately achieved via follow-on agreements at the local level.	
Toward employee commitment and union-management cooperation			Conrail: Significant gains in work rules, with relationships generally improving over the 1980s.

for fostering solely on the basis of a substantive agenda. However, the carriers' objectives with respect to a social agenda clearly correlate with strategic choice. At one end of the spectrum was Guilford, which placed little value on continuing the existing relationship; at the other end was UP, which wished to improve attitudes as a first step in a change program. In between was CSX, which decided to capitalize on already good working relations to push ahead with integrative bargaining.

Expected response from labor. In the case of CSX and the unions, the social relationship was sufficiently positive that management expected the unions to be willing to come to the table on an exploratory basis. Management had invested substantial resources to cultivate an atmosphere that would allow the union leaders to embark upon a very different approach to negotiations. Generally, however, for most of the carriers in the railroad industry, the state of labor relations falls into the arm's-length category. And they found that it was extremely difficult to engage in a fostering process, given the large

Table 6.5 Strategic Periods and the Factors Proposed to Influence Strategic Choice

| | Factors Proposed to Influence Strategic Choice | | |
Strategic Periods	Management's Priorities	Management's Expectations of Labor's Responses	Management's Perceptions of the Labor-Management Power Balance
Guilford			
Period 1: unrestrained forcing	Management had an ambitious agenda for work-rule concessions. It had no social contract objectives.	Labor was not expected to be persuaded of the need for substantive change.	Management was confident it could force change.
UP			
Period 1: fostering	Management had no clear substantive agenda but did desire better relations	Labor was expected to be somewhat open to social initiatives.	(Power balance not applicable to fostering)*
CSX			
Period 1: fostering	Management had an agenda for significant work-rule changes as well as a desire for better relations.	Labor was expected to be somewhat open to social initiatives.	(Power balance not applicable to fostering)*
Conrail			
Period 1: mixture of forcing and fostering	Management had an agenda for significant work-rule and economic changes as well as a desire for better relations.	Labor was expected to be persuaded of the need for substantive changes and to be receptive to social initiatives.	Given the government's role, management was confident of its ability to force change.
Period 2: fostering	Management had an agenda to realize additional work-rule changes and to build on base of positive relations	Labor was expected to continue to support cooperative relations.	(Power balance not applicable to fostering)*

*Note that in Chapter 3 we did not propose a hypothesis relating power and fostering (see Table 3.2).

number of unions: it took only one union to block progress (as illustrated by the outcome at CSX).

Participation in anything resembling labor-management cooperation creates deep ambivalence for most union leaders. With the possibility of criticism from above and below, or from other craft unions, the response to most overtures for engaging in a fostering process is likely to be negative or noncommittal. In an industry with a standard technology and common procedures, any change, albeit acceptable to the workers directly affected, might be labeled opportunistic or a breach of faith by office-seeking unionists.

Power equation. In two cases, the choice of strategy appeared to be heavily influenced by power factors. For example, management at Conrail was confident it could take advantage of the compelling circumstance of bankruptcy and was thus able to use a form of forcing that made the case for the required changes very credible. Guilford management reasoned that it possessed the power to compel compliance since it operated in one small region of the country and felt it could hire the necessary replacements and see its forcing strategy through to completion. Similarly, the unions at Guilford also reasoned that they could successfully employ countervailing power to stop management from executing its strategy.

At CSX, key managers were doubtful they could actually force the changes they sought; moreover, they believed they had the vision and the process skills necessary to fashion an innovative and integrative agreement and to create understanding and concurrence within and across the various regions.

Choice of Separate versus Industry Negotiations

In a fundamental way, each of the four cases represents a departure from the traditional approach of achieving change via industry-level negotiations. Guilford's unrestrained forcing approach could only take place outside of "national handling." Conrail also found it necessary to separate itself from the employers' association in order to reach agreement on substantive terms that would enable it to survive and avoid bankruptcy.

CSX and Union Pacific (the two fostering examples) remained in national handling, although CSX presumably would have opted out of the 1988 round of negotiations if it had been successful with its joint planning exercise. In the case of Union Pacific, no dilemma existed, at least in the early stages of the task force approach. In this respect, the strategy followed by UP resembles other "local" strategies that a company can pursue simultaneously while remaining in industry-level negotiations.

How do we explain a company's decision to embark upon a strategy that requires separation from the industry group? A company following an unrestrained forcing strategy, such as Guilford, seeks to bring about major substantive changes on a rapid timetable even though social relations will deteriorate and the tenor of the relationship may resemble all-out war. Internal differences within the organization will likewise be exacerbated.

Conrail appears to have found a better solution in that there are no negative consequences to leaving the national negotiations in order to fashion an agreement to avoid bankruptcy (but few carriers would choose to be in that predicament in order to avail themselves of a superior change strategy). While the CSX approach failed to deliver fully on substance, it did produce major gains in social relations. Union Pacific's task force approach also delivered some gains in social relations, but the accompanying level of significant substantive improvements was lower.

Conducting a joint planning exercise of the sort engaged in by CSX and the craft unions requires plentiful resources. More important, it is not even possible to embark upon such an exercise in the first place unless there exists a substantial degree of trust. Top officials at CSX invested considerable time over many years before broaching the idea of a joint planning exercise. Most of the carriers engaged in an arm's-length relationship at the national level find that it is not feasible to enlist their union leadership in a search for integrative solutions.

The task force approach pursued by Union Pacific is generally available to all carriers. It does not require the existence of a cooperative relationship: indeed, one of the major purposes of this approach is to move local-level relations in a more accommodative direction. However, the unions' response will depend on how they perceive the carrier's motivations. If the carrier is seen as genuinely interested in improving communications and talking about common problems, then the response is likely to be positive, although guardedly so. However, if the carrier is spinning off branch lines, subcontracting work away from the core business, and engaging in other moves that weaken the unions' institutional base, then the union response is likely to be negative as increasingly has been the case. (A point to be elaborated on, shortly).

COMPARISON OF YIELD FROM CARRIER-LEVEL STRATEGIES VERSUS NATIONAL HANDLING

While the carrier initiatives were being shaped and implemented during the 1980s, the pace of change made possible by the 1986 and 1991 agreements accelerated, although this new trend was not readily apparent even after the 1986 agreements, which lengthened in increments the mileage limits for operating crews, had been signed. Key executives continued to argue that progress was too slow—prompting a wide range of local efforts to realize breakthroughs in staffing levels and work rules.

By the mid-1990s, however, with the 1991–1992 agreements in place, it was clear to most observers that a "sea change" had occurred in operating practices—or at least in the opportunity presented to carriers to implement long sought-after changes.

Among other items the 1991–1992 agreement provided for the following:

1. Immediate reduction of crew size for through freight to one brakeman, with eventual complete elimination. Disputes handled by local arbitration (binding), with the parties paying the costs. These crew changes estimated to eliminate 30,000 positions eventually.

2. Senior brakemen bought out at $50,000–$70,000, with other brakemen assigned to reserve pool and eligible to receive 75% of normal pay.

3. The length of work day for road engineers and trainmen increased in stages, resulting in a reduction of annual pay of approximately $5,000 per worker. By 1994, the standard run, which had been 100 miles in 1986, would be 130 miles.

4. Regional and systemwide districts for road workers were created, thereby requiring longer traveling times from home to work.

5. Craft workers in the shops required to perform other functions, up to two hours per day.

Commenting on the cumulative impact of national negotiations, R. E. Swert, vice president of labor relations at Conrail, in private correspondence noted that "The last two rounds (1986 and 1991) of national bargaining have produced far greater work-rule changes than at any other time in our history."

Significantly, Conrail's labor costs as a percentage of revenue, which were flat (about 41 percent) during most of the 1980s, started to decline and by 1993 stood at 36 percent. Similar drops were evident for the other major freight carriers.

Does this mean that all the carrier-level efforts of the 1980s were not necessary. On the contrary, the case can be made that local experimentation set the stage for the national agreements, especially the 1991–1992 edition. As a result of a decade's experience in operating special trains with reduced crews (in part, made possible by expediter agreements) and implementing buyout programs that established a "fair price" for personnel to leave the industry, the parties were able to build a base of experience that led to the principles contained in the 1991–1992 agreements.

Another function of local strategies, especially of the fostering variety, was to keep labor-management relations from completely "going sour" in the face of declining employment and union membership. Although with the benefit of hindsight, it seems that the prospect for cooperative relations was not bright. Specifically, a number of union leaders responded positively to overtures by individual carriers to fashion win-win packages. While these breakthroughs were usually accompanied by an improvement in working relations, eventually the tide turned against the union leaders who had been involved in cooperative programs, e.g., the presidents of both TCA and BMWA were replaced by insurgents, and by the early 1990s unions in general had withdrawn from quality and productivity-type committees.

Although pay and benefits remained intact for those continuing to work, the cumulative impact of changes in crew size, length of the standard day, and distance traveled to work—combined with the increasing downward trend in employment—meant that there were enough angry union members to create a political environment where "hardliners" were able to dominate the leadership ranks of the railroad unions.

NOTES

1. Amy Andrews and Rod Bloedow were especially helpful in conducting field interviews and developing data on which these cases are based.
2. If ton-miles is taken as the best measure of total freight movement in the United States, then the share carried on railroads has declined from approximately 40 percent in 1970 to about 36 percent in 1987, accompanied by a corresponding gain in the share carried via over-the-road trucking.
3. Emergency Board No. 172, "Report to the President" (December 13, 1968).
4. Gerard J. McCullough, "The U.S. Railroad Industry after Deregulation," in *The Transformation of Industrial Relations in Transportation*, ed. Robert B. McKersie and Gerard J. McCullough (Cambridge, Mass.: Center for Transportation Studies, MIT, 1989).
5. See Seth H. Bramson, "Florida East Coast Railway," in *Encyclopedia of American Business History and Biography: Railroads in the Age of Regulation, 1900–1980*, ed. Keith L. Bryant, Jr. (New York: Facts on File, 1988), 162–163. Also, for a more extensive discussion, see Seth H. Bramson, *Speedway to Sunshine: The Story of the Florida East Coast Railway* (Erin, Ontario: Boston Mills Press, 1984).
6. McCullough, "The U.S. Railroad Industry after Deregulation."
7. Basically, the issue is whether the guidelines of the ICC or those of the Railway Labor Act govern such a transaction. If ICC procedures apply, then the parent railroad would be free to make the changes (perhaps with the requirement that the affected workers be protected for six years), but there would be no need to put the unions on notice and to bargain over the changes. However, if RLA procedures apply, then the change process would be governed by the procedures of the National Mediation Board, and the companies would be required to give notice and work through the lengthy procedures of the board.
8. For a good description of this period of labor history in the railroads, see the chapters dealing with union-management cooperation in railroads in Sumner H. Slichter, *Union Policies and Industrial Management* (Washington, D.C.: The Brookings Institution, 1941).
9. D. W. Collins, "The Labor-Management Task Force on Rail Transportation," in *Productivity in U.S. Railroads*, ed. A. D. Kerr and A. L. Kornhauser (New York: Pergamon Press, 1980), Chapter 8.
10. The unions other than UTU that had represented workers in the various operating divisions after the Springfield Terminal reorganization banded together and appealed to the National Mediation Board for a recertification of their bargaining rights, utilizing a craft council concept. Several unions, such as BMWE and the BLE, were successful in re-establishing their role as bargaining agents for respective crafts, but they were required to accept the terms of the Springfield Terminal agreements.
11. When railroad buffs first hear the term *Springfield terminal*, they mistakenly

assume that the subsidiary must be based in Springfield, Massachusetts. In fact, the subsidiary—which, in 1987, employed virtually no workers—was located in Springfield, Vermont, and had served as a small switching railroad for the products of Jones and Lamson, a major machine tool company that had fallen on hard times. Actually, when one of the authors visited the property, all that could be seen was a roundhouse with rusty rails and uncut grass.

Part III

Understanding Strategic Choices

We found many combinations of change strategies in our three industries and 13 case histories. Our primary focus in Part III is on explaining the factors that shape these strategic choices. What have we learned about why one party chooses to force change, another decides to foster, and still another opts to escape? And what causes a party to shift from one strategic orientation to another—for example, from forcing to fostering?

Our theory identifies two types of considerations that might enter into strategic choice: first, the desirability of the potential benefits associated with the implementation of a particular strategy and, second, the feasibility of successfully implementing it. In practice, do negotiators give these two broad considerations equal weight? Alternatively, is their choice more strongly influenced by the priority they assign to a strategy's potential benefits, or is it more strongly influenced by feasibility factors?

Some factors that affect potential benefits and feasibility are common to all companies and unions in the same industry, whereas other factors are specific to a particular plant or company location or to an individual negotiator. Chapter 7 analyzes the different tendencies for management in our three industries to rely on escape, forcing, and fostering. This will contribute to our understanding of the general factors that influence strategic choice. It turns out that feasibility factors unique to an industry do help explain the industry's general strategic proclivities but that potential benefits do not.

Then, in Chapter 8, we compare our 13 cases, including different episodes within a particular case history. This company-level analysis indicates that *both* the desirability of potential benefits and feasibility factors contribute to an explanation of specific strategic choices. This combination of industry, case, and episode analysis helps explain the factors that shape the choices parties make about broad change strategies.

But do strategies make a difference? Chapter 8 also presents a systematic comparison of the strategies used in the 13 cases and their outcomes. To do this, we first group our case histories by the strategy or strategies employed and find that they fall into four different scenarios. When we map these scenarios against the outcomes, we find a strong tendency for the case histories in scenarios that include *both* forcing and fostering executed either sequentially or in parallel to be associated with better outcomes for both management and labor.

Chapter 7

Strategic Decisions in Context:
An Industry-Level Analysis

Companies in all three of the industries we have been examining faced significant competitive pressures for change in their labor relations. Yet their managements tended to rely on different strategies. For example, managements in paper forced more often than they fostered; in auto supply, they forced and fostered with nearly comparable frequency; and in railroads, they fostered somewhat more than forced. And auto supply managements were alone in making significant use of escape strategies.

Why these—and other—differences? What *industrywide conditions* predispose management for or against a particular strategy?

Our theory differentiates between factors that influence the desirability of the potential benefits a negotiator might associate with a strategy under consideration and factors that influence the feasibility of implementing the strategy. We will examine the evidence from our three industries—focusing first on benefits and then on feasibility.

ASSESSING THE POTENTIAL BENEFITS OF ALTERNATIVE STRATEGIES IN THREE INDUSTRIES

Given an assumption that negotiators will select strategies based in part on the desirability of the potential benefits that would result from their successful execution, we proposed that management would tend to force when it placed high priority on achieving ambitious objectives for changes in work rules and the economic package and low priority on moving toward commitment and cooperation.

Examination of our comparative industry data confirms that forcing and fostering do in fact tend to yield different benefits, and it produces two additional findings relevant to the proposition. First, the analysis indicates that conditions in the three industries should logically lead to differing management priorities and therefore provides a basis for predicting the use of different strategies. Second, the predictions fail—suggesting that *in this industry-level comparison*, potential benefits are not dominant considerations in making strategic choices.

Different Strategies Yield Different Potential Benefits

Our industry cases confirm the theoretically based expectations that forcing can achieve some benefits but not others. Successful forcing by management can decrease payroll costs and increase management's contractual right to make flexible labor assignments and to raise work standards. In addition, it can limit the union's influence in challenging other day-to-day actions by management. However, the potential benefits of forcing strategies, by themselves, are limited. Despite an increased contractual right to make flexible assignments, forcing often results in a failure to exercise the flexibility permitted by the revised contract. Forcing strategies may also increase workloads but fail to achieve increased labor effort in the sense of working smarter as well as harder. Moreover, while weakening the union's influence in certain areas, forcing tactics may also heighten the union's resistance in other areas—for example, causing the union to limit worker involvement in quality improvement programs.

Successful fostering offers a contrasting pattern of potential benefits. It is less likely than forcing to lead to reduced payroll costs and formal changes in work rules and workloads, at least in the short term, but more likely to lead to other benefits—those that derive from commitment and cooperation, such as working more effectively to improve quality, machine uptime, and raw-material utilization.

Thus, forcing offers management more significant benefits when labor costs are a big percentage of the cost of goods and contractual flexibility can be readily implemented. Fostering is more advantageous when quality, productivity of capital, and utilization of raw materials are more important than payroll costs. We now expand these points for our three industries. They differ in terms of the economic significance of labor cost reduction, increased contractual flexibility, and the types of increased effectiveness that come from worker cooperation, leading us to expect differences in their relative use of change strategies.

Potential Benefits Differ by Industry

In principle, the more significant benefits for paper companies are those associated with fostering cooperation and commitment because of the technical process uncertainties in pulp and paper manufacturing. Fostering is more likely to yield a workforce that will work harder and smarter to fully utilize the highly expensive equipment and costly raw materials. Forcing usually requires management to rely on compliance techniques with workers and jeopardizes yields and throughput. Because labor costs (as a percentage of cost of goods) in paper manufacturing are relatively low, the benefits of forcing economic concessions are also relatively modest. There-fore, just considering the potential benefits, we would expect paper man-agements to rely more on fostering than on forcing.

Railroads offer the most interesting contrast with paper. Railroad compa-nies have a more urgent need for decreased payroll costs and formal work-rule reform that might derive from successful forcing and less need for the type of performance improvements that can derive from commitment and cooperation. Thus, just on the basis of the potential benefits, we might expect more forcing than fostering by railroads.

Auto parts companies are an intermediate case. They can achieve major benefits from *both* forcing and fostering. Payroll costs are a significant factor, and yet to compete effectively, these companies also need the various types of improvements that can derive from fostering cooperation and commit-ment. Based on this analysis alone, we would expect auto parts manage-ments to rely equally on forcing and fostering.

Our analysis thus far has compared industries in terms of the potential benefits of two strategies—forcing and fostering. Our third strategy, escap-ing to a greenfield site, appears to offer comparably high potential benefits to companies in all three industries. It enables management to emphasize revision of whatever terms of employment are important competitively—such as labor costs, flexibility, and participation. It can, for example, shift wage and benefit packages from industry patterns to local labor market standards. Newly hired workforces also have proven to be fertile grounds for policies promoting employee participation and work assignment flexibil-ity. Transferring operations also provides management with leverage for both forcing and fostering activities being pursued in continuing operations. Based just on this analysis, we would expect all three industries to utilize escape as a strategy.

Thus, *based strictly on potential benefit considerations*, we would expect relatively more use of fostering in paper and relatively more use of forcing in railroads. We would expect uniformly high reliance on escape throughout our three industries. (See Table 7.1, particularly the top row for each indus-try.)

Differences in Potential Benefits Do Not Explain the Strategic Patterns

In fact, these assessments of industry differences in potential benefits provide remarkably little help in accounting for the actual pattern of stra-tegic initiatives (which we discussed in part II and summarize in Table 7.1, particularly in the second row for each industry). For example, escape offers high potential benefits to all three industries, but it is observed relatively infrequently in paper and railroads. Paradoxically, forcing offers more po-tential benefits in railroads, where it is used infrequently,[1] and less sig-nificant benefits in paper, where it is used more extensively. Fostering offers high potential benefits to both paper and auto parts and would therefore

Table 7.1 Potential Benefits (Desirability) of Strategic Options and Their
Observed Frequency in Three Industries

	Strategic Options		
Industry	Escape	Forcing	Fostering
Paper			
Potential benefits	High	Moderate	High
Observed frequency	Low	High	Moderate
Auto parts			
Potential benefits	High	High	High
Observed frequency	High	High	Moderate
Railroads			
Potential benefits	High	High	Moderate
Observed frequency	Low	Low	Low to moderate

appear to warrant more extensive use than is characteristic of these industries.

Clearly, the attractiveness of potential benefits alone is not helpful in explaining the strategies employed by management in paper, auto parts, and railroads. We turn next to an analysis of how feasible it is for managements in each of our industries to successfully implement the several strategies in their particular contexts.

ASSESSING THE FEASIBILITY OF STRATEGIC OPTIONS IN THREE INDUSTRIES

We assume that negotiators will select strategies based in part on their likelihood of success. In particular, we proposed that management's judgments about the feasibility of executing any one of the several strategies—forcing, fostering, and escape—would be based on (1) labor's expected response to the changes requested by management, (2) estimates of its own relative bargaining power, and (3) the existence of other conditions that could enable implementation of tactics associated with each strategy.

Our comparison of the three industries produced two broad findings that bear on this overall feasibility proposition. First, paper, auto supply, and railroads did, in fact, differ in terms of labor's characteristic response, bargaining power, and other enabling conditions, and these differences therefore provided a basis for anticipating differences in the extent to which managements in each industry would tend to rely on forcing, fostering, and escape. Second, the observed tendencies are generally consistent with the overall feasibility proposition. Thus, to underscore a key finding discussed later, feasibility considerations were generally far more influential than desirability (potential benefit) considerations in explaining differences between industries.

Labor's Responses to Management's Objectives Differ by Industry

Management's proposals for changes in substantive and social terms elicited characteristically different responses from labor across the three industries.

Consider labor's response to management requests for work-rule changes and economic concessions. Auto supply unions—operating in an environment with tough foreign competition—were generally more likely than unions in paper and railroads to see a competitive necessity for these changes and therefore accept them as in labor's own interests.

The three industries contrasted even more systematically in terms of the attitudes of their respective unions toward changes in the social contract. One indicator of a union's receptivity to social changes that either management or labor might initiate by fostering was its stance regarding quality of work life (QWL) and employee involvement (EI) programs.

The United Auto Workers (UAW), the predominant union in the auto supply industry, became very supportive of such joint efforts within many firms as early as the 1970s. While the issue is still a subject of significant internal debate in this union, some of the nation's first QWL experiments and some of the longest-lasting efforts have been developed with full support from the UAW.

On the other hand, until at least 1990, the United Papermakers International Union (UPIU) took the position that QWL was not needed because such matters should be considered within the regular channels of labor-management relations. With regard to worker flexibility and team organization, the UPIU claimed that the practice was already in place with the tradition of the "crew" in the paper mills.

The railroad unions took a similar stance, given the importance of the crew in that industry as well. In some unions, such as the Brotherhood of Maintenance of Way Employees, certain local chairmen and national leaders sought to achieve more flexibility in specific terminals or in the utilization of outside employees for inside work during the winter months, but these initiatives were more the exception than the rule.

Our theory suggests that these general differences in labor's characteristic responses to the types of substantive and social contract changes sought by management in the competitiveness era would enhance the feasibility of fostering most in auto supply and diminish it in paper and railroads.

Power and Other Enabling Factors Differ by Industry

Power factors and other conditions that we proposed would affect the feasibility of escape, forcing, and fostering also vary across the three industries. Here, we focus on power factors identified in our theoretical propositions: the availability of escape, the relative sources of economic power in bargaining (and especially at impasse), and other factors such as the degree of centralization in bargaining.

An important condition with direct implications for escape (and indirect implications for forcing and fostering) is management's ability to transfer operations. Companies in the auto supply industry find it easier than companies in the other two industries to shut down unionized operations and start up new operations in greenfield sites. The heavy capital investment of paper companies in infrastructure and equipment that have productive lives measured in terms of decades and that cannot be transferred from one location to another causes management not only to preserve existing mills but also to locate expanded capacity at these sites rather than building new greenfield mills. In railroads, the construction of new railbeds is even rarer than the construction of greenfield mills in paper. Escaping unionization in this industry takes the form of spinning off a branch line and rolling stock to another business entity. Thus, we find that differences in the use of the escape option can be explained by the fact that escape is simply less available in paper and railroads, not that its potential benefits are any less desirable.

Forcing strategies depend on economic power. Management's power to force substantive change in the longer term is enhanced when the escape option, just discussed, is available, as is the case in auto supply. Other sources of power with direct implications for forcing vary across our industries. The power to force change is enhanced when management can operate a facility during a strike or sustain the costs of a shutdown. Operating with management personnel is most feasible in the paper industry and least feasible in the labor-intensive auto parts manufacturing industry. To anticipate our conclusion, this particular feasibility factor helps explain why paper companies relied relatively more heavily on forcing, despite this strategy's more modest potential benefits.

The analysis of other sources of relative power also helps explain the low incidence of forcing in railroads. The power of railroad unions to resist is relatively high, given the unions' legal right to conduct secondary boycotts and the solidarity of the railroad brotherhoods. Another factor discouraging railroad management from pursuing a forcing strategy is the federal government's penchant for intervening and requiring a return to the status quo ante, thereby effectively blunting the exercise of managerial determination to act and persevere. In fact, the procedures for government intervention tend to act as a broad conservative force that discourages the use of either extensive forcing or fostering to bring about major change and encourages the parties to continue to rely on traditional bargaining modes.

The degree of centralization of traditional bargaining structures, which varies widely among our three industries, also has implications for forcing and fostering. The relationship between bargaining structure and strategic choices is complex. Indeed, in the recent history of these three industries, decentralization has generally promoted both management's power to force change *and* its ability to foster change. However, we judge the greater effect to have been its enabling of fostering—allowing for the identification of local problems and the development of local relationships.

Collective bargaining has always been highly decentralized in the paper industry (almost entirely plant- or facility-level negotiations), moderately decentralized in the auto supply industry (a mix of companywide and plantwide, depending on the size of the firm, its philosophy, and the union that represents its members), and highly centralized in railroads (always companywide and sometimes industrywide). The current trend toward decentralization in the three industries does not change this ordering.

Thus, we would expect this structural feature to have enabled fostering most in paper and least in railroads. This is only partly consistent with the observed tendencies—since the most fostering occurred in auto supply rather than in the more decentralized paper industry.

Feasibility Factors Explain the Strategic Patterns

Based on our broad feasibility proposition and on our comparative analyses of feasibility factors, how much would we expect each industry's management to utilize escape, forcing, and fostering? Do the observed patterns confirm these expectations?

The *ability to transfer operations* in auto supply but not in paper and railroads made the escape option much more feasible for auto supply management. And indeed, it was the only industry to make significant use of the escape strategy.

The *ability to continue operations* during a strike, which makes forcing more feasible, was most available to paper management and least available to auto supply. When this power factor is combined with the ability to transfer operations (which has a secondary effect of enhancing forcing), the combination produces the following implications for management's power to force. Compared to railroad management, paper and auto parts managements have relatively favorable power positions. Paper managers cannot easily transfer operations, but they can operate during a strike; auto supply managers cannot easily operate during a strike, but they can transfer operations. This contrasts with railroad managers, who can do neither. This reading of the feasibility of forcing matches the actual pattern of forcing in the three industries.

The *receptivity of labor to change proposals* and the *decentralization of the negotiating structure* both enable fostering. Labor in the more competitive auto parts industry was relatively more receptive to management's change proposals than was labor in the other two industries. Paper's structure was the most decentralized, auto supply's was moderately decentralized, and railroads' was highly centralized. Thus, auto supply had a combination of these two factors slightly more favorable to fostering than paper, and railroads had the least favorable conditions. These assessments of the relative feasibility of fostering are generally consistent with the fostering tendencies in these three industries.

Interestingly, while railroad managements faced relatively unfavorable conditions for each and every strategy—compared to the other two industries—they nevertheless engaged in some fostering. Fostering may be difficult to implement in railroads due to a centralized bargaining structure accompanied by many craft unions, but it is nevertheless the approach that is most feasible, and consequently, most of the change efforts that have emerged recently in the industry, ranging from CSX's joint planning exercise to the local task forces of many railroads, all fall within the fostering rubric.

SUMMARY AND CONCLUSIONS

Table 7.1 compared the potential benefits of the various strategic options with their observed frequency; Table 7.2 expands that comparison to include the feasibility factor. When we array our assessments of potential benefits, feasibility, and observed frequency in this fashion, the evidence strongly suggests that differences in feasibility exerted the dominant influence.

The explanation for differences among industries emphasized the implications of fundamental economic and technological factors and collective-bargaining structures, together with the ideologies of international

Table 7.2 Potential Benefits (Desirability) of Strategic Options, Feasibility of Implementing Them, and Their Observed Frequency in Three Industries

	Strategic Options		
Industry	Escape	Forcing	Fostering
Paper			
Potential benefits	High	Moderate	High
Feasibility	Low	High	Moderate
Observed frequency	Low	High	Moderate
Auto parts			
Potential benefits	High	High	High
Feasibility	High	High	Moderate to high
Observed frequency	High	High	Moderate
Railroads			
Potential benefits	High	High	Moderate
Feasibility	Low	Low	Low to moderate
Observed frequency	Low	Low	Low to moderate

unions—all exercising their influence by affecting the feasibility of implementing strategic options. Thus, our main finding at the industry level highlights the importance of feasibility and the relative unimportance of desirability. Do the same patterns hold at the company or facility level? This will be our focus in the next chapter.

NOTE

1. The observed frequency of forcing in the railroad industry refers to carrier-level strategies. Unlike those in paper and auto supply, negotiations in railroads also occur at the industry level. From this perspective, a moderate degree of forcing has occurred as the employers have relied on the procedures of the Railway Labor Act to bring about a steady revision of work rules and pay arrangements—with increasing benefits accruing from this approach in the late 1980s and early 1990s.

Chapter 8

Negotiating Strategies: How They Are Shaped and How They Affect Outcomes

We are in an era of competitiveness in which management has reached beyond tactical moves in the context of a traditional social contract. Forcing, fostering, and mixed change strategies are aimed at revising substantive and/or social contracts—with labor adopting its own strategies in response. Our analysis in this chapter, which builds on propositions developed in Chapter 3, focuses on two issues: how strategies affect outcomes and how negotiators decide which strategy to adopt.

The first issue centers on the relationship between strategies and negotiated outcomes. We begin this chapter by summarizing the wide variation in substantive and social contract outcomes in our cases. Then we examine how negotiators' strategic choices help explain these outcomes. Because strategic choices do not account for all the variation in outcomes, we will continue to explore in subsequent chapters how tactical choices can also help account for these outcomes.

A second puzzle—to which we devote the latter portion of this chapter—digs deeper: How can we explain the variations in strategic choices themselves? Whatever its overall trends in utilizing the three change strategies, each industry employed all three strategies to at least some extent. And the cases we drew from each industry include examples of forcing, fostering, and combined forcing/fostering. Why did some negotiators initiate change by forcing, others by fostering? Why did some follow forcing with a period of fostering whereas others did not? Why did a few choose to combine forcing and fostering in the same time period?

The analysis driven by these two puzzles enables us to draw conclusions about theory and practice. Regarding negotiations theory, this chapter illustrates and extends our understanding of propositions in Chapter 3 that posit how outcomes are influenced by strategic choices. Regarding practice, this chapter (and the next three chapters, which deal with negotiating tactics) will identify effective approaches.

Table 8.1 Changes in Substantive and Social Contracts from Management's Perspective

Net Change in Social Contract	Net Change in Substantive Contract			
	Negative	Small or None	Moderate Positive	Large Positive
Toward containment and compliance				Jay Guilford
No change from compliance and arm's-length accommodation		Bidwell UP	AP Parts CSX	
Toward *employee* commitment only				De Ridder
Toward employee commitment and union-management cooperation			Pensacola Adrian Budd	Anderson Packard Conrail

This chapter shifts the focus from the industry context, treated in Chapter 7, to actual choices and their consequences at the company or plant levels in our 13 cases, a focus we maintain throughout the rest of the book.

OUTCOMES AND THEIR RELATIONSHIP TO STRATEGIC CHOICES

In our 13 case histories we identify six different sets of substantive and social contract changes. These cases can also be grouped in terms of the strategy, or combination of strategies, employed. We summarize these variations in outcomes and strategies and then explore how much they correlate.

Negotiated Outcomes

Each industry chapter concluded with a matrix summary of the four or five company case histories in terms of the amount of net change in their social contracts and the amount of substantive change favorable to management, the moving party (see Tables 4.5, 5.5, and 6.4). Each of these chapters also commented on whether the substantive changes, if any, benefited labor in these cases. Table 8.1 combines the findings about outcomes (from management's perspective) for all 13 cases.

In examining the pattern of changes in Table 8.1, we need to note that the baseline combination of outcomes is "small substantive change (or none)/no change from compliance and arm's-length accommodation." Bidwell and UP occupy this cell. Two companies—AP Parts and CSX—changed moderately in substantive terms but not in their social contracts. The other nine companies (or mills) experienced significant changes in substantive and social contracts during the period of observation—for better or for worse.

The amount and direction of changes experienced in these nine cases are diverse. For example, in seven of the cases, the parties moved toward greater mutuality, whereas in two of the cases —Jay and Guilford—the parties moved in the opposite direction, toward greater adversarialism. Among those moving toward greater mutuality, all but De Ridder revised the social contracts with both employees and the union. De Ridder renegotiated the social contract only with employees.

As we emphasized earlier, the distribution of our 13 cases across these various categories is not necessarily representative of the distribution of outcomes in any larger population of labor-management relationships. For example, we have only 1 case (De Ridder) in which management sought and achieved new relations with the workforce but not with the union. In fact, we know from independent field experiences and research that such a combination is a relatively common event. We array the cases in this way so as to indicate which combinations of social and substantive outcomes will become the focus of our analysis.

We should also note that the social contract outcomes (by definition) take into account the implications for both labor and management. In contrast, the substantive outcomes listed in Table 8.1 are assessed only in relation to management's interests. In order to assess the implications from labor's perspective, we have developed Table 8.2, which parallels the structure of Table 8.1. Broadly speaking, it indicates that labor's substantive outcomes were never positive when management achieved no substantive change or when the social contracts were oriented around containment and compliance. On the other hand, positive outcomes for labor were observed in the cases in which social contracts were oriented around commitment and cooperation.

Returning to the perspective of management as reflected in Table 8.1, we note that the 13 cases fall into 6 different cells of the 16 possible combinations of substantive and social change. Now we array these 6 sets of outcomes primarily along a spectrum from adversarialism to mutuality in terms of the direction and degree of change in the social contract:

Outcome set 1: shift toward adversarialism (containment and compliance), combined with major substantive change advantageous to management (and disadvantageous to labor). Two cases: Jay and Guilford.

Outcome set 2: no net change in social contracts, combined with a moderate amount of substantive change favorable to management. Two cases: AP Parts and CSX. (In AP Parts, the substantive changes were disadvantageous to labor; in CSX, they were advantageous.)

Table 8.2 Changes in Substantive and Social Contracts from Labor's Perspective

Net Change in Social Contract	Net Change in Substantive Contract			
	Negative	Small or None	Moderate Positive	Large Positive
Toward containment and compliance	Jay Guilford			
No change from compliance and arm's-length accommodation	AP Parts	Bidwell UP	CSX	
Toward *employee* commitment only			De Ridder	
Toward employee commitment and union-management cooperation			Pensacola Adrian Budd	Anderson Packard Conrail

Outcome set 3: no net change in either social or substantive contracts. Two cases: Bidwell and UP.

Outcome set 4: movement toward employee commitment (without changing the union-management relationship), combined with major substantive change highly favorable to management and at least moderately favorable to labor. One case: De Ridder.

Outcome set 5: movement in social contracts toward employee commitment and union-management cooperation, combined with moderate substantive change favorable to management and labor. Three cases: Pensacola, Adrian, and Budd.

Outcome set 6: movement toward commitment and cooperation, combined with major substantive change favorable to management and major or moderate substantive change favorable to labor. Three cases: Anderson, Packard, and Conrail.

How do these six patterns of outcomes relate to the negotiating strategies used? To facilitate our analysis of this relationship, we group our cases into strategic scenarios.

Strategic Scenarios

Almost all our cases began with the company's first major strategic departure from its traditional compliance/arm's-length accommodation pattern.[1] We analyze four different scenarios illustrated by our 13 cases, including 2 cases we picked up only *after* management had already made its first major initiative. The exceptions are Adrian and Packard Electric.

Scenario 1: Unrestrained forcing only.   Three cases—Jay, AP Parts, and Guilford—began with unrestrained forcing, marked by the use of harsh tactics, including the hiring of permanent replacements for striking employees. Jay and Guilford were continuing in this general mode at the end of our observation period. In AP Parts, the unrestrained forcing period had ended, with the parties having restored the traditional compliance/arm's-length relationship. Significantly, while the future may produce fostering initiatives, none of these three unrestrained forcing cases had evolved to that point. This last observation is consistent with our findings about the profound bitterness that often accompanies an unrestrained forcing campaign and persists after such a campaign has ended. Our analysis of strategic choice in this chapter attempts to explain the occurrence of these unrestrained forcing periods. Then, in Chapter 9, we examine how unrestrained forcing tactics decrease the likelihood of subsequent fostering.

Scenario 2: Fostering only.   Four cases—Bidwell, CSX, UP, and Anderson—began with fostering. The Bidwell fostering effort ended within a few years of its initiation. When we concluded our observation, Anderson Pattern had already logged six years of fostering in a way mutually productive for management and labor. CSX and UP represent intermediate examples. After several years of fostering, UP still had not hit pay dirt (in either substantive or social terms) but was nevertheless continuing the effort. CSX had achieved moderate progress in working on substantive changes.

None of these four fostering efforts had transitioned into a different change strategy. The apparent explanations for this vary among our cases. Anderson Pattern was achieving both major substantive change and a transformation of the social contract, with its substantive change being of the type achieved by other managements in our sample only through forcing or combined forcing/fostering. Bidwell management lacked the determination to produce change. CSX and UP were motivated to produce change, but as we noted in our analysis of the railroad industry in Chapter 7, management faced major obstacles in shifting from the prevailing pattern of gradual change. These ideas are further developed below in our analysis of management choices to foster.

Scenario 3: Forcing followed by fostering.   Three of our cases—Pensacola, De Ridder, and Adrian—involve forcing followed by fostering.

In two cases, Pensacola and De Ridder, management began its first change initiative with forcing, which was then followed by fostering. Two factors appear to be significant. First, in both cases, the forcing tactics were more restrained than in the other forcing cases mentioned above: the De Ridder case involved a strike but not the hiring of permanent replacements, and the Pensacola case did not involve a strike. Second, in both cases, forcing achieved either all or most of management's high-priority objectives for substantive change. The combination of these two conditions increased the likelihood of the subsequent fostering initiatives—and their success. In the Pensacola case, fostering, in turn, was followed by a third distinct period: management returned to the negotiating table to force an additional substantive concession from labor while it also continued to foster a continuation of the newly established cooperation and commitment. That it was successful in combining forcing and fostering is explained by—and illustrates—the robustness of the change that had occurred in the social contract and the skill with which the parties executed the combined strategy. We explore this explanation further in Chapter 11.

Adrian also conformed to the scenario of forcing followed by fostering, but it differed from Pensacola and De Ridder in that our observations began after a prior period of forcing. The scenario differs in another way as well: it included *un*restrained forcing. The conflict was bitter and violent but did not involve hiring replacements for the striking workers. Because it provides our only example of unrestrained forcing followed by fostering, our explanation for the fostering period should be especially instructive.

Scenario 4: Combined forcing/fostering followed by fostering. Management in two cases—Budd and Conrail—began its change efforts with combined forcing and fostering followed by fostering. Our Packard Electric story also included these two periods, differing only in that we judged significant fostering to have already occurred before our period of observation. This scenario is closely related in form and explanation to the "forcing followed by fostering" scenario. The major difference is, of course, the inclusion of fostering in the initial period, which we will attempt to explain in our analysis of these particular periods.

Relationship between Outcomes and Negotiating Strategies

We are particularly interested here in assessing the relationship between outcomes and negotiating strategies. However, before addressing this question, we should acknowledge the array of factors other than the choice of negotiating strategy that may have influenced negotiated outcomes in our 13 cases and indicate where these other factors are addressed later in this chapter and elsewhere in the book. We identify three other types of factors influencing outcomes.

First, at the starting points we chose for the periods studied in the 13 companies or mills, each labor-management pair had inherited a unique set of circumstances affecting the relative difficulty of negotiating substantive and social change. We treated many of these circumstances in our case histories, and some of them will figure in our subsequent analysis of the factors that influenced strategic choice. That is, factors such as labor's skepticism regarding the business rationale for management's proposals influences not only the latter's choice of whether to force or foster but also the range of probable outcomes.

Second, the choice of tactics and the skill with which they are executed will affect the dynamics and outcomes of negotiations. The influence of tactical choice is the main focus of Part IV (Chapters 9, 10, and 11).

Third, the duration of our periods of observation—which varied widely in our sample of cases—obviously affected the amount of opportunity for the parties to produce significant change. For example, our studies of Conrail and Packard Electric covered a much longer segment of their histories than was covered by our studies of Jay, Bidwell, and UP. The time frame of our studies is particularly pertinent to the instances in which fostering was the only strategy in use. Specifically, these cases tended to be of a shorter duration. Therefore, we have not allowed for the possibility of pure fostering's being followed by some emphasis on forcing. We will return to this point later, when we evaluate the generally weak results from pure fostering. We need to keep this artifact of time frame in mind as we interpret the association between outcomes and strategies below.

We have constructed a matrix in Table 8.3 to facilitate our consideration of the relationships between strategic choice and outcomes: we array across the top of the matrix the four strategic scenarios and along the side of the matrix the six distinct combinations of substantive and social contract outcomes for management discussed earlier.

The first pattern that appears, in the upper-left-hand corner of this matrix of strategies and outcomes, is clear and readily interpretable. The scenario of "unrestrained forcing only" (Jay, Guilford, and AP Parts), which included bitter strikes that were *not* followed up by any strategic initiative by management to generate cooperation and commitment, produced substantive change and yielded either no net change in the social contract or greater adversarialism. The persistence or intensification of highly adversarial relations, in turn, limited management's ability to obtain the benefits of the work-rule changes it had negotiated and to even remotely tap the reservoir of skills, experience, and ingenuity of its workforce. Thus, the performance gains these managements achieved in practice were less than would be suggested by the substantive changes they won through forcing.

The strategy of unrestrained forcing emerged in some cases from what the parties may originally have hoped would be a more moderate forcing campaign, a dynamic that is partly explained by our analysis below (e.g., ambitious substantive agendas and *both* sides' confidence in their own bargaining power), and it is further examined in the analysis of tactical choices in Chapter 9. Certain tactics not only help precipitate an unrestrained forcing episode but make it especially difficult to follow up with subsequent fostering—difficult but not impossible, as is shown by the Adrian experience, in which unrestrained forcing *was* followed by a successful fostering effort. But we are getting ahead of the story.

A second pattern is also relatively straightforward. Four cases—Bidwell, UP, CSX, and Anderson—conformed to the scenario of "fostering only." This scenario included fostering initiatives that neither followed strategic forcing nor were combined with it. In Bidwell and UP, it yielded neither substantive

Table 8.3 Strategic Scenarios and Outcomes

| Outcomes | Strategic Scenarios | | | |
	Scenario 1: Unrestrained Forcing Only	Scenario 2: Fostering Only	Scenario 3: Forcing Followed by Fostering	Scenario 4: Combined Forcing/ Fostering Followed by Fostering
Set 1: Shift toward more extreme adversarialism, combined with large change in substantive contract	Jay (S) Guilford (S)			
Set 2: No change in social contract, combined with moderate change in substantive contract	AP Parts (S)	CSX		
Set 3: No change in either social or substantive contracts		Bidwell UP		
Set 4: Major shift toward employee commitment only, combined with large change in substantive contract			De Ridder (S)	
Set 5: Major shift toward commitment and cooperation, combined with moderate change in substantive contract			Pensacola Adrian (S)	Budd
Set 6: Major shift toward commitment and cooperation, combined with large change in substantive contract		Anderson		Packard Conrail

Note: (S) = strike.

nor social contract changes, and in CSX, it yielded only moderate substantive change, suggesting the weakness of a change strategy based strictly on fostering. As we explore below, in the discussion of the next two patterns, when fostering follows forcing or is combined with forcing, it appears to have more potential for producing change. However, before turning to these strategic patterns, we need to acknowledge that Anderson experienced both major substantive change and a strong movement toward commitment and cooperation. Our explanation for Anderson's change results—developed in Chapter 10—centers on the especially effective tactical execution of fostering and recognizes some other circumstances favorable to fostering in the Anderson case, such as the organization's relatively small size and high skill profile. Also important by way of a contrasting object lesson was the utilization of forcing and escape strategies by other area firms in this closely knit industry.

A third pattern associates the scenario of "forcing followed by fostering" with changes in both the substantive and social contracts (toward mutuality). Within this combination of outcomes, there is considerable diversity of experiences. The forcing component of Pensacola's scenario did not precipitate a strike; De Ridder's involved a strike but not unrestrained forcing tactics; and Adrian's was unrestrained. Thus, Pensacola and Adrian achieved similar outcomes by different strategic and tactical routes. In addition, during the fostering period of this scenario, De Ridder's social change concentrated on employees, whereas in Pensacola and Adrian, it embraced both employees and the union. Chapter 11 examines the role of tactical choices in explaining the diversity of outcomes associated with forcing followed by fostering.

The patterns associated with the fourth scenario—"forcing/fostering followed by fostering"—are similar to the patterns associated with the third scenario. In both scenarios, a period of predominately fostering activity follows a period in which some substantive changes have been forced by management. Thus, the parties have put behind them the tough, tension-laden forcing process involving changes especially unpleasant to labor and pursued full-fledged fostering. The third and fourth scenarios together account for six of the seven cases involving both moderate to large substantive change and a successful effort by the parties to create employee commitment and (except for De Ridder) union-management cooperation. (The seventh, Anderson, has already been discussed.)

The distinctive aspect of the fourth scenario—that the first half of our observation period was marked by *combined* forcing/fostering—reflects in part the degree of competitive urgency that both parties were feeling when management undertook its initial change effort. We have noted earlier that this applies especially to Conrail and Budd and that Packard Electric had already engaged in fostering activities as a backdrop to the periods we observed in this case. The amount of change in these three scenario 4 cases slightly exceeded the amount of change associated with scenario 3 for several reasons: the competitive urgency, the longer period of time observed, and the imaginative implementation of tactics.

Given the strong (but not complete) association between strategic scenarios and outcomes in our cases, we need to learn what factors helped shape the three strategic choices comprising these scenarios.

FACTORS THAT SHAPE NEGOTIATING STRATEGIES

Our 13 cases included 20 separate time periods, each characterized by a particular management negotiating strategy. In each period, negotiators made choices among several action alternatives: to continue working within their traditional pattern, to force change, to foster new conditions, or to engage in a strategy combining both forcing and fostering (see Table 8.4).

We have proposed that these negotiating choices by management are influenced by at least three types of factors: the first is the nature of management's actual desires—its agenda and its priorities; the second and third relate to feasibility—its expectations of labor's responses and its perception of power relations. These three factors are, in turn, reflections of underlying situational conditions such as economic necessity, the existing level of trust between the parties, the basic philosophical beliefs of leaders, and the skill of negotiators.

In our treatment of each case in Chapters 4, 5, and 6, we offered an explanation for the strategic choice or choices it contained. The aspects of these analyses that related strategic choice to management's priorities, expectations, and power perceptions were summarized in Tables 4.4, 5.4, and 6.5. In the following sections, we combine these summaries and organize them by type of strategy in Tables 8.5 (forcing), 8.6 (fostering), and 8.7 (combined forcing/fostering).

We begin by reviewing the evidence related to the adoption of forcing strategies.

FORCING CAMPAIGNS

Six of the 20 periods predominately involved forcing: 4 periods were characterized by "unrestrained forcing" and 2 by a more limited form of forcing, which we refer to as either "controlled forcing" or simply "forcing."

Unrestrained forcing evolved in four periods: Jay period 1, Guilford period 1, AP Parts period 1, and Adrian Fabricators period 1. All four cases involved bitter strikes. In the first three cases, the key management tactic that caused us to define the forcing episode as unrestrained was the hiring of permanent replacements, which posed a basic threat to labor. In the fourth—Adrian—we defined the forcing episode as unrestrained because it involved a similarly dramatic threat to labor in the form of a refusal to recognize the union and the firing of a union official. In all cases, labor reciprocated with the most aggressive tactics it could muster.

Although, in other respects, the instrumental tactics as well as the circum-

Table 8.4 Cases, Time Periods, and Strategies

Cases Grouped by Strategic Scenario	Period	Strategy
Scenario 1: unrestrained forcing only		
Jay (1987–1989)	1	Unrestrained forcing
AP Parts (1984–1989)	1	Unrestrained forcing
Guilford (1986–1990)	1	Unrestrained forcing
Scenario 2: fostering only		
Bidwell (1981–1984)	1	Fostering
Anderson Pattern (1984–1990)	1	Fostering
CSX (1986–1990)	1	Fostering
UP (1986–1989)	1	Fostering
Scenario 3: forcing followed by fostering		
Pensacola (1985–1988)	1	Forcing (1985)
	2	Fostering (1985–1988)
	3	Forcing/fostering (1988)
De Ridder (1983–1990)	1	Forcing (1983–1984)
	2	Fostering (1985–1990)
Adrian Fabricators (1985–1990)	1	Unrestrained forcing (1985–1986)
	2	Fostering (1987–1990)
Scenario 4: Combined forcing/fostering followed by fostering		
Packard Electric (1977–1990)	1	Forcing/fostering (1977–1980)
	2	Fostering (1980–1990)
Budd (1982–1990)	1	Forcing/fostering (1982–1986)
	2	Fostering (1987–1990)
Conrail (1976–1990)	1	Forcing/fostering (1976–1987)
	2	Fostering (1988–1990)

stances associated with these four unrestrained forcing cases vary widely, the explanations for the forcing strategies, discussed below, have much in common.

The forms of forcing we observed in two other cases—De Ridder and Pensacola—were more restrained and less threatening to the security or survival of one or both parties than those described above. During the 1983–1984 contract negotiations, the De Ridder strategy included relatively aggressive forcing in the preparation and execution of the strike. However, the critical exercise of restraint related to management's decision *not* to hire permanent replacements (although it had considered doing so) nor to engage in other overt tactics that would have threatened the union as an institution. Pensacola mill management forced significant changes in the contract during the 1985 negotiations, with both sides agreeing that management had "shoved it down the union's throat." However, the forcing was even more restrained than in the De Ridder case.

Objectives That Drive and Constrain Forcing Campaigns

We expected to find that forcing strategies would typically be strongly influenced by the desirability of potential benefits—specifically, that they would be driven by a management agenda of ambitious objectives for substantive change with no intention to revise the social contract toward commitment and cooperation. What did we actually find? (See Table 8.5.)

Factors driving the decision to force. A review of management agendas in the six forcing periods shows that in almost all instances, management was ambitious in its objectives for substantive change and in its aspirations for revising the balance of power and control.

Managements in Jay, AP Parts, Guilford, and Pensacola had exceptionally aggressive substantive agendas. Each sought to gain sufficient economic concessions in particular and to break the past pattern of economic settlements in general. In addition, these four companies sought revisions in work rules important to the union. In a fifth case, De Ridder management also had aggressive substantive objectives, but they were focused entirely on work-rule changes; management was willing to provide for normal, or perhaps even generous, economic gains.

We infer that managements in these five cases also hoped to revise the power equation with the union that had existed over the past decade or more. For example, once International Paper had entered into its confrontation with the UPIU (if not before), management appeared to want to demonstrate to the union that bargaining power had shifted from labor to management. And management succeeded in this respect. In the case of AP Parts, UAW leaders explicitly interpreted the hard bargaining as potentially the leading edge of a regional realignment of power between small auto parts companies and the union.

In any event, management sought the work-rule changes in these cases not merely to achieve specific forms of operational efficiency but also to enhance management control over operations in general. In some cases, the work-rule changes were intended to establish a containment relationship with the union.

De Ridder, in which management specifically confined its objectives to work-rule changes, provides insight into the type of enhanced latitude and control management sought in several of the forcing episodes we studied. First, De Ridder management assessed its problems. It not only had agreed in the 1970s to contractual provisions that restricted its operational decisions (presumably because of greater union bargaining power) but also had ceded to the union the translation of these provisions into practice, apparently because of the union's more careful monitoring. The union's daily pursuit of protective work rules was both more systematic and more effective than management's attention to its own interests. Because of the high turnover among upper-level managers, there was little managerial oversight in this area, which allowed department foremen and supervisors wide latitude in making agreements with employees and union representatives on the mill floor. As a result, management agreed to local practices that were inconsistent with each other. The union, for example, kept better records of agreements than did management and could focus on the agreements that served labor's immediate purposes; moreover, the union's officers generally had greater job stability than did management.

Then, in 1983, with the informed support of Boise Cascade corporate executives, De Ridder mill management set out to reverse this situation entirely. The boldness of management's agenda was reflected in the zipper clause and team concept it achieved in contract negotiations. The zipper clause completely eliminated the agreements and practices that De Ridder managers believed had hampered their ability to manage successfully: "The elements of Team Concept supersede all conflicting limitations on management rights provided in the labor agreement, and all preexisting rules, commitments, understandings, work practices, past practices, grievance settlements, arbitrations or side agreements written or unwritten." The ambitious intent of the team concept language was set forth in the new contract as well: "Team Concept simply means the company has flexibility in how it assigns employees."

Our sixth forcing episode was Adrian Fabricators period 1. It was in certain respects characterized by the least ambitious management *change* objectives. Management's positions were highly disagreeable to labor primarily because *labor's expectations* had changed. Under ESOP, the workers had become owners; they expected economic benefits, not sacrifices, and they expected to exercise more personal influence, not to be subjected to a continuation of authoritarian management practices. When management violated these new expectations—for example, by not recognizing union representatives—many workers struck.

Except for Adrian, the types of objectives that management sought to

Table 8.5 Periods in Which Management Forced

Hypothesis	Proposed Conditions That Promote Management Forcing	Unrestrained Forcing (periods)			Controlled Forcing (periods)		
		Jay (1)	Guilford (1)	AP Parts (1)	Adrian (1)	De Ridder (1)	Pensacola (1)
Potential Benefits							
Management change objectives:							
Priority for—and ambitiousness of—substantive change?	High	High	High	High	Medium to low	High	High
Priority for creating commitment/cooperation?	Low	None	None	None	None	Commitment was a goal, but was not actively pursued during this period.	None

Feasibility					
Labor's expected response:					
Probability of labor's being persuaded by business rationale for ambitious substantive proposal?	Low	Low	Low	Low	Medium
Labor's expected initial response to commitment and cooperation goals, if any?	Negative	N.A.*	N.A.	Labor wanted changes; management did not.	Labor was unaware of management's goal.
Power equation:					
Management confident it can force substantive change?	Confident	Confident	Confident	Confident	Confident

* N.A. (not applicable) refers to the fact that management was not currently pursuing commitment and cooperation.

achieve through forcing probably could not reasonably have been achieved through fostering—at least not within the same time frame.

Existence of inhibiting objectives. All but one of the pure forcing cases was marked by a glaring absence of any evident intention on management's part to move toward commitment and cooperation. In the exception—De Ridder—management's social objectives did not preclude forcing strategies, but they did appear to exercise a moderating influence on the choice of forcing tactics. Management placed high priority on a smooth and complete implementation of the contractual flexibility it sought to force. This (future) priority and the concern about attitudes that accompanied it prompted management to be generous in its economic offer and also disinclined to use permanent replacements during the forcing period.

Summary. Thus, as we expected, our forcing periods generally appeared to be driven by ambitious substantive objectives and unconstrained by a desire to move toward commitment and cooperation. Equally interesting are several other patterns not covered by our stated hypotheses about the role of objectives in forcing decisions: in five of the forcing episodes, management's objectives went beyond making substantive changes in the contract and involved containing the union's bargaining power and its influence over operations. Not surprisingly, three of these five episodes evolved into unrestrained forcing. In one case—Adrian—management found itself in a forcing period not so much because it had an ambitious new agenda but because its traditional approach violated the workers' changed expectations based on their new status as employee-owners.

How Labor's Expected Response Affects Forcing Decisions

We proposed that forcing is more likely to be the strategy of choice when management expects labor to be unpersuaded by the company's business rationale for its substantive agenda and to respond negatively to any fostering activities management might initiate.

Expected response to substantive proposals. Forcing periods were accompanied by an expectation that labor would *not* accept the business rationale for the substantive proposals. For example, IP was profitable and enjoying a cyclical upswing when the Jay contract dispute occurred. The De Ridder mill, while failing to meet management's performance expectations, was not in any sense threatened. Even in cases in which management could make a more compelling argument for the business necessity for some change, such as with AP Parts, it was unlikely that the rationale for the *amount* of change sought by management would have been convincing to both union officials and members.

In only one forcing case—Pensacola period 1—did management expect labor to be at least partly persuaded by the business rationale for its substantive proposals. The new owners had shut down paper machines and a bag plant, helping to make the case that changes were required in order for the mill to become competitive; nevertheless, labor remained unconvinced that many of the proposed changes were justified.

Expected response to a social agenda. As noted above, in only one of our six forcing episodes did management aspire to a new social contract with employees based on commitment. In this case, De Ridder management decided it had to force substantive change first and worry about promoting commitment later. Until the strike was behind it, management did not expect labor—either union officials or members—to be receptive to any initiatives to promote commitment.

Summary. Our forcing periods were, as expected, characterized by pessimism regarding labor's response to proposals for *substantive* changes. However, the general absence of management objectives to promote commitment and cooperation in these cases denied us significant evidence bearing on the idea that pessimism regarding labor's response to proposals for new *social* relations would help predispose management toward forcing.

Role of Power in Decisions to Force

Here we are interested in the parties' *perceptions* of power rather than any after-the-fact assessment of actual bargaining power.

Management's perceptions and decisions to force. We proposed the obvious— that management is more likely to force when it is confident of its own power—and indeed, in all six of our forcing periods, management was confident it could force the substantive change it sought.

The primary bases of management's confidence did, however, vary across our cases. For example, going into the Jay mill negotiations, IP management had succeeded in achieving similar gains in several of its southern plants and had witnessed Boise Cascade's recently having forced a comparable change on labor in the neighboring mill at Rumford, Maine. At the De Ridder mill, the confidence of Boise Cascade management was based less on recent precedents than on a more basic assessment of underlying power—the combination of its own strike preparations and its ability to bring the power of the entire corporation to bear on any economic contest with one mill local in a southern state. In the Adrian case, the fact that workers were also owners under the newly formed ESOP encouraged management's belief that the workforce would be too divided to pull off a successful strike.

In these and other forcing cases, management's confidence in its bargaining power undoubtedly entered into its decision to force—first bolstering its hope that the union would concede without a strike and then supporting its belief that it could win a strike.

Labor's perceptions and escalation to unrestrained forcing. We proposed that forcing would tend to escalate to an unrestrained form when *both* parties were confident of their relative power.

Indeed, this condition did help precipitate all four cases of unrestrained forcing we observed. Of course, in each case, one or both of the parties probably miscalculated. We have already mentioned several assumptions underlying management's confidence in the Jay case. For its part, the UPIU eventually bet on an innovative corporate campaign and the pooling of several mills to support a belief that the union could defeat management's change agenda. In the end, management prevailed. In this case, the union clearly miscalculated. Perhaps management did as well.

By contrast, the AP Parts management, which ended up gaining only a portion of its substantive objectives, probably made the larger miscalculation. The union survived by making a number of key tactical moves, including not striking when management expected it to and elevating the dispute by bringing in the union negotiators involved in national negotiations at General Motors and Ford as a demonstration of solidarity.

The Pensacola forcing period is also consistent with the pattern being considered here. Management was confident and labor was doubtful about its own power, which helps explain why forcing did *not* escalate.

One forcing period does not fit the general pattern. At De Ridder, forcing did not escalate despite the fact that both parties were initially confident of their bargaining power. This appears to be attributable to the nature of management's future intentions to promote commitment, mentioned above, and also to the fact that the union folded before management found it necessary to play its permanent-replacement card.

Summary. With one exception, the forcing periods fit the expected pattern: all six were characterized by management confidence in its bargaining power. In addition, the four unrestrained forcing periods were all characterized by *both* labor and management confidence in their own bargaining power, whereas one of the two moderate forcing cases was characterized by management confidence and labor doubt. An exception to this pattern—De Ridder—had strong potential to escalate into unrestrained forcing, but it did not, for reasons discussed elsewhere.

FOSTERING EFFORTS

Ten periods were characterized by a predominately fostering strategy on management's part.

Fostering initiatives in our cases took many forms. Fostering at Bidwell and UP began with management's making climate-changing overtures to union officials, which were followed at Bidwell with employee involvement. At Pensacola, similar initiatives were successful and paved the way for participative redesign of work and negotiation of new wage schemes.

At Anderson and CSX, management initiated fostering with a strong focus on common problems or opportunities. Anderson's successful fostering continued over a long period of time, centering on new technology but encompassing a wide range of other issues as well. CSX's fostering first occurred within a structure that brought all unions into a common problem-solving process, but when this initial process broke down, the carrier dealt individually with each union in parallel fostering activities.

The fostering periods at Adrian and De Ridder were similar in that they occurred against a backdrop of vigorous forcing. In addition, new leaders on the management side played key roles in creating credibility for the fostering initiatives. The tactics differed significantly in that, at Adrian, fostering was aimed at both union leaders and employees, whereas, at De Ridder, it was aimed exclusively at employees. Only in the De Ridder case did management focus its attention strictly on the individual level and treat institutional relations with benign neglect.

At Packard and Budd, both of which had already experienced major change periods involving combined forcing/fostering, fostering took similar forms. Not surprisingly, fostering in these two companies was characterized by many different activities at both the institutional and individual levels. It included top-level labor-management committees serving in a joint governance role for certain issues (such as subcontracting, training, health and safety, and health care costs) and selected problem-solving forums during collective bargaining. Other activities included formal employee participation groups, team-based work reorganization, employee-focused statistical process control programs, and just-in-time delivery processes.

Fostering at Conrail also followed a forcing/fostering period but involved a less ambitious set of activities.

We now turn to an explanation for these fostering decisions. (See Table 8.6.)

Objectives behind Fostering Efforts

We proposed that the fostering strategy would tend to be employed when management placed a high priority on revising the social contract toward commitment and cooperation and a low priority on achieving ambitious substantive change. Considering first the social contract objectives, in all ten fostering periods, management placed at least medium priority on such objectives, and in half of the periods, management placed high priority on them. When we turn to substantive objectives, we find a weaker pattern: five of the ten periods are marked by low priority for ambitious substantive change, as expected, but three feature substantive agendas with medium priority and two with high priority.

To illustrate what we mean by low, medium, or high priority in social and substantive agendas, consider the cases of Anderson, Bidwell, and CSX. Anderson is a case in which high priority was placed both on substantive changes (seeking to eliminate contract language limiting flexible work assignments) and on building cooperation and commitment (as reflected in the high levels of information sharing and the free granting of profit shar-

Table 8.6   Periods in Which Management Fostered

Hypothesis	Proposed Conditions That Promote Management Fostering	Fostering (periods)									
		Bidwell (1)	UP (1)	CSX (1)	Anderson (1)	Conrail (2)	Pensacola (2)	Adrian (2)	Budd (2)	Packard Electric (2)	De Ridder (2)
Potential Benefits											
Management change objectives:											
Priority for—and ambitiousness of—substantive change?	Low	Low	Low	High	High	Low	Low	Medium	Medium	High	Low
Priority for creating commitment/co-operation?	High	Medium	Medium	Medium	High	Medium	High	High	High	High	High/low[*]

Feasibility

Labor's expected response:

Probability of labor's being persuaded by business rationale for ambitious substantive proposal, if any?	High	N.A.†	N.A.	Medium	High	N.A.	N.A.	Medium	Medium	High	N.A.
Labor's expected initial response to commitment and cooperation goals, if any?	Positive	Neutral	Neutral	Positive	Positive	Negative	Positive	Negative	Positive	Positive	Negative

*High/low = high priority for employee commitment and low priority for union cooperation.
†N.A. (not applicable), in relation to "labor's expected response," refers to the fact that management did not currently aspire to ambitious substantive change.

ing). In contrast, CSX placed high priority on substantive changes (work-rule flexibility) but only medium priority on the social contract (wanting to build positive relations but not to forge a joint partnership). Bidwell is among the least ambitious combinations of social and substantive objectives, seeking no significant contractual change and only moderate changes in labor relations.

We find that the duality of "high" and "low" conditions prescribed in our original proposition was literally met only in Pensacola period 2, but it was closely approximated in De Ridder period 2 (the high priority for social change focused on employees and not union officials). Interestingly, both these periods occurred in the fostering phase of the "forcing followed by fostering" scenario. Pensacola and De Ridder managements had already achieved the substantive changes they required.

However, if we consider the *relative* priority management placed on social contract and substantive changes, another six fostering periods would fit this general pattern. In the cases of Bidwell period 1, UP period 1, Conrail period 2, Adrian period 2, Budd period 2, and Packard Electric period 2, the priority for social contract changes was higher than the priority for substantive changes. The relative differences in priorities among these case may reflect the different industries, with auto supply requiring high (and sustained) levels of cooperation and commitment, combined with at least medium levels of substantive change (building on higher levels of change in earlier eras). In all cases, however, the higher priority placed on achieving social contract changes helps us understand the choice of a fostering strategy.

Labor's Expected Response and Decisions to Foster

How will labor respond to management's change objectives for which fostering might be employed? We proposed that if management expects labor to be persuaded by the business rationale for substantive proposals and to be receptive to attempts to promote commitment and cooperation, then management is more likely to utilize fostering.

Expected response to substantive proposals. In five of the ten fostering periods, management placed no more than low priority on major substantive change, and therefore, these periods offer no relevant test for this idea; however, in the other five periods, in which management placed medium or high priority on ambitious substantive change, it did expect labor to be slightly to significantly persuaded by the business rationale for the changes.

By period 2 in Packard Electric, for example, labor and management had discussed in depth over a period of years the severity of the evolving business situation and the role of labor costs in the competitiveness of segments of the business. Management believed that union officials especially would grasp the validity of the business rationale, even though they might not be willing to agree to management's proposals.

Also, at Pensacola during period 2, there were some important differences among unionists in their attitude toward commitment and cooperation activities. Although, at the time, the stance of the international union and one influential local president toward such innovations was generally negative, the union's regional international representative had experienced such change in other paper mills and found himself in philosophical agreement with many of its features, as long as traditional union safeguards against managerial abuse remained intact.

Expected response to the idea of commitment and cooperation. There is meager support in our data for the idea that management must anticipate labor receptivity before it will decide to foster. In only five of our ten fostering cases did management initially expect a positive response. In three, it expected no more than a neutral response; and in two, it actually expected the initial response to be negative.

In three of the cases in which labor receptivity was anticipated—Conrail, Budd, and Packard Electric—the basis for management's expectations is easy to understand: the expectations were formed going into the second phase of a scenario in which a combined forcing/fostering period was followed by a fostering period.

The two examples of negative expectations, drawn from the Pensacola and De Ridder cases, are equally comprehensible: fostering occurred on the heels of a major forcing episode in which labor had reluctantly acceded to management demands. Despite the unfavorable expectations about labor's initial response, managements nevertheless proceeded, presumably because they had confidence in their own fostering skills and believed that ultimately the new social contract they envisioned would prove mutually beneficial to both labor and management.

STRATEGIC PERIODS THAT COMBINE FORCING AND FOSTERING

Four episodes involved a combination of forcing and fostering. The renovation of Conrail during 1976–1987 involved a more or less continuous synthesis of controlled forcing and fostering. Both the forcing and the fostering reflect the large scale of the corporate reorganization, the highly public and political nature of the process, and the deep financial pressures facing this railroad. Labor and management had to work together to be effective in their dealings with Congress, banks, and other stakeholders, but these same stakeholders placed requirements and time constraints on the parties that, in effect, compelled a degree of forcing.

The mix of controlled forcing and fostering at Budd during period 1 reflected severe economic pressures, a workforce that was not yet persuaded of the severity of these pressures, and ongoing activities regarding a formal employee participation program. Initially, economic concessions were forced under threat of layoffs. When the workforce in most locations rejected a second round of concessions, layoffs did occur. At the same time, however, resources were devoted to employee participation efforts, yielding some economic performance gains.

The experience at Packard Electric during period 1 was similar to that at Budd. Concessions were sought, but it ultimately took large layoffs to "educate" the workforce regarding management's economic concerns. An employee participation program preceded the layoffs and subsequently became a springboard for joint planning related to subcontracting, multitier wages, and employment security.

Pensacola management's forcing in the mixed forcing/fostering negotiations in 1988 (period 3) was even more restrained. Although the corporate agenda to eliminate premium pay for Sunday as such required company negotiators to force this "bitter pill" on labor, management sweetened the overall settlement with an unrequested 401(k) plan and employed tactics that were as nonprovocative as possible.

What factors appeared to underlie management's strategy of combined forcing/fostering? (See Table 8.7.)

Objectives, Expectations, Power Perceptions, and Combined Strategies

We did not develop any specific propositions to cover strategies that combined forcing and fostering in the same time period. However, the patterns we observed make sense in terms of management's priorities and its expectations of labor's response.

First, we find that all four combined periods occurred when management placed medium to high priority on *both* substantive change and movement toward commitment and cooperation. Clearly, this dual-track agenda was driving the combined forcing/fostering strategy. For example, Packard Electric was facing severe cost pressures, but the workforce was not fully educated (and resisted learning) about these pressures—which required a measure of forcing. At the same time, the quality and continuous improvement mandates of the business, combined with an institutional history and norms established around QWL, pointed toward concurrent fostering initiatives.

Second, we find that management had expected labor to be at least somewhat persuaded by its business rationale for the proposed substantive change in three of the four periods and to be neutral to positive in response to its social agenda in all four periods. Again, this confidence in labor's receptivity would appear to be a critical condition favoring a decision to combine forcing/fostering. For example, in the cases of both Budd and Packard Electric, the mixed periods involved early experiences with the movement of equipment out of a plant on the premise that certain operations were no longer competitive. These events proved to be highly salient learning experiences that built a measure of receptivity to later discussions of economic pressures.

Third, management was confident or moderately confident of its power to force change in the combined strategy periods in all four cases, suggesting that combined strategies were more likely when management believed it could pursue a forcing-only strategy.

FACTORS THAT SHAPE STRATEGIC CHOICES: REVIEW OF THE EVIDENCE

To this point, our review of factors influencing management's strategic choices has focused on one type of strategy at a time. Now, we summarize the evidence, focusing in turn on each of the propositions about the factors shaping strategic choice. We follow this with a review of the more objective factors that often underlie management's priorities, such as external economic pressure. Finally, we review other specific conditions that enable forcing or fostering.

Propositions about Forcing and Fostering Choices

Our propositions about the factors influencing management's strategic choices deal with management's priorities, its expectations about how labor will respond to these priorities, and how its own bargaining power compares to the union's.

Potential benefits: management priorities. In Chapter 3, we proposed that management was more likely to force and to employ severe forcing tactics when its objectives included high priority for an ambitious agenda of work-rule and economic changes and low priority for a new social contract based on commitment and cooperation. Conversely, we proposed that management would tend to foster when its priorities were reversed. These factors were moderately to strongly helpful in explaining the strategic choices represented by our 20 case periods.

Consider the ten periods in which forcing occurred (including combined forcing and fostering). Management placed high priority on achieving ambitious substantive change in seven of these periods and medium priority in three. This contrasts with the periods of predominant fostering, in which management placed either high or medium priority on such objectives in only five of the ten episodes. Thus, higher priority for an ambitious substantive agenda was obviously a major driving consideration in decisions to force. However, lower priority for substantive change was a weaker explanation for decisions to foster: indeed, five of the ten pure fostering cases occurred despite medium to high priority for this type of change. While this range may impair predictions, it does suggest that fostering strategies may be quite robust (with appropriate tactics) across a range of substantive change objectives.

Management's social contract objectives show a clearer pattern. All four unrestrained forcing episodes were marked by an absence of any manage-

Table 8.7 Periods in Which Management Combined Forcing and Fostering

Hypothesis	Proposed Conditions That Promote Management Forcing	Proposed Conditions That Promote Management Fostering	Combined Forcing and Fostering (periods)			
			Conrail (1)	Budd (1)	Packard Electric (1)	Pensacola (3)
Potential Benefits						
<u>Management change objectives:</u>						
Priority for—and ambitiousness of—substantive change?	High	Low	High	Medium	High	Medium
Priority for creating commitment/cooperation?	Low	High	Medium	Medium	High	High

Feasibility

Labor's expected response:					
Probability of labor's being persuaded by business rationale for ambitious substantive proposal, if any?	Low	High	High	High	Medium	Low
Labor's expected initial response to commitment and cooperation goals, if any?	Negative	Positive	Neutral	Neutral	Neutral to positive	Positive
Power equation:					
Management confident it can force substantive change?	Confident	—*	Confident	Moderately confident	Moderately confident	Confident

*No hypothesis.

ment intentions to revise the social contract toward commitment and coop-eration. (In fact, in several cases, management wanted to revise power relations—in effect, containing the union.)

The other two (controlled) forcing periods present a more varied picture. In Pensacola period 1, there was no social agenda, but in De Ridder period 1, management wanted to begin to move the social contract with employees toward commitment. In De Ridder, these social contract concerns served to inhibit the severity of forcing tactics.

All ten of the fostering periods and all four of the combined forcing/fos-tering periods were characterized by at least medium priority for a man-agement agenda of negotiating cooperation and/or commitment. This is perhaps the least noteworthy finding because of the strong logical relation-ship between fostering and these changes in the social contract.

Thus, the high priority given to a social contract change objective, if any, is confirmed to be a major consideration in strategic choice. Indeed, in contrast to our findings in Chapter 7, this analysis supports the general proposition about the role of desirability (potential benefits) in strategic choice.[2]

Labor's expected response. Our second proposition takes into account la-bor's probable reaction to management's objectives—its reaction to the business rationale for proposed change and to any management aspiration to promote commitment and cooperation. If management expects favorable responses, then it is more likely to foster; otherwise, it is likely to believe forcing is a necessary step to achieve it substantive objectives.

Management's expectation that labor will not be persuaded by the com-pany's business performance rationale for its substantive proposals does help explain the strategic choices. Management perceived labor to be skep-tical in all but one of the forcing periods. This contrasts with the four combined forcing/fostering periods, three of which were characterized by an assumption that labor would be at least slightly persuaded.

Labor's perceived receptivity to management's social contract objectives, if any, appears to have exercised little influence on management's choices. Overall, there is an absence of any clear pattern in both the predominantly forcing and predominantly fostering periods. This finding suggests, con-trary to our expectations, that the lack of confidence in labor's receptivity to the social contract agenda is *not* a strong factor leading to forcing and that such confidence is *not* an essential precondition to fostering initiatives.

Power equation. The third proposition introduces the role of power per-ceptions in strategic choice. In all of the periods involving some measure of forcing (including the combined periods), managements were confident of their distributive bargaining power—a condition that we proposed would be consistent with their decisions to force. A condition that we proposed would point to unrestrained forcing—*both* parties' being confident of their power—did indeed characterize all four unrestrained forcing cases but only one of the other two forcing cases. Management in De Ridder period 1, as we said before, relied on *controlled* forcing for several reasons: its ambitious change objectives were confined to work rules and complemented by generous economic proposals, its objective was to build positive relations, and labor eventually recognized the inadequacy of its bargaining power.

Summary of support for the propositions. How helpful were the forcing propositions in explaining the choices observed in our studies? To what extent did our findings support the propositions?

Overall, we judge a relatively high level of consistency between the propositions and our findings. But naturally, some cases were explained more easily than others by the propositions.

Some of the forcing decisions were consistent with virtually all the conditions hypothesized to favor them. For example, in all four of the unrestrained forcing periods, the initial decision to force was very strongly indicated by the hypotheses, and the conditions favoring unrestrained forcing were also present.

At the other end of the spectrum, two management strategies combining forcing and fostering occurred under conditions that would not necessarily have indicated forcing. While Packard Electric in period 1 and Budd in period 1 sought ambitious substantive changes, union officials generally accepted that these changes were justified by business pressures; moreover, both parties were doubtful of their power to force. Thus, while forcing itself was not indicated, one might expect that if it did occur, it would be coupled with fostering.

There was more variation in the way the fostering cases lined up with our propositions, perhaps reflecting the broad range of tactics and initiatives that we have included under the fostering umbrella. Still, we clearly see that management's placing medium to high priority on social contract objectives is central to a fostering strategy. Ironically, even though our propositions did not contemplate the considerable variation in the substantive contract objectives and in labor's expected response to the forcing initiatives, these observations do point out the range of circumstances under which fostering is initiated.

Factors Underlying Priorities, Expectations, and Power Perceptions

We have been exploring management's strategic choices as they reflect management's own objectives, its expectations about labor's response, and its assumptions about bargaining power. Each of these separate judgments can be based on innumerable underlying conditions—conditions that are either more fundamental or more enduring than the judgments themselves. We note several such conditions—economic pressure, management philosophy, and the prevailing level of trust. The latter two factors are especially salient aspects of the interpretive frames of management negotiators.

External economic pressures. In our sample, one of the most obvious underlying factors potentially affecting several management judgments is the degree of economic pressure on the enterprise or business unit involved.

A comparison of the three sets of strategic periods—forcing, fostering, and combined—indicates that the economic pressures generally were highest in the periods in which managements elected to combine forcing and fostering and lowest in the periods of fostering only. Intermediate amounts of economic pressure accompanied pure forcing. The differences among the average levels of pressure were relatively small, especially between the two sets involving combined forcing/fostering periods and pure forcing periods. Considerable variation existed within each of these two sets. For example, two of the managements under the most pressure were in the set combining controlled forcing and fostering. They were Conrail, which in period 1 faced bankruptcy, and Packard Electric, which in period 1 needed to cut labor costs dramatically or lose major pieces of business. However, one of the other managements employing the combined strategy—Pensacola in period 3—was not under extreme pressure; on the contrary, the mill's business was in a strong and improving financial state.

The seven periods in which management faced especially strong economic pressures included Conrail period 1 and Packard Electric periods 1 and 2, already mentioned; Adrian periods 1 and 2; AP Parts; and Budd period 1.

Economic pressures could influence strategic choice through any of several possible mechanisms. First, we expected stronger economic pressure to be associated with high-priority objectives for ambitious substantive change, which we did *not* find. Second, we expected stronger pressure to be accompanied by an objective to revise the social contract. In fact, again, there was no systematic tendency for managements facing these seven periods of strong economic pressure to be more interested than other managements in our sample in revising the social contract. Third, under strong economic pressure, we expected labor to be viewed as more readily persuaded by the business rationale for management's substantive proposals. Here we did find a slight tendency in line with our expectations. This mechanism appeared to be particularly important for the managements of Conrail in period 1 and Packard Electric in period 1, both of which utilized a combination of fostering and forcing.

Management and union leadership philosophy. Another underlying factor is the philosophy of management embraced by key managers and the leadership philosophy of union leaders. A strong linkage exists between social contract objectives and certain underlying management philosophies and union ideologies. Interestingly, the management linkages in our sample were sharpest in the cases in which labor relations decisions were being made by a top line manager (company CEO or plant manager) who also had the power to shape the management philosophy. The best management examples from our forcing periods are Guilford (CEO) and Adrian Fabricators period 1 (company president), while the strongest union leadership in a forcing case was demonstrated at AP Parts (regional director). The most striking examples from our fostering or combined strategy periods are

Anderson (company president and union business agent), Adrian period 2 (company president and union international representative), De Ridder (plant manager), and Packard Electric (union chairman).

Prevailing levels of trust. A third underlying factor is the prevailing level of trust between the parties at the beginning of the period. We expected this factor to influence managements' social contract aspirations and whether they expected labor to be receptive to these social aspirations and persuaded by the business rationale for substantive proposals.

Clearly, the average prevailing level of labor-management trust at the beginning of the ten periods characterized by a fostering strategy was higher than in the six periods characterized by a forcing strategy. Also, the level of trust that prevailed in the combined forcing/fostering periods was higher than in the forcing periods. Specifically, the prevailing levels of trust at the beginning of Pensacola period 3, Packard Electric period 1, and Budd period 1—each combining forcing and fostering—were among the highest in our sample of 20 periods. This trust helps especially to explain why labor was relatively more persuaded by the company's business rationale for proposed changes—*which made the combination of forcing and fostering not only desirable but also feasible for management.*

Other Conditions Enabling Forcing and Fostering

We also proposed generally that management is more likely to adopt a particular strategy when other specific conditions would enable its tactical implementation.

All of the forcing instances, for example, coincided with contract expirations. Similarly, both the uncontrolled forcing at Jay and the controlled forcing at De Ridder represented instances in which there was a pent-up desire for change within management, evidence of success in achieving such changes in other locations, and a strong resolve to pursue the change agenda in these locations.

A fostering strategy is enabled by other conditions. A decentralized structure's enabling effects on fostering in paper were well illustrated by the Pensacola case. Plant management and the local unions cooperated to modify work designs and other practices in ways that probably would not have been approved by the UPIU's council representing all of Champion's unionized mills.

Other conditions enabling the tactical implementation of fostering include the existence of credible and simple common goals, such as the goal of improving safety at De Ridder; structures that permitted local integrative bargaining, such as the one maintained at Pensacola; and the introduction of new technologies that give credible grist to participation mechanisms, such as occurred at Anderson. These are only a few examples of the specific conditions that can make fostering tactically more feasible. Our cases include many such enabling conditions, which, in certain instances, were central to the fostering. For example, at Anderson Pattern, investment in new technology provided a focal point for a key series of fostering interactions.

SUMMARY AND CONCLUSIONS

In this chapter, we have observed strong correlations between strategies and outcomes. Forcing strategies varied in the degree to which they produced the intended substantive changes, but most did achieve some change. Also, with two notable exceptions (De Ridder period 1 and Adrian Fabricators period 1), the forcing strategies were consistent in producing social contracts with employees rooted in compliance and social contracts with unions that either remained arm's-length or involved containment. In contrast, the pure fostering strategies mostly led to little or no substantive or social change (with the exception of Anderson Pattern in both regards). The cases in which forcing was followed by fostering, as well as the cases in which mixed forcing and fostering periods were followed by fostering, featured moderate to large changes in substantive agreements and shifts to social contracts based on cooperation and commitment.

In addition, we have identified key considerations that help to explain the observed strategic choices. The choices are rooted in management's initial ambitions or objectives (regarding social and substantive contracts), the feasibility of those objectives in terms of labor's expected response, and the power equation (expressed in terms of each side's initial confidence in its ability to force). In many ways, we have seen that strategic choices are "overdetermined": two and sometimes all three of these factors are aligned around a given strategy.

While the overall links between strategies and outcomes seems clear, some exceptions have been noted above. As we will discuss in Chapters 9, 10, and 11, these exceptions can best be understood by examining tactical moves within the context of a given strategy.

NOTES

1. As noted earlier, we selected our cases based on a generalized knowledge about some aspect of the situation—specifically, that it involved either forcing or fostering. We developed an understanding of the more complex sequence of negotiating strategies that had occurred in our cases only *after* we had selected the situations and investigated them. At that point, we decided to use the strategic period as an analytic unit. Using this device clarified that we had in our sample seven simple cases (comprising only one strategic period) and six compound cases (comprising a sequence of different strategies over two or three time periods). In general, we have attempted to capture in each case the company's (or plant's) history, beginning with management's first significant effort to negotiate a major change in the social or substantive contract and concluding with the most recent activities we could document in this project. There are

exceptions to this (Adrian and Packard Electric), which we discuss in the body of the text.

2. How do we explain this anomaly? First, it may be related to our use of different operational measures of desirability at the two levels of analysis. In our industry-level analysis in Chapter 7, we defined desirability by the *logical* priority we researchers assigned to potential benefits, given an industry's particular work technology and factor economics. For example, we reasoned that given certain paper industry characteristics—high capital intensity, costly raw materials, process uncertainties that made mill performance especially sensitive to worker skills and attitudes, and labor costs that were a low percentage of total cost—management had more to gain by improving relations with labor than by reducing payroll costs. Therefore, when we observed that management forced a reduction in payroll costs before it attempted to foster cooperation, we concluded that desirability factors were overwhelmed by feasibility considerations. In contrast, in our company-level analysis, we used the *actual* priorities of specific company managements. One would expect a closer alignment between choices and actual priorities. Because, in our industry-level analysis, we did not have any way to determine actual priorities, and in our company-level analysis, we did not attempt to infer the logical priorities based on the company's unique situation, we can draw no firm conclusions about the implications of using these different operational measures of desirability.

A second possible line of explanation for the different findings at the two levels of analysis is perhaps more interesting. There may be more actual variance in feasibility than in desirability factors across our three industries. Conversely, within each set of cases drawn from the same industry, there may be more variation in managements' priorities than in their assessment of the feasibility of achieving them.

In any event, the differences in the roles of desirability and feasibility factors in the analyses in Chapters 7 and 8 are thought-provoking and hopefully will trigger additional research or analysis.

Part IV

Tactical Choices and Negotiating Dynamics

Forcing and fostering refer to broad change strategies. Putting these strategies into practice requires appropriate tactics. Negotiators make tactical choices related to each of three processes—bargaining, shaping intergroup attitudes, and managing intraparty differences. And they can also make tactical choices about the structure in which their interparty interactions take place.

Chapters 9, 10, and 11 examine, in turn, the implementation of forcing, fostering, and combined forcing/fostering. For each of these several strategic orientations, we illustrate implementing tactics and the dilemmas and other dynamics they generate. We also examine the tactical risks associated with the execution of each strategy. In the process, we attempt to derive lessons from our studies about what works and what doesn't.

In addition to their more direct role of describing and analyzing the tactical execution of forcing and fostering, these chapters also assess aspects of the theory of strategic negotiations. The theory proposes that for a given strategic orientation, the choices regarding each of the three processes tend to be predictably correlated and that strategies combining forcing and fostering generate equally predictable dilemmas. Moreover, the theory proposes that structural features play a role in facilitating or frustrating the implementation of strategic choices. Now we turn to what we found in our field studies.

Chapter 9

Implementing a Forcing Strategy: Tactics and Dynamics

Forcing strategies involve the mobilization and deployment of power. In all of our cases, management was the moving party, though labor usually responded to forcing initiatives with its own forcing tactics. Forcing involves more than distributive bargaining within a traditional, arm's-length labor-management relationship. It involves an especially vigorous set of distributive tactics as well as supporting tactics in the other two negotiating processes affecting intergroup attitudes and intraparty differences. Therefore, whether intentionally or not, a forcing strategy invariably impacts the social contract as well as the substantive contract. The purpose of this chapter is to explain how forcing strategies work: the process and structural factors that are designed to implement them, the dynamics that commonly accompany them, and thus, how they achieve their intended—and unintended—consequences.

We begin the analysis by assessing the tactical risks facing parties engaged in forcing. The balance of the chapter is then devoted to a range of tactical considerations that have direct bearing on these risks and benefits.

We draw our illustrative material from the six forcing periods in our studies (see Table 9.1). Four periods were characterized by strategies that escalated into unrestrained forcing: Jay, Guilford, AP Parts, and Adrian Fabricators period 1. Two other periods involved more controlled forcing: De Ridder period 1 and Pensacola period 1.

COMMON PATTERNS AND VARIATIONS IN THE FORCING CAMPAIGNS

In the cases we studied, whenever management forced, labor invariably resisted the change proposals and forced back. Its forcing tactics included overt and covert concerted activities (such as strikes and work-to-rule). Leaders on both sides actively heightened intergroup hostility and pro-

Table 9.1 Periods of Forcing, Fostering, and Forcing/Fostering

Case History	Strategic Periods		
	1	2	3
Paper mills			
Jay (International Paper)	Unrestrained forcing		
De Ridder (Boise Cascade)	Forcing	Fostering	
Bidwell (disguised name)	Fostering		
Pensacola (Champion Paper)	Forcing	Fostering	Forcing/fostering
Auto supply companies			
AP Parts	Unrestrained forcing		
Adrian Fabricators	Unrestrained forcing	Fostering	
Packard Electric	Forcing/fostering	Fostering	
Budd	Forcing/fostering	Fostering	
Anderson Pattern	Fostering		
Railroads			
Guilford	Unrestrained forcing		
Union Pacific	Fostering		
Conrail	Forcing/fostering	Fostering	
CSX	Fostering		

moted internal solidarity. Although the hierarchical organization of management is less vulnerable to internal divisions than the political organization of unions, some unions did attempt to create disagreement within the employer side—for example, through corporate campaigns.

In none of the six forcing periods was the union ever persuaded that either management's new agenda or its new negotiating tactics were "legitimate." Thus, in each case, management had developed no route to change other than forcing it. As a result, management's initial actions were determined largely by the strength of its aspirations, by its estimate of bargaining power, and by its willingness to sustain the costs inherent in its actions. Its subsequent tactics were influenced not only by these considerations but also by the union's responses and unfolding dynamics. Finally, management in several cases took active steps to bolster its own internal consensus and create divisions within labor.

There was some variation across forcing firms in their apparent concern

Table 9.2   Roles Played by Tactical Processes in the Six Forcing Periods Studied

- *Distributive bargaining:* In all cases, management built and tactically exploited bargaining power in order to achieve ambitious substantive changes. And in some cases, it sought to demonstrate that the power balance had fundamentally shifted in management's favor. It met resistance from labor on both counts. Five of the six forcing periods were marked by strikes, all but one of which involved the use of unrestrained forcing tactics.

- *Managing internal differences:* Management sought to ensure that members of its own organization understood and supported its objectives and forcing strategy. In most instances, it also sought to create divisions within labor, thereby weakening the union's position. For their part, union negotiators always worked to increase labor solidarity and sometimes took steps to weaken consensus on the company side.

- *Shaping intergroup attitudes:* In one of the six forcing periods, management clearly wanted to minimize the adverse effects of hard bargaining on intergroup attitudes, especially employee attitudes. In the remaining forcing periods, management seemed willing to add to intergroup hostility. In all cases, union officials attempted to arouse anger and hostility toward the company in order to promote labor solidarity. In any event, the parties had to contend with the escalation of tension, whether induced inadvertently or deliberately.

about the consequences of souring attitudes. Generally, management sought to divide labor and did so in ways—such as hiring permanent replacement workers—that were almost certain to leave a poststrike legacy of negative attitudes. Only De Ridder evidenced noticeable concern about poststrike attitudes, and its concern was primarily focused on the attitudes of employees—not union officials. In our 13 cases, when management was deeply concerned about attitudes in the present period and still felt that it needed to force change, it usually engaged in mixed forcing/fostering. Those cases are considered in Chapter 11. Table 9.2 summarizes the roles of the three negotiating processes in the overall forcing effort.

The six forcing episodes under scrutiny replay confrontational patterns common to an earlier era in the United States, such as imaginative power tactics, impasses, mutual costs, and eventual compromises. However, they include not only classic distributive-bargaining tactics[1] but also tactics more severe than the practices prevailing in recent decades. Consider, for example, the mix of labor and management tactics instrumental to forcing in our case involving International Paper's (IP's) mill in Jay, Maine:

- The lockout by International Paper management in the Mobile, Alabama, mill, which increased the credibility of its willingness to take a strike at Jay

- The United Papermakers International Union's (UPIU's) response of creating a pool of four mills, whose contract negotiations were kept open concurrently, including Jay, Mobile, and two other mills

- IP's decision to hire permanent replacements to operate the Jay mill and the other two striking mills

- The UPIU's employment of Ray Rogers to conduct a corporate campaign—pressuring IP directors through adverse publicity and pressuring companies that dealt with IP through veiled secondary boycotts

- The UPIU's rally in Maine, featuring Jesse Jackson, and its caravan throughout New England to generate support for its cause

- The help provided by the UPIU's Jay local in obtaining an OSHA levy of $250,000 in fines for hazardous plant conditions

- The town of Jay's UPIU-supported ordinances banning strikebreakers, restricting temporary housing, and appropriating funds for Maine environmental law enforcement

- The unfair labor practice charges filed by both sides

In general, our forcing episodes illustrate the following dimensions that differ from past conflict patterns:

- Management, not labor, made the demands (for major work-rule and economic concessions).

- Management manifested a strong readiness to take a strike and operate during the strike.

- Management appeared willing to sustain, at least temporarily, new levels of antagonism in employee relations as a price for achieving substantive concessions.

- Labor often recognized the limitations of the strike as an economic lever and sought nontraditional forms of leverage to augment the strike.

- Labor felt that its very institutional existence was threatened—by either the movement of work out of a facility, the hiring of permanent replacement workers, or encouragement of a decertification vote.

The forcing periods contain many differences: they embraced a variety of negotiating objectives; they relied on forcing tactics that ranged in the severity of threats employed; they were characterized by a variety of techniques for managing intergroup attitudes and internal differences; they occurred within varied structures; they generated different dynamics and followed different paths; and they produced a range of outcomes in terms of both costs and benefits.

RISKS OF FORCING

Our analysis of management decisions to force in Chapter 8 emphasized the role of certain objectives—specifically, high priority for achieving ambitious substantive changes and perhaps for rebalancing the future power relationship, and low priority for increasing mutuality in the social contracts with labor. It also underscored how management's strategic choices were influenced by expectations about how strongly labor would remain opposed to its proposals and by judgments about bargaining power. The major strategic risk for management was that it might have totally miscalculated its ability to force the changes it sought.

If the above are strategic considerations in a forcing decision, what are the tactical concerns that come to the fore in implementation? The concerns involve certain predictable costs and the risks of these costs getting out of hand—risks that are intensified by the interactions among the three negotiating processes. We found four types of risks: escalation, defeat or stalemate, a residue of distrust, and a legacy of internal friction.

Risk of Escalation

Whenever the strike (or a similar economic weapon) is the primary enforcement mechanism, the forcing strategy involves direct costs. Each party has to incur costs to make threats credible. Management may build inventory, take extra steps to reassure its customers of continued service in the event of a strike, and train supervisors and replacement workers to operate equipment. The union may build a war chest, engage in alliances that would otherwise be unnecessary, and suspend activities such as joint safety programs that are in labor's own interest.

A risk for both parties is that early distributive bargaining may fail to produce a solution, a strike may ensue, and the costs may escalate—with a cessation of both production and weekly paychecks, for example. The forcing can escalate even further, becoming what we have termed unrestrained, draining the company of a trained workforce, destroying the livelihood of individual workers, and undermining the institutional security of the union.

The escalation of conflict and its attendant costs is produced in part by several dynamic interactions among the three forcing subprocesses. Escalation can occur, for example, when negotiators whip up animosity toward the other side in order to achieve solidarity among their constituents—which is intended to enhance their distributive-bargaining position. In this case, the intergroup animosity tends to be reciprocated and take on a life of its own, becoming a driving force in the distributive bargaining rather than merely a form of tactical support for it. Escalation may also be fueled by another dynamic. When a negotiator attempts to foment internal divisions in the other party's organization in order to weaken its bargaining power, the other side may see the tactic as a threat to its institutional security, thereby requiring a major counterattack.

These and other escalation dynamics were observed in some but not all of our forcing episodes. Our six cases contained variation in the amount of escalation. As we review the tactical choices involved in forcing, we can look for clues about why forcing episodes escalated to unrestrained forcing at Jay, Guilford, AP Parts, and Adrian but did not do so at De Ridder and Pensacola (and why De Ridder experienced a strike but Pensacola avoided this type of showdown).

Although we treat more controlled forcing and unrestrained forcing as different strategies, the critical unrestrained-forcing threshold sometimes presented itself to management as a result of an escalation after it had first decided to force. Thus, we will analyze which forcing tactics triggered escalation and which served to contain it.

Risk of Defeat or Stalemate

Distributive bargaining is inherently a win-lose-compromise game. Forcing strategies usually involve high-stakes distributive bargaining. Thus, while the objective of initiating a forcing episode may be to win major substantive changes over the opposition of the other party, the other party may not concede the changes. There is, of course, a similar risk of defeat for the party resisting the changes.

The risk of defeat or stalemate is a by-product of many of the same dynamics that are involved in escalation itself. For example, many tactics that heighten the stakes of distributive bargaining—such as making ambitious substantive proposals that dismay the other side or using divide-and-conquer tactics—also heighten the intergroup hostility and, in turn, tend to rigidify bargaining positions. These dynamics render obsolete each party's earlier predictions about the terms the other party would probably accept.

Our cases varied in terms of whether management achieved the primary objective behind its decision to force. Specifically, management prevailed in some forcing episodes—Jay, De Ridder, and Pensacola—but was denied the "win" it sought in others, such as Adrian and AP Parts. Why? What tactical triumphs or defeats were critical to the differences in these outcomes? We will analyze in particular how effectively the parties developed their bargaining power and how well they achieved the necessary internal consensus.

Risk of a Legacy of Distrust

The dynamics described above not only limit the parties' ability to compromise in distributive bargaining and to engage each other in integrative bargaining during the forcing episode but also risk leaving a legacy of intergroup hostility after the forcing episode had ended. This residue of bitterness can limit the parties' flexibility to implement fostering activities in the period following the forcing campaign—a dynamic that was critical in some of our cases but not others. In our analysis of forcing tactics, we will explore clues about why Jay and Guilford persisted in a forcing mode and an intensified adversarial pattern, whereas AP Parts restored a traditional relationship of accommodation and De Ridder, Pensacola, and Adrian transitioned into a fostering mode. Do certain aspects of the tactical choices during forcing help explain the variation in subsequent developments and the eventual outcomes?

Risk of a Legacy of Weakened Solidarity

The dynamics described above, especially those related to developing or undermining internal consensus in order to affect the distributive-bargaining process, contain an additional risk for the parties. Each side's assaults on the other's internal solidarity can have effects that continue beyond the forcing episode. In addition, because constituents extend support to their negotiators based in part on the premise that their negotiators will achieve their objectives, a win-lose outcome may produce new fissures in the defeated party. Thus, we will explore why labor in some instances—especially in the Jay case but also in De Ridder, AP Parts, and Guilford—ended up more internally divided than when the forcing episode began.

In the five sections that follow, we examine a series of tactical choices that the parties make during a forcing period—from the early preparation phase through the conclusion of a forcing campaign. We highlight instances in which the tactics can be shown to relate to one or more of the risks described above and in which their execution helps explain the dynamics and outcomes of the forcing campaigns in which they occurred.

MANAGING THE SUBSTANCE OF DISTRIBUTIVE BARGAINING

Early in a forcing campaign, the initiating party (management in all of our cases) formulates its objectives, frames the negotiating agenda, and justifies its position. The other party (the union or unions in all of our cases) responds in similar terms. Both sides also usually take steps to develop internal support for their bargaining positions.

Formulating Objectives and Framing the Agenda

Both the ambitiousness of the moving party's objectives and the way it frames the agenda can inadvertently trigger escalation. Choosing the level of aspiration is a threshold issue relevant in the decision about whether to force in the first place (which was discussed in Chapter 8), but these substantive choices also have tactical implications (which are our primary concern in this chapter).

Management often underestimates the labor opposition that will be generated by its demands for economic and work-rule concessions. While management may believe that the case for concessions is compelling and self-evident, labor will tend to focus on the way these concessions nullify decades of hard-won gains, threaten workers' standards of living, and undermine the union's strength and self-respect. Anticipating such reactions by the other party enables the negotiator to understand the hostility engendered and take steps to contain it or to avoid reciprocating it.

When management's demands are not carefully delimited, the union frequently misinterprets management's intentions, inferring that the demands for concessions are more than just a straightforward attempt to improve productivity and reduce costs. Labor often concludes—sometimes too quickly—that management has embarked on a campaign to get rid of the union. The union's conclusion that its institutional interests are threatened involves complicated judgments because even if management would prefer to be rid of the union, that does not mean its forcing actions are necessarily part of a plan to achieve this result.

Management's basic objectives at both Jay and AP Parts were especially ambitious, covering a wide range of economic and work-rule concessions. As a result, the substantive proposals—in themselves—were provocative. By contrast, managers at De Ridder pushed hard for radical work-rule changes but did not press their advantage by seeking wage concessions. They tempered what could have been a multiyear escalation of conflict by focusing their forcing effort where change was most needed while holding back on change that would have been of less importance to management but of central importance to labor. Our comparative analysis of De Ridder and Jay in Chapter 4 concluded that this difference in management's objectives explained in part why De Ridder was able to end the strike after several months and follow up with successful fostering, whereas Jay's strike lasted a year and a half and was followed by continued tension.

In addition, the agenda that management places on the table in negotiations not only reflects its underlying objectives but can also become a major tactic in distributive bargaining. It signals management's seriousness. It is an attempt to shape the other party's expectations. And often, it is intended to intimidate.

Our cases indicate that while the aggressive agendas management used to launch forcing campaigns may have had these several intended effects, they also antagonized labor and mobilized oppositional processes—increasing the risk of escalation. In Jay, De Ridder, Guilford, and AP Parts, management's agenda had the following effects on labor: because the company's proposals were unprecedented, they generated surprise and dismay; and because they were so ambitious, they were threatening. While the ambitious proposal did successfully intimidate labor in the Pensacola forcing episode, in other cases, such proposals tended to infuriate as well as intimidate, thereby contributing to the escalation that marked the forcing periods in these latter cases. The tactics of AP Parts management, discussed next, are illustrative.

Signaling the need for deep changes: AP Parts. AP Parts management signaled the need for deep changes right at the outset of the 1984 negotiations. The company violated the union's expectations regarding both substance and procedure. Procedurally, the company broke from traditional norms, such as the union's making most of the opening demands or the employer's refraining from direct communication with union members. As one union leader characterized the opening of the 1984 negotiations:

> It was at the opening meeting that they dropped the entire proposal on us.
> We weren't expecting anything like that. At the same time they had supervisors in the plant passing out handbills stating that "we are committed to staying in Toledo."[2]

Management's ambitious substantive demands also surprised the union. The company apparently requested $5.84 per hour in wage and benefit concessions, the replacement of the individual incentive system with a measured daywork system, the elimination of the 30-and-out pension provision, the freedom to subcontract, the redefinition of job classifications, and the reorganization of the plant around work cells. These demands would eliminate or scale back long-standing union gains and introduce new, controversial work practices.

The opening round of bargaining at AP Parts became a pivotal event due to management's demands for far-reaching substantive change and its departure from established norms. Through what it said and how it said it, the company set the agenda—and it set a much broader agenda than had been the case in past negotiations. Whether intentionally or not, management threw the union off balance. For its part, the union responded by closely studying every action taken by AP Parts. It was looking to see whether the crisis was as severe as the company suggested or whether the crisis had been exaggerated as a tactic to wrest substantial concessions from the workforce and possibly undermine the union itself.

Providing Justification for Proposals

A forcing strategy by management is more likely to be successful if, despite labor's opposition to the proposed changes, it comes to accept that management has a credible business rationale for them. On the other hand, if labor believes that ambitious demands are arbitrary, then escalation and stalemate become more likely.

The pulp and paper industry provides a negative example of this point. Management's efforts to force a reduction in the rate of payroll cost increases never was presented to labor in a credible manner. The UPIU saw management's demands as especially unjustified in the mid- to late 1980s, when paper companies were generating record profits. To the union and workers, it appeared that paper companies were simply availing themselves of new (and perhaps temporary) bargaining power advantages to squeeze labor. In fact, management in the paper industry could have made a better case for forcing a change given the trend line of payroll costs. Employees had fared relatively well over several decades compared to shareowners in this industry. While paperworkers' earnings ranked favorably against those in other industries, returns on shareholder investments in paper compared unfavorably to the returns in other American industries. Paper management probably had more justification for its concern about payroll costs and flexibility than it succeeded in communicating.

Thus, in our case studies, the absence of a management rationale credible to labor increased the likelihood of the strike at De Ridder and the unrestrained forcing at Jay. In Pensacola's forcing negotiations, which did not escalate to a strike, the mill's vulnerability gave *some* credence to management's demands.

One explanation for why the proposals by paper industry managements were not seen as credible is that, given the isolated environments of paper mill towns, it would take very effective communications to break through and to convince the workers and their union representatives that a new era had dawned. By contrast, it would probably be easier for an auto supply company to gain worker acceptance of the need for change, given the fact that its workers have witnessed considerable disruption in the major manufacturing centers, although even auto supply faced difficulties in creating credibility, as demonstrated by the following example from the early phases of Budd.

Failed attempt to make the case for change: Budd. In 1981, before implementing a large layoff, Budd management pressed for concessions. The local union leadership was persuaded that adjustments were needed and agreed to a midcontract reopener. The parties reached an agreement, which provided for wage and benefit concessions. When the agreement was presented to the membership, it was also made clear that a "no" vote would mean the loss of the plant's wheel and drum business (which accounted for over half the plant's workforce).

Although the local union president recommended ratification, labor was not convinced of the threat, and more than 95 percent of the membership voted against the agreement. Following the rejection, the local union president resigned, and the business was indeed shifted out of the Detroit plant, resulting in a layoff of more than 900 employees. As one union leader commented on the membership's vote against the concessions: "We had a ferocious membership meeting. Talk about being scared, we had to be escorted out of the meeting. . . . They [the membership] never believed it until the machines were disassembled."[3]

This early attempt at revising the contract proved costly to both sides. The union and the membership suffered the loss of jobs. The company incurred all the costs associated with shutting down nearly 100,000 square feet of productive capacity. The experience, which was repeated in other Budd facilities, illustrated the limitations imposed by each side's frame of reference. Management assumed that the need for change was self-evident and that its statements would be taken seriously. Many union members interpreted the statements as merely stronger versions of past rhetoric, but not as real threats.

Thus, simply promulgating information about what management perceives as compelling circumstances that warrant change does not guarantee that the recipients of this information will accept the proposed changes as justifiable. Our cases contain many other examples in which "rational" arguments appeared to fall on "deaf ears." AP Parts, for example, attempted to use the leverage of a new contract with Ford to secure important changes in operating practices, and many railroads announced plans to sell off branch lines unless they achieved substantial changes in work rules. Because the unions regarded these arguments as insufficient to justify the proposed changes, they set the stage for escalated resistance to the initiatives.

Developing Early Internal Support

The development and maintenance of internal support for a party's negotiating position is a key tactical requirement for both parties. The party that fails in this respect increases its risk of defeat.

One of our cases, De Ridder, illustrates an especially systematic effort by management relative to this tactical requirement, and internal management support was a key ingredient in the company's successful handling of the strike.

Convincing constituents of the need for forcing: De Ridder. Boise Cascade corporate executives and De Ridder mill managers convinced themselves that the company's objectives (flexibility rights) were not only justified but important to the future of the mill as a business entity. The analysis of why the De Ridder mill was underperforming as an asset served to convince managers that it was worth taking a strike to achieve the desired changes in management's rights to assign work.

Several other De Ridder activities—e.g., internal planning and preparation committees and the communications to all managers and employees about economic performance—also helped to promote internal cohesion in the management organization. The cohesion translated into support for the action plans for the strike itself and the poststrike period. The informed support of mill management and management personnel elsewhere in Boise Cascade was especially important because they were to play a key role in implementing the company's bargaining plan—by walking through picket lines and operating the equipment.

INFLUENCING THE STRUCTURE OF DISTRIBUTIVE BARGAINING

In deciding how to force (and counterforce), the parties also manage the structure—by selecting the level of centralization, establishing the channels and frequency of communication, as well as enlisting additional parties in partisan causes. This manipulation of the bargaining structure for tactical purposes reverses the traditional view that structure is a fixed element of negotiations.

Selecting the Level of Centralization

Although the degree of centralization is often a static feature of collective bargaining, varying by industry, we found that in some cases, negotiators could and did modify this structural feature on the margin in order to serve a forcing strategy. In the context of forcing, each party tends to seek the degree of centralization that maximizes its relative bargaining power. Needless to say, when one party seeks decentralization to aid a forcing strategy and the other seeks centralization to counter that strategy, this form of bargaining over how to bargain takes on great importance.

Our case involving the IP paper mill at Jay, Maine, illustrates how two parties engaged in forcing can differ in their preferences about bargaining structure. Bargaining in the paper industry has traditionally been on a mill-by-mill basis, with certain companies, including IP, setting the pattern for the entire industry. IP sought to preserve this structure in its sustained effort to negotiate work-rule and pay concessions because this structure gave it bargaining power advantages. The UPIU locals, for their part, sought to enhance their power by "pooling" the negotiations across mills and, indeed, did succeed in keeping four negotiations open concurrently.

As the strike progressed, IP not only employed permanent replacements to operate the striking mills but also was able to bring all the resources of the corporation to bear on the conflict, which involved only a small fraction of its system of mills and plants. When the UPIU found it could not expand the pool beyond the original four mills to include other IP mills whose contracts were scheduled to terminate, it lost both the struggle over bargaining structure and the negotiation itself.

The IP-UPIU episode illustrates how several types of forcing risks are associated with the tactical use of structure. First, the party that loses the skirmish over the structure and must work within a disadvantageous structure—as the UPIU eventually did—experiences an increased risk of failure in the distributive bargaining. Second, a bid by one party to alter the degree of centralization may trigger an escalating tactic by the other side. Indeed, the UPIU's bid to pool the plants was the trigger for management's maneuver of hiring permanent replacements for Jay and the other striking mills. Third, a party's bid to centralize increases the scope and difficulty of building and maintaining its internal consensus. And should the bid fail, the party may be left with a legacy of internal conflict in the postforcing period. When the UPIU failed to maintain and build the pool to counter IP's power, the net result was a union not only defeated but weakened internally. More on this third risk below.

Structuring the Channels and Frequency of Communications

The number of communications channels and the frequency of interactions are two related aspects of structure. A major change in either feature represents a shift in the structure of bargaining. In our cases, these features shifted together and could be combined for analytic purposes.

Our six forcing episodes involved contract talks, and the parties confined their contacts almost exclusively to representatives within a limited number of institutional channels. This sort of structure is characteristic of traditional, arm's-length collective bargaining, though during forcing episodes, the channels often become even more formal and constrained. Almost all of the six periods were characterized by decreased institutional channels/interactions. For example, in the case of AP Parts, meetings were highly formalized, including one stage featuring elaborate procedures by which small language changes would be handed to top negotiators for inclusion in common three-ring binders. Furthermore, traditional, informal backdoor channels were closed off during these negotiations.

Confining contracts to limited channels during periodic formal negotiations can facilitate a forcing strategy. Specifically, these features allow a negotiator to control information in order to bluff and create bargaining chips in distributive bargaining. They also permit a negotiator to characterize the positions and posture of the other party when speaking to constituents and therefore to stimulate adversarial attitudes toward the other party (thus managing internal differences). In the process, of course, these features also minimize the parties' ability to identify and work on common problems.

Enlisting Additional Parties

Collective bargaining has traditionally been viewed as an archetypical example of bilateral, or two-party, negotiations. Increasingly, however, other parties are being brought into the picture—in either traditional or new roles. These additional parties include the government, a firm's customers, local communities, service providers, and employers or unions in the same industry but not directly involved in the negotiations. Any additional party brings with it the potential to fundamentally change the structure of bargaining from bilateral to multilateral negotiations.

In the context of a forcing strategy, particularly unrestrained forcing, additional parties may be brought in by either the initiating or responding party. All four of our instances of unrestrained forcing involved additional parties. Some companies used customer/market pressures (and even brought in customer representatives) as a way of framing the negotiations in terms of competitive survival. Such a tactic was common in our auto supply cases. There was some risk that the customer's interests would not be identical to those of the employer (and this is an avenue sometimes exploited by unions), which would be destabilizing to the forcing initiative. However, in most cases, employers were confident that they could manage the presentation of customer needs in such a way as to minimize the risks.

Additional parties were enlisted not only by management to bolster forcing strategies but also by unions to thwart such strategies. For example, at Guilford, AP Parts, and IP (Jay, Maine), the unions sought assistance from other local and international unions by positioning their disputes as being ominous harbingers of a more general trend toward forcing by employers in the industry or the region. In addition, other employers and top managers with ties to the forcing firms were targeted. During the AP Parts strike, demonstrations were held at the headquarters of one of the company's main customers (General Motors), and the international union broke off talks at both GM and Ford in order to join the picket line at the AP Parts facility in Toledo, Ohio. In the case of the IP strike in Jay, Maine, a corporate campaign targeted a wide range of business and community interests that could influence IP management.

In other cases, additional groups enter the negotiations as neutral third parties. For example, the area labor-management committee in Toledo and the local mayor both sought to be of assistance as neutral mediators of the AP Parts dispute. Similarly, by March 1988, the strike between IP and the UPIU was weakening both sides, but there was little pretext for either side to come forward with a new offer. As will be developed later in the chapter, a former undersecretary of labor took the initiative to bring the parties together in an effort to find common ground.

These tactics to enlarge the number of involved parties are not particularly new, and they vary in the degree to which the additional parties fully joined the negotiations. Still, they were each designed to serve a forcing strategy, and they each took on added significance in the present era in which customer, supplier, and community interdependencies are more salient.

When the directly involved parties seek to involve additional parties in order to increase their own bargaining power, they may risk further polarizing the situation. The stakes expand to include issues of organizational survival for both the company and the union. Previously risky alliances (such as close ties with customers, the community, competitors, and other unions) may look attractive and even essential to one of the parties. Even third parties will be pressured to take on partisan roles. These "neutral" parties become the target for appeals, making it difficult for any party to remain neutral regarding basic questions of survival. For example, during the AP Parts strike, the parties placed high priority on wooing public opinion and harnessing community resources in the service of their respective agendas. Similarly, in the cases of AP Parts, Guilford, and the Jay mill, the unions sought interventions by relevant government officials and arbitrators by arguing that the very institution of collective bargaining was under attack. Management representatives responded (in a variety of governmental forums) that the companies' actions were not only legal, but necessary given the competitive climate.

MOBILIZING AND DEPLOYING BARGAINING POWER

As we have already indicated, the way parties state their substantive proposals and how they design the structure for their negotiations have important implications for bargaining power. Here we take up some of the more overt power tools and techniques, such as threatening to transfer operations, preparing for and waging strikes, hiring permanent replacements, and employing in-plant tactics and corporate campaigns. The primary risks associated with these tactics are, on the one hand, defeat (when they don't work) and, on the other hand, escalation and a legacy of distrust (when they are not only coercive but also highly provocative).

Using the Escape Option Tactically

In developing a bargaining plan, management often considers whether to make tactical use of escape. In this sense, the escape option is employed as a tactical maneuver in which management's willingness and ability to carry out such a threat will vary, as will labor's assessment of management's willingness to take such risks. For example, prior to the strike at AP Parts, management moved contracts with aftermarket customers to the firm's Goldsboro, North Carolina, facility and shifted the Toledo, Ohio, facility to OEM production. The move itself was not executed as an escape strategy (since alternative work was brought into the Toledo facility). However, it had important tactical implications for the subsequent forcing since the shift provided justification to the community for the hard stance that AP Parts was taking in negotiations.

Strike Preparations

Strike preparations are often instrumental to building power. Like other power tools, they have direct and indirect effects. They can not only bolster the credibility of the company's bargaining position but also indirectly add to the contentiousness of the labor-management relationship and thereby increase the likelihood of escalating economic warfare. While the notion of strike preparations is not new to collective bargaining, the techniques used (and their implications) have been redefined in recent years. The process has been formalized through the input of management consultants and advanced to the point where the preparations have become a highly visible, well-orchestrated tool—as important a source of intimidation as the actual event itself. Also, with the increased use of permanent replacement workers (which is addressed below), strike preparations take on very serious implications. In fact, one indication of the current polarization in labor-management relations is the lack of a middle ground on the strike preparations issues: if management prepares for a strike, this move serves as a forcing tactic (regardless of whether a strike occurs), and if management doesn't prepare for a strike, then this can send a powerful fostering signal.

Thorough planning for a strike at De Ridder.   Preparation for a possible strike at De Ridder was especially systematic and thorough—and provocative. To build the company's bargaining power, a management group carefully planned for the following: continuation of the inflow of raw materials and the outflow of finished product, operation of the mill during a strike with managers from other Boise Cascade mills, training of potential replacements with skills not readily available, temporary housing for replacements, and mill security. The group also constructed a new access road to the plant—a road that avoided the union hall, which was located on the regular access road.

To ensure that the company actually realized the benefits of contractual changes (which managers assumed the workforce would surely resist), another management group planned how to introduce and sustain the changes. In effect, managers prepared for the continuous negotiations they expected with workers and the union to determine what the new contractual terms would mean in practice.

Management supplemented these other planning efforts with a plan for communications within its own organization, to the workforce, and to the community. This preparation, together with the ambitiousness of the company's proposals, helped convince labor that management was, indeed, serious; however, instead of generating a willingness on labor's part to make concessions, it triggered reciprocal efforts by labor to prepare for the economic showdown. These dynamics were equally evident in the AP Parts case.

Provocative fences and security guards at AP Parts.   One union leader described some of AP Parts' preparations and labor's reaction to them as follows:

> They erected a chain link fence around the plant on the same day that we sat down to begin negotiations. There had not been one prior to that. The company took down a sign outside the personnel office indicating there was no hiring and replaced it with a sign requesting employment applications. Nuckles Security [a private security firm] brought in a van load of big, ugly men in uniforms. They tried to put fear in the guys, but these were the wrong people for that. They got a reaction—they got a lot of hate, but these were the wrong guys for fear.[4]

Once the union concluded that its institutional security was at risk, it began counteracting management initiatives. One union official characterized the union strategy as follows: "We played tit for tat. We reacted to what they did. If they sent a four page letter to all employees, we would come back with a five page letter."[5]

Hiring Permanent Replacements for Striking Employees

Once a strike deadline is reached, the forcing dynamics become complicated and subject to a series of pivotal events. In several of our cases at this juncture, management decided to hire replacement workers—with profound risks for escalating the conflict out of control and for souring labor relations over the long term.

Permanently replacing workers on the Guilford Railroad. Negotiations between Guilford and its union came to an impasse over the handling of furloughed employees. At this point, the union announced a strike, which it saw as a routine event in the industry—anticipating that a settlement would ultimately be reached via arbitration or the appointment of an emergency board. The company, however, saw the strike as a destructive act against a carrier in a fragile economic situation—which provided justification for hiring permanent replacement workers to keep the railroad operating. The union immediately escalated the strike to the national level, utilizing the secondary boycott pressures that are legal under the Railway labor Act. Ultimately, the strike was settled when Congress legislated the recommendations of the emergency board. But replacement workers continued working, and the damage to the labor-management relationship was substantial.

Within any particular negotiation, the hiring of permanent replacement workers represents a pivotal event and is the tactic that most vividly illustrates what is meant by "unrestrained forcing." From labor's perspective, this marks a point of no return—wherein the stakes become institutional survival.

In-Plant Tactics by Labor

Given the shift in the power equation that tends to accompany the onset of a strike, unions are increasingly resorting to pressure tactics short of leaving work. These tactics include work-to-rule and more aggressive actions designed to impair the regular, daily functioning of business operations. This is one of the forms of escalation on labor's side. The AP Parts case illustrates this struggle as well as the dynamics of the ensuing strike.

Severe counterforcing at AP Parts. By the contract expiration date in the negotiations between AP Parts and the UAW, the membership had rejected the package and management had erected a security fence, advertised for replacement workers, and hired a firm associated with decertification efforts. The union had anticipated that management expected a strike, and in a surprise tactic, the union members showed up on the day the contract expired ready to work under the terms of managements's final offer. Reportedly, they found security guards hurriedly packing up food, cots, and other supplies that might be used to sustain replacement workers stuck overnight in the factory. While management's extreme opening demands marked an initial pivotal event that gave management an advantage at the outset of the AP Parts negotiations, the union's decision not to strike represented a second pivotal event, in which labor reestablished control over the situation. This tactical move by the union stemmed from its conclusion that it would have greater bargaining leverage by continuing to work than by going on strike.

While working under the terms of management's final offer, the union members engaged in a variety of tactics designed to frustrate the regular flow of business operations. For example, they reportedly inflated records of accumulated inventory so that management would underestimate how long it would take to meet customer needs under these circumstances.

For its part, management directed security guards to regularly videotape work activities (to which workers responded with taunts). In accordance with the terms of management's final offer, wages and benefits were cut by $5.84 per hour, and new shop rules giving management more freedom to assign work were instituted. During the next month, more than 150 workers were laid off (bringing plant employment to 232). More than 80 employees received more than 200 disciplinary notices for violations of new work rules with other infractions during the three-week period following the contract expiration—an example of forcing at the individual level of the organization.

Violence and Escalation during Strikes

When strikes do occur, the stakes are usually high for both sides—especially if permanent replacement workers are utilized. Violence flares and relations deteriorate. The experience at AP Parts also illustrates these dynamics.

Rapid deterioration of relations at AP Parts. After an unfair labor practice charge filed by the union was rejected in April 1984, the union called the workers out on strike. AP Parts then brought in the first group of 40 replacement workers, who were met by approximately 125 picketing union members. As a result of punctured car tires, broken windshields, and other such activities, a court order was issued the next day limiting union picketing.

Over the next several weeks, the conflicts between picketing strikers, security guards, and replacement workers intensified, with daily taunting, stone throwing, and other exchanges. Periodically, there were public demonstrations outside the facility as well, the largest of which was in May 1984, to protest the company's announced reward of $10,000 for information concerning vandalism during the strike.

The demonstration, involving about 3,000 people, turned violent. A group of demonstrators attempted to break through the plant gate with an 18-wheel semi truck. The Toledo police used tear gas canisters to break up the protest, which generated a public outcry since some of the canisters contained printed warnings that they could be deadly. One union official reflected on the experience and the overall strike as follows: "This was a war, full of wounds. Vietnam was easy compared to this, I was over there. It was like a goddamn tour of duty. Imagine nine months with no income. We had suicide, alcoholism and divorce."[6]

The demonstration vividly illustrated that the labor-management relationship (and any prior sense of a stable, arm's-length social contract) had collapsed. Formal negotiations were officially broken off, and the parties settled into a contest of extreme unrestrained forcing.

Corporate Campaigns

In their efforts to gain leverage in the face of a forcing strategy, several unions embraced a series of tactics that have come to be called "corporate campaigns." The corporate campaign has roots that go back to labor's earliest struggles and public pronouncements against financiers and management trusts. However, it was the textile union's campaign against J. P. Stevens in the 1970s that marked the modern-day use of leverage (including veiled secondary boycott threats) against members of a corporation's board of directors, banks serving the corporation, and other key stakeholders. While such tactics have usually not been as potent as management's use of permanent replacement workers, they often mark a comparable point of no return for the labor-management relationship.

Corporate campaign against International Paper. Perhaps the most complex and important UPIU activity in its dealings with International Paper was the corporate campaign following the onset of the strike in Jay, Maine. By early 1988, the campaign was in full swing. Strikers were organized into caravans that traveled through Maine, and then to other parts of New England, to garner support. In February 1988, they appeared in Boston, where the Democratic mayor declared "UPIU Local 14 Solidarity Day"— and also pledged to avoid buying IP products for the city. Democratic presidential candidates Michael Dukakis and Jesse Jackson vied to express their support. The union identified several major companies—including Coca-Cola, Avon, Anheuser-Busch, and a Boston bank—that bought paper from IP or shared directors with IP, and orchestrated picket lines, boycott lists, and letter-writing campaigns.

The union's goal was to demonstrate to board members that they would be treated as integral parts of IP management in every aspect of their lives. Board members encountered pickets everywhere. Political debate spread from the Maine legislature to the Democratic presidential campaign. And the Maine governor drafted a bill that would keep non-Maine companies from providing strikebreakers.

MANAGING INTERNAL RELATIONS IN THE HEAT OF FORCING

The degree of consensus within an organization is of paramount importance to its leaders. The strength of management's internal agreement and cohesiveness is a major ingredient in the organization's ability to get work done effectively and efficiently. Similarly, for labor officials, solidarity is fundamental to the union's institutional strength. Thus, both management and the union are concerned about internal consensus regardless of whether they are engaged in interparty negotiations. However, under the pressures of negotiations, both the tolerance for internal dissent and the building of consensus take on added tactical significance.

We have already explored tactical efforts to generate early support for a party's bargaining position, as illustrated by De Ridder management's systematic development of the rationale for its forcing. Once the process has moved to the stage of all-out forcing—characterized by the use of replacement workers, corporate campaigns, and strident appeals to third parties—each side usually devotes considerable energy to bolstering support within its own organization and often seeks to create divisions within the ranks of the other party.

The tactical risks here are several: a party that fails to garner internal support is more likely to lose the forcing campaign; a party that attempts to divide the other side risks an escalation it may regret; and the side that gets internal support for positions it must later abandon may suffer weakened solidarity in the postforcing period.

In our sample, labor was the party whose bargaining was most often weakened by failure to generate internal consensus—a not surprising pattern given the reality that a union is a political organization, in contrast to the more hierarchical nature of the business organization. Union members not only elect officers, they usually vote on proposed agreements before they are put into effect, whereas managers neither elect their representatives nor vote on proposed agreements.

Labor's shortfalls in managing internal differences in our sample included the rivalry between the UTU and the craft unions at Guilford, the division among worker-owners during the strike at Adrian Fabricators, and breaks in the solidarity of UPIU strikers in the Jay negotiations. Management benefited in each case.

Opportunistic Moves to Affect Internal Consensus

Typically, forcing campaigns are characterized by a panoply of internal relations tactics often devised during the battle to take advantage of any opportunity to weaken the other's consensus or bolster one's own. The "end run" by management is perhaps the most vivid tactic used by one party to sow divisions in the other side.

Direct appeals to union members—a classic end-run maneuver. Management's communicating directly with employees—as an end run around the union—characterized many of our forcing cases. For example, management at AP Parts sent all employees a four-page letter detailing its version of the negotiations (whereupon the union responded with a five-page letter presenting its own version). At De Ridder, management made sure that all employees were aware of its offers—especially since the offers contained some features that were very attractive financially. Each of these moves was designed to promote splits between union members and union leaders.

Interweaving activities to unite one's own party and divide the other: Jay. Each party in the UPIU-IP negotiations took many steps to strengthen its own unity and undermine the other party's internal consensus. IP successfully sued the UPIU for injunction violations—and then proceeded to distribute the proceeds to strikebreakers and employment agencies. The usual heckling of strikebreakers continued—answered on paydays by the employed workers' brandishing of their paychecks. UPIU members also attempted to undermine support for IP's position by appealing to shareholders and board members. In turn, IP tried assiduously to break the power of the corporate campaign by reaching settlements at other locations. Each side went to great lengths to demonstrate the destructiveness, self-serving nature, and ultimate hopelessness of the other side's strategy—in large part to unite its own constituents.

Interestingly, the greatest effect of the UPIU corporate campaign, discussed earlier as a pressure tactic, was probably *within* the union's multi-level organization. Out of 1,250 UPIU members, fewer than 70 strikers returned. Although the availability of unemployment insurance for an extended period blunted the necessity of returning to work, observers suggested that, in large part, this modest hireback reflected the power of the corporate campaign—especially as a means for focusing and reinforcing labor's anger at IP and its resolve not to give up the strike. In a small town in which the same extended family could include both hourly workers and managers, the corporate campaign allowed strikers to fix upon new faces and to conduct antagonistic encounters in other locations.

On management's side at Jay, the primary effort to sow divisions within the local union was the "carrot and stick" message implicit in its handling of replacements and job openings—specifically, its November 1987 announcement that it had hired 988 permanent replacements and that 12 jobs were still open to returning strikers. The carrot message: "You can apply for one of these 12 positions." The stick: "If you don't apply, your job can be gone forever."

The threat of the permanent loss of jobs created divisions not only locally in Jay but also among the other UPIU locals that were invited to join an expanded pool as their contracts expired. In the end, the UPIU failed to achieve the solidarity it needed to support an ultimate test of strength with IP, and therefore, the union acceded to management's demands and ended the forcing episode.

MANAGING THE ENDGAME OF FORCING CAMPAIGNS AND THEIR LEGACIES

By the latter stages of a forcing campaign, when both parties have decided it is in their best interests to resolve the dispute, they face a number of challenges—most of which are by-products of the tactics already discussed.

Restoring Working Relations

Unless management decides to pursue a strategy of escape, sooner or later it and the union will have to attend to their relationship, especially in situations in which the mobilization of bargaining power has led to a breakdown in communications.

While the first challenge for a negotiator employing a forcing strategy is to avoid unwanted escalation of the conflict, the second challenge is to temper the effects of such escalation when it does occur. In most of our cases, the parties met the second challenge no more successfully than the first. Chapter 11 analyzes tactics used to shift from a period of forcing to a period of fostering. It will be helpful here to anticipate one portion of that discussion by examining some of the tensions and complexities associated with the reconstruction of relations during or in the aftermath of an escalating conflict.

In the following subsections, we examine a number of instances in which the major tactical objective was to restore working relations, sometimes with the help of third parties, either during or immediately following negotiations. First, however, we use the forcing period at Pensacola to illustrate how the mere fact of a forced solution, even if the forcing tactics themselves were mild, leaves a legacy of resentment.

Attitudinal effects of forced solutions: Pensacola, 1985. We have been considering the attitudinal effects of various forcing tactics. But forced solutions per se usually produce lingering antagonism.

The Pensacola case provides an example. It was characterized by a general absence of provocative tactics by management beyond the "shocking" effect of the ambitious demands. Management's bargaining power inhered in the context of the situation (new management, subsequent downsizing of the mill, and a pervasive sense of insecurity among the workforce), and therefore, management had no need to take other potentially antagonistic steps to mobilize power or bolster the credibility of its bargaining positions.

The atmosphere at the final Pensacola negotiating session—traditionally used by the parties to move from the adversarial posturings of the bargaining table to the more congenial relationships characterizing day-to-day mill life—was clouded by the union team's sense that the company had taken advantage of the mill's immediate situation by aggressively gaining greater control over labor deployment in the mill. While company negotiators expected that employees' elation over the large capital investment at Pensacola would overshadow negative union reactions to the manner in which management had pressed its advantage in contract negotiations, the union team felt that it had been forced without notice to play an old game by new rules. A member of the company negotiating team observed:

> They felt really used at that time. I can recall the final session that they had. . . . [I]t was a very depressing situation. Typically, final sessions—there's handshakes, congratulations on a job well done. This was very tense, cloudy; you could cut the air with a knife. Union people made comments to me to the effect that we just raped them. . . . It was pretty bitter—that we had, in essence, shoved it down their throats.

Company negotiators had written provisions for a joint union-management steering committee into the new contract, but fear of the potential for vocal opposition in this ready-made forum led managers to exclude union representatives from early implementation planning.

Unsuccessful de-escalation attempt at AP Parts. Having built tension to a fever pitch, the AP Parts negotiators found that they had to take special steps to de-escalate the tension just to permit talks to resume. But diminishing the provocative dynamics proved difficult.

In mid-June, secret talks—initiated by the company—began in Ann Arbor, Michigan. A new group of management lawyers was brought in, and meetings started with an open and informal tone, signaled by casual attire on both sides. The new lawyers indicated, however, that the negotiations were to start from scratch—AP management would not honor any existing tentative agreements. The use of distributive tactics such as this was accompanied by renewed tension. For example, the company brought large binders with proposed new contract language. The union resented the considerable time devoted at the beginning of each meeting to replacing pages in the binders, each of which featured only minor wording changes. In response, the union handed out its own large binders with its own proposals. The debate then centered on whose binders would be the basis for discussions.

By mid-August, the negotiations again came to a halt. We do not know how serious the company was about seeking resolution at this stage, but it is clear that the binder tactics and other such acts undercut communications and, hence, substantive discussions.

Third-party initiatives to de-escalate conflict: Jay. Our forcing cases contain many examples of third-party initiatives intended to break escalation patterns or bargaining impasses. The negotiations between IP and the UPIU involving the mill in Jay, Maine, are illustrative. By March 1988, the nine-month-old strike and the bruising and expensive conflict attending it had wearied both parties. Management was losing production and profits at a steady rate, and the union faced a loss of intraorganizational consensus. Yet neither side could readily make an unsolicited offer.

Enter former Undersecretary of Labor Malcolm Lovell. He engineered a resumption of contract talks in Knoxville, Tennessee, and announced he was prepared to expand the mediating role he had already played. Simultaneously, IP was reported to have a "genuine desire" to reach a settlement, and the UPIU president issued a statement reflecting a new sense of optimism about the potential for integrating the company's and employees' interests: "[The UPIU is ready] to begin developing a positive, long-term relationship dedicated to the competitiveness of the company and the welfare of employees."

In addition, Rogers' corporate campaign was suspended; of course, IP announced that it had been "terminated" while the UPIU declared that it had merely been put "on hold." Although this particular set of talks did not itself produce an agreement, it did play an important role in thawing the relationship between the leadership of the two sides. A similar intervention by the mayor of Toledo served to lessen (but not eliminate) tensions between AP Parts and the UAW.

Reconstructing relations following mutually costly strikes at AP Parts, Adrian, and De Ridder. The strike at AP Parts was costly to both sides. Management succeeded in implementing an agreement that featured deep concessions in wages and work rules, but only after an extended period of below-normal production, a break with the management community in Toledo, and a disruption of relations with key customers. The union succeeded in preserving most of its members' jobs and demonstrated its creativity in devising its own forcing tactics, but at a great personal cost to most of the workers who had been on strike and at the risk of alienating the very customers that it now depended on for continued work. How did the parties then halt the escalating conflict and reconstruct traditional relations in such a context?

The first break in the tension—following the contract settlement—involved changes in key individuals on both sides of the table. The plant manager, personnel director, and many supervisors left the company—with new individuals hired to take their places. Within the union, a new slate of leaders was elected on a platform of moving beyond the strike and working with management. When the firm's main customers expressed concern about future labor strife, the parties then negotiated an early agreement covering a period of several years. While the bargaining process did not feature high levels of problem solving, neither was it extremely contentious. A traditional, arm's-length relationship had been reestablished within two years of the parties' having been involved in all-out warfare.

The new management team still continued to employ traditional control-oriented approaches (rather than participative management principles). In response, the union's membership returned to office a group of union leaders who had played key roles during the strike—replacing the leaders who had run on a more collaborative platform. Also, management was constructing a new facility in Indiana that would have similar productive capacity and would be operated on a nonunion basis. Both parties remained determined to avoid the tensions associated with the strike, and they showed remarkable resilience in reestablishing traditional relations; but there were still tensions in the relationship, and it was unclear whether the arm's-length relations would be stable, deteriorate, or move toward increased cooperation.

The reconstruction process also depended on new faces at Adrian Fabricators and De Ridder—both of which involved key changes in top management. The process was further aided at Adrian Fabricators by technical assistance from the state of Michigan and conciliatory overtures by the union (such as covering the cost of all windows broken during the strike). Thus, escalating dynamics that emerge in the context of forcing strategies can produce long-term tensions in labor-management relationships, but these unanticipated conflicts can also be tempered and even reversed over time.

Dealing with the Internal Fallout of Forcing

Often, even "successful" forcing—especially if it's mutually costly—occurs at the ultimate expense of internal agreement. In a forcing campaign, the losing side in particular experiences new and exacerbated divisions, while the winner may increase its internal cohesiveness.

For example, the UPIU's failure to recruit new locals to expand the pool and build pressure on International Paper not only resulted in the union's decision to yield to management's terms but also created a residue of regret and shame on the part of those who declined to join their "brothers in the good fight." The "lessons learned" undoubtedly made the UPIU leaders more cautious about future forcing strategies similarly dependent on inter-local solidarity.

Consider also the De Ridder case. Within a year of the strike, in which the company prevailed, there was a complete change of union leadership, interpreted by managers as an indictment of the strike itself. One remarked, "It was a reaction against the strike. They were saying, 'We were as misled by the union as we were mistreated by the company.'" While the president of the maintenance union continued in office, the production local experienced a turnover of three presidents. Mill managers explained this in terms of the union's changing posture and significance at De Ridder, since the old mechanisms of grievances, arbitration, contract demands, and strikes had come to look far less central to employee well-being, and the union had failed to devise any new modes of interaction with management.

As noted earlier, there was a similar turnover in union leadership at AP Parts, though this was followed by a second turnover that returned former strike leaders to union office—reflecting a continuation of tensions from the forcing period.

SUMMARY AND CONCLUSIONS

The forcing tactics available to management and labor in the present era are many—as are the accompanying risks. We have reviewed management tactics, including ambitious concessionary demands, end runs to the union membership, hiring replacement workers during a strike, and threatened (or actual) movement of work out of a facility. Counterforcing by the union includes in-plant tactics, corporate campaigns, pooling contract expirations, and just acting in unexpected ways (such as not striking at contract expiration). As potent as these and other management and union tactics may be, the majority of our cases also illustrate their bluntness.

All of our forcing cases involved some degree of escalation and unanticipated dynamics. In the cases of unrestrained forcing, the escalation included violence and the building of deep-seated antipathies. While management in each of our cases surely expected some measure of resistance, it is not clear that any of the managements fully anticipated the degree to which unions would feel threatened by such tactics as the hiring of replacement workers. Thus, the gains from forcing were often offset (at least in the short run) by substantial costs.

The risk of inadvertent escalation is also increased by a set of dilemmas associated with the management of internal differences. Maintaining solidarity was particularly important and difficult for unions (as political organizations), which inspired a variety of attitudinal tactics aimed at identifying a common enemy—thereby fueling distributive tensions.

Structure—usually a fixed aspect of negotiations—proved an important tactical tool. Parties engaged in forcing sought to manipulate the degree of centralization, the number of parties, and the channels for information flow. The negotiations over structure involved high stakes, since a loser would have to bargain within a structure established by (and favorable to) the other side.

Although, in some instances, management's gains may have fallen short of expectations, in all cases, management did succeed in establishing its capacity to utilize force as a lever for change. In contrast to the mixed forcing and fostering periods (which are discussed more fully in Chapter 11), this demonstration of power was not easily harnessed as the foundation for a new social contract.

When recovery from the escalating dynamic did occur, the process was complex and dependent on tactical overtures and other related changes. For example, in the one case of unrestrained forcing that subsequently shifted to mutual fostering—Adrian Fabricators—the de-escalation of tension required symbolic gestures, the turnover of key leaders, third-party technical assistance, and the fortuitous coincidence of an upturn in business. At AP Parts, the restoration of relations returned matters to traditional, arm's-length dealings. But this, too, involved changes in union and management leadership, as well as substantial moderation by management in the next round of negotiations. De Ridder was a case of controlled forcing that best illustrates the use of tactics to anticipate recovery (such as pressing for work-rule concessions while still offering a relatively attractive wage package), but as we discuss in Chapter 10, this success also depended on many unique features of the case (such as the turnover of top management at the plant and a concerted effort to address safety issues in the plant).

At a practical level, there are many tactical lessons for labor and management. First, it would be hard for management to overestimate the hostility engendered by demands for major substantive change. Second (and relatedly), substantive proposals should be accompanied by credible justification. The development of internal support is clearly critical to forcing (and counterforcing), though it requires careful tempering. Similarly, altering the bargaining structure is a tempting, but high-stakes, lever in a forcing campaign.

In sum, forcing change offers the promise of producing major gains within a relatively short time frame. Also, it is possible for the labor-management relationship to recover from a forcing campaign—even a very harsh one. However, success in forcing requires extraordinarily careful attention to tactical details and their consequences.

NOTES

1. We do not attempt here to provide a comprehensive catalog of the tactics that may be used to implement a forcing strategy. With a few exceptions, we confine our treatment to the tactics that played an important role in our 13 cases. Other distributive-bargaining tactics described in *A Behavioral Theory of Labor Negotiations*, 2d ed. (New York: ILR Press, 1991) are still potentially relevant today.
2. Joel E. Cutcher-Gershenfeld, Robert McKersie, and Richard Walton, *Pathways to Change: Case Studies in Strategic Negotiations* (Kalamazoo, Mich.: W. E. Upjohn Institute for Employment Research, forthcoming), Chapter 2.
3. Ibid., Chapter 5.
4. Ibid., Chapter 2.
5. Ibid., Chapter 5.
6. Ibid., Chapter 2.

Chapter 10

Implementing a Fostering Strategy: Tactics and Dynamics

In describing change efforts based on fostering, one practitioner stated, "The process takes longer, but the result is stronger." Why does it take longer? In what ways can the result be stronger? Our analysis of the tactics and dynamics associated with fostering points to predictable dilemmas and critical linkages that help explain why fostering points to predictable dilemmas and critical linkages that help explain why fostering change is both difficult and attractive.

Whereas most of our forcing cases were centered on tactics directly related to contract negotiations, the fostering strategies we examine were initiated both at and away from the bargaining table. Either way, they inevitably involved long-term processes for managing change. Fostering negotiations are subtle and complex: they call for creative structural adaptation, skillful management of process tactics, and careful attention to unfolding dynamics.

Fostering is usually designed to negotiate greater mutuality into the social contract and to address common problems in that spirit. What major risks must negotiators consider in implementing a fostering strategy? And what tactical choices are critical to successful fostering? For example, a negotiator must decide how much, if any, effort to invest in improving working relations before initiating work on substantive issues and whether to target initial fostering directly at employees or at union leaders. The other party must decide how to respond to such overtures. Each party must decide how far to go in attempting to muster internal support before engaging in joint fostering activities and what techniques to employ. These are some of the important choices the negotiators in our cases had to make.

We will describe and illustrate what negotiators in our cases actually did in these tactical areas and assess their actions in terms of whether they minimized the tactical risks of fostering and whether they contributed to good outcomes. We draw from the ten predominantly fostering periods in our cases (see Table 10.1). Four of these periods—Bidwell mill, Anderson

Table 10.1 Periods of Forcing, Fostering, and Forcing/Fostering

Case History	Strategic Periods		
	1	2	3
Paper mills			
Jay (International Paper)	Unrestrained forcing		
De Ridder (Boise Cascade)	Forcing	Fostering	
Bidwell (disguised name)	Fostering		
Pensacola (Champion Paper)	Forcing	Fostering	Forcing/ fostering
Auto supply companies			
AP Parts	Unrestrained forcing		
Adrian Fabricators	Unrestrained forcing	Fostering	
Packard Electric	Forcing/fostering	Fostering	
Budd	Forcing/fostering	Fostering	
Anderson Pattern	Fostering		
Railroads			
Guilford	Unrestrained forcing		
Union Pacific	Fostering		
Conrail	Forcing/fostering	Fostering	
CSX	Fostering		

Pattern, Union Pacific, and CSX—featured the first initiative by management to negotiate major change, whether by fostering or by forcing. In all four of these cases, this was the only period we studied. The Bidwell effort was abortive. UP and CSX were continuing in a fostering mode when our observation ended. The fourth fostering effort—that of Anderson Pattern—was very successful and ongoing. The other six fostering periods were second periods in our studies, with three following a forcing period and the other three following a combined forcing/fostering period. These six periods were all productive to some degree.

The analysis in this chapter begins with a review of the diverse patterns that are associated with fostering strategies—patterns that offer the potential for all three tactical subprocesses to play critical roles. Then, we review the key benefits, costs, and tactical risks associated with fostering and set forth the various structural options that support fostering efforts. In the second half of the chapter, we examine, in turn, each negotiating subprocess, with attention to particular tactics that are illustrative of that process. These tactics will be familiar to most readers; they include off-site retreats, employee information briefing sessions, employee involvement programs, interest-based bargaining techniques, total quality management efforts, and many others. Although many of these tactics are themselves the subject of vast literatures, we examine them through a negotiations lens—which yields some distinctive insights.

COMMON PATTERNS AND VARIATIONS IN THE FOSTERING PERIODS

Whereas we regard distributive bargaining as the single defining process for a forcing strategy and treat the other two processes as supportive of it, we find fostering more complicated. The cornerstone for a fostering strategy can be either intergroup attitude change or integrative bargaining or some combination of the two processes. Of course, for successful fostering as for successful forcing, all three tactical processes, including the management of internal differences, must be coordinated and skillfully executed.[1]

A typical fostering effort can be illustrated by a quick review of some of the tactics used in the Anderson Pattern case:

- The offer of profit sharing by Anderson Pattern's president, who requested no *quid pro quo*
- A restructuring of union-management negotiations from areawide to company-specific in order to deal with profit sharing and subsequent proposals adaptive to the company's competitive situation
- A limited experiment to relax the one-person, one-machine staffing requirement for two new pieces of equipment
- A company-sponsored trip for employees to see new equipment at a trade show prior to agreeing to experiment
- The deliberations about whether to expand the successful staffing pattern from an experiment to general practice, leading to an agreement to do so after labor's job security and training concerns were addressed
- The extensive, regular sharing of information on sales, quality, market conditions, safety, and other matters

We see in this partial review of tactics in the Anderson case not only integrative bargaining (such as the search for arrangements that both permitted more efficient staffing practices and dealt with the employees' training and employment security needs) but also initiatives to promote new intergroup attitudes (the profit-sharing overture) and internal consensus within labor's ranks (the trip to a trade show to learn about the new equipment, which paved the way for union-management agreement). Indeed, all of our fostering episodes involved at least some management

Table 10.2   Roles Played by Tactical Processes in the Ten Fostering Periods Studied

- *Integrative bargaining:* In some cases, management drove fostering with an integrative agenda; in other cases, it drove the effort with successful relationship work and then followed up with integrative bargaining. In a few cases, the parties paid little or no attention to this process. Integrative bargaining, which benefits from the involvement of diverse elements within each party, sometimes exacerbated the problems of maintaining internal consensus.

- *Managing internal differences:* In most cases, negotiators paid major attention to developing internal support for fostering, whether it was driven by integrative bargaining or intergroup attitude-change activities. Nevertheless, deficiencies in managing internal consensus often limited the overall effectiveness of the fostering efforts.

- *Shaping intergroup attitudes:* In many cases, management initiated the fostering period with attitude-change activities, usually following up with integrative bargaining. In a few cases, attitude-change effects were incidental to integrative bargaining.

attention to the tactical requirements of all three processes. However, the similarities end there.

Worth noting at this point are three specific types of differences: in labor's responses, in the role played by each tactical process, and in the outcomes of the fostering period.

First, labor's reaction varied widely. When the fostering period represented management's first initiative toward major change, labor's *initial* responses were skeptical and cautious. In contrast, when management fostered against a prior period of combined forcing and fostering, then both parties engaged in the process of reciprocating fostering initiatives.

Second, the sequence in which the parties attended to the three processes varied from case to case. In about half our cases, the interparty work first emphasized integrative bargaining, whereas in the other half, it first emphasized reshaping intergroup attitudes. Although work on internal consensus usually comes into play at various points throughout a fostering episode, in a few instances, one or both of the parties attempted to build internal consensus before undertaking any significant interparty work. This occurred as a distinct phase in both Bidwell and Pensacola. Table 10.2 summarizes the roles of the three tactical processes in the overall fostering effort.

Third, as noted earlier, the success of the fostering efforts in achieving change varied widely across our ten periods. We hope to help answer the following questions regarding this variation:

- Why did fostering clearly help produce changes in both the substantive and social contracts at Anderson, Boise Cascade's mill at De Ridder,

Champion's mill at Pensacola, Conrail, Adrian Fabricators, Budd, and CSX?

- Why, in contrast, did fostering at UP and Bidwell fail to achieve significant changes in either the substantive or social contracts? Specifically, why was Bidwell's effort abandoned and UP's encapsulated?
- Why and how did fostering produce relatively more significant substantive change in some cases, such as Anderson, than in others, such as De Ridder, where the fostering effort produced significant social change but only minor substantive change?
- Why and how did De Ridder's successful fostering produce employee commitment but not union-management cooperation, whereas successful fostering in other cases involved changes in the social contracts at both levels?

RISKS OF FOSTERING

Fostering can lead to beneficial changes in the collective agreements and/or social contracts. Either type of change can be the driving rationale. The analysis in Chapter 8 of decisions to foster emphasized a management desire to move toward cooperation and commitment. In about half of our fostering periods, management pursued major substantive changes as well. Our analysis also noted that decisions to foster were enabled by expectations that labor would be receptive to management's cooperation and commitment initiatives and that it could be persuaded by the business rationale for the company's substantive proposals, if any. A strategic risk, of course, is that management may be overly optimistic about labor's potential receptivity and its effort may yield no result. Another strategic risk for management is that it may cultivate better feelings without producing any fundamental change in the substantive or social contracts.

Accompanying the strategic considerations are several additional concerns that help shape the tactical implementation of fostering. We found three broad concerns, each related to a particular process. We refer to these concerns as "risks," which can be managed more or less effectively.

Creating positive intergroup attitudes and integrative bargaining represent a natural pair of processes; each can reinforce the other—indeed, each is fully effective only if it *is* reinforced by the other. Therefore, two key risks are that one or the other process may not be implemented in a timely and coordinated manner. It is also necessary to develop internal consensus in *both* parties in support of positive intergroup relations and integrative work if these two interparty processes are to be brought to fruition. Therefore, the third risk, which is composed of many different sources of risk, is that one or both parties may fail to develop adequate internal consensus. Our cases illustrate achievements as well as shortcomings in fostering efforts that can be traced to the management of all of these tactical challenges. The most common deficiency in our fostering episodes related to the third risk—the failure to develop and maintain adequate *internal* support throughout the change effort.

Let us consider these three types of risk and how they relate to tactical maneuvers and outcomes in our cases.

Risk of Insufficient Work on Relationships

Management sometimes attempts to define and address common problems without also taking steps to develop the trust and respect that are required in order for the parties to speak candidly about their respective interests and concerns and to explore a range of alternative solutions.

During the 1980s, American managers became especially aware of this important component of fostering. And in our sample of fostering efforts, this challenge was the one least often ignored. For example, even in our less productive fostering periods—Bidwell, UP, and CSX—there was no evidence that inadequate or poorly timed work on intergroup attitudes was a major problem. Moreover, relationship work was often not only timely but also implemented imaginatively and effectively.

For example, in their comments, many managers revealed a sophisticated perspective on how the process of sharing economic data with union leaders and employee groups is instrumental to building intergroup trust. They reported that a period of up to six months is usually required before any serious discussion and debate are begun around the data; another period that could extend up to or beyond six months is often characterized by detailed challenges concerning the data; and finally—after perhaps a year or more of regularly sharing information—the data would be seen as a credible basis for joint problem solving and improvement in operations.

Several successful fostering periods, such as at Pensacola and Packard Electric, were characterized by especially effective management initiatives to work on intergroup relations with both union officials and employees. These included formal off-site sessions, informal dinners, special study groups, and numerous initiatives designed to build understanding and trust. The fostering efforts of De Ridder management also illustrate well-designed and well-executed work in reshaping employee-manager attitudes at that level.

Risk of Insufficient Work on Substantive Issues

Management sometimes becomes so focused on the attitudinal aspect of fostering that it fails to address the substantive issues with integrative potential, such as work rules, job design, employment security, training, and pay schemes. A fostering effort dedicated to "relationship for relationship's sake" soon runs out of steam. At first, participants may be relieved to be able to give and receive signals of trust and respect, but unless these new attitudes are put to work on common problems, the new relations will not be reinforced and maintained.

This potential deficiency appeared to be part of the reason why fostering at Bidwell and UP was not productive. On the other side of the ledger, Anderson, Budd, and Packard Electric provided examples in which especially effective integrative bargaining played a key role in successful fostering.

A more fundamental reason for the lack of progress on substantive issues may stem from the dilemma created by the relationship work that accompanies a fostering strategy. Ultimately, the resolution of certain substantive issues can require a measure of distributive bargaining—and in some situations, this shift may create considerable dissonance. Consequently, another risk is that in some situations, the pursuit of fostering may make it difficult to initiate the distributive bargaining that the circumstances require.

Risk of Inadequate Internal Support

A major risk during the implementation of fostering is that although labor and management representatives may develop mutual respect and engage in effective integrative bargaining, the process and the outcomes it produces may not be supported within one or both parties. Negotiators can fail to develop internal support among their constituents for a variety of reasons. This particular process may receive too little attention, or it may not be addressed in a timely manner. In some cases, the situation itself is inherently complex and marked by a diversity of viewpoints. In other cases, some fostering tactics themselves complicate the management of accord.

Consider this dilemma: on the one hand, the negotiators open up multiple channels between the labor and management organizations in order to promote positive intergroup attitudes and integrative bargaining, but on the other hand, the diversity of perspectives brought into play within one or both sides prevents the achievement of the necessary internal accord, resulting in too little consensus to achieve an interparty agreement.

The risks associated with managing internal differences presented major challenges in nearly every fostering period we studied. They were especially crucial to the nonproductive fostering at Bidwell and in the first round of fostering at CSX, and were key complicating factors in the fostering efforts at Budd, Packard Electric, Pensacola, and De Ridder. On the other hand, these risks were especially well managed at Anderson.

CHOOSING THE STRUCTURE FOR FOSTERING

The party initiating fostering must decide to whom fostering will be aimed and by what channels of interaction. Let's review several important tactical issues:

- Probably the most important tactical choice for management embarking upon a new fostering effort is whether to begin by giving more emphasis to the individual level (relations with employees) or the institutional level (relations with union officials).

- If management wants to target union relations, it must decide what level of the institutional structure of labor-management relations to emphasize—industry, company, plant, or work unit.

- The parties must decide how many channels of interaction they wish to open up for attitude-change and problem-solving activities.

These are not the only structural questions involved in the implementation of fostering, but they are the ones that commonly arise relatively early in a fostering effort.

Choices along each of these structural dimensions have major implications for the parties' ability to manage all three processes—their ability to establish a favorable climate for interparty work, their ability to identify and address the potentially integrative issues, and their ability to secure and maintain internal support for the other two processes.

In the following subsections, we briefly review each of these structural choices, how they were managed in some of our cases, and their implications for the dynamics and outcomes of fostering.

Individual versus Institutional Initiatives

Fostering can take place at either an institutional level (including various forms of union-management cooperation and joint problem solving) or an individual level (including employee involvement and other forms of "shop-floor" problem solving). Typically, fostering at one level is intended to be matched by subsequent fostering at the other level, which sets the stage for a key strategic choice. Fostering that begins at the institutional level can be the start of a "top-down" strategy, while fostering that begins at the individual level can be the start of a "bottom-up" strategy.

A top-down fostering approach by management relies primarily on efforts to convince union leaders first and rank and file second of the mutual benefits of cooperation. A contrasting bottom-up approach reverses the emphasis, conducting activities aimed at improving relations with workers in advance of a serious effort to change the institutional relationship with the union. A "balanced individual/institutional" approach gives roughly equal and simultaneous attention to fostering change at both tiers. The initial fostering effort typically emphasizes either the institutional or individual level, whereas ongoing fostering typically settles into a balanced pattern of activities. Our study contained at least one example of all three approaches.

Top-down fostering. In our sample, top-down fostering was the most common approach, with early emphasis on improving the attitudes of management and union officials toward each other, followed by defining and addressing common problems. For example, Bidwell and Pensacola managements first met with local union leaders to secure their agreement and establish joint structures to enable employee participation. Similarly, the president of Anderson Pattern raised proposals with union leaders before attempting to engage employees in the dialogue. In two other instances, CSX and Union Pacific, management also started at the top but still had not significantly involved workers in fostering activities by the end of our study. The geographic dispersion of railroad work sites complicated individual-level fostering.

Why did management in these cases start fostering with union leaders? The premises underlying this approach were that union officials would need to agree to any substantive changes management was seeking, in such areas as job design and payment schemes, and/or that union leaders were assumed to have the political will and clout to serve as attitudinal gatekeepers for the workforce, meaning that they could effectively prevent management from improving worker-manager relations or assist in developing these relations.

The main risk of top-down fostering is that as attitudes become more positive between management and union representatives, rank-and-file union members may suspect their leaders of being co-opted by management. If union members become worried that their leaders will "sell out," the leaders may decide to redistance themselves from management. In any event, the parties will find integrative bargaining difficult. While this risk was a matter of potential concern in all our cases, it was more salient at CSX and UP, where fostering remained focused on union officials.

Bottom-up fostering. During the 1980s, bottom-up fostering was a common tactic in American industry. It is intended to create changes in the attitudes and expectations of the rank and file and thereby modify the political realities for their elected representatives. In some cases, it is part of a strategy to marginalize the union. In other cases, it is simply designed to improve employee relations without disturbing the existing union relations. In most cases, however, it is merely intended to be the first phase of a fostering move toward both employee commitment and union-management cooperation. In the latter case, union officials who observe changes in members' attitudes are expected to become more receptive to a cooperative relationship at their level. The risk, of course, is that whatever management's purpose in promoting closer relations with employees, the union may find this initiative threatening and choose to try to stop or neutralize it.

Our cases included only one example of fostering aimed initially at the individual level. De Ridder management undertook a major effort to foster commitment with plant workers without also attempting to generate cooperation with union officials. This effort was sustained for six years after the 1983 strike. Interestingly, in this particular case, neither management nor the union officials ever made a bid to foster a cooperative relationship. Furthermore, the local union officials themselves made only limited attempts to bar worker participation in fostering activities.

Balanced fostering at both levels. Balanced fostering is ideal if it can be realized because, in most cases, management will eventually need to change relationships at both levels; moreover, this approach presents the least risk of either employees or their representatives getting too far out in front in developing more cooperative attitudes—leading to a backlash. Balanced fostering occurred in our sample in the second periods at Budd and Packard Electric, when the parties had already engaged in fostering combined with forcing over a sustained period.

Indeed, in virtually all of our cases in which fostering outcomes would be judged positive—e.g., Pensacola, Budd, Packard Electric, and Anderson Pattern—the parties eventually utilized a balance of individual- and institutional-level change processes. In the Pensacola case, the unfolding employee involvement process was jointly managed in parallel with integrative-bargaining processes. Similar balancing occurred at Packard Electric, linking strong employment security language and wage flexibility with shop-floor problem-solving activity. At Budd, the linkage was visible in the confluence of shop-floor innovations (such as the die transition teams and the Phoenix Project) with ongoing subcommittees within the collective-bargaining process (addressing issues such as health care, cost containment, product quality, and employment security). At Anderson Pattern, increased worker autonomy and training emerged in parallel with integrative bargaining around work rules, new technology, and employment security.

Managing the Degree of Centralization

In our cases, we observed a general tendency to move toward more decentralized structures to facilitate fostering. Decentralization complements fostering by allowing for the emergence of innovative "local" solutions. Concurrently, however, decentralization produces dilemmas involving the effective management of local variation.

Fostering between Anderson Pattern and the union produced a series of agreements that contained *quid pro quos* substantially different from the union's agreements with other area firms—a significant break from a long tradition of centralized bargaining in the community. In 1984, approximately two years after a new co-owner became president of Anderson Pattern, the collective-bargaining agreement expired. This agreement involved Anderson Pattern and the three other unionized pattern-making firms in the community, all negotiating with the Pattern Makers' Association of Muskegon. Although most negotiations were conducted on an areawide basis, a proposal to establish a profit-sharing plan, raised by the new president, was of no interest to the other area employers. As a result, discussions and a later agreement on this concept proceeded bilaterally between the union and Anderson Pattern. Subsequent discussions and agreements concerning new technology and employment security were also of no interest to the other employers and hence conducted on a bilateral basis.

Fostering at CSX and Bidwell initially involved all of the unions representing their respective workforces. In both cases, however, key unions withdrew from the fostering dialogue. As a result, both employers shifted emphasis to a more decentralized form of fostering on a union-by-union and work-area-by-work-area basis.

Another form of decentralization (motivated by the limitations of centralized dialogue) can be found in the negotiations between Budd and the UAW. For certain issues, such as the crafting of language on the die transition team in Detroit and the Phoenix Project in Philadelphia, plant-level bargaining was judged to be a more appropriate forum compared to a tradition of channeling key issues to corporate headquarters and the international union. The facilitating role of decentralization can also be seen in the fashioning of expediter agreements in railroads.

Decentralization offers some advantages for integrative bargaining and attitudinal structuring, but it creates the potential for increased differences within comparable units. For example, at Packard Electric, decentralized decision making produced a wide range of work organizations and compensation schemes to match the varying competitive conditions of different units of the Warren, Ohio, manufacturing complex. Inevitably, such variations raised tensions among units around equity. The job of the union steward then expanded to include mediating the internal conflicts and identifying instances in which the tensions over the variations were intolerable. The response to the tensions created by such variations often involves some form of recentralization.

Establishing New Patterns of Interaction

While all of our forcing initiatives centered on contract bargaining, many of our fostering initiatives featured the application of integrative techniques to regular daily, weekly, or monthly interactions. For example, Packard Electric, Budd, Anderson Pattern, Bidwell, and Pensacola established formal employee involvement or quality circle programs, under which groups of employees would get together periodically to identify and address common problems. In some cases, the groups were organized by functional work areas in a facility, and in other cases, they were established to bring together a cross section of individuals from different areas.

While there is a large literature on worker participation, our focus here is on the negotiating processes involved in such initiatives. We know that employee involvement groups are typically encouraged to address relatively minor issues on which early successes are likely. In time, however, if the groups are successful, they will be tackling issues of greater and greater significance—which brings the promise of achieving increased integrative gains but also the complexity of surfacing contradictory views among various factions within labor and management.

For example, at an early stage of the employee involvement process at Budd, a group identified the outside storage of dies as a threat to quality if they were later reused in production runs. Shifting to internal storage of the dies was relatively uncomplicated and uncontroversial. In contrast, after a decade's experience with worker participation at Packard Electric, the union's continued commitment to the effort became linked to demands for job security. The issue was made quite salient in the Warren branch operations by the work of the jobs committee, involving more flexible work rules and other changes in work organization—all of which produced lower staffing levels than would have occurred if exceptions had not been made to the regular contract. The corporation's concurrent investment in new production facilities in the South and in Mexico further sharpened the issue. Tackling union demands for employment security, however, required a multiyear series of interactions that culminated in a set of formal quid pro quos at the collective-bargaining table around a multitier wage system and greater use of part-time workers. The outcome had many integrative features but required a dramatic new substantive agreement.

A more common form of continuous negotiations involves the establishment of ongoing or periodic forums for midcontract dialogue in the context of a longer-term agreement. For example, the Budd Company negotiated a four-year agreement (one year longer than had traditionally been the case) and established a top-level labor-management committee to conduct quarterly meetings.

Many of the issues that are "on the table" in the present competitiveness era are complex and politically charged, and require continuing attention during the term of the agreement. To tackle such issues at the "main table" would be time-consuming and potentially compromising for the chief negotiators on both sides. As a result, collective-bargaining negotiations in the fostering context are increasingly characterized by the creation of joint committees that serve as an adjunct to the main-table exchanges. In many of our sites, for example, joint committees were established to investigate the health care cost containment issue, generate options, and report back to the principals.

Employing Third Parties

In a fostering context, additional parties are generally sought to provide legitimacy, expert knowledge, and other resources. For example, in the cases of Bidwell, Budd, Adrian Fabricators, Pensacola, Conrail, and CSX, outside parties helped facilitate the initiatives. In some cases, these were independent, private consultants or traditional third-party neutrals (such as arbitrators or mediators). But there were also some nontraditional facilitating parties. In the case of Conrail, for example, the federal government played a key facilitating role through the infusion of capital and its emphasis on flexible work arrangements. During the strike at AP Parts, the local mayor and area labor-management committee assumed a mediating role. In the case of Adrian Fabricators, it was state government that assisted—first in establishing the ESOP and four years later in urging a greater emphasis on employee participation. In the cases of Budd, Adrian Fabricators, and Packard Electric, it was internal and external customers that framed many aspects of the fostering efforts through their insistence on employee involvement processes, statistical process control techniques, just-in-time delivery, and participative management. In some cases, the customers even provided technical assistance in these areas. Another nontraditional participant was Muskegon Community College, which custom-designed an associate's degree program for Anderson Pattern employees—in effect, taking on the functions of a training department.

Sometimes, labor resists the presence of additional parties (when it is management that is seeking to foster change). In this case, labor's concern is not so much that outsiders have no legitimate role in the relationship but, rather, that additional parties—even well-meaning ones—may produce unintended consequences. For example, unions are often concerned that consultants who are brought in to help foster employee participation may unintentionally (or intentionally) serve employee needs in ways that bypass or undercut the union. If it becomes clear that the additional parties are sensitive to such concerns and that they can contribute information, expertise, or resources that might also be of value to labor, then their entry into what has been a bilateral relationship can be relatively smooth. Otherwise, this intervention designed to aid the fostering effort may instead become a point of contention.

The structural choices we have been examining involve where and when interactions take place. We turn now to the interactions themselves and start by examining tactics designed to shape intergroup attitudes.

MAKING OVERTURES TO ESTABLISH—AND REINFORCE— THE CLIMATE FOR FOSTERING

Implementing a fostering strategy requires continuous attention to how actions affect the levels of mutual trust and confidence between the parties. Many actions designed for other purposes, especially integrative work on common problems, provide major reinforcement for positive attitudes. Our interest here is in the efforts of one or both parties directly aimed at intergroup attitudes, and especially those efforts early in a fostering episode intended to create the right climate.

The nature of this challenge varied in our cases—from reversing distrust and resentment in cases such as De Ridder, in which fostering followed on the heels of aggressive forcing; to creating a new level of trust in cases such as Anderson, in which the prevailing relationships were generally amicable; to merely maintaining and deepening a trusting climate in cases such as Budd and Packard Electric, in which fostering followed a period of forcing/fostering.

Many of the overtures designed to establish or reinforce an appropriate climate for fostering involve familiar tactics, including pursuing common social or community activities, making joint visits to other locations and conferences, scheduling an off-site retreat, jointly developing a mission or philosophy statement, taking symbolic actions, and holding information briefings and listening sessions. Examples of these sorts of tactics will be woven throughout our analysis.

Symbolic Actions to Convert a Skeptical Workforce

Nearly every action taken by each side against the backdrop of a forcing period assumes symbolic significance. Particularly if the action is a fostering overture, it will be studied to determine whether it is genuine.

Sustained and skillful cultural change at De Ridder. De Ridder's fostering effort continued over time to rely most heavily on promoting attitude change and reinforcing the spontaneous work behaviors that accompany increased commitment. Thus, after the mill manager's initial efforts to unfreeze hostile attitudes (which we discuss in Chapter 11), he orchestrated a continuous stream of initiatives aimed at securing worker commitment. Many of the initiatives, including the following, carried a strong symbolic message:

- An Employee Assistance Program was formed (with the help of a specialist from the UPIU's national headquarters, but without local union participation).

- The Bridge Committee—a peer contact point to provide direction for help with personal troubles, substance abuse, and other problems—was launched.

- Hourly employees made customer visits, which provided independent evidence of quality issues and market factors.

- The new mill manager made significant and visible expenditures on maintenance to address productivity, safety, and quality of work life issues

The new mill manager built a training center—once again seeing it both as a practical means to develop necessary skills and as a symbol of management's intentions. He also hired 15 additional operators to permit employees to rotate off the floor to help analyze training needs and develop training materials. Whole working crews came into the new training center to advise their coworkers and check the materials, making the entire process, in the words of one manager, "a very powerful tool" for change and involvement. We can infer, as well, that this training-development process was an arena in which supervisors and hourly employees were, at the same time, renegotiating their working relationships, on the mill floor, since the materials being developed had to embody job content within the new team concept work structure.

The mill manager, who orchestrated all these changes, took equally systematic steps to change supervisory behavior (and presumably supervisors' attitudes) toward workers. These initiatives simultaneously ensured internal management coherence and promoted intergroup cooperation. We will explore these activities below in our consideration of the management of internal differences.

The local union leadership was consciously left out of both the earlier "thawing" overtures and the change effort just described. The union leaders raised objections to some of the activities involving direct interactions between managers and employees but could neither deter management from these initiatives nor persuade workers to boycott them. Management took no overtly hostile actions toward the union officials or the union as an institution. In fact, the human resources manager stated that he left his door open to the union officers and gradually built personal relationships with them, but that he continued to depend on what we have called individual negotiations: "Throughout this entire period, my group and I have dealt with the union officers on anything they want [ed] to deal about. We've negotiated a third extension [of the 1983 contract, with few changes] until 1995. By the time they come to me, I've usually heard everything at the listening sessions."

Launching Fostering within an Amicable Relationship

When labor relations are already generally friendly, the initial climate-setting initiatives may take many different forms. They can, for example, involve concrete proposals or actions that, in the absence of an amicable relationship, might be misinterpreted.

The profit sharing proposed by the president of Anderson Pattern provides a case in point. The union was initially skeptical, but when it became clear that management was not asking for any *quid pro quo* from labor, the union agreed to it. The offer served as tangible evidence of the company president's intention to foster new relations.

Even if there is a history of amicable relations, fostering overtures eventually surface some skepticism. In this case, the response derives from the attitude "If it's not broken, don't fix it." The fostering party is, in effect, seeking to replace such an attitude with an orientation toward continuous improvement in operations as well as in the tenor of labor-management relations.

Reinforcing a Fostering Effort

In several cases, the predominantly fostering period followed a period of combined forcing/fostering. In cases such as these, in which movement toward cooperation had already occurred, the challenge was to deepen relationships. There are an almost unlimited number of steps that can reinforce a movement toward greater mutuality. To illustrate, we describe the development of "guiding statements" by the IUE and Packard Electric and the symbolic actions at Budd.

Guiding statements for the IUE and Packard Electric. In May 1978, Packard Electric and the IUE established a jobs committee, based on the union's insistence that it be involved with a recently established management productivity task force. At the outset, the committee drafted a statement of purpose, which was to "develop an ongoing union-management approach that will maintain job security and identify opportunities for hiring in the Warren operations."[2] The statement was particularly important as a vehicle for shaping union members' attitudes: it was designed to identify valued goals that would build member tolerance for the close dialogue that union leaders would be having with managers.

By February 1979, the jobs committee successfully reached an agreement that involved the creation of 100 new jobs—the first new hiring in Warren since 1973. These employees were to work in surrounding communities in new "branch" facilities, where there would be reduced job classifications, job rotation, and an emphasis on teamwork. In order to further shape attitudes regarding the branch facilities, top union and management leaders crafted an "operating philosophy" statement for these facilities, which read as follows:

> We believe that every business has a responsibility to its customers, its employees, and the community in which it exists, and shall strive to satisfy the needs and security of each.
>
> We share in the belief that a successful business provides and maintains an environment for change and is built on a foundation of trust, where every person is treated with respect and offered an opportunity to participate. We are totally committed to the patience, dedication, and cooperation necessary to build this foundation.
>
> We also believe that it can be accomplished through a functioning partnership built on the wisdom, the knowledge, and the understanding of the employees, the union, and management.[3]

Needless to say, this statement is clearly designed to codify shared understandings between top leaders and to elicit "patience, dedication, and cooperation" from others in both the labor and management organizations.

Symbolic actions at Budd. Sometimes, both parties will together make significant symbolic moves. For example, labor and management leaders in Budd's Detroit plant agreed to construct a special room for union-management meetings, but they were very careful about designing the table for the room. They rejected a rectangular table as too adversarial and a round table as too cooperative. Finally, they settled on a curved, oblong table with one end squared for the labor and management committee cochairs. This design symbolized their working together but retaining separate identities.

MUSTERING EARLY INTERNAL SUPPORT

It eventually becomes crucial for both parties to develop an adequate level of internal consensus supporting a new relationship between union and management and the outcomes of joint problem solving. Parties vary in the extent to which they attempt to garner internal support for joint activities early in the fostering episode.

Several tactics for building internal support are illustrated by our cases, including holding separate meetings prior to joint meetings, conducting an indoctrination effort within management, using hierarchical control techniques, educating the workforce, and involving nontraditional stakeholders in the negotiations. To some degree, these tactics were utilized in all of our fostering cases. Where the tactical initiatives were far-reaching, they were instrumental to the fostering strategy. Where their scope was limited, fostering suffered.

Holding Separate Sessions Prior to Joint Meetings

Holding separate meetings for labor and management often represents a key first step in a fostering initiative. Even if the ultimate goal is to work together, each side needs "off-line" time so the leadership and internal constituents can assess readiness for change, identify possible areas of resistance, and formulate the change strategy.

Working toward internal consensus at Bidwell. At Bidwell, the fate of fostering depended crucially on the management of internal differences on both sides. And both sides took steps early in the process to build internal consensus for proceeding with a QWL project.

Prior to initiating the company's contact with the union, the plant manager sponsored several activities to help management get its act together. First, all salaried employees attended a one-day QWL orientation session, which yielded a mixture of interest, curiosity, and skepticism. Second, managers participated in a series of two-day supervisory skills training sessions, which were well received. Third, the management staff was surveyed, and feedback sessions were held on a unit-by-unit basis. The success of these sessions was mixed, but in several units, they led to problem-solving meetings.

The leaders of the four local unions arranged to attend a session of the aforementioned QWL orientation workshop conducted by the same consultant. One union's officers remained opposed to the program but decided to participate in another meeting with management.

While the agreement within both mill management and local unions was sufficient to proceed, it was not adequate to enable the fostering effort to be sustained, especially when it was jostled by other events.

Conducting a Preparatory Indoctrination Effort

Sometimes, one side or the other has a fairly ambitious agenda of internal consensus building. The focus will be not just on informing but on engaging internal constituents in a way that builds commitment to the fostering process.

Internal indoctrination at Pensacola. After the 1985 negotiations at Pensacola in which management forced major changes in work rules, a corporate policy endorsed participative management, and the Pensacola mill was asked to take the lead among Champion's ten union mills.

Implementers decided that in order to be successful, the new system had to be driven by line managers. Several meetings were held early in 1985 to explain the new contract to supervisors, to begin to enlist line manager support for fewer rules and more participation, and to assist department managers in presenting information to their own departments. Key managers traveled to participatory mills (including a new Champion nonunion greenfield mill). Although the emphasis on participative management was not voluntary for the Pensacola managers, the meetings and mill visits were designed to produce genuine supervisor commitment to a participatory style, which, in turn, was intended to help improve relations at the individual level—between workers and supervisors.

The meeting most Pensacola mill managers regard as the real start of management change was held off-site, in March 1986. Attending were 40 managers and supervisors. The major corporate negotiator during the 1985 negotiations and some corporate staffers from headquarters were also invited in recognition of the need for corporate support of such efforts. Those attending received reading material contrasting traditional "control" management with the desired "participative" style, and they read and discussed descriptions of participative programs at other companies. These activities were designed to explain the concept of participative management and enlist the enthusiastic, informed support of the mill's managerial corps.

Although, because of numerous in-mill explanatory and planning meetings during this period, most key agents of change (or resistance) in the mill already understood the nature of participative management before the "buying-in" meeting, this session was larger and more public and reflected attention to the need to enlist the support of major actors at all management levels.

Using Hierarchical Control Techniques

Within management, hierarchical controls provide an important means of building internal support for a fostering initiative. While many fostering activities are voluntary for unions and union members, these same activities are often mandatory for managers.

Hierarchical reinforcement of fostering at De Ridder. The new mill manager at De Ridder used hierarchical tools to make the internal management changes needed to ensure implementation of the intergroup initiatives. He made safety performance a key criterion in a newly established management-by-objectives system. Then, when supervisors used poor judgment in safety matters, they were disciplined, even severed in some extreme cases. The human resources manager said later: "The safety issue was a thing they could grasp. People knew safety was bad there, and a lot of supervisors would just say, 'It's dangerous making paper.' Supervisors would say that all accidents arose from 'unsafe acts.'" The new mill manager commented: "The most important thing is we disciplined supervisors who gave unsafe orders; in extreme cases, some of them were eventually terminated or suspended."

By the end of the new manager's first year, many supervisors had left the mill, reportedly in reaction to reduced merit raises and other new performance demands. They were largely replaced from within De Ridder. Again, these appointments at once altered the composition of the managerial corps in directions supportive of change, rewarded supervisory flexibility, and demonstrated the depth of top management's commitment to change.

Communicating and Educating

If all the constituents have the same information as their representatives about the rationale behind the proposals subject to integrative bargaining, they are more likely to support integrative solutions, including those that inflict some pain. This is a particularly crucial issue for labor. Often, the question becomes: Who communicates the "bad news," if that's the key to developing internal consensus in the union—managers or union representatives?

Facilitating internal consensus at Anderson Pattern. During the negotiation over a proposed relaxation of the one-worker, one-machine rule for two new pieces of equipment, the president of Anderson Pattern provided a creative answer to the question of who communicates the bad news—let the employees inform themselves. In parallel with a series of union-management meetings, the issue was being hotly debated among this small organization's entire workforce. As previously mentioned (and we will return to this example), the president of Anderson Pattern suggested that interested employees travel to Chicago to see the proposed equipment at a trade show that was then under way. Although only 25 machine shop employees would be directly affected by this new technology, almost the whole workforce chose to go to the trade show. According to the union's business manager, the workers returned with a vivid understanding of how the computer-controlled equipment could be operated with fewer workers. Moreover, he reported that most workers were persuaded that the equipment not only required fewer workers but also could "make us competitive enough to increase volume so that we wouldn't have to eliminate people."

Educating both union leaders and members at Budd. Budd provides an interesting example in which management's initial effort at communicating the need for change failed, but subsequent efforts succeeded. The experiences in the local negotiations at the Detroit plant illustrate the critical role that information sharing can play in integrative bargaining.

In the fall of 1988, the Budd Company approached the UAW about initiating early negotiations at the national and plant levels in order to assure the firm's customers of continuity. Management's approach represented a significant departure from the traditional norms of collective bargaining. As a plant personnel official recalls: "The local agreement was very different from what I'd seen before. We had 18 items on the table and the union had only one."[4]

This aggressive approach, which was paralleled in other plants at the national level, came as a surprise to the union and led to an initial collapse of the early bargaining effort. A regional UAW official described the process as follows: "This was not traditional negotiations. The whole process was different. I was shocked by their demands. . . . They came out demanding and I don't like bargaining that way. It was 'this or else,' with the demise of a couple of plants as a possibility held over our heads. We got to the point of no return. We told them to bag their ass."[5]

The breakdown in negotiations reflected the complexity of management's asking the union to be more responsive to its competitive situation (by agreeing to early negotiations) and at the same time using distributive tactics once the union came to the table.

Following the winter holidays, management concluded that a reopening of the negotiations depended on extensive sharing of information about the competitive pressures facing the plant and the company. Both parties were well aware of the similar situation a few years earlier when management had focused on educating local union leaders in the Detroit plant, only to have union members in overwhelming numbers reject a concessionary agreement. Therefore, this time around, management sought to educate the entire workforce. The corporate vice president for industrial relations offered this description of the task: "The communications process is the key element. One of our jobs is to meet the expectations of not only the UAW but also, for lack of a better word, the lowest member of the organization.

We must communicate to individual workers, not just Solidarity House. Our workers can't expect to get what Ford gets and we must communicate this."[6]

As one union leader commented, the communications after the collapse of the first round of early negotiations were a significant break from traditional practice: "I was a bit surprised by the early negotiations, but more surprised by the company talks. Roth and Harper [corporate and division executives] met with hourly workers beforehand and let them know what was going on with the company. They were being honest and that was different."[7] A labor relations official in the Detroit plant said of these sessions: "Roth met with groups of about 100 employees in Detroit and Philly. He talked to them face-to-face about the potential loss of the Lincoln and Econoline jobs. Something happened here. I saw a reaction and some scared people."[8]

In all, the communications and information sharing included informational meetings between management and the bargaining committee as well as plant meetings in which the division president spoke to all employees and "state-of-the-plant" meetings involving local union and management leadership. Printed communications included the plant newsletter, which became more business-oriented, and "Budd Bulletins" at a corporate level (with additional economic information). A UAW vice president spoke to management and helped increase understanding regarding the UAW's interests, and further meetings were held with corporate labor relations staff and staff from the international union. A member of the UAW international staff concluded: "These were the most updated long-run forecasts that the company had ever given us. Everybody's eyes were wide open going in. It's not like they said 'trust me.' When the top guy in stamping comes in and says 'I'm not going to bullshit you,' we knew what he was going to say. It was a sellable approach."[9]

The information sharing signaled a different tone from management, which brought the union back to the bargaining table at both the national and local levels. One union leader explained the resumption of negotiations after the Christmas holidays by noting that the company was "not as demanding." In fact, the extensive information sharing had shaped attitudes within the union, enabling it to be more receptive.

Involving Nontraditional Internal Stakeholders in Negotiations

A key means of managing internal differences is to widen the scope of constituent involvement in various aspects of formal negotiations. Consider the additional stakeholders that might be included in collective-bargaining negotiations. For management, this might mean that the industrial relations managers would be joined by representatives from finance and line management. For the union, it might mean that more people would be sought out in soliciting issues and to serve as members of internal committees working on the preparation for bargaining or even in the collective-bargaining process itself. Although the inclusion of these additional internal stakeholders increases the likelihood of internal splits and tension, it also helps assure that the integrative processes are rooted in more complete information and greater accountability on the part of all stakeholders.

WORKING SUBSTANTIVE ISSUES

We turn now to what is usually the major payoff activity of fostering—addressing common problems via integrative and mixed (integrative/distributive) bargaining.

Integrative bargaining can either lead, follow, or occur in parallel to activities designed to shape attitudes. It, like attitudinal work, can take place at both the institutional and individual levels. Stylized forms of what we have called integrative bargaining have been developed by practitioners. These approaches—which are variously termed "interest-based bargaining," "mutual gains bargaining," and "win-win bargaining"—all build on core principles that include sharing information fully; focusing on underlying interests, not stated positions; and creating options that would result in mutual gain.

We called attention earlier to the risk of the parties' remaining preoccupied with improving the attitudinal component of their relationship and not addressing their common problems in a timely way. We cited Bidwell and UP managements as perhaps having failed to initiate integrative bargaining in a timely way in their fostering efforts and referred to the especially effective integrative bargaining between the parties at Anderson, Budd, and Packard Electric. These latter cases provide us with many of our positive examples of integrative-bargaining tactics.

Two characteristics of bargaining in the service of fostering are especially important. The first is that the parties must find new *quid pro quos* that recognize both their common problems and their distinct interests, and that this search process must develop momentum, thereby giving fostering a life of its own, hopefully as robust as the escalation cycles we discussed in the forcing chapter. We use Anderson to illustrate this possibility. The second critical characteristic that supports effective integrative and mixed bargaining is flexibility—about both form and substance. This is underscored by our discussion of Budd's "hit-to-hit" campaign.

In reviewing the two characteristics of integrative bargaining in a fostering context, our examples will touch on a number of familiar institutional arrangements, including the use of formal employee involvement groups or task forces, formal problem-solving processes, and interest-based approaches to collective bargaining, as well as the creation of systems or structural change via a total quality management (TQM) or sociotechnical systems (STS) design process or an employee stock ownership plan (ESOP).

Gaining Momentum in the Search for Quid pro Quos

We begin our examination of the bargaining involved in fostering change by reviewing a few rounds of the fostering activity that occurred at Anderson Pattern between 1984 and 1990. Anderson provided us with one of the most successful fostering periods in our sample. Indeed, as we have stated earlier, Anderson accomplished as much substantive and social change over the six-year period of sustained fostering as any of our other companies, including those such as De Ridder and Pensacola that first forced substantive change and then fostered a new social contract. The histories at Anderson, De Ridder, and Pensacola covered roughly the same time period.

After Anderson management had altered the tone of the relationship by offering a profit-sharing scheme, the next major issue—the introduction of new technology—was addressed first via a relatively low-risk experiment in which exceptions to contractual work rules were allowed for two pieces of equipment. When the experiment proved a success, management proposed expanding its scope to all operations. The union then raised deeper concerns around job security and training, which were addressed—an especially significant management response in such a small firm. Although the parties continued to address some issues, such as health care costs, via a more adversarial process, the social and substantive contracts were dramatically revised with respect to a remarkable array of issues, including the reward system, new technology, worker training, communications and information sharing, worker autonomy, and social activities. In each case, a pattern emerged in which a new relationship was constructed *bit by bit*. With each successive new agreement and understanding, the firm increased its competitive capability, and the union was able to play a larger role in more aspects of the business. We summarize here two of these many groundbreaking agreements.

Bargaining over the introduction of new technology at Anderson Pattern. Historically, Anderson Pattern has always upgraded equipment—periodically replacing lathes and drill presses and adding computer numerical controls (CNC). While machine tolerances and consistency improved, the organization of work did not fundamentally change. In 1985, however, the president of Anderson Pattern offered the union a unique *quid pro quo*.

He said he would be willing to purchase a state-of-the-art machine center and coordinate measuring machines if the union would permit the flexibility to run the equipment with fewer workers (with each running multiple operations). At issue was Article XIX in the contract, which allowed operators to run more than one "automatic" machine only if no workers were laid off at the time and, even then, only for certain combinations of machines. This same contract language was at issue in a two-year strike against another firm in the area, which ultimately ended in the decertification of the union in that location. Thus, the issue was controversial, and it surfaced deeper issues of forcing and escape.

This matter was not only addressed in formal union-management meetings but also hotly debated among all the employees in this small firm. A second event described earlier—an employee trip to Chicago to see the proposed equipment on display at a trade show—proved pivotal in generating labor support for the idea. On May 10, 1985, the parties signed two letters of understanding—each pertaining to a specific piece of equipment. The letters waived the "one-employee, one-machine" rule and guaranteed that programming and other such work would be performed in the bargaining unit.

The integrative bargain was responsive to labor's concerns in several ways. First, management only asked for the exception to apply to two pieces of equipment—it did not push for the complete elimination of the contract language. Second, these exceptions would only apply during the term of the existing collective-bargaining agreement—allowing for a future chance to examine the experience before formulating the new contract language. An additional issue of importance to the union involved the new work associated with programming and maintaining the equipment, which it wanted to keep in the bargaining unit. Management was responsive to this concern as well.

The agreement marked another pivotal event, taking the parties a step further down a fostering path. They were, in effect, jointly conducting a two-year experiment that was a fundamental departure from established machine operation procedures.

In reflecting on the agreement, the union's then business manager (who negotiated the agreement) commented:

> Until recently, pattern making was 99 percent unionized. Restrictive work rules didn't matter because we all worked under the same rules. That changed in the 1980s. Now an employer will only spend a half-million dollars on a new machine if that machine can be fully used. What do we gain if, instead, that investment goes to a nonunion shop? The best thing to do was to negotiate training arrangements so that our people learn the latest technology.[10]

Clearly, the forcing and escape alternatives being used elsewhere served as a backdrop for labor's positive engagement in integrative bargaining.

Also, note that the parties did not fully depart from a traditional norm emphasizing contractual specificity. While allowing for increased flexibility, they were very precise that the scope would be limited to two particular machines, the time frame would be limited to just two years, and the programming would be done by bargaining unit employees. Thus, the agreement represented a dramatic shift substantively but a less dramatic shift procedurally. The parties had departed from the areawide bargaining structure, but other norms around contractual specificity remained unchanged.

Bargaining over flexibility and security at Anderson. When the collective-bargaining agreement expired in 1987, so did the letters of understanding allowing increased flexibility in the staffing of the two new pieces of equipment. The parties were thus faced with the question of whether to abandon their experiment or continue to expand it.

Management proposed completely eliminating Article XIX, which restricted staffing on all machining equipment. Further, it proposed establishing a new form of work organization around work cells, defining operators' work relative to multiple machines—a highly controversial issue for the union. While the two new pieces of equipment had generated a sufficient increase in volume to maintain the existing workforce, it was much harder to assess the potential impact of completely eliminating the contact language. What would be the implications of such a change in the event of a downturn? Further sharpening this concern was the fact that within the pattern-making profession, layoffs are generally made not on the basis of seniority but on the basis of work requirements and worker skills. Management's proposal thus surfaced deep job security concerns among the entire workforce.

Job security is never an easy issue to address, but it was particularly challenging for a small firm in the cyclical auto supply industry. It had no slack resources or alternative work available in the face of declining demand. Nevertheless, the union's position was firm—unless management addressed job security, it would not agree to the work cells or the elimination of Article XIX.

Anderson Pattern management felt it could not make a blanket no-layoff pledge, but the parties found a way to ensure that no individuals would disproportionately suffer the consequences of increased flexibility. The parties agreed that in the event of a downturn, a worker could not be laid off for longer than two months unless 75 percent of the workers in that work area had been laid off for more than two months. With this degree of job security, the employees agreed to eliminate Article XIX. Summing up the union's justification, the current union business manager asked: "Do we want to protect jobs and skills that are becoming noncompetitive or do we want to provide the opportunity for our members to learn new and more competitive skills?"[11] He also noted that highly skilled pattern makers "would go nuts if their only job was to program a machine and watch it operate."

Eliminating Article XIX and introducing job security language were both highly significant substantive changes, but they also signaled movement away from traditional regulatory approaches to issues. The parties were, in effect, moving beyond positional bargaining (how many machines could one person operate) and toward a more integrative, problem-solving approach centered on underlying interests (flexibility and job security). It is important to note that management's fostering overtures on flexibility occurred in a context in which forcing and escape were realistic alternatives. Similarly, the union's response involved taking a strong position on the principle of job security. Thus, the success of the fostering effort was rooted in distributive as well as integrative dynamics.

Demonstrating Flexibility in Addressing Issues

As new issues arise in the context of a fostering initiative, the parties often discover that traditional forms of interaction are inadequate for achieving agreement. For example, the traditional norm in collective bargaining calls for each side to independently establish target and resistance points on a given issue; then each develops an opening position; and ultimately, the resolution generally lies somewhere between the two opening positions (assuming there is a positive range for settlement). However, for a complex issue such as work reorganization or the implementation of new technology, a simple dance between opening positions may not generate any mutually acceptable options. In fact, it may even be hard to generate an opening position that will be acceptable to the various factions within one side. As a result, considerable skill and ingenuity are required in the way issues are surfaced and formulated. The Budd case provides a striking illustration in this regard.

Crafting new language at Budd. Local negotiations at Budd's Detroit facility began early, paralleling early national negotiations. The negotiations initially collapsed due to forceful management demands but were then resumed after extensive management briefing sessions for the workforce. At this point, the local discussions focused on die transition—a key factor in the economic performance of a stamping plant. The large metal dies (some weighing as much as 20 tons) had to be removed from presses at the end of a production run and replaced with new dies for stamping a different part. Improving the die transition process was not an easy issue to address in the context of traditional collective bargaining.

The parties focused on the establishment of a "hit-to-hit" labor-management committee that might oversee autonomous teams of approximately 20 craft employees that would be responsible for changing dies. The die transition teams were to reduce the time between the last good stamping, or "hit," in one production run and the first good hit in the next run.

Roughly half of the local negotiations (which lasted about four months) involved discussions regarding the hit-to-hit committee. The parties did ultimately draft a letter of agreement on the creation of a hit-to-hit committee that would, in turn, help create the autonomous die transition teams of hourly workers, but the process was quite difficult. As the plant manager in Detroit commented, new language was required to draft the letter: "We tried to do it the old way, but it didn't work. It could not be developed in traditional bargaining language. Thus, we got rid of the 'may,' which has always been interpreted as something I don't have to do, and the 'shall,' which is something I must do."[12]

The task of drafting the letter first fell to the plant's industrial relations department, but as the director of industrial relations commented: "The die transition letter was important. We really struggled with that and modified our proposal 3 or 4 times. They didn't like it. We told them 'You do it! If you don't like it then you write one up.' . . . It was surprising, they came back with an almost perfect letter."[13]

A UAW international representative recalled that the union was able to draft the letter on the basis of experiences in other locations: "The company told us that one of the major problems was die transition teams. We put together language, which was out of the norm for us. They acted like they won a million bucks. They called a caucus right away. We had a smooth flow after that point."[14]

Thus, by being flexible and departing from established norms of interaction, the parties crafted an integrative solution.

As an integrative exercise, the hit-to-hit committee was a great success. The die transition teams in action were dramatic to behold: a group of a dozen or more people representing a range of crafts would descend in an almost choreographed fashion on a line of huge stamping presses (some weighing as much as 100 tons) and change a series of dies (each weighing as much as 20 tons). Downtime for die changes was cut by more than 50 percent as a result of the coordination achieved within this autonomous work team structure (in contrast to the previous linear process, in which the work of one craft had to be completed before the work of the next would begin). In the process, however, unanticipated splits emerged between line and staff management, as well as within the line management hierarchy. We discuss this complication in the following section.

COPING WITH UNANTICIPATED INTERNAL SPLITS

We discussed earlier how negotiators may attempt to line up internal support in the initial stages of a fostering effort. Here, we examine another aspect of this process of managing internal support—dealing with differences that develop as a result of other tactical initiatives.

As noted, one of the techniques for generating internal support for interparty problem-solving and relationship-building processes is to widen the extent of constituent involvement in them. In management's case, this may mean having the industrial relations managers joined by representatives from finance and line management. In the union's case, it may mean involving more people as members of internal committees working on the preparation for bargaining and even on the bargaining team itself.

These more inclusive approaches may help minimize complications with the ratification and administration of an agreement, but they also bring a greater diversity of views into the negotiating process. Thus, in managing internal differences in the spirit of a fostering initiative, potential tensions are added to the negotiations.

Internal differences emerged in most of the fostering efforts we studied. We present five examples: one in which differences emerged within the management organization, three in which differences developed within labor, and one in which differences developed in both labor and management.

Internal differences in Budd's hit-to-hit campaign. We discussed earlier how the negotiations over the creation of what became the hit-to-hit committee brought line management into a leadership role. One union official characterized the role of local staff and line management in the bargaining as follows: "In the local negotiations it was clear that local company IR guys were not running the show. The production manager had more clout than the local IR people. In the past there would be labor relations people and no one else in the room. Production people put positions across. This is still ongoing."[15] This negotiation marked the beginning of an unanticipated split between line and staff management.

In establishing and overseeing the hit-to-hit committee, the plant production manager and his staff took an activist role, which included dealing directly with the workers and the union on daily administrative issues. As one line manager commented:

> Certain groups are excluded from hit-to-hit. You are better off without their [IR's] involvement. It eliminates face-to-face discussions because for some groups it is best not to communicate. All people have labels in the company. IR does not do well in certain situations. A group will assume the personality of the individuals. When it gets down to the nitty-gritty, the key is partnership. The relationship has been building. The union has trust in [production management].
>
> We make sure that all the parties play by the initial rules created by the union and company in negotiations. We rule on particular areas. I guess it has taken over the traditional union/management role. During the meetings there are a lot of discussions and negotiation. It's not really negotiations, it's mostly discussions. IR has no authority at HTH [hit to hit]. What do you really need a labor relations department for in this setting?[16]

The local union president echoed the manager's comments: "When I'm in the plant, sometimes I go through the right channels and sometimes I go directly to managers. I know my job is to go through IR managers and not to the floor, but I have an advantage having worked with most of the people before."[17] In a conversation with the production manager, these relations were confirmed:

> I communicate with the union all of the time. I go with Herb [the local union president] to seminars and get the union presidents in all three plants to go to high-level quality and hit-to-hit meetings. It is difficult to get the okay for them to go. Vice presidents and presidents don't understand why you would want to bring the union. I get them involved in everything I do . . . . I don't ignore IR, but I look to do the job myself.[18]

The stronger links between line management and union leadership send implicit signals that interactions are to be driven more by functional needs than by a formal protocol—a key shift. A new rule is being established—that line management will take the lead on bargaining issues that relate to production operations. That logic even extends to relations within line management, as this statement by the plant's production manager suggests: "We originally wanted two superintendents on the Hit-to-Hit Committee, but the only way the union would get involved was if I was involved. HTH meets with great resistance by management. It's a revolution. There is no supervision with die transition. It scares the hell out of people."[19]

The success in managing internal differences played a key role in the success of the hit-to-hit committee.

Cross-facility complexity at a Budd retreat. In 1986, top managers and union leaders at Budd and the UAW were anxious to codify and advance the various plant-level initiatives around employee involvement and labor-management cooperation. An off-site session was scheduled involving corporate and international union leadership, along with leadership from the union and management bargaining committees in many different plants. The early parts of the retreat were valuable for providing common technical information and statements of support from top leaders. The later part of the retreat involved representatives from all of the plants in an exercise of self-assessment and planning for the future. As discussion proceeded, important ideological differences surfaced among local union leaders regarding their views on such issues as employee involvement and relaxation of certain work rules. To avoid open debate, union participants became very restrained in their comments, and the meeting, which had begun promisingly, ended on a much less enthusiastic note. All the participants gained valuable information regarding the future complexity of managing fostering initiatives across multiple facilities, but this very complexity prevented the off-site session from achieving its initial goal of pointing the way toward the future.

Platform for employment security demands at Packard. By 1983, the IUE and Packard Electric had established regular, annual off-site meetings of top union and management leaders. It was at such a meeting that Nick Nichols, then an outspoken union steward, made a bold move. He had been an early proponent of the quality of work life initiative and was concerned that current company investment in Mexico was undercutting what he understood to be a management commitment that no jobs would be lost as a result of the QWL effort. Fellow union leaders had counseled him not to press the issue—seeing little hope of a firm no-layoff guarantee and, consequently, little value in a battle over the issue. To the surprise of both the union and management leadership at the retreat, Nichols arranged for an overhead projector to be delivered to the room and presented detailed excerpts from management's public statements in the 1970s on the job security issue. The move split the union, placed the employment security issue squarely on the table, spearheaded Nichols' election as chief steward (and the defeat of all the other members of the bargaining committee), and ultimately led to the negotiation of an unprecedented lifetime job security guarantee in exchange for a multitier way system and work-rule flexibility. Thus, the off-site meeting, which had been intended to promote problem solving and closer relations, triggered new interparty issues and internal splits that neither party had anticipated but that proved pivotal to the unfolding relationship.

Difficulties encountered in 1988 negotiations at CSX. CSX provides a classic case of internal divisions' undermining integrative or mixed bargaining in a fostering effort and illustrates how fragile integrative bargaining can be within the framework of a traditional arm's-length relationship. The entry of CSX and its many unions into a negotiation process without constraining deadlines was intended to facilitate the development of innovative and integrative solutions to the company's competitive problems and labor's need for equitable treatment. The negotiators developed mutual trust and produced innovative proposals, but when internal consensus on labor's side cracked and one of the unions—the UTU—refused to go along, the concerted effort was derailed.

Several of the unions had followed procedures designed to keep the rank and file abreast of developments. Specifically, the BMWE involved all general chairmen in briefing sessions and included many of them on task forces. The TCU followed a similar approach, with the expectation that the general chairmen would keep the membership posted. Stories in the various union newspapers also helped the internal communication process. The UTU, in contrast, did not engage in any of these activities; consequently, it was not surprising that this union's general chairmen rejected the proposed agreement when it was presented to them.

Unraveling of internal support on both sides at Bidwell. Despite the fact that each of the parties at the Bidwell mill took carefully designed steps early in the fostering process to develop an internally consistent approach to the other party, internal divisions developed on both sides, causing the effort to founder.

When a new mill manager, installed by new owners, reviewed the con-

cerns of his managers, he discovered deep differences about the QWL program. Labor's tenuous commitment to the QWL fostering process also unraveled at about the same time, partly in response to its sense of management's ambivalence.

The dissenting union, which had agreed to wait and see how the program evolved, decided to actively attack the program and the other labor officials who supported it. If management had been cohesive and strongly committed, the QWL effort might have weathered the opposition of one of the unions; but in the absence of a firmer management commitment and stronger actions to make that commitment credible, officials in the more receptive unions also backed away from the program. Cohesion on the union side was further weakened by the fact that some officers who had been involved in establishing QWL had lost their reelection bids or opted not to run for reelection.

SUMMARY AND CONCLUSIONS

For many readers, this discussion of fostering may have been equivalent to the Shakespearian character who aspired to be a poet and one day discovered, with great satisfaction, that in his regular conversations, he had actually been "speaking prose." In many cases, parties may be engaged in fostering strategies for renegotiating social and substantive contracts—though they are likely using such labels as employee involvement, total quality management, sociotechnical systems design, grievance mediation, and interest-based bargaining. Examining these change efforts through a negotiations lens reveals a number of key insights.

First, we have learned that many fostering initiatives encourage and are supported by decentralization in work practices and policies. The result can be innovation that is better matched to local needs, whether "local" means the needs of a given facility, a work area within a facility, or a particular stakeholder group. However, with the decentralization comes a dilemma—increased variation in practice.

Second, we have seen that fostering initiatives can begin at either the institutional or the individual level. The majority of our cases featured top-down strategies, reflecting the gatekeeper role played by most unions. In these cases, however, the top-level dialogue depended on the movement downward of communications and problem-solving activities so that individual union members and first-line supervisors would also experience tangible benefits from the fostering. The one example of a bottom-up strategy (De Ridder) depended on the fact that the union was weakened (after a debilitating strike). Even then, the effort could not stay at the individual level; ultimately, corporate executives decided they had reached a critical juncture at which diffusion of employee commitment programs to other plants depended on the support of local union leaders.

Third (and in contrast to forcing strategies), all three negotiating processes represented viable points of departure for a fostering initiative. In fact, though it was often logistically difficult to attend to all three, they reinforce one another in critical and positive ways (again in contrast to forcing, in which the reinforcement often led to unintended excesses).

Fourth, the management of internal differences emerged as the linchpin for a fostering strategy. On the union side, the management of internal differences was critical, given that union leaders are elected to their positions and thus very sensitive to internal splits. Interestingly, the internal dynamics also proved pivotal for management since fostering processes often called for input across functional areas and were inherently unpredictable in their output—a virtue of problem solving but an anathema in many corporations.

Fifth, the structuring of interparty attitudes was the focus of key tactical efforts in all our cases. These efforts went far beyond informal trust building; they included formal programmatic initiatives such as off-site retreats and joint educational efforts. We found that such structuring efforts, though a necessary component of the fostering strategies, were insufficient since they were not designed to produce substantive value for the parties.

Finally, many of the risks associated with a forcing strategy relate to what might be called an "overalignment" of the three processes, whereas the major risks involved in fostering are primarily related to their "misalignment." Recall that Chapter 9 developed the argument that the risks of forcing largely derive from such mutually reinforcing dynamics as the following: the intergroup hostility stimulated in order to promote the internal solidarity required to enhance distributive bargaining is further exacerbated by hard-bargaining power tactics, which fuel an escalation; the escalation, in turn, adds to the costs of conflict, increases the risks of stalemate, and leaves a constraining legacy of distrust. Our analysis in this chapter specified the types of misalignment among integrative bargaining, shaping intergroup attitudes, and developing internal support that constitute major risks associated with the implementation of fostering strategies. In forcing, then, the major risks derive from errors of commission; in fostering, they derive from errors of omission.

NOTES

1. As in our treatment of forcing tactics, we do not provide a comprehensive listing of tactics that could be used to implement fostering. With a few exceptions, we emphasize the tactics actually employed in our case studies. For other potentially relevant tactics, see Richard E. Walton and Robert B. McKersie, *A Behavioral Theory of Labor Negotiations*, 2d ed. (New York: ILR Press, 1991).
2. Joel E. Cutcher-Gershenfeld, Robert McKersie, and Richard Walton, *Pathways to Change: Case Studies in Strategic Negotiations* (Kalamazoo, Mich.: W. E. Upjohn Institute for Employment Research, forthcoming), Chapter 5.
3. Ibid.
4. Ibid.
5. Ibid.

6. Ibid.
7. Ibid.
8. Ibid.
9. Ibid.
10. Ibid., Chapter 3.
11. Ibid.
12. Ibid., Chapter 5.
13. Ibid.
14. Ibid.
15. Ibid.
16. Ibid.
17. Ibid.
18. Ibid.
19. Ibid.

Chapter 11

Implementing a Coordinated Forcing and Fostering Strategy: Tactics and Dynamics

In the preceding two chapters, we have examined the tactics associated with the relatively distinct strategies of forcing and fostering. In most American companies in the current era, labor and management at least contemplate implementing *both* forcing and fostering strategies. Management's priorities often include payroll cost reduction and increased flexibility (for which forcing often seems necessary) as well as the enhancement of quality and worker commitment (for which fostering is the appropriate avenue). Labor's priorities typically include the preservation of living standards and the protection of jobs and the union's institutional security (for which forcing is often necessary) as well as increased influence over long-range business planning and the quality of work life (for which fostering is the more likely route). Thus, both parties are likely to at least contemplate forcing, and both are likely to engage in some exploration of fostering.

Recalling our scenario analysis presented in Chapter 8, which related outcomes to negotiating strategies, it is significant that neither scenario 1 (forcing by itself) nor scenario 2 (fostering alone) produced outcomes as good as those yielded by the two other scenarios that involved some coordination of two strategies: scenario 3 (forcing followed by fostering) and scenario 4 (a period of combined forcing/fostering followed by fostering). Here, we analyze the cases in which some coordination of forcing and fostering occurred in order to better understand the additional dilemmas and process dynamics involved.

Table 11.1 identifies the cases and time periods that can be classified as coordinated strategies. We have highlighted six case histories that involved either a combination of forcing and fostering during the same period or an especially instructive transition from one strategy to another or both. This chapter explores these two types of strategic coordination plus a related form of tactical coordination.

Table 11.1   Periods of Forcing, Fostering, and Forcing/Fostering, Together with Instructive Transitions from One Period to Another

	Strategic Periods		
Case History	1	2	3
Paper mills			
Jay (International Paper)	Unrestrained forcing		
De Ridder (Boise Cascade)	Forcing	→ Fostering	
Bidwell (disguised name)	Fostering		
Pensacola (Champion Paper)	Forcing	→ Fostering	→ Forcing/fostering
Auto supply companies			
AP Parts	Unrestrained forcing		
Adrian Fabricators	Unrestrained forcing	→ Fostering	
Packard Electric	Forcing/fostering	Fostering	
Budd	Forcing/fostering	Fostering	
Anderson Pattern	Fostering		
Railroads			
Guilford	Unrestrained forcing		
Union Pacific	Fostering		
Conrail	Forcing/fostering	Fostering	
CSX	Fostering		

This chapter starts by considering how the two strategies—forcing and fostering—both complement and contradict each other.

Then, we examine the implications of coordinating forcing and fostering strategies when they are implemented concurrently. We observed these "combined periods" in four cases: the first periods of the Packard Electric, Budd, and Conrail cases and the third period of the case involving Champion's Pensacola mill.

Before turning to the second major type of strategic coordination, we explore a type of tactical coordination whereby, in the context of executing one strategy, the negotiator incorporates tactics usually associated with the other. For example, the negotiator may engage in distributive bargaining within an overall fostering period or engage in integrative bargaining within a forcing regime. We refer to these as "mixed tactics."

The final section of the chapter examines the coordination involved in implementing the two prototypical strategies in sequence. Three of our cases—De Ridder, Pensacola, and Adrian Fabricators—involved forcing followed by fostering. Although we have no cases in which forcing followed fostering, we address the implications of this sequence as well, since we know of many instances outside of our study in which this sequence has occurred.

FORCING AND FOSTERING: COMPLEMENTARITIES AND CONTRADICTIONS

We can examine the relationship between forcing and fostering at two levels: at the level of the goals these strategies serve and at the level of the tactics used to implement them. Interestingly, the two activities can be complementary and/or contradictory at both levels.

Consider how the goals of forcing and fostering can be complementary. Management may decide to force the changes in employment terms that are the most disagreeable to labor and also foster a climate with labor in which these changes can be implemented effectively and in which labor and management can devise other integrative changes in employment terms and work organization. This pattern of complementarity of management goals is illustrated by Budd, Packard Electric, De Ridder, and Pensacola (periods 2 and 3).

In other cases, the goals of forcing and fostering may be mutually contradictory. For example, if management seeks not only to change the collective-bargaining agreement but also to contain or avoid the union, then forcing can serve both purposes and the idea of fostering cooperative union relations is logically contradictory. Jay, Guilford, AP Parts, and Adrian (period 1) seem to fit this pattern.

The contradictory relationship between forcing and fostering tactics is specified in the theory itself. Forcing involves various forms of information control in the bargaining process, whereas fostering requires open information flow. Forcing is often assisted by sharpening intergroup hostility, whereas fostering requires the promotion of mutual trust and respect. Forcing often involves exploiting divisions within the ranks of the other party, whereas fostering depends on building basic consensus in both parties (while recognizing, of course, the value of internal differences during the search for integrative solutions). These types of contradictions generate most of the dilemmas and risks encountered during strategic transitions, especially from forcing periods to fostering, and in periods that combine both strategic orientations. They also create the challenge of mixing integrative and distributive bargaining within either a forcing or fostering regime.

The opposing thrusts of the two sets of tactics also make them potentially complementary—in the sense that each set may help ameliorate certain

Table 11.2 Possibilities of Complementarity between Forcing and Fostering Tactics

Limitation of One Strategy	Ameliorating Potential of Tactics of the Other Strategy
Forcing	*Fostering*
The risk of escalation and a deterioration of the relationship (social)	← Fostering's emphasis on developing positive intergroup attitudes can help the parties maintain satisfactory relationships.
The emergence of distrust and the difficulty of pursuing integrative bargaining (substantive)	← Fostering's emphasis on engaging relevant stakeholders can help the parties overcome the animosities present at the main table and develop creative solutions to common problems that have a high probability of being implemented.
Fostering	*Forcing*
The risk of stagnation and a lack of concrete change (substantive)	← Forcing's emphasis on distributive bargaining (e.g., the use of deadlines) can enable the parties to produce minimally acceptable levels of change.
Lack of support by the rank and file for both the process and solutions associated with fostering (social)	← Forcing's emphasis on generating internal agreement and solidarity can enable bargaining representatives to secure the support of the principals.

extremes or risks inherent in the other. A theme of Chapter 9 was the risk of escalation inherent in implementing a forcing strategy. Fostering tactics that focus on preserving relationships during a forcing campaign can decrease that risk. We have also noted, in Chapter 10, that with fostering, the parties run the risk of improving the attitudinal component of their relationship but failing to put that trust and respect to work in solving significant problems involving matters such as quality, productivity, and employment security. Forcing tactics that focus on substance can help overcome this deficit. (See Table 11.2.)

We begin our exploration of these many potential relationships between forcing and fostering activities by focusing on strategies that combine both orientations in the same time frame.

COMBINED FORCING AND FOSTERING

Whereas a potential benefit of a combined strategy lies in the ability of one party to force rapid change on a matter disagreeable to the other party while still sustaining a fostering process, considerable risks are associated. As noted earlier, forcing may lead to unanticipated escalation, while fostering may result in excessive delay in achieving tangible changes. Managing each of these risks requires great skill when a single strategy is used exclusively; the challenge is even greater when they are combined.

The concurrent utilization of forcing and fostering strategies carries two core risks. First, there is the risk that the forcing will undercut the fostering activities. In all four of our combined periods, this did occur to some extent. The damage, however, was neither great nor permanent. In three cases, the combined period was followed by a period of fostering (the fourth instance—Pensacola—marked the end of the period under study, but we do have additional information to indicate that fostering activities have been resumed following the difficult round of collective bargaining in 1988).

Second, there is the risk that concurrent fostering will undermine the firmness of the party's stance in its forcing effort. In fact, we found little evidence of management's becoming so "soft" as a result of the fostering experience that the forcing objectives were abandoned or substantially undercut. We did find many instances, though, in which the scope and nature of the forcing were tempered as a result of concurrent fostering. For example, at Packard Electric, the integrative experiment with the branch plants represented a contrast to management's original approach (which was to move work to the South)—and significantly, it still accomplished the objectives of reduced cost and increased flexibility.

Combined Strategies as a Prelude to Fostering

In the cases of Budd, Packard Electric, and Conrail, we observed combined strategies that proved to be a prelude to a period in which the predominant strategy was fostering. The process by which the strategy shifted from a combined strategy to a fostering strategy reflects a de-emphasis on the forcing and an increased emphasis on the fostering.

In the cases of Budd and Packard Electric, there was initially a distinct separation between the concurrent forcing and fostering strategies. The fostering initiatives in both cases began as employee involvement (EI) or quality of work life (QWL) problem-solving programs. While the programs were certainty designed to help improve quality and reduce costs, the driving goals in the late 1970s and early 1980s were primarily centered around improving working conditions and building worker commitment. As a result, when both firms experienced extreme competitive pressures in the early 1980s, EI and QWL were not seen as the primary vehicles for responding to the crisis. Instead, both firms resorted to massive layoffs, combined with threats and then action to move work to lower-cost locations—all standard responses to competitive pressures in the auto supply industry at the time.

The experience under EI and QWL with joint labor-management oversight committees helped set the stage for increased management efforts to educate local union leaders about the severity of the competitive crisis. In

1981, at Budd's Detroit pant, for example, the president of the local union was persuaded that the situation was serious and went so far as to endorse a concessionary agreement. The membership did not share this view, however. The agreement was rejected by a vote of more than 90 percent, and key union leaders who had endorsed the agreement were turned out of office in the next local elections. Management also carried out its threat to remove work from the facility—leading to a layoff of more than 900 workers.

The remaining workforce at Budd was deeply affected by the loss of so many jobs. The next few years saw two additional mass layoffs and an initial decline in EI activities. Overall, between 1979 and 1982, the size of the bargaining unit in the Detroit plant was reduced by more than half, from 2,800 to 1,200. In time, however, the number of EI groups rose, and these groups became increasingly focused on improved quality and economic performance. By the mid-1980s, much of the corporate downsizing was complete (removing a major issue requiring forcing activity), and the fostering under EI had become more central to the firm's economic success. It was the combination of both circumstances that allowed for a fostering strategy to emerge out of this combined period at Budd. Thus, the forcing created turbulence that initially undercut the parallel fostering activities, but ultimately, fostering (with a shifted focus) increased to such a point that it became the dominant strategy.

In Conrail, the combination of forcing and fostering was more tightly interwoven from the outset since each strategy derived from congressional pressure as part of the bailout and reconstruction of the company. Congress called for the establishment of various labor-management committees, and management placed great priority on communications about the overall situation, the retraining of workers at risk of displacement, and the provision of generous severance payments for those who were displaced. Yet Congress and management also called for the elimination of key work rules (especially involving crew size), the consolidation of maintenance shops, wage concessions, and other controversial changes. The committees were approached as fostering initiatives, while the changes in work rules, benefits, and other areas were experienced as concessionary bargains. Although both activities derived from the same source, the implementation of the strategies proceeded separately from each other. In fact, since both the forcing and fostering were triggered by a third force, some of the contradictions between the two were tempered. Following the period of extensive congressional oversight, management did not continue with an ambitious forcing agenda, which set the stage for the subsequent period of fostering.

Thus, in all three cases in which the combined period led to a period of fostering, the combination of forcing and fostering involved an acceptable accommodation of concurrent, but separate, tactical endeavors. In the two cases in which the strategies were not externally imposed, the coexistence of forcing and fostering strategies surfaced predictable tensions. While the tensions were less evident in the Conrail case—in which the forcing was externally imposed—it, too, was an unstable situation. We conclude from these time periods that there are limits to the extent to which forcing and fostering can coexist as combined strategies because of the conflict inherent in the goals at stake in forcing as well as the contradictory nature of the forcing and fostering tactics.

Combined Strategies after Fostering

In one case, Pensacola, we observed a combined period that followed a period of fostering. In this case, management sought certain changes in the collective-bargaining agreement that would roll back long-established union gains. Specifically, management was under corporate pressure in the 1988 negotiations to eliminate Sunday premium pay and some other special pay allowances. It felt compelled to force these changes despite its nearly three-year experience with successful employee involvement and joint work re-design efforts—cooperative activities that management in fact wanted to sustain and reinforce. Thus, although management anticipated having to engage in some measure of forcing around the pay changes, it still hoped to continue the fostering activities.

The Sunday premium pay issue had come to symbolize management forcing in the paper industry since this was a key strike issue in some of the most notable industry confrontations during the past decade. Labor at Pensacola was therefore disappointed when this issue appeared as a management priority, given both the history of cooperation and the fact that mill performance was improving. Labor was not persuaded by any economic arguments offered by management on the pay issue and essentially tele-graphed to management that the only avenue available was to force the concession. Further, labor was unwilling to engage in joint dialogue on language relating to cooperation and participation: it preferred that management present its language and that labor be granted a separate conces-sion for agreeing to such language. Thus, while management hoped to keep the forcing carefully limited to the pay changes, the climate created was such that even the language on cooperation and participation was ap-proached by the union in a traditional, adversarial fashion.

This instance of combined forcing and fostering at Pensacola is distinct from the other combined periods in a number of respects. Perhaps because it followed a period of sustained fostering (which, in turn, followed a period of forcing), there was a greater initial effort to keep the scope of the forcing within bounds. The scope was limited in two ways: it was limited substan-tively to a few issues (premium pay on Sundays and other special pay allowances), and it was limited in temporal terms since it was advanced within the context of contract negotiations. Thus, the combined period of fostering and forcing at Pensacola was relatively short-lived: it was centered on the bargaining of the 1988 contract.

Appraising the Tactics of a Combined Period

Given the fact that the four cases just reviewed (Budd, Packard, Conrail, and Pensacola) experienced some of the best outcomes, it is appropriate to identify the elements that made for success. As mentioned earlier, the simultaneous presence of forcing and fostering activities can ameliorate the risks inherent in the distinct strategies. The following subsections illustrate this crossover of the tactical processes for forcing and fostering in several of our cases.

Packard. Again, the backdrop of employee involvement activities at Packard did not prevent a crisis and the possibility of escalation, but the quality of the relationship meant that when critical choice points were reached as a result of distributive-bargaining moves by the company (the unilateral creation of the task force and the hiring of temporary workers), the union leadership's response was more akin to integrative than distributive bargaining (its demand to convert the task force into a joint jobs committee and its willingness to reexamine the agreement governing temporary workers).

The significant point is that while the two strategies of forcing and fostering existed in different arenas at Packard, they did exert reciprocal and complementary influence on each other. If Packard had just pursued QWL-type activities in a kind of bottom-up change program, the results would have been very slow to materialize. Or if it had just engaged in hard deadline tactics, matters would probably have continued to escalate as they did for a period in the early 1980s.

With a backdrop of EI and with the formal joint jobs committee in place, each side could press ahead with its primary objectives (the company seeking flexibility and the union seeking to stem outsourcing) without endangering the relationship and escalating matters in a nonproductive fashion.

Conrail. In Conrail's case, the ability to combine both strategies was made possible by the strong role of a third party (the federal government). But significantly, while the company possessed considerable power to coerce change as a result of the bankruptcy and the mandates coming from Washington, it chose a course of restraint, emphasizing constructive dealings with the union leadership and a problem-solving process to shape its transition to a restructured carrier.

Pensacola. In the Pensacola case, the impetus for change disagreeable to labor was supplied by corporate headquarters' requirement that local mills eliminate the premium pay for Sunday. However, the distributive bargaining was not allowed to escalate. By emphasizing the positive elements of the local relationship, the parties were able to work within both a forcing and fostering frame, as the following behaviors illustrate:

- While union leaders opposed the company's position on eliminating premium pay for Sunday, they did not attempt to whip up the rank and file; in fact, they disseminated company arguments and rationale.

- While the union initially indicated that it would agree to a memorandum on labor-management cooperation only if the price were right, toward the close of negotiations, its leaders proposed language on cooperation that became the basis for the final draft.

A true synthesis of forcing and fostering contains many elements, as illustrated by the 1988 negotiations at Pensacola. The following crossover elements were involved:

Management pursued forcing in a way sensitive to its newly improved relations with the union leadership:

- It sponsored joint trips to a QWL conference.
- It openly acknowledged that the Sunday premium issue was advanced by "those folks at the corporate headquarters."
- It delayed positional bargaining (the company did not present its final offer until after the meeting of the union council).

For its part, the union leadership appeared to be setting the stage for the inevitability of the change ("We fought as hard as we could") and not whipping up opposition within the rank and file.

As a result, management did not try to "one-up" the following forcing tactics:

- Initially, the union refused to discuss participation.
- The union demanded profit sharing in exchange for new language on participation.
- Throughout the negotiations, the union continued to say, "We are not giving up our opposition to changing premium pay for Sunday."

While the company tried to maintain the relationship, its negotiators nevertheless remained adamant about the requirement of reaching agreement by the deadline.

As a result of this combination of tactics, a number of innovative proposals emerged as the deadline approached, and the parties settled some tough, contentious issues without undermining their new relationship.

MIXED TACTICS WITHIN A DOMINANT STRATEGY

The cases of combined strategy just examined represent full-fledged examples of the side-by-side implementation of forcing and fostering. In other situations, the coordination involved a more modest mixing of tactics. While the parties were engaged in one strategy, they found it advantageous to introduce tactics normally associated with the other strategy.

Integrative Bargaining within a Forcing Context

Though there are constraints on integrative bargaining in a forcing context, it is still possible (and perhaps advisable) for parties to seek ways to add an integrative dimension. It should be noted, however, that the UAW attempted this in the AP Parts case with little success. The union in that instance asked management to distinguish among its concession demands, offering to work with management more closely around improving productivity if management would back off from its demands for wage and benefit reductions. Perhaps the offer was never stated clearly enough, or it was not believed in the context of the union's counterforcing, or there was never really full internal agreement within the union to support such integrative discussions, or management judged all of its demands to be necessary, or management had an additional agenda of undercutting the union—for whatever reason, it proved difficult within a forcing frame for the union to introduce an integrative dimension.

Thus, in most of our forcing cases, we find little evidence of either the union's or management's seeking to introduce a measure of integrative bargaining as a counterpoint to forcing or as a boundary around it. When this does happen, it usually sets the stage for subsequent fostering. That being the case, this tactic depends on a party's having in mind a broader strategy in which the forcing is part of an intended sequence that also includes fostering.

Distributive Bargaining within a Fostering Context

Once a fostering initiative has begun, the parties often face difficult choices in the management of subsequent distributive issues. Among our cases, this tactic was most common in negotiations occurring outside of collective bargaining. For example, many of our cases featured employee involvement or quality of work life programs, and some featured experiments with total quality management programs. All of these fostering initiatives involved problem-solving discussions by employee groups or functional work teams. Inevitably, before some of the proposed solutions could be implemented, other issues needed to be confronted.

For example, at Budd's Kitchener, Ontario, plant, the efforts of many EI groups were impeded by a bottleneck in the engineering department, which was not prepared for the additional workload associated with a large number of group suggestions. Both the EI facilitators and the union leadership confronted the engineering department about its priorities—in turn, surfacing a deeper systems issue around required resources in engineering. Ultimately, distributive bargaining was required to obtain an increase in staff for the engineering function. Thus, the success of the integrative efforts depended to a significant degree on the capacity of employees, group facilitators, managers, and union leaders to engage in an effective confrontation that addressed the distributive issue while not undermining their cooperative efforts.

Another successful example of the crossover occurred at Adrian after the ESOP program had been instituted and the parties were in their fostering phase. The workers quite openly expressed their resentment at differential rewards and surfaced the issue of financial fairness. The result was a revision of the plan that more adequately met the parties' objectives. Within a positive social relationship, raising an issue in a distributive fashion can be productive when the forms of power utilized are not overtly coercive and the parties have the ability to turn a perceived inequity into a starting point for problem solving.

Another example of distributive bargaining in a fostering context is the handling of temporary workers at Packard Electric. In this case, management had sought contract language allowing for the use of temporary workers so that it could manage effectively in a context in which the core workforce had lifetime employment security. In fact, when groups of temporary workers were brought in on three separate occasions, both parties experienced unanticipated difficulties in handling the contrast between full-time and temporary workers' doing equivalent jobs while facing different career opportunities. This proved to be an unexpectedly difficult issue, and the parties still had not found a satisfactory solution at the end of the period we examined.

The Bidwell case presents another vivid example in which, within a fostering context, a distributive issue surfaced—but was not addressed as such. Although the primary reason for the decline of the fostering effort at Bidwell was more directly related to unresolved internal differences in both management and labor, the effort was weakened by management's failure to recognize the occasional need for distributive-bargaining structures and processes. For example, when managers discovered that the two parties appeared to have different preferences for the timing of the start of QWL activities, they failed to caucus (or confirm in some other way the interparty differences) and decide how to negotiate them. The unaddressed differences had a deleterious effect on the process.

Labor responded to management's stated bid for new relationships with workers and with their representatives by making a number of requests. Management acceded to some of labor's requests, such as the accelerated start of QWL activities, but not others, such as removing time clocks and acting to correct the behavior of supervisors who were not attuned to the QWL philosophy. These failures by management to negotiate acceptable terms for labor's commitment and cooperation were probably just another reflection of management's own ambivalence and disunity. Nevertheless, these omissions underscored the need for both parties to have understood more explicitly that fostering efforts such as the QWL program were indeed a negotiation process—one in which they had to be capable of resolving contentious issues as well as handling integrative problem solving and in which they had to be capable of utilizing tough intraorganizational resolution processes as well as of achieving attitude change.

Though it is clearly difficult to deal with distributive issues in the context of a fostering initiative, success in doing so typically proves to be a pivotal event in the relationship. For example, the distributive confrontation about job security at Packard Electric marked the inauguration of the sustained period of fostering that the parties have since pursued. The initial confrontation was controversial for both the union and management, but it provided the foundation for a unique agreement in which management was afforded a multitier wage structure and work-rule flexibility in exchange for a guarantee of lifetime job security.

The fact that considerable strain and tension can result from the use of forcing behaviors within a basically cooperative relationship is also well illustrated by an episode from the Budd case.

Campaign to increase discipline in the context of a fostering program: Budd. At Budd's Kitchener plant, the production manager and general foreman decided, in November 1985, to initiate a program aimed at increasing the fraction of the day that workers spent on their job. In the production manager's words, this was ". . . [a] program to ask people or convince people that they should start work on time, they should work up to the break, they should be back after the break, they should be back after lunch, and they shouldn't leave their job early. We're paying for that, we expect that. We have to have it to remain a viable corporation in the long run."

Under the program, general foremen held meetings in their respective work areas to explain that competitive pressures required employees to work steadily from the bell at the beginning of each work period to the bell at the end of that period. Privately, the supervisors were instructed to refrain from disciplining workers who arrived late or left early; they were just to explain the importance of the change.

Most workers complied with the request—no longer leaving early for breaks or washing up early at the end of the day. However, a small group of informal shop-floor leaders (mostly skilled trades workers) continued to leave early—reportedly as a test of management's resolve. Thus, some workers saw the competitive pressures and company request as legitimate, while others interpreted the issue as one of power and control. The request became, in effect, a battle for allegiance between production management and the shop-floor leaders, with most workers initially complying and then reverting back to past practices. In response, management planned a second round of meetings to reemphasize the "bell-to-bell" concept.

Before the second round of meetings was held, however, a dispute arose around relief time. Specifically, a group of press shop foremen began enforcing a 1978 memorandum stipulating that workers should not spend relief time in the cafeteria. In March, a press operator asked his foreman whether he could use his relief time to eat his lunch in the cafeteria. The foreman showed him the rule and denied the request. The operator went anyway. In the cafeteria, he was approached by the general foreman and told to return to his job. The employee finished his lunch before returning and was disciplined by the general foreman. After the episode, the union bargaining committee requested a meeting with management on the relief-time issue, at which management upheld the disciplinary action.

Subsequently, the production manager and the general foreman decided to include a restatement of the rule on relief time in their planned second round of meetings on working from bell to bell. During the first of these meetings, the discussion of working bell to bell passed without incident. As soon as the foreman mentioned the relief-time issue, however, the workers began booing. According to one worker who was at the meeting, a group of five or six of the more vocal workers followed the booing with a request to see the production manager, and "then, all of a sudden . . . there's 50 guys sitting down."

At that point, the union committeeman for the area went to find the production manager, who said he would meet with the workers the next day. Other groups of workers attending the second round of meetings accepted the relief-time message without incident. The following day, rumors circulated that the production manager might not be able to meet with the group. At the first break, the workers in this area decided *not* to resume production after the break until management agreed to meet with them. In response, the general foreman set up a meeting with the production manager later that morning. At the meeting, the production manager recalls restating the company's official position but also telling people, "You use a little common sense on your relief time, and we'll use a little common sense in administering guidelines."

Following the meeting, there were no subsequent relief-time incidents, but the employee involvement group in the area threatened to quit the EI process. The local union president met with the group, and at his request, they chose to continue meeting. In discussing the incident, one worker commented:

> On one side, they come in and say, "We need a participative management, we want your input, you've got to do this." And on the other side, they slap you. Now I don't think those two go hand in hand. If I participate and I give up 100 percent production for a day, . . . you're going to come and tell me that "you've got to stay right here." Where is this leading? What is coming out of it?

Both the threatened withdrawal of the EI group and the comments of the above worker raise issues of consistency that go to the heart of the social contract. The negotiations over working bell to bell first surfaced the issue in its simplest form. That is, had the social contract around the shop-floor relations been revised so that workers would accept competitive pressures as sufficient justification for breaking with past patterns of leaving their work stations early? While management's request to work from bell to bell represented a highly restrained form of forcing, the second issue, involving relief time, represented more direct forcing. Enforcement of the relief-time rules could not be justified (or was not presented) as part of the competitive response. Rather, it emerged as what would otherwise have been a routine struggle between labor and management over work practices. In this context, however, the relief-time issue became entangled with the issue of working from bell to bell and even produced tensions in the EI process. As a result, much broader issues around the social contract were raised.

MANAGING THE TRANSITION TO A CONTRASTING STRATEGY

Given the complexity of managing the coordination of forcing and fostering within the same period, it is not surprising that in many of our cases containing both strategies, they were deployed on a sequential basis. In a fundamental sense, the guiding principle is coordination through time differentiation. In this connection, we should note that even for some of the combined cases (especially Budd and Packard), another type of differentiation (by level of the organization) was employed.

It should also be noted that we have already examined the transition from a combined strategy to pure fostering. In this subset of cases, the dilemmas are minor. Assuming that the parties have been successful in handling the dilemmas involved in utilizing both strategies in the first time period, then the shift to pure fostering in the second time period is rather straightforward. When the combined period occurred during contract negotiations and the fostering period during the implementation phase, then it is easy to see how the deadline and signing of the new agreement served as the marker for the shift in strategies.

We now turn to a consideration of several cases in which the deadline served as a marker but the management of the transition was not easy nor straightforward. Specifically, these were our cases in scenario 3, forcing followed by fostering.

Transition from Forcing to Fostering

When forcing is followed by fostering, dilemmas arise around all three negotiating processes. First, the tactics of distributive bargaining will have revealed power differences, producing winners and losers on various issues. If this is to be followed by integrative bargaining, it is helpful if the "winners" are seen as not having pressed their power advantage fully (leaving some value "on the table"). For example, De Ridder management pressed hard during the strike for work-rule changes, but it did provide for a wage increase and classification combinations that produced additional wage gains for most workers. These choices made during the forcing period greatly facilitated subsequent fostering at the individual level.

Second, the soured attitudes produced by forcing present the most difficult challenge in the transition to fostering. The uncertainty and mistrust engendered during the forcing can be quite counterproductive during fostering.

Third, intraorganizational pressures may pose still another barrier to making the shift from forcing to fostering. Constituents on each side may see in the shift evidence that their leadership has weakened since they are now working closely with people who had recently been characterized as the enemy in a forcing contest. Clearly, some type of demarcation or signal that the frames are changing is helpful in managing the transition. A change in key players and the signing of a contract, for example, represent clear opportunities for signaling such a shift.

When the forcing involves a strike, the transition can be especially challenging. Obviously, the event itself can serve as a marker, but the extremely hostile attitudes that often accompany a strike can impede a shift to fostering. The additional steps required to turn the social equation around are well illustrated by episodes from Adrian, De Ridder, and Pensacola.

Repairing relations after a bitter strike at Adrian Fabricators. The strike at Adrian pitted worker-owners against one another—creating great resentment on both sides. Immediately following the strike, the union made an important symbolic gesture—specifically, by covering the cost of repairing plant windows that had been broken during the strike. Then, state officials helped facilitate a series of off-site retreat meetings in which sources of tension were aired and the parties moved to identify areas of mutual understanding. A key enabling factor at this time was the departure of the highly authoritarian CEO and his replacement by the company's former comptroller, who was known for practicing a much more participative management style.

Setting a constructive tone and listening at De Ridder. We noted in the forcing chapter that Boise Cascade's forcing at the De Ridder mill was limited both procedurally (permanent replacement workers were not used) and substantively (demands for concessions were confined to work rules). These factors, plus the fact that the company offered generous economic terms and employment security, encouraged mill managers to believe they could turn around the bitterness that they inherited in the poststrike period. They planned the immediate aftermath of the acrimonious strike carefully with a view to first neutralizing and then reversing hostility. Supervisors were instructed not to act on their own pent-up frustrations, which had grown during the strike when they operated the mill and were the targets of hostile actions. They were coached not only on how to *avoid* gloating over the company's victory but also on how to conduct professional discussions of the work to be done. The first day workers spent back on the job was devoted entirely to classroom activities, during which management was able to manage the initial contacts and set a constructive tone.

The mill manager and human resources manager, both of whom had recently been appointed to their positions, soon began meeting with work groups. These meetings, known locally as "listening sessions," were scheduled so that over a short period of time, the two managers met with all shifts in all departments. This process gave De Ridder employees an opportunity to express their views, which at the time were ferociously negative. The mill manager either addressed the problems identified by employees or explained any delays. We noted in Chapter 10 how the mill manager followed up these "icebreakers" over the next half decade with a systematic attitude-change program.

Joint trips and meetings at Pensacola. Whereas the above tactics at De Ridder were directed at employee-manager relations, the early efforts to make the transition from forcing to fostering at Pensacola emphasized institutional relations. Pensacola initiated several activities in which managers and union officials participated jointly.

In the early stages of the fostering period at Pensacola, union-management groups attended various labor-management conferences. One conference brought union officers and local officers from another Champion Paper mill together under company sponsorship, a precedent-setting occurrence. The union's international president even appeared as a presenter at the conference. Pensacola's four union local presidents returned to the mill energized by the vision of a cooperative future without confrontations and union busting—but still cautious about whether this would become a reality in their location.

The joint attendance at conferences where relevant information could be independently checked by both parties was a constructive move for Pensacola, as it has been for many other pairs of union officials and managers taking their first steps toward greater cooperation. Such events are most effective in restructuring attitudes when the parties have a full opportunity to raise questions or concerns and otherwise investigate the implications of changes they are considering.

Another climate-setting event occurred early in the fostering period at Pensacola, when management, local and regional union officials, and consultants met off-site. The session was specifically designed to solicit informal, preliminary union support for the proposed changes. The time seemed ripe since managers and union leaders had both been involved in change-oriented meetings during the previous two months. The UPIU international representative surprised some present by delivering a rousing speech in support of participative management, and the union officials who attended expressed support of the mill's movement in that direction.

Fostering Followed by Forcing

Among our cases, we had no instances of pure forcing that followed fostering (although we did have one combined period that followed fostering—at Pensacola, discussed earlier in the chapter). However, we are aware of numerous instances in other settings in which concession bargaining or other forcing initiatives have followed a period of fostering activity. The dilemmas that arise are essentially the reverse of the issues noted above.

Distributive bargaining that follows a period primarily characterized by integrative bargaining will likely be seen as taking unfair advantage and as being contrary to the spirit of the prior period. Trust can evaporate quickly, and a "we-they" attitude soon colors intraorganizational relations. The challenge in such a case is not so much making the shift to a forcing strategy, since this can be done with relative ease. Rather, the dilemma arises if the forcing party subsequently wishes to shift back to a fostering strategy or is concerned about minimizing the escalation of conflict.

SUMMARY AND CONCLUSIONS

The essence of a coordinated strategy involves the following supportive elements from the three tactical processes:

- *Bargaining:* emphasis on realizing substantive change within a specified timetable
- *Managing internal differences:* involvement by key constituents who are fully aware of both the major issues and the processes required for their resolution
- *Shaping intergroup attitudes:* relationships that are supportive of using both power and problem-solving techniques for resolving issues

Combining forcing and fostering to achieve this balance represents the most difficult and yet the most central domain of labor-management relations in the present era. The distinct strategies (forcing and fostering) can be employed concurrently or sequentially. When the strategies are employed concurrently—even for ostensibly separate reasons—some dissonance or interference does occur. The tension often results in a deterioration of the fostering or a delimiting of the forcing (confining it to specific issues and/or a bounded time period). At the same time, the juxtaposition of the two strategies can produce positive outcomes by minimizing forcing's tendency to produce escalation and fostering's to produce stagnation.

A focused introduction of elements of one strategy into the context of the other strategy can also yield positive outcomes. For example, the use of integrative bargaining during a forcing campaign is the primary vehicle by which a sequential shift to fostering can be achieved, though such tactics depend on a clear long-term strategy. The use of distributive bargaining during a fostering initiative is a predictable necessity if the parties want to avoid the sequential or combined use of forcing and fostering. Such distributive bargaining requires great tactical skill, however, and when employed effectively, can often prove to be a pivotal event in a relationship.

When the strategies are employed sequentially, we found that a tempering of forcing initiatives is critical for subsequent fostering success and that prior fostering imposes clear limits on subsequent forcing (given the ultimate desire to reestablish a fostering strategy).

In general, it is easier to implement forcing and fostering in sequence; however, if there is time pressure (e.g., Conrail) or if the parties have already moved along the road toward cooperation and commitment (e.g., Pensacola), then it is feasible to employ the two strategies simultaneously.

Chapter 12

Conclusion: Value Added by the Proposed Theory

We have advanced the theory proposed in this book as a contribution to two bodies of literature in the applied social sciences: negotiation and planned social change. Does this theory, grounded with our case histories, add value in each of these fields?

We examine first the general advantages of using negotiation as a lens for viewing social change of the type occurring in the American workplace and second the particular contributions of our theory to an understanding of negotiations.

ADVANTAGES OF VIEWING SOCIAL CHANGE THROUGH A NEGOTIATION LENS

The question we address here is how the negotiation concept helps an analyst or a change agent notice, understand, and anticipate critical realities in workplace change. In other words, does it provide an especially good lens for viewing this social phenomenon? Before arguing the advantages of a negotiation perspective, we take note of two alternative perspectives on workplace change: organizational development and industrial relations.

The literature on planned organizational change and development often emphasizes the role of the change agent in orchestrating change activities such as organizational diagnosis, environmental scans, envisioning and planning workshops, participation, and training. A typical formulation of social change in this literature would cite management's decisions to better utilize the capabilities of employees, its recognition of the need to involve and empower people in new ways, and the mechanisms it establishes to accomplish these objectives. Formulated in this way, the focus would be on how management plans, implements, and evaluates change.

The literature on transformation in industrial relations has emerged in recent years in response to fundamental shifts in the field. This literature is rooted in the documentation of developments in practice so as to identify implications for theory, practice, and policy. A typical formulation in this literature would focus on various institutional arrangements (such as labor-management committees, work teams, and joint training programs), with further attention given to the changing roles of labor and management and the implications for organizational performance and union institutional security.

Our formulation—that the changes are manifested in revisions in the social contract between labor and management and that these revisions are negotiated—complements these other perspectives by giving more attention to many important realities. We explore seven of these realities under two headings:

1. The role of power and other factors affecting the feasibility of change.

2. The indeterminacy of the change process

We propose how the theory of negotiated change clarifies these properties of the social change phenomenon.

Role of Power and Other Factors Affecting the Feasibility of Change

Whether change attempts are made and whether they succeed depend on many factors that have nothing to do with how much the change is desired by the initiating party. The approach used here clarifies this.

Reality 1: Change management is a negotiated process, not a directed one. The most fundamental distinction of the "strategic negotiations" framework we employ is signaled by the framework's label itself. Many theories of social system change posit an individual change agent or a group initiating and directing the change process from beginning to end. Negotiations theory emphasizes not only that other stakeholders have interests that must be taken into account, but also that they will be active in advancing their interests. It assumes that while one party may initiate changes, the change process is best understood as a process of *mutual influence*, with initiatives often shifting back and forth among stakeholders. The framework permits us to acknowledge and analyze the mixed-motive relationship between the initiating party and other key stakeholders, a mixture that is constantly shifting.

One can pay a price for failing to recognize that workplace reform is a negotiated process. Bidwell mill managers, for example, approached the implementation of a quality of work life program as a directed process. They apparently failed to recognize that the changes in the social contract at Bidwell implicit in the proposed QWL program required a mixture of distributive as well as integrative bargaining. The most striking evidence of this failure occurred when management allowed the timing decision about launching the program—a decision that involved a conflict of interest between management and the unions—to be made without first caucusing. Recall that at the time of the decision to move ahead, management strongly preferred a fall launch and the unions wanted to start in the summer. Management felt that the consultant had tilted the decision situation in favor of the unions.

The Budd case offers a sharply contrasting positive example. Management needed to radically improve the efficiency of replacing tools and dies and recognized that this sort of change in production methods—normally the province of industrial engineers and production superintendents—would not yield the best results if approached as a directed process. The parties first negotiated the creation of a joint hit-to-hit committee, which, in turn, revised the contractual classifications for skilled trades and established die transition teams. Finally, it was within the teams that workers negotiated new methods. Although the path sounds complicated—not exactly the shortest distance between two points—Budd management was much more successful because it had recognized almost from the outset that this type of social change must indeed be negotiated.

Reality 2: Change agent influence is an essential, yet highly contingent, resource. Most social change theories recognize that the manager of change needs to possess influence commensurate with the scope of change he or she seeks and that this influence has multiple sources. Negotiations theory assigns this question a central role. It gives more explicit emphasis to the various ways in which power, authority, and legitimacy can be developed as well as used. It clarifies how the net strength of the various forms of influence is conditional on both the particular objectives being pursued at a given time and the stance of the other party.

A comparison of the De Ridder and Jay cases illustrates the *contingent* nature of management influence. Managements in both instances attempted to force substantive change and succeeded to some extent. Both had to sustain a strike to achieve their immediate objectives for contract negotiations. However, De Ridder's strike was shorter and its aftermath more conducive to efficient mill operations. De Ridder management was the more successful in imposing the changes it wanted.

But De Ridder management did not necessarily have more raw bargaining power than Jay management; rather, the former's power produced a more satisfactory outcome only because its objectives were more limited. De Ridder management's objectives were confined to flexibility regarding work rules, whereas Jay management's objectives embraced concessions on both work rules and economics.

The De Ridder story also illustrates the crucial influence of a key leader—specifically, the new plant manager who arrived on the scene as the workers ended the strike and the implementation of the new agreement commenced. The pivotal role of leaders is apparent in most of the cases in which the outcomes were superior. For example, the success of the change effort at

Anderson must, in large part, be credited to the leadership of the president, who took the initiative to embark upon a constructive program of change.

Reality 3: Change efforts are shaped as much by considerations of feasibility as by considerations of desirability. The negotiation lens clarifies another key aspect of change, one we will merely note here because we explore it in more depth elsewhere in this chapter. The amount of change effort expended by the initiating party is, of course, determined both by the significance of what it expects to gain and by the obstacles it expects to encounter. Negotiations theory helps show why the latter, the factors affecting feasibility, is often equally or even more important in explaining why change does or does not occur than the former, the attractiveness of the potential benefits from successful change. This contrasts with theories of planned change that emphasize the moving party's goals, the strength of its own motivation to change, and the positive and logical steps required to reach the goal.

Indeterminacy of the Change Process

Many factors that characterize social change of the type examined here— in which one party initiates change that would not only serve its own interest but also affect other stakeholders—contribute to uncertainty in the change process. This uncertainty makes such change particularly challenging to practitioners and interesting to social scientists.

Reality 4: Outcomes are often unanticipated and unwelcome, not merely disappointing. The negotiation framework clarifies the sources of uncertainty within the change process and is therefore more realistic than most change theories about the amount of uncertainty in outcomes. Change theories generally acknowledge that the outcome of an action cannot be predicted precisely based on information about a situation existing at the time the action is initiated. Typically, they do assume, however, that planned action will result in movement toward the goal, usually allowing only for the possibility of shortfalls.

Inherent in the negotiation framework is an acknowledgment of even more uncertainty about the outcomes of change initiatives: not only may actual changes fall short of objectives, but they may be the *opposite* of those intended. IP's negotiations at the Jay mill resulted in mixed outcomes. While IP achieved the economic concessions it sought, it undoubtedly lost rather than gained ground in terms of efficient and effective mill operations. First, it needed to train replacement workers inexperienced in operating a paper mill; then it had to cope with the inevitable tensions between these "strike-breakers" and the strikers who gradually returned to the mill after the strike. The reasons some of the outcomes were the opposite of those sought included the union's unexpectedly strong resistance and the continuing consequences of using permanent replacements to break the strike.

The assumption of high uncertainty in outcomes derives from certain other social dynamics captured by the negotiation framework, such as the changing nature of contexts and the active and rational nature of the resistance to change. They are the next two realities we discuss.

Reality 5: Contexts are dynamic, not a set of "givens." Negotiations theory allows for contextual factors and their effects to be almost as dynamic as the change process itself. Most theories of change acknowledge that contextual factors exercise a general supportive or inhibiting influence on the proposed change. Negotiations theory goes further and proposes an intricate relationship between many contextual factors, the change objectives, and the efficacy of certain initiatives.

For example, the settlements of prior negotiations in the industry or elsewhere in the same company tend to affect the aspirations and expectations of labor and management in a local negotiation. The pattern or precedent affects how strongly and boldly the parties will act to impose or resist similar proposals in their own negotiations. However, the precise influence of prior settlements on the parties' resoluteness and on the outcome depends on the success each has in shaping the other's perceptions.

A vivid example of a contextual shift with implications for the bargaining process occurred at Packard Electric when a sharp market downturn led the company to abrogate what labor perceived as its guarantee of employment security. The employment security guarantee was, of course, a linchpin in the new social contract that the company was forging with the union. Even though the company presented persuasive evidence that it had miscalculated in its ability to promise lifetime job security, a team of local union officials was voted out of office and trust between employees and the employer deteriorated substantially. Under a more traditional social contract, the market downturn and subsequent layoffs would have been routine events. In this case, however, the change in the economic context proved a serious challenge to the social contract.

Reality 6: Resistance to change is often active and rational, not merely passive and emotional. Negotiations theory contrasts with theories of change that postulate the classic "resistance to change"—referring to passive resistance based on emotional or irrational impulses—and prescribe methods for "overcoming" such resistance. The premises of negotiations theory are that the interests of employees and their unions are partly independent of management's interests, that the sources of resistance include rational as well as irrational and emotional bases, that the resistance will probably be active and persuasive as well as passive, and that successful change will depend on how management *modifies* its change proposals to accommodate labor's interests as well as its attempts to reduce labor's resistance to the proposals as they were originally formulated.

Our cases were filled with illustrative labor responses to management's change initiatives. Guilford management encountered imaginative union tactics within a framework of laws and regulations—tactics that were designed to frustrate the company's change program and were motivated by a clear and unambiguous conclusion that it was in labor's best interests to resist the changes. Aspects of the Jay IP case could be summarized with the same words. In one or both cases, labor may have largely lost its cause, but in neither case could one argue that its response was strictly emotional or irrational. To overcome the resistance in these cases, managements needed not only to employ all the power at their disposal and be willing to pay substantial, if not unaffordable, prices but also to modify their positions toward accommodation of labor's interests.

Reality 7: Change scenarios are marked by pivotal events and other dynamics that render plans obsolete. Negotiations theory does not even flirt with the assumption implicit in some theories of change that a carefully developed plan can be implemented in a predetermined sequence. Planning is important in the negotiation framework, but it is recognized that events will soon render a comprehensive plan irrelevant.

Plans may be made obsolete because of relatively straightforward miscalculations. AP Parts provided a case in point. Management underestimated the UAW's resistance to its proposals, which the international union officers saw as potentially a leading edge for the erosion of union gains in the northern Ohio region. When management considered the potential use of replacement workers and other aspects of a forcing strategy, it surely anticipated strong resistance from the local union. It failed to anticipate, however, the high priority the international union would give to this strike at a relatively small, independent supplier. Management was reportedly surprised when Don Ephlin and Steven Yokich broke off UAW negotiations with GM and Ford, respectively, in order to join the striking AP workers on the picket line in Toledo, Ohio. Thus, the international union and the firm's major customers became central elements in the power equation for each side—all because of how seriously the union took this particular conflict.

Plans are also made obsolete by more complicated dynamics—both strong momentum dynamics that take parties further along a path than contemplated and pivotal events that abruptly alter the direction of change activities. Momentum can mount when an episode takes on a life of its own; for example, new conflict tactics used by one side beget new tactics by the other, resulting in an escalation of the conflict. Equally important, the change can take a new direction at any time. Discontinuities, triggered by pivotal events, can arise as planned or unplanned occurrences.

Leaders of change who understand that they are negotiators are better prepared for events that gather momentum and can use these dynamics to their advantage. They are also better prepared to create or seize upon events to change the direction of action. They accept that the change path often takes a zigzag course.

Both the pathways to change and the eventual outcomes are highly emergent, dependent on relatively unpredictable responses of stakeholder

groups to each other. Thus, a management that envisions an eventual cooperative relationship may unexpectedly find itself engaged in interactions the
effects of which—at least, for the time being—represent an intensification
of adversarial relations.

Our analysis of the Bidwell case identified three pivotal events that
rendered change plans obsolete. The first event was mill management's
decision to undertake the QWL program in the absence of informed leadership commitment to the change. The lack of internal management consensus undermined the integrative program at several stages. A second event
was the QWL timing decision referred to above. Among its several implications, this event strengthened labor's sense of ownership of the program
and weakened management's. A third pivotal event was the attack on QWL
by the leaders of one of the four unions. The division among unions helped
take the steam out of the change effort.

Similarly, at Budd, a pivotal event arose in negotiations over die transition
at the Detroit plant. The event was precipitated by the apparent inability of
the labor relations staff or the union leadership to draft language that would
be enforceable as part of the contract. When line management (in the form
of the plant manager and the production superintendent) took over the lead
in the negotiations, a fundamental shift occurred within management. In
the aftermath of negotiations, line management increasingly worked directly with the union to address critical issues involving the relationships
between the contract and production requirements. Labor relations no
longer played the key intermediary role that it once did.

In summary, we believe that a negotiations perspective offers many advantages in addressing critical dimensions and dynamics of workplace
change.

We turn now to an assessment of how the particular theory of strategic
negotiations proposed here contributes to the negotiations field. We keep it
brief because we are reviewing conclusions about findings already summarized at the end of chapters in Parts III and IV.

POWER OF THE THEORY TO DEAL WITH STRATEGIC NEGOTIATIONS

Our theory of negotiations differs in many respects from existing theories
(including *A Behavioral Theory of Labor Negotiations*, published by two of us
in 1965). Most of these differences derive from our examination of the nature
of current labor-management relations. Existing theories focus on the substantive stakes—how to create and claim material value. We set out to
formulate a theory that deals with major change in social contracts as well
as substantive agreements—what we call strategic change. The theory was
also designed to take into account other empirical observations, such as the
actual change strategies observed in the field, the tactical maneuvers commonly used to implement them, and the characteristic dynamics they set in
motion.

We select for summary several major lessons about strategic negotiations supported by our study.

Interrelationship of Substantive and Social Contracts in Strategic Negotiations

Our strategic negotiations framework helps capture the richness of the interests at stake. Negotiating frameworks that focus only on the substantive agenda overlook the profound variations in the longer-term implications of different change efforts. The idea that management and labor are negotiating not only substantive changes but also the terms of their relationship enables us to encompass more of the complexities of the changes that were negotiated. We discovered that the social and substantive aspects of negotiations can be interrelated in many ways.

First, we found that major differences in the social contracts that managements were attempting to negotiate affected their levels of aspiration on the substantive issues, their negotiating tactics, the outcomes of contract negotiations, and subsequent developments. The contract negotiations at IP's Jay mill in 1987 and Champion's Pensacola mill in 1988 are illustrative. In each case, corporate executives wanted to continue settlement patterns that they had launched in earlier negotiations at one of their other mills. These companies differed, however, in the broader social contracts they were actively promoting. Pensacola labor and management had already begun to move away from traditional arm's-length accommodation and toward commitment/cooperation. Although definite, the movement was still modest and tenuous, and management was anxious to avoid derailing the favorable trend. At Jay, no comparable past developments and management concerns were present. As a result, Pensacola's controlled behavior contrasted sharply with Jay's unrestrained forcing and work stoppage. Pensacola management consciously moderated its aspirations, relied on integrative bargaining and highly restrained distributive tactics, and—without a strike—achieved a contract that was reasonably acceptable to both sides. Pensacola had preserved a context in which the parties could continue their journey toward commitment/cooperation.

Second, we observed that when management seeks major changes in the substantive agreement, it must also revise the social contract with labor—either by defeating the union, as in the cases involving the Jay mill and the Guilford railroad, or by making it a full partner, as in the cases involving Packard Electric and Anderson Pattern.

Third, a direct effort to change the social contract invariably requires major changes in the substantive contract. De Ridder management increased the payout from its wage scheme to reflect workers' increased responsibility for performance under the new relationship based on mutual commitment. Packard Electric could only go so far in negotiating union cooperation and employee commitment without agreeing to formally provide for certain measures of employment security. In contrast, the efforts at Bidwell and UP appeared to aspire to only minor revisions in the social contract and did not involve a major substantive agenda.

Thus, the effective strategic negotiations we observed involved an orchestration of major revisions in both the social and substantive contracts.

Strategic Change Options—Force, Foster, and Escape

Efforts to effect major changes in the substantive and social contracts involved one of three major management strategies or some combination of them: to *force* labor to accept unwanted substantive terms and/or weaken the union's influence in the workplace, to *foster* the solution to common problems and new attitudes of labor-management mutuality, or to *escape* the current labor-management relationship by transferring operations. Forcing and fostering were of more interest because they are negotiating strategies.

Our distinctions about strategy proved useful in contrasting and comparing our cases. Our four cases of unrestrained forcing (drawn from all three industries) had more in common with each other than each had with other cases of negotiated change within the same industry. The same point can be made for the cases involving forcing followed by fostering and those involving combined forcing/fostering. Only the pure fostering cases showed extraordinary diversity: Anderson involved both substantive and social negotiations and produced major change, whereas Bidwell and UP produced little or no change. CSX was an intermediate case.

We found that for a given strategy—either forcing or fostering—negotiators' thrusts in each of the three tactical processes tended to be correlated as predicted:

- Forcing involves the following alignment of the three tactical processes: (1) distributive bargaining; (2) the heightening of intergroup tension, either intentionally or unintentionally; and (3) the promotion of solidarity in one's own organization and divisions in the other organization.

- Fostering involves the following alignment of the three tactical processes: (1) integrative bargaining; (2) the enhancement of intergroup trust; and (3) the promotion of internal consensus in both parties.

Moreover, we found that the implementation of each of the two strategies involved certain risks, which we believe are also predictable. The tactical risks common to the implementation of forcing were the risks of uncontrolled escalation, defeat, a legacy of intergroup distrust, and severe internal disunity in the negotiator's *own* organization. We characterized these risks as resulting from errors of commission—overly aggressive implementation of one or more of the three tactical processes.

The tactical risks common to the implementation of fostering were the risks of insufficient relationship work, inadequate substantive work, or too little internal consensus to support interparty problem solving and a change in intergroup relations. Thus, the tactical risks associated with fostering are errors of omission—failing to align the three processes.

Negotiations involve tactical choices about structure as well as process. Although some structural features, such as industrywide bargaining, may be fixed for a particular change episode, negotiators can usually influence the structural design in some respects, including adjusting the degree of centralization, multiplicity of channels, frequency of interaction, and number of parties.

We found that structural features did play important roles, either facilitating or complicating the execution of a preferred negotiating strategy. Only one structural feature appears to have a straightforward relationship to strategy: structures that provide for more channels between the parties and more frequent interactions tended to facilitate fostering but not forcing. The other structural features had complex, but nevertheless potent, implications for the implementation of a strategy.

Crucial Role of Managing Internal Differences

Distributive bargaining is the cornerstone of forcing. Constructive intergroup attitudes and integrative bargaining are virtually defining processes for fostering. Therefore, we generally anticipated the importance of these two types of processes, although we could foresee neither how they would be executed nor all of the dynamics and risks associated with them.

Our learning about the third negotiating process—managing internal differences—was even greater. The tactical roles of managing internal differences in forcing and fostering each were generally prescribed by the theoretical framework we took into the study. However, we did not anticipate how crucial this tactical arena would be in determining the effectiveness of both strategies in action.

The outcomes of several forcing campaigns hinged on the successful or unsuccessful influencing of internal differences. In the negotiation involving IP's mill in Jay, Maine, management used "carrot-and-stick" maneuvers to exploit divisions in the ranks of the Jay mill and to deter additional UPIU mills from joining the original pool of four mills when this pool of union locals was facing defeat. In contrast, at a crucial point in the forcing campaign at AP Parts, the display of support by International UAW Vice Presidents Don Ephlin and Steven Yokich helped promote solidarity in the local and enabled the union to avoid defeat.

Consider also our fostering cases. Fostering in the Bidwell mill foundered primarily because of internal divisions within both parties: managers remained divided about the QWL effort, and one of the four mill unions began to actively attack the program. CSX's fostering also received a major setback when one of the railroad unions, the UTU, decided it could not proceed with the integrative-bargaining effort.

Fostering succeeded at Anderson Pattern because the company president used imaginative initiatives to deal with different interests within the union and to build consensus for proposals that were on the table. An example was the Chicago bus trip for employees to see the proposed new equipment—which helped them to imagine how the equipment would preserve rather than eliminate jobs.

Especially interesting paradoxes are associated with fostering. Although fostering can stumble because of internal differences, the strategy usually involves opening up more channels of interaction among more participants from each organization, which, in turn, introduces more diverse perspectives and complicates the management of differences. Our clearest example of this developed around the hit-to-hit committee in the Budd case. As noted earlier, the integrative solution to the challenge of finding quicker ways to change tools and dies was assisted by the direct involvement of line manufacturing managers, but their involvement complicated both the role of the industrial relations managers and the IR managers' relationship with line management and the union.

Although this process of managing internal differences plays a strictly supportive role in the overall negotiations process, it clearly must be a part of any comprehensive negotiations theory, and its importance and subtlety warrant more study.

Rationales for Strategic Choices to Force or Foster

The choices about what change strategy to pursue appear to be influenced by a variety of considerations. We begin with a review of these considerations as "advantages" and "disadvantages."

For management, the strategic advantage of forcing is the possibility of achieving more profound revisions of the substantive contract and a more favorable balance of bargaining power along with greater shop-floor control. The disadvantages derive from the *tactical* risks of forcing outlined above—namely, the risk of a costly conflict-cycle dynamic, the failure to identify integrative potential, and the lack of commitment in implementation.

For management, the strategic advantages of fostering are the potential to solve common problems and serve complementary interests, the promise of commitment in implementation, and the potential for a self-reinforcing dynamic involving trust → integrative solutions to problems → trust, and so on. The disadvantages of fostering are that even when the effort is successful, the substantive changes often come relatively slowly and the norm of cooperation may stifle healthy conflict. Additional disadvantages are the tactical risks that ineffective work on either substance, attitudes, or internal consensus will result in a waste of the parties' time and effort.

Another type of analysis of the considerations influencing strategic choice distinguishes between "desirability" factors and "feasibility" factors. Our findings emphasize how important it is for negotiators to consider a strategy's feasibility, not just the desirability of the benefits likely to flow from the strategy if it is successful.

First, consider the role of potential benefits—desirability factors. Our analysis of 20 strategic periods supported the idea that management tends to use forcing strategies if its priorities emphasize major substantive changes in economics and work rules (and downplay a movement toward cooperation and commitment) and if it would like to rebalance the power equation with labor. Conversely, management tends to use fostering strategies if it has a contrasting set of priorities.

Second, management judgments regarding feasibility also appeared to play an important role in the 20 strategic decisions to force or foster. Management's choices to force were correlated with its beliefs in its own power advantage and with its perceptions that labor would find management's proposals very disagreeable and its rationale for them weak. Management's choices to foster were moderately correlated with its expectations that labor would be receptive to cooperative overtures and would be persuaded of the business rationale for the company's proposals.

We also analyzed these considerations at the industry level. This analysis relied on the logical, as opposed to actual, priorities of management and general feasibility considerations (such as the ability to operate facilities during a strike and the union's ideological stance toward employee participation) rather than actual management judgments of feasibility. Interestingly, we again found that feasibility considerations were influential (they explained the different patterns of reliance on strategies in the three industries) but desirability factors were not (they failed completely to help explain these patterns).

Need for—and Challenges of—Employing Both Forcing and Fostering

Given the preceding discussion of the different advantages of each strategy, it is not surprising that managements often decide they must both force and foster. Although all 13 cases were initially selected as an example of either forcing or fostering, when we developed the case histories, we found that about half of them actually involved both forcing and fostering during the periods of concerted change effort. Some involved a sequence of forcing followed by fostering, and others involved a combination of forcing and fostering in the same time period. Significantly, better outcomes were associated with case histories that involved both forcing and fostering rather than only one or the other.

Also, given the opposing tactical requirements of forcing and fostering in each of the three negotiating processes, we could anticipate the many dilemmas associated with coordinated strategies. Our cases show, for example, that forcing commonly leaves a legacy of intergroup antagonism that can constrain management's options to foster in subsequent periods.

Interestingly, some of the contrasting tactical thrusts of the two strategies can be made complementary in coordinated forcing and fostering. For example, managements can limit forcing's tendency to escalate and leave a legacy of distrust by passing up the immediate bargaining power advantage that accrues from demonizing the other side or exploiting divisions within the other side's organization. In fact, negotiators sometimes actually make positive overtures to maintain trust, as Pensacola mill management did, for example, during its forcing/fostering negotiations with the UPIU local.

Emergent Distinctions in Negotiating Strategies

We began our study utilizing the distinctions between two forms of strategic negotiations—forcing and fostering. Both were recognized as departures from bargaining over incremental substantive changes within the existing social contract. During the course of our study, we found it useful to make further distinctions in both forcing and fostering.

In forcing, we developed the distinction between a controlled form of forcing and "unrestrained forcing." Four of our six forcing episodes had evolved into unrestrained forcing. While one could argue that the moving parties gravitated into unrestrained forcing rather than planned it, they nevertheless made explicit choices that redefined the negotiating strategy. We chose to incorporate this "controlled versus unrestrained" distinction into the formal theory at a relatively early stage of the study, and our subsequent analysis confirmed that the distinction was a significant one in terms of the antecedents and consequences of the choice and the tactical dynamics and risks associated with it. This distinction between controlled and unrestrained forcing strategies probably deserves a place in a general theory of strategic negotiations; it certainly deserves further study.

In fostering, we developed an appreciation for a major distinction that we elected not to incorporate into the formal theory—namely, the distinction between top-down and bottom-up fostering, which we continued to treat as a tactical choice.

Most of our fostering periods were characterized by top-down fostering—with management focusing initially on improving relations with union officials and subsequently extending fostering to employees. The rationale for this sequence was that it was desirable to get the union officials on board because their participation was necessary in order to revise the collective agreement and/or because they could help (or hurt) management's efforts to promote employee commitment. The perceived risk of this form of fostering was that union members might charge their leaders with being co-opted by management.

We found only one instance of the opposite form of fostering, although we know it is common in industry today. Normally, bottom-up fostering is designed to improve employee relations as a way of changing the political realities for union leaders, in the hope that these leaders will conclude sooner or later that it's to their advantage to respond positively to management's fostering. The risks of this approach are that union leaders might feel threatened by this management bonding with employees and attempt to undermine it or retaliate in other ways.

Our one example of bottom-up fostering, De Ridder, offered a relatively extreme example of this strategic choice: De Ridder managers focused *all* of their fostering on employees for *almost the entire period* covered by our observations. It was only in 1991, after corporate management decided to explore partnership relations with the UPIU, that De Ridder mill managers began to make cooperative overtures to the leaders of their local union.

The distinction between top-down and bottom-up fostering may also deserve to be incorporated into a general theory of strategic negotiations and be subject to further investigation.

Thus, we conclude that the negotiations framework helps clarify a number of aspects of the type of social change studied here. It appears to be especially helpful in recognizing the different interests of stakeholders and their potentially active roles in opposing or supporting change; explaining why outcomes are often at variance from those intended by the initiating party; showing the dynamic interaction between the context for change, the change process, and the outcomes; clarifying the forces of momentum that can give a dispute a life of its own and the pivotal events that can alter the basic course of the change trajectory; and demonstrating the conditional and changeable nature of the initiating party's influence.

Our conclusion is that social analysts and labor and management practitioners themselves can benefit from applying the negotiations theory outlined here to the changes occurring today in the American workplace.

Appendix A

List of Case Histories Included in the Study

The 13 cases presented in this book were purposely selected to illustrate extremes of fostering and forcing strategies in each of three industries. The following sections provide an overview of these cases.

PULP AND PAPER INDUSTRY CASES

The four pulp and paper industry situations were selected initially to illustrate two instances of forcing and two instances of fostering. Upon closer examination, two of the case histories actually involved combinations of forcing and fostering. The paper industry background and cases were developed jointly by Kathleen Sharf and Richard Walton.

International Paper mill in Jay, Maine, and the UPIU: This case focuses on the dispute between International Paper (IP) and the United Papermakers International Union (UPIU) during 1987 and 1988 involving the Jay, Maine, mill and three other IP facilities. Management sought major economic and work-rule concessions, and the union decided to go all out in resisting management's demands. The result was a negotiation characterized by unrestrained forcing, which produced mutually costly results for the parties. We based this case history largely on published accounts, supplemented by conversations with industry observers.

Boise Cascade mill in De Ridder, Louisiana, and the UPIU: The De Ridder mill case covers two major periods. During the 1983–1984 contract negotiations, management demanded major work-rule changes, and the union struck. This forcing episode, which produced considerable anger and bitterness, was followed by a concerted and successful effort by management to negotiate employee commitment. We based this case history on our fieldwork and on reports prepared by Casey Ichniowski.[1]

Bidwell mill and the UPIU: The case history involving the Bidwell mill (a

353

disguised name) focuses on a management-initiated quality of work life (QWL) program. The negotiations between labor and management involved labor's cosponsoring the QWL program, the timing of the program's launch, and management's support for the effort. After a briefly successful start, the program was aborted. We based our case history wholly on an account published by Susan Mohrman,[2] although given our particular purpose, our analysis and interpretation of events differ in some respects from hers.

Champion mill in Pensacola, Florida, and the UPIU: The Pensacola mill case covers three periods, each characterized by a different management negotiating strategy. The first period centers on the 1985 negotiations, in which management took advantage of concerns over the mill's viability in order to force major work-rule changes. The second period—between the 1985 and 1988 contract negotiations—involved an effort to foster more cooperative relations with union leaders and more commitment on the part of employees. In the third period, during the 1988 contract negotiations, management attempted to force substantive changes strongly resisted by labor at the same time that it attempted to foster a continuation of the improved relations generated during the second period. This case history resulted from our own field research and general knowledge of the Pensacola situation. One of the researchers, Richard Walton, is a member of Champion's board of directors.

AUTO SUPPLY INDUSTRY CASES

Five auto supply cases were selected to illustrate a mix of forcing and fostering strategies across a range of suppliers—including two smaller independent suppliers, two medium-to-large independent suppliers, and one internal supplier at an original equipment manufacturer. One case illustrates a pure forcing period, a second illustrates a pure fostering period, and the others feature a mixture of periods involving forcing and fostering strategies. One case—Packard Electric—was based heavily on a published account. The others were produced by our field research. The auto supply background and cases were developed by Patrick McHugh and Joel E. Cutcher-Gershenfeld.

AP Parts in Toledo, Ohio, and UAW Local 14: AP Parts is a medium-sized independent producer of auto mufflers and other stamped and welded components. Our focus is on the Toledo facility, where the workforce is represented by UAW Local 14. The story begins with the collapse of relations into a highly acrimonious strike in 1984, traces the escalation of conflict into open warfare, and describes how the parties reestablished a traditional arm's-length collective-bargaining relationship and negotiated an early contract in 1987.

Adrian Fabricators in Adrian, Michigan, and UAW Local 963: Adrian Fabricators is a small, independent manufacturer of metal bins used in assembly-line operations; its workforce is represented by UAW Local 963. This story also begins with a highly contentious strike. Adding to the intensity was the fact that this is a small firm in which the majority of the stock is owned by the employees, who were, in effect, striking against themselves. In this case, the parties also reestablished relations and went on to build a cooperative partnership between the plant management and the union leadership.

Packard Electric in Warren, Ohio, and IUE Local 717: Packard Electric is an auto supply division of a major automobile manufacturer; its workforce is represented by IUE Local 717.[3] The case begins with fostering efforts focused on improving the quality of work life through employee participation—which occurred concurrently with layoffs and the movement of work to locations in the southern United States and Mexico. Over time, and through a series of pivotal events, the focus of the fostering broadened to include the negotiation of a no-layoff pledge, a multitier wage system, and a range of experiments in new forms of work organization.

Budd Company in Detroit; Kitchener, Ontario; and Philadelphia; and multiple UAW locals: The Budd Company, a large independent parts manufacturer, followed a pattern similar to Packard Electric. The story begins with concurrent QWL efforts and massive layoffs, followed by the construction of a new labor-management partnership. Even though the Budd Company is large for an independent supplier, its efforts were constrained in comparison to Packard Electric (which could draw on the resources of General Motors Corporation). Also, because of the Budd Company's multiplant structure, the case illustrates multiple levels of interrelated negotiations.

Anderson Pattern in Muskegon, Michigan, and the Pattern Makers Association of Muskegon: Anderson Pattern is a small firm with a highly skilled workforce that produces molds, castings, and other design-related products. Early in this case, fostering focused narrowly on the introduction of new technology. The process evolved into the granting of substantial contractual flexibility in exchange for some employment security protection combined with a major infusion of capital into the business. Critical to the case is the unique context of a highly skilled, autonomous workforce and the presence of strong union and management leaders.

RAILROAD INDUSTRY CASES

We highlight four railroad cases—one illustrating forcing, two illustrating forms of fostering, and one featuring a mixture of forcing and fostering. The cases were developed from interviews and on-site observations.

Guilford in New England and multiple unions: The Guilford case portrays a series of episodes in which management sought to achieve major revisions in work rules and union representation. As a result, the parties engaged in unrestrained forcing. The eventual outcomes were not yet clear, given the extensive litigation that was still under way.

Conrail in the northeast corridor and multiple unions: The Conrail case covers two time periods: the negotiations to avoid bankruptcy (under government auspices) and the carrier's subsequent return to the private sector. The intense period of activity to avoid bankruptcy involved the federal government as well as management and labor, and the process was characterized by a mixture of forcing and fostering. After the carrier returned to financial health, a fostering strategy continued via a number of joint programs in health, quality, and productivity.

Union Pacific in the western United States and multiple unions: The UP case is typical of the many fostering efforts made by labor and management to improve relationships on a yard-by-yard basis by engaging in problem solving outside of collective bargaining. The Labor Management Process (LMP) spread to four yards before it was eclipsed by several other programs initiated by top management, especially a total quality effort.

CSX in the Midwest and multiple unions: The CSX case presents the most ambitious example of fostering undertaken in the railroads during the last decade. A comprehensive package of staffing reductions, work-rule changes, and gain sharing was not implemented due to one major union's failure to ratify the agreement. The company has since decentralized its fostering strategy by reaching agreement for changes on a regional, union-by-union basis.

Notes

1. See Chapter 4, note 8.
2. See Chapter 4, note 9.
3. See Chapter 5, note 38.

Appendix B

Study Methods

The primary purpose of this project was to develop a theory of strategic negotiations. This development process comprised formulating theory, applying it to field cases, assessing the strength of the evidence supporting the theoretical framework in general and the formal hypotheses in particular, and elaborating the theory based on the study's findings. We describe here how we performed this developmental work.

SOURCES OF HYPOTHESES

The most basic set of inherited hypotheses are those included in *A Behavioral Theory of Labor Negotiations*—a strictly process-oriented theory. This theory, published in 1965, proposed that social negotiations, such as labor-management negotiations, were composed of four parallel and interacting subprocesses: distributive bargaining, integrative bargaining, attitudinal structuring, and internal bargaining. The present theory of strategic negotiations also utilizes this idea but treats bargaining as one subprocess that can take two contrasting forms depending on the negotiating strategy. Thus, we use three negotiating subprocesses, or "processes," as we decided to call them.

We began this study with several additional concepts and broad propositions, each based on prior research and other observations of practice. First, we had formulated two major negotiating strategies (fostering and forcing) and another change strategy (escape) that we had observed being employed to achieve major change in labor-management relations. We envisioned how each of the three negotiating processes would tend to be managed in support of forcing and in support of fostering. Second, based on our observations of contemporary industrial relations, we also expected structural features of collective bargaining to figure importantly in the transformation. Third, based on case study research at Xerox and other locations, we saw

357

organizational change as an unfolding process marked by pivotal events in which key negotiations occurred.[1] Fourth, based partly on a comparative study of the development and diffusion of workplace innovation,[2] we expected contextual conditions (economic, social, and institutional factors) to play an important role in reshaping labor-management relations.

Thus, the general theoretical framework presented in Chapter 3—which combines propositions about strategy, structure, and context with our earlier theory of negotiating processes—is grounded in prior observations.

The more specific hypotheses also presented in Chapter 3 were derived by deductive logic from the broad theoretical propositions. These include the hypotheses about the specific factors we expected to influence the choices of strategies, process tactics, and structural features. Some of these propositions were formulated in formal terms after the project was well under way but before we undertook the relevant comparative analyses of the 13 cases and 20 strategic periods—the analyses that we ultimately used to help assess the strength of the propositions.

One important distinction contained in our propositions did emerge during the analysis phase of the study. We decided to make a formal distinction between forcing strategies that were unrestrained and those that were more controlled in terms of the severity of forcing tactics used. We incorporated this distinction in Chapter 3 and included a few specific hypotheses utilizing it; however, we suspect that it is only one among many strategy distinctions that might take on comparable importance in another set of sites.

Notwithstanding our use of prior theory outlined above, the study was equally designed to generate new concepts and insights. Indeed, many broad findings reported in this book were not in any way hypothesized in advance of analysis. Examples include the relative importance of feasibility factors in influencing the pattern of strategic choices, reported in our industry analysis in Chapter 7; the various ways in which structural features are modified to serve negotiating strategies, reported in Chapters 9 and 10; and the critical role played by managing internal differences in determining the success or failure of both forcing and fostering strategies. In Chapters 9 and 10, we also identified the *tactical* risks associated with the execution of forcing and fostering and found four major risks that had to be managed in forcing and three major risks in fostering.

Potentially the most important set of findings was not anticipated by a hypothesis. It dealt with the connection between strategies employed by managements and the outcomes achieved. Managements that first forced in one period and then fostered in the next period achieved relatively good results. So did managements that combined forcing and fostering in one period and then fostered in the following period. With one exception, poor results were achieved in those cases in which management relied strictly on either forcing or fostering. For unions, the pattern held as well (with the most beneficial results being achieved primarily in the context of concurrent or sequential strategies), though the results for unions and workers were generally worse than for management on average—reflecting management's power advantages in the present era.

Our strategy for assessing whether this expanded theoretical framework was relevant and useful for describing and analyzing contemporary cases of major changes in labor-management relations includes (1) utilizing the framework to guide clinical analyses of particular sites and (2) applying the specific hypotheses to a comparative analysis across multiple sites. We discuss next our units of analysis.

UNITS OF ANALYSIS: INDUSTRY, COMPANIES, AND TIME PERIODS

We analyzed negotiating phenomena at several levels. Our study embraces three industries, 13 separate companies, and 20 strategic periods, with each company case history comprising 1, 2, or 3 strategic periods.

For some analyses, we focused on the industry. In the first part of each industry chapter in Part II, we described and analyzed labor negotiations in that industry, and then in Part III (Chapter 7), we compared the three industries. These analyses were especially useful in assessing the role of contextual factors.

Our clinical analyses of case histories in Part II focus on one or more episodes of negotiated change over some significant history. Our comparative analysis in Part III (Chapter 8) compared these 13 case histories of labor-management relations. Specifically, we evaluated outcomes based on the results of the entire histories covered by our cases.

Our third unit of analysis was a specific episode or defined time period within a case history. Time periods were marked by shifts in strategy. Thus, if we observed no changes in strategy during the history covered by our study, we treated it as one period. Some case histories contained two or three periods. The periods within a case history were not completely independent observations, in that they included common features and each subsequent period was influenced by the preceding one(s). The comparative analysis of time periods in Chapter 8 is aimed at assessing the role of various factors in shaping strategic choices.

This third level of analysis represented an important methodological step. While it is common to find comparative analysis of industries or companies, it is less common to find comparative analysis of distinct strategic time periods. The time periods in fact proved especially helpful in the analysis. When we initially attempted to compare only company cases, we found that we were trying to lump together highly contrasting time periods. This led us to the deeper classification, which makes the research more than a series of case studies.

SELECTION OF STUDY SITES

Our "selection" of industry sites—the paper, auto supply, and railroad industries—was strongly influenced by the fact that each of us was already familiar with one of these industries. We were satisfied with this set of three industries because they offered significant diversity—in terms of the amount of effort expended to renegotiate social contracts, the strategies relied on, and the structures that characterized them as well as differences in other contextual factors.

Our choices about particular cases to investigate were based primarily on two criteria. We wanted a balance of forcing and fostering cases. And we wanted to be opportunistic, taking advantage of situations to which we could readily obtain access. In auto supply, we also attempted to achieve variation in our cases that would parallel the variation in the industry in terms of company size. In each industry, we ended up with a set of cases that reflected to a remarkable extent the diversity we found in the industry as a whole—in terms of outcomes as well as strategies. We were fortunate in this respect because we understood neither the overall industry patterns nor the actual nuances of the strategies and outcomes of our cases until we had gathered our data.

Nevertheless, we did not intend the 13 cases to be a representative sample of American industry, nor can we claim that they are in retrospect. In places throughout the book, we call attention to certain types of situations that we know to be important but that are not illustrated by any of our cases. For example, we have no case histories that include a fostering period followed by pure forcing.

ANALYSES AND THE NATURE OF EVIDENCE FOR THE FINDINGS

The industry-by-industry and company-by-company clinical analyses reported in Part II and then extended in Part IV confirmed to our satisfaction that the theory of strategic negotiations provides a useful framework for describing and analyzing the changes and change activities we studied. Readers will decide for themselves how helpful they find the framework in interpreting the events reported.

Our comparative analyses in Part III were conducted to assess where our findings supported the theory and where they did not. The grist for the comparative analyses included discrete judgments we had already made in Part II about each industry and each company case based on clinical analysis: for each industry, we assessed the level of pressures for change, the desirability and feasibility factors related to strategic choice, and the relative frequency of the use of the several different change strategies; and for each company case, we judged the outcomes over the periods covered by the history, categorized management's strategy as either forcing or fostering or mixed, inferred how the parties had perceived their bargaining power early in the period in question, and so on. Thus, in Part III, we were able to analyze how these factors and others we had assessed in earlier chapters were interrelated.

To help ensure the independence of these discrete clinical judgments, so that we could draw the appropriate theoretical inference from relationships we found among them, we critiqued each other's judgments of the evidence in each case. Although there was a high level of interrater reliability in the first round of judgments, certain cases required more discussion before we agreed on particular judgments.

Despite our best efforts, the subjectivity of our judgments causes us to treat the evidence produced by the comparative analyses as suggestive rather than definitive.

PERSONAL BELIEFS OF THE AUTHORS

Several personal beliefs are relevant to the study. We believe that a change in the social contract is required. This belief influenced the selection of the topic. We also believe that society will be healthier if labor and management move toward commitment and cooperation while preserving the integrity and strength of their respective institutions. This belief could potentially have influenced our judgments—for example, causing us to underestimate the outcomes in cases in which the parties were *not* attempting to negotiate commitment and cooperation. To supplement our own efforts to minimize any such distortion, we asked others acquainted with the cases in question to help us detect any such bias.

NOTES

1. Joel E. Cutcher-Gershenfeld, "Tracing a Transformation of Industrial Relations," BLMR 123 (Washington, D.C.: U.S. Department of Labor, 1988).
2. Richard E. Walton, *Innovating to Compete* (San Francisco: Jossey-Bass, 1987).

Index